Teacher's Answer Key

Vocabulary Workshop

Introductory Through Complete Course

HOLT, RINEHART AND WINSTON

Austin • *New York* • *Orlando* • *Chicago* • *Atlanta*
San Francisco • *Boston* • *Dallas* • *Toronto* • *London*

CONTENTS

Using *Vocabulary Workshop*: An Introduction for Teachers

INTRODUCTORY COURSE

FIRST COURSE

SECOND COURSE

THIRD COURSE

FOURTH COURSE

FIFTH COURSE

COMPLETE COURSE

USING *VOCABULARY WORKSHOP:* An Introduction for Teachers

Welcome to a new edition of *Vocabulary Workshop*!
As you will see, we have created a new kind of vocabulary textbook, one that
- helps students to discover independently the meanings of new words,
- encourages students to think about the different definitions and uses of words,
- introduces new words in the context of a variety of stimulating topics,
- gives students practice in the kinds of vocabulary items they will encounter on national and regional standardized tests.

The following is a description of the instructional model on which the series is based.

Teaching Vocabulary: The Holt Model

Both teachers and researchers agree that vocabulary instruction works best if an interactive, student-centered model is adopted. Teachers realize that vocabulary is most effectively taught in context. Instead of providing students with alphabetized lists of words to be memorized, more and more teachers prefer to present words in groups, in the context of interesting subject matter.

Teachers also recognize that vocabulary can be built in a variety of ways. Strategies such as brainstorming and analyzing context clues are thus often used in the classroom. (For more on vocabulary instruction, see especially the following studies: Dale D. Johnson, guest editor. "A Themed Issue on Vocabulary Instruction." *Journal of Reading* 30 (1986); Margaret C. McKeown and Mary E. Curtis. *The Nature of Vocabulary Instruction.* New Jersey: Lawrence Earlbaum, 1987; Richard Sinatra and Cornelia A. Dowd. "Understanding Syntactic and Semantic Clues to Learn Vocabulary." *Journal of Reading* 35 (1991): 224–229.)

After reviewing the formal research and talking with classroom teachers about vocabulary acquisition, we designed the model below.

The Holt Model of Vocabulary Instruction

The goals of vocabulary instruction are listed in the center of the circle:

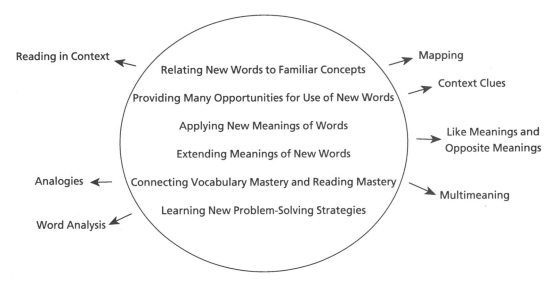

Relating New Words to Familiar Concepts
Students will be able to examine their own prior knowledge as they encounter new vocabulary words. They will be encouraged to relate new words to familiar concepts.

Providing Many Opportunities for Use of New Words
Students will be exposed to each new vocabulary word a number of times in each volume of *Vocabulary Workshop*. They will also encounter these new words in a variety of ways and contexts. Thus, students will have many opportunities to work with new words.

Applying New Meanings of Words

Students will be able to use new vocabulary in a variety of test situations and reading contexts.

Extending Meanings of New Words

Students will be able to elaborate their uses of vocabulary. *Vocabulary Workshop* exposes students to multiple meanings of words and to the subtle variations these meanings can take so that students can extend their knowledge of these words.

Connecting Vocabulary Mastery and Reading Mastery

By presenting vocabulary words in the context of reading passages, *Vocabulary Workshop* helps students learn new words and become better readers at the same time.

Learning New Problem-Solving Strategies

Vocabulary Workshop enables students to develop problem-solving strategies that they can employ when encountering an unfamiliar word. Thus, students will become more reflective in their approach to reading new texts and to the vocabulary therein.

The Design of Vocabulary Workshop

To achieve these goals of vocabulary instruction, we have divided each volume of *Vocabulary Workshop* into the following sections: *Making New Words Your Own, Connecting New Words and Patterns,* and *Reading New Words in Context.* Introductory Course, First Course, and Second Course contain an additional section, *Understanding New Words and Their Uses.*

Each grade level of *Vocabulary Workshop* uses a list of three hundred words. Because students retain vocabulary best when the words are introduced in smaller groups, we have divided each group of three hundred words into three broad context areas, each of which deals with one hundred words. For example, in Introductory Course, the three one-hundred-word context areas are titled "Amazing Nature," "People and Places," and "Ecology and Environment." These three large groupings are further broken down into clusters of either ten or twenty words.

The chart below, which covers the first third of Introductory Course, gives an overview of the flow of vocabulary instruction in *Vocabulary Workshop.*

CONTEXT: Amazing Nature			
Making New Words Your Own	Formative Assessment	Understanding New Words and Their Uses + Connecting New Words and Patterns + Reading New Words in Context	Summative Assessment
1 (first 10 words) 2 (second 10 words)	1 2	1 (first 20 words)	1 (first 100 words)
3 (third 10 words) 4 (fourth 10 words)	3 4	2 (second 20 words)	
5 (fifth 10 words) 6 (sixth 10 words)	5 6	3 (third 20 words)	
7 (seventh 10 words) 8 (eighth 10 words)	7 8	4 (fourth 20 words)	
9 (ninth 10 words) 10 (tenth 10 words)	9 10	5 (fifth 20 words)	

(Left vertical label: Test/Lesson Number)

- In *Making New Words Your Own,* we introduce students to the vocabulary words through mapping and context clue items. In Introductory Course, First Course, and Second Course, students also encounter like meanings and opposite meanings items, while Third Course through Complete Course provide students with sentence completion items. Students work with ten new vocabulary words in each of the thirty lessons in this section.
- *Understanding New Words and Their Uses* appears in Introductory Course, First Course, and Second Course. Each of the fifteen lessons in *Understanding New Words and Their Uses* gives the students an opportunity to work further with ten of the twenty words presented in two corresponding lessons in *Making New Words Your Own.* In this section, we provide exercises in multimeaning and word analysis.
- Each of the fifteen lessons in *Connecting New Words and Patterns* gives the students additional opportunities to work with ten of the twenty words presented in two corresponding lessons in *Making New Words Your Own.* These fifteen lessons provide practice in word analogies.
- In *Reading New Words in Context,* we provide fifteen reading passages. Each of the fifteen lessons presents twenty vocabulary words and corresponds to two lessons in *Making New Words Your Own.*

The exercises in *Vocabulary Workshop* are designed to reflect state-of-the-art testing practices. *Making New Words Your Own, Understanding New Words and Their Uses,* and *Reading New Words in Context* in Introductory Course, First Course, and Second Course reflect the kind of items students will encounter in the Iowa Tests of Basic Skills, the Stanford Achievement Test, and the Comprehensive Test of Basic Skills. *Reading New Words in Context* in Third Course through Complete Course has been especially influenced by New Jersey's new High School Proficiency Test, as well as new test formats on the SAT-I. *Connecting New Words and Patterns* is designed to introduce students to the kind of logical thought items that they may eventually encounter on the SAT-I.

Assessment Booklets

Each volume of *Vocabulary Workshop* includes an accompanying assessment booklet containing both formative and summative tests.
- Each *Assessment Booklet* contains thirty formative tests for ongoing evaluation. Each formative test corresponds to one ten-word lesson in the *Making New Words Your Own* section of **Vocabulary Workshop.**
- Each *Assessment Booklet* also contains three summative tests for testing mastery. The elaborate summative tests are modeled on state and national tests and use the same contexts covered in the accompanying **Vocabulary Workshop** lessons. The summative tests for Introductory Course, First Course, and Second Course test the students' mastery of vocabulary through the use of context clue, like meanings, opposite meanings, word analysis, and multimeaning items. The summative tests for Third Course through Complete Course test students' vocabulary mastery through reading passages and context clue items, sentence completion items, and analogies items.

The answers for each test are included in the *Teacher's Answer Key* that accompanies the **Vocabulary Workshop** series. The point scoring for each test follows the directions for each part of that test. The total score for each test is 100 points.

Using the Vocabulary Workshop *Program in the Classroom*

You may wish to work with this innovative series in one of two ways.
- Proceed through each of the thirty lessons in *Making New Words Your Own.* In this way, you will introduce students to the entire three-hundred-word list, ten words at a time. After students complete each lesson in *Making New Words Your Own,* administer the accompanying formative test. If the mean score on these tests is 80% or above, you may not find it necessary to work through the remaining sections. However, if the mean score is below 80%, or if your goal is to prepare students for standardized tests, you may wish to assign *Connecting New Words and Patterns, Reading New Words in Context,* and, for Introductory Course, First Course, and Second

Course students, *Understanding New Words and Their Uses*. After working through ten lessons of *Making New Words Your Own* and the five corresponding lessons in each of the remaining sections, administer the accompanying summative test.

- Work with twenty words at a time, beginning by working through two lessons in *Making New Words Your Own*. For example, for the Introductory Course, First Course, and Second Course students, work through Lessons 3 and 4 of *Making New Words Your Own*, then proceed directly to Lesson 2 of *Understanding New Words and Their Uses*, Lesson 2 of *Connecting New Words and Patterns*, and Lesson 2 of *Reading New Words in Context*. After completing ten lessons in *Making New Words Your Own* and each of the five corresponding lessons in the remaining sections, administer the accompanying summative test.

Conclusion

This new edition of *Vocabulary Workshop* has been designed to help students learn vocabulary independently and become better readers. We believe that you will find *Vocabulary Workshop* a flexible program that will complement your own approaches to teaching vocabulary in the classroom.

Norbert Elliot
January 1993

Introductory Course

Lesson 1   pages 3–6
Exercise 1   Mapping
Your Guess and Definition answers will vary. Possible responses to Other Forms items follow.

1. *n.* definition, definiteness, definitiveness; *vt.* define, defines, defined, defining; *adj.* definitive; *adv.* definitely, definitively
2. *n.* denial; *vt.* denies, denied, denying
3. *n.* descent, descendant; *n. pl.* descendants; *vi.* or *vt.* descend, descends, descended, descending
4. *n.* doubtfulness, doubter; *vi.* or *vt.* doubt, doubts, doubted, doubting; *adj.* doubtable; *adv.* doubtingly, doubtfully
5. *n.* majoritarianism; *n. pl.* majorities; *adj.* majoritarian
6. *n.* navigation, navigability; *n. pl.* navigators; *vi.* or *vt.* navigate, navigates, navigated, navigating; *adj.* navigable; *adv.* navigably, navigationally
7. *n.* reliability, reliableness, reliance; *vi.* rely, relies, relied, relying; *adj.* reliant; *adv.* reliably, reliantly
8. *n.* symbolism, symbolist, symbolization, symbolizer, symbology; *n. pl.* symbols; *vt.* symboled, symboling; *vi.* or *vt.* symbolize, symbolizes, symbolized, symbolizing; *adj.* symbolic, symbolical, symbolistic; *adv.* symbolically, symbolistically
9. *adj.* twilit
10. *n.* vividness; *adv.* vividly

Exercise 2   Context Clues
11. (E) majority
12. (D) definite
13. (I) symbol
14. (C) doubtful
15. (J) navigator
16. (F) vivid
17. (H) deny
18. (G) twilight
19. (A) descendants
20. (B) reliable

Exercise 3   Like Meanings and Opposite Meanings
21. B   22. A   23. D   24. C   25. B   26. C   27. B
28. C   29. A   30. D

Lesson 2   pages 7–10
Exercise 1   Mapping
Your Guess and Definition answers will vary. Possible responses to Other Forms items follow.

1. *n.* astonishment; *vt.* astonishes, astonished, astonishing; *adj.* astonishing; *adv.* astonishingly
2. *n.* conferrer, conferee, conference; *n. pl.* conferences; *vi.* or *vt.* confer, confers, conferred, conferring; *adj.* conferable
3. *n.* innumerableness, innumerability; *adj.* innumerous; *adv.* innumerably
4. *n.* interviewer, interviewee; *n. pl.* interviews; *vi.* or *vt.* interviews, interviewed, interviewing
5. *n.* journalist, journal, journalese; *adj.* journalistic; *adv.* journalistically
6. *n.* legendry; *n. pl.* legends; *adj.* legendary
7. *n.* quotation, quotability, quoter; *vi.* or *vt.* quotes, quoted, quoting; *adj.* quotable; *adv.* quotably
8. *n. pl.* sessions; *adj.* sessional
9. *n.* summary, summation, summarist, summariness, summarization, summarizer; *n. pl.* summaries; *vt.* summarizes, summarized, summarizing; *adv.* summarily
10. *n.* unexpectedness; *adj.* unexpected

Exercise 2   Context Clues
11. (G) astonish
12. (A) legend
13. (D) interview
14. (J) unexpectedly
15. (E) quote
16. (B) innumerable
17. (I) conference
18. (F) journalism
19. (H) sessions
20. (C) summarize

Exercise 3   Like Meanings and Opposite Meanings
21. B   22. A   23. D   24. A   25. C   26. C   27. B
28. C   29. A   30. A

Lesson 3   pages 11–14
Exercise 1   Mapping
Your Guess and Definition answers will vary. Possible responses to Other Forms items follow.

1. *n.* collapsibility; *n. pl.* collapses; *vi.* or *vt.* collapses, collapsed, collapsing; *adj.* collapsible
2. *n.* collision; *vi.* collides, collided, colliding
3. *n.* disaster; *adv.* disastrously
4. *n.* fatality, fatalism, fatalist; *n. pl.* fatalities; *adj.* fatalistic; *adv.* fatally, fatalistically
5. *n.* founder; *n. pl.* foundations; *vi.* or *vt.* found, founds, founded, founding; *adj.* foundational
6. *n.* ignorance, ignorer; *vt.* ignores, ignored, ignoring; *adj.* ignorant; *adv.* ignorantly
7. *n.* incidence; *n. pl.* incidents; *adj.* incidental; *adv.* incidentally
8. *n.* mischief, mischievousness; *adv.* mischievously
9. *n. pl.* nuisances
10. *n.* prediction, predictability, predictor; *vi.* or *vt.* predicts, predicted, predicting; *adj.* predictable, predictive; *adv.* predictably, predictively

Exercise 2   Context Clues
11. (J) mischievous
12. (A) foundation
13. (C) disastrous
14. (D) nuisance
15. (G) collide
16. (E) predict
17. (F) incident
18. (I) collapse
19. (H) fatal
20. (B) ignore

Exercise 3   Like Meanings and Opposite Meanings
21. D   22. A   23. B   24. C   25. D   26. B   27. A
28. D   29. A   30. A

Lesson 4 pages 15–18
Exercise 1 Mapping
Your Guess and Definition answers will vary. Possible responses to Other Forms items follow.

1. *n.* aviator, aviation, aviator; *vi.* aviate, aviates, aviated, aviating
2. *n.* bombardier, bombardment; *vt.* bombards, bombarded, bombarding
3. *n.* declaration, declarer; *vi.* or *vt.* declares, declared, declaring; *adj.* declarative, declaratory, declarable; *adv.* declaredly, declaratively
4. *n.* demonstrator, demonstrability, demonstrableness, demonstrativeness; *n. pl.* demonstrations; *vi.* or *vt.* demonstrate, demonstrates, demonstrated, demonstrating; *adj.* demonstrable, demonstrative; *adv.* demonstrably
5. *n.* departee; *n. pl.* departures; *vi.* or *vt.* depart, departs, departed, departing; *adj.* departed
6. *n.* detective, detector, detection; *vt.* detects, detected, detecting; *adj.* detectable, detectible
7. *n.* disturbance, disturber; *vt.* disturbs, disturbed, disturbing
8. *n.* exceptionality; *n. pl.* exceptions; *adj.* exceptional, exceptionable, exceptive; *adv.* exceptionally, exceptionably
9. *n.* locale, locality, location, localism, localite, localization; *vt.* localize, localizes, localized, localizing; *adj.* local, localizable
10. *n.* miracle, miraculousness; *adv.* miraculously

Exercise 2 Context Clues
11. (E) aviation	16. (J) declared
12. (A) disturb	17. (F) exception
13. (H) miraculous	18. (I) demonstration
14. (B) locally	19. (C) detect
15. (D) bombard	20. (G) departure

Exercise 3 Like Meanings and Opposite Meanings
21. D 22. A 23. C 24. D 25. B 26. D 27. A
28. A 29. D 30. C

Lesson 5 pages 19–22
Exercise 1 Mapping
Your Guess and Definition answers will vary. Possible responses to Other Forms items follow.

1. *n.* cautiousness; *vt.* cautions, cautioned, cautioning; *adj.* cautious, cautionary; *adv.* cautiously
2. *n.* congratulation, congratulator; *vt.* congratulates, congratulated, congratulating; *adj.* congratulatory
3. *n.* dreadfulness; *vi.* dreads, dreaded, dreading; *adj.* dreadful; *adv.* dreadfully
4. *n.* erroneousness; *n. pl.* errors; *adj.* erroneous; *adv.* erroneously
5. *n.* generator; *n. pl.* generations; *vt.* generate, generates, generated, generating; *adj.* generative, generational
6. *n.* gratefulness; *adj.* grateful; *adv.* gratefully
7. *n.* hero, heroine, heroism; *n. pl.* heroics; *adj.* heroical; *adv.* heroically

8. *n.* involvement; *vt.* involves, involved, involving; *adj.* involved
9. *adv.* previously
10. *n.* separatist, separator, separatism, separability; *n. pl.* separations; *vi.* or *vt.* separate, separates, separated, separating; *adj.* separable, separative, separatory; *adv.* separately, separably

Exercise 2 Context Clues
11. (E) gratitude	16. (G) heroic
12. (J) caution	17. (B) generations
13. (F) involved	18. (H) separation
14. (I) error	19. (A) dread
15. (D) congratulate	20. (C) previous

Exercise 3 Like Meanings and Opposite Meanings
21. A 22. C 23. B 24. D 25. C 26. C 27. A
28. D 29. A 30. C

Lesson 6 pages 23–26
Exercise 1 Mapping
Your Guess and Definition answers will vary. Possible responses to Other Forms items follow.

1. *n. pl.* abdomens; *adj.* abdominal
2. *n. pl.* commotions; *vt.* commove, commoves, commoved, commoving
3. *n.* competitor, competitiveness; *vi.* compete, competes, competed, competing; *adj.* competitive; *adv.* competitively
4. *n. pl.* escorts; *vt.* escorts, escorted, escorting
5. *n.* flexibility; *adv.* flexibly
6. *n. pl.* foes
7. *n. pl.* hoists; *vt.* hoists, hoisted, hoisting
8. *n.* maximization, maximizer; *n. pl.* maximums, maxima; *vt.* maximize, maximizes, maximized, maximizing; *adj.* maximal; *adv.* maximally
9. *n.* mobility, mobilization, mobilizer; *vi.* or *vt.* mobilize, mobilizes, mobilized, mobilizing; *adj.* mobilizable
10. *n.* paralyzation, paralyzer; *n. pl.* paralyses; *vt.* paralyze, paralyzes, paralyzed, paralyzing; *adj.* paralytic

Exercise 2 Context Clues
11. (D) abdomen	16. (E) foes
12. (A) hoist	17. (B) flexible
13. (F) escort	18. (G) paralysis
14. (J) mobile	19. (I) maximum
15. (H) commotion	20. (C) competition

Exercise 3 Like Meanings and Opposite Meanings
21. D 22. B 23. A 24. C 25. B 26. B 27. B
28. D 29. A 30. B

Lesson 7 pages 27–30
Exercise 1 Mapping
Your Guess and Definition answers will vary. Possible responses to Other Forms items follow.

1. *n.* daintiness; *n. pl.* dainties; *adj.* daintier, daintiest; *adv.* daintily
2. *n. pl.* discomforts; *vt.* discomforts, discomforted, discomforting

3. *n.* discouragement; *vi.* or *vt.* discourages, discouraged, discouraging; *adj.* discouraging; *adv.* discouragingly
4. *n.* earnestness; *adv.* earnestly
5. *n.* inhalant, inhaler, inhalation, inhalator; *vi.* or *vt.* inhales, inhaled, inhaling
6. *n.* lingerer; *vi.* lingers, lingered, lingering; *adj.* lingering; *adv.* lingeringly
7. *n.* regulator, regulation; *vt.* regulates, regulated, regulating; *adj.* regulatory, regulable
8. *n. pl.* requirements; *vt.* require, requires, required, requiring; *adj.* requisite
9. *n. pl.* vacuums, vacua; *vi.* or *vt.* vacuums, vacuumed, vacuuming; *adj.* vacuous
10. *n.* vaulting; *n. pl.* vaults; *vi.* or *vt.* vaults, vaulted, vaulting; *adj.* vaulted, vaulting

Exercise 2   Context Clues
11. (D) lingered
12. (H) discomfort
13. (C) vault
14. (I) inhale
15. (E) earnest
16. (G) discouraged
17. (A) requirement
18. (B) dainty
19. (F) vacuum
20. (J) regulated

Exercise 3   Like Meanings and Opposite Meanings
21. A   22. D   23. C   24. D   25. B   26. C   27. A
28. C   29. B   30. C

Lesson 8   pages 31–34
Exercise 1   Mapping
Your Guess and Definition answers will vary. Possible responses to Other Forms items follow.
1. *n. pl.* assaults; *vi.* or *vt.* assaults, assaulted, assaulting; *adj.* assaultive
2. *n.* concealment, concealer; *vt.* conceals, concealed, concealing; *adj.* concealable
3. *n.* disguisement, disguiser; *n. pl.* disguises; *vt.* disguises, disguised, disguising; *adv.* disguisedly
4. *vi.* or *vt.* gasps, gasped, gasping
5. *n.* hibernation, hibernator; *vi.* hibernates, hibernated, hibernating
6. *n.* imitation, imitator, imitativeness; *vt.* imitates, imitated, imitating; *adj.* imitative, imitable; *adv.* imitatively
7. *n.* imposter, imposture; *n. pl.* impostors
8. *n.* portioner; *n. pl.* portions; *vt.* portions, portioned, portioning; *adj.* portionless
9. *n. pl.* references; *adj.* referent, referential; *adv.* referentially
10. *n.* termination, terminableness, terminator; *vi.* or *vt.* terminate, terminates, terminated, terminating; *adj.* terminable, terminative, terminational; *adv.* terminably, terminally

Exercise 2   Context Clues
11. (G) gasp
12. (E) assault
13. (H) portioned
14. (F) impostor
15. (B) terminal
16. (I) disguise
17. (J) hibernate
18. (C) conceal
19. (A) references
20. (D) imitated

Exercise 3   Like Meanings and Opposite Meanings
21. C   22. A   23. D   24. B   25. D   26. A   27. C
28. C   29. A   30. D

Lesson 9   pages 35–38
Exercise 1   Mapping
Your Guess and Definition answers will vary. Possible responses to Other Forms items follow.
1. *n.* bureaucrat, bureaucracy, bureaucratese, bureaucratization; *n. pl.* bureaus, bureaux; *vi.* or *vt.* bureaucratize, bureaucratizes, bureaucratized, bureaucratizing; *adj.* bureaucratic; *adv.* bureaucratically
2. *n.* lunarian, lunation; *adj.* lunate, lunated; *adv.* lunately
3. *n. pl.* particles
4. *n.* pharmacist, pharmaceutical, pharmacology, pharmacologist, pharmacopoeia; *n. pl.* pharmacies; *adj.* pharmacologic, pharmacological, pharmaceutical, pharmacopoeial; *adv.* pharmacologically, pharmaceutically
5. *n.* piercer; *vi.* or *vt.* pierces, pierced, piercing; *adj.* piercing; *adv.* piercingly
6. *n.* receiptor; *n. pl.* receipts; *vt.* receive, receives, received, receiving; *adj.* receivable, received
7. *n.* resignation, resignedness; *vt.* resigns, resigned, resigning; *adj.* resigned; *adv.* resignedly
8. *n.* statics; *adj.* staticky; *adv.* statically
9. *n.* surgeon; *n. pl.* surgeries; *adj.* surgical; *adv.* surgically
10. *vt.* unman, unmanned, unmanning

Exercise 2   Context Clues
11. (E) pierce
12. (A) surgery
13. (H) bureau
14. (D) receipt
15. (F) resign
16. (J) particle
17. (G) unmanned
18. (C) static
19. (B) pharmacy
20. (I) lunar

Exercise 3   Like Meanings and Opposite Meanings
21. B   22. B   23. D   24. C   25. A   26. A   27. A
28. D   29. A   30. B

Lesson 10   pages 39–42
Exercise 1   Mapping
Your Guess and Definition answers will vary. Possible responses to Other Forms items follow.
1. *n.* automatization, automaton, automatism, automatist; *vt.* automate, automates, automated, automating; *adj.* automatic; *adv.* automatically
2. *n.* flammability
3. *n.* gossiper; *vi.* gossips, gossiped, gossiping; *adj.* gossipy
4. *n.* licensee, licenser, licensor, licensure, licentiate, licentiateship; *n. pl.* licenses; *vt.* licenses, licensed, licensing; *adj.* licensable
5. *n. pl.* nephews
6. *n.* prier, pryer; *n. pl.* pries; *vi.* or *vt.* pries, pried, prying; *adv.* pryingly
7. *n.* ransomer; *vt.* ransoms, ransomed, ransoming
8. *n.* strayer; *n. pl.* strays; *vi.* strays, strayed, straying
9. *n.* suspiciousness, suspect; *n. pl.* suspicions; *vi.* or *vt.* suspect, suspects, suspected, suspecting; *adj.* suspicious; *adv.* suspiciously
10. *n.* tollage; *n. pl.* tolls; *vi.* tolls, tolled, tolling

Exercise 2   Context Clues

11. (G) stray
12. (E) automation
13. (C) toll
14. (A) license
15. (D) pry
16. (F) suspicion
17. (I) nephew
18. (H) gossip
19. (J) ransom
20. (B) flammable

Exercise 3   Like Meanings and Opposite Meanings

21. D   22. A   23. A   24. C   25. B   26. B   27. A
28. B   29. D   30. A

Lesson 11   pages 43–46
Exercise 1   Mapping

Your Guess and Definition answers will vary. Possible responses to Other Forms items follow.

1. *n.* analysis, analyst, analyzer, analytics; *vt.* analyzes, analyzed, analyzing; *adj.* analytic, analytical, analyzable; *adv.* analytically
2. *n.* careerist, careerism; *n. pl.* careers; *vi.* careers, careered, careering
3. *n.* debater; *n. pl.* debates; *vi.* or *vt.* debates, debated, debating; *adj.* debatable
4. *n.* documentation, documentary, documentarian, documentarist; *n. pl.* documents; *vt.* documents, documented, documenting; *adj.* documental
5. *n.* essentiality, essentialism; *n. pl.* essentials; *vt.* essentialize, essentializes, essentialized, essentializing; *adv.* essentially
6. *adj.* identic; *adv.* identically
7. *n. pl.* offspring, offsprings
8. *n.* public, publicist; *vt.* publicize, publicizes, publicized, publicizing
9. *n.* reactance, reactant, reactivity, reactiveness; *n. pl.* reactions; *vi.* or *vt.* react, reacts, reacted, reacting; *adj.* reactional, reactionary, reactive; *adv.* reactively
10. *n.* thoroughness; *adv.* thoroughly

Exercise 2   Context Clues

11. (A) essential
12. (E) thorough
13. (D) publicity
14. (J) debate
15. (B) identical
16. (I) reaction
17. (F) documents
18. (H) careering
19. (C) offspring
20. (G) analyzing

Exercise 3   Like Meanings and Opposite Meanings

21. B   22. B   23. C   24. A   25. D   26. C   27. A
28. C   29. B   30. D

Lesson 12   pages 47–50
Exercise 1   Mapping

Your Guess and Definition answers will vary. Possible responses to Other Forms items follow.

1. *n.* biographer; *n. pl.* biographies; *adj.* biographic, biographical; *adv.* biographically
2. *n.* destiny; *n. pl.* destinations; *vt.* destine, destines, destined, destining
3. *n.* determinant, determiner, determinism, determinist; *vi.* or *vt.* determine, determines, determined, determining; *adj.* determined, determinable, determinative, deterministic; *adv.* deterministically

4. *n.* generosity, generousness; *adv.* generously
5. *n. pl.* notions; *adj.* notional; *adv.* notionally
6. *n.* professional, professionalism, professionalization, professor; *n. pl.* professions; *vt.* professionalize, professionalizes, professionalized, professionalizing; *adj.* professional; *adv.* professionally
7. *n.* respectability, respecter; *vt.* respect, respects, respected, respecting; *adv.* respectably
8. *n.* routinism, routinist, routinization; *n. pl.* routines; *vt.* routinize, routinizes, routinized, routinizing; *adv.* routinely
9. *n.* scholarship; *n. pl.* scholars; *adj.* scholastic, scholastical; *adv.* scholarly, scholastically
10. *adj.* self-confident; *adv.* self-confidently

Exercise 2   Context Clues

11. (C) notion
12. (J) self-confidence
13. (D) determination
14. (E) respectable
15. (B) biography
16. (F) generous
17. (I) destination
18. (H) profession
19. (A) scholar
20. (G) routine

Exercise 3   Like Meanings and Opposite Meanings

21. D   22. C   23. A   24. D   25. B   26. A   27. C
28. A   29. B   30. C

Lesson 13   pages 51–54
Exercise 1   Mapping

Your Guess and Definition answers will vary. Possible responses to Other Forms items follow.

1. *n.* ceremoniousness, ceremonial; *n. pl.* ceremonies; *adj.* ceremonial, ceremonious; *adv.* ceremoniously
2. *n.* conductor, conductorship, conduction, conductivity, conductibility, conductance; *vi.* or *vt.* conducts, conducted, conducting; *adj.* conductive, conductible, conductorial
3. *n.* consensus; *vi.* consents, consented, consenting; *adj.* consensual, consentaneous, consentient; *adv.* consensually, consentaneously
4. *n.* fragrance, fragrancy; *n. pl.* fragrancies; *adv.* fragrantly
5. *n.* ignition, igniter, ignitor; *vi.* or *vt.* ignites, ignited, igniting; *adj.* ignitable, ignitible
6. *n.* interruption, interrupter; *vt.* interrupt, interrupts, interrupted, interrupting; *adj.* interruptive, interrupted
7. *n.* manager, managership, managerialism, manageability, manageableness; *vi.* or *vt.* manage, manages, managed, managing; *adj.* manageable, managerial; *adv.* managerially, manageably
8. *n.* plea, pleader; *n. pl.* pleadings, pleas; *vi.* or *vt.* pleads, pleaded, pled, pleading; *adj.* pleadable; *adv.* pleadingly
9. *n. pl.* quarantines; *vt.* quarantines, quarantined, quarantining; *adj.* quarantinable
10. *n.* schemer; *n. pl.* schemes; *vi.* schemes, schemed, scheming; *adj.* schematic, scheming; *adv.* schemingly

Exercise 2   Context Clues

11. (C) conduct	16. (G) interrupt
12. (D) schemed	17. (I) consent
13. (A) quarantined	18. (H) fragrant
14. (F) ignited	19. (E) pleaded
15. (J) ceremony	20. (B) management

Exercise 3   Like Meanings and Opposite Meanings

21. A   22. B   23. A   24. D   25. B   26. A   27. D
28. A   29. B   30. A

Lesson 14   pages 55–58

Exercise 1   Mapping

Your Guess and Definition answers will vary. Possible responses to Other Forms items follow.

1. *n.* architecture; *n. pl.* architects; *adj.* architectural, architectonic; *adv.* architecturally, architectonically
2. *n.* betrayal, betrayer; *vt.* betrays, betrayed, betraying
3. *n.* desperation, desperateness; *adv.* desperately
4. *n. pl.* districts; *vt.* districts, districted, districting
5. *n.* eternity, eternalness, eternization; *vt.* eternize, eternizes, eternized, eternizing; *adv.* eternally
6. *n. pl.* glimpses; *vi.* or *vt.* glimpses, glimpsed, glimpsing
7. *n. pl.* realms
8. *n.* sacrificer; *n. pl.* sacrifices; *vi.* or *vt.* sacrifices, sacrificed, sacrificing; *adj.* sacrificial; *adv.* sacrificially
9. *n.* victimizer, victimization; *n. pl.* victims; *vt.* victimize, victimizes, victimized, victimizing
10. *n.* victor, victory; *adv.* victoriously

Exercise 2   Context Clues

11. (B) architects	16. (A) eternal
12. (I) desperate	17. (H) victims
13. (E) glimpse	18. (G) realm
14. (C) sacrifice	19. (F) districts
15. (J) betray	20. (D) victorious

Exercise 3   Like Meanings and Opposite Meanings

21. B   22. A   23. D   24. B   25. A   26. A   27. B
28. A   29. C   30. A

Lesson 15   pages 59–62

Exercise 1   Mapping

Your Guess and Definition answers will vary. Possible responses to Other Forms items follow.

1. *n.* abundance; *adv.* abundantly
2. *n. pl.* barriers
3. *n.* description, descriptiveness, describer; *vt.* describe, describes, describing; *adj.* descriptive, describable; *adv.* descriptively
4. *n.* desirability, desirableness; *vi.* or *vt.* desire, desires, desired, desiring; *adj.* desirous; *adv.* desirously, desirably
5. *n.* establishment, establishmentarian, establisher; *vt.* establishes, established, establishing; *adj.* establishmentarian
6. *n.* geologist; *n. pl.* geologies; *vi.* or *vt.* geologize, geologizes, geologized, geologizing; *adj.* geologic, geological; *adv.* geologically

7. *n.* possession, possessiveness, possessor; *vt.* possesses, possessed, possessing; *adj.* possessive, possessed, possessory; *adv.* possessively
8. *n.* prehistorian, prehistory; *adj.* prehistorical; *adv.* prehistorically
9. *n.* surveyor, surveying, surveillance; *n. pl.* surveys; *vt.* surveys, surveyed, surveying
10. *n. pl.* terrains

Exercise 2   Context Clues

11. (E) descriptive	16. (J) survey
12. (C) geology	17. (H) possess
13. (F) terrain	18. (G) barrier
14. (B) abundance	19. (I) prehistoric
15. (A) establish	20. (D) desirable

Exercise 3   Like Meanings and Opposite Meanings

21. A   22. B   23. A   24. C   25. D   26. C   27. A
28. B   29. D   30. A

Lesson 16   pages 63–66

Exercise 1   Mapping

Your Guess and Definition answers will vary. Possible responses to Other Forms items follow.

1. *n.* drama, dramatics, dramatist, dramatization, dramaturgy; *vi.* or *vt.* dramatize, dramatizes, dramatized, dramatizing; *adv.* dramatically,
2. *n.* extraordinariness; *adv.* extraordinarily
3. *n. pl.* feats
4. *n.* irregularity; *adv.* irregularly
5. *adj.* leisured; *adv.* leisurely
6. *n.* lieutenancy; *n. pl.* lieutenants, lieutenancies
7. *n. pl.* marvels; *vi.* or *vt.* marvels, marveled, marveling; *adj.* marvelous; *adv.* marvelously
8. *n.* numerousness; *adv.* numerously
9. *n.* satisfaction, satisfier, satisfactoriness; *vt.* satisfies, satisfied, satisfying; *adj.* satisfactory; *adv.* satisfactorily
10. *n.* vicinage; *n. pl.* vicinities

Exercise 2   Context Clues

11. (B) dramatic	16. (I) numerous
12. (C) marvels	17. (E) feat
13. (F) irregular	18. (D) vicinity
14. (J) satisfied	19. (H) extraordinary
15. (G) leisure	20. (A) lieutenant

Exercise 3   Like Meanings and Opposite Meanings

21. C   22. A   23. B   24. C   25. D   26. A   27. C
28. B   29. A   30. B

Lesson 17   pages 67–70

Exercise 1   Mapping

Your Guess and Definition answers will vary. Possible responses to Other Forms items follow.

1. *n.* ambition; *adv.* ambitiously
2. *n.* enviousness, envier; *vt.* envies, envied, envying; *adj.* envious, enviable; *adv.* enviously, envyingly
3. *n.* exclamation, exclaimer; *vi.* or *vt.* exclaims, exclaimed, exclaiming; *adj.* exclamatory

4. *n.* heiress, heirdom, heirship; *n. pl.* heirs
5. *n.* honor, honoree, honorableness, honorability; *adj.* honorary; *adv.* honorably, honorarily, honorifically
6. *n. pl.* oaths
7. *n.* portraiture, portraitist, portrayal, portrayer; *n. pl.* portraits; *vt.* portray, portrays, portrayed, portraying; *adj.* portrayable
8. *vi.* reigns, reigned, reigning
9. *n. pl.* wardrobes
10. *n.* yachting, yachtsman, yachtsmanship, yachtswoman; *n. pl.* yachts, yachtsmen, yachtswomen

Exercise 2   Context Clues

11. (C) heirs	16. (H) exclaimed
12. (D) envied	17. (F) oath
13. (E) portrait	18. (G) yacht
14. (I) wardrobes	19. (A) reigned
15. (B) ambitious	20. (J) honorable

Exercise 3   Like Meanings and Opposite Meanings
21. D   22. A   23. B   24. C   25. D   26. A   27. C
28. A   29. D   30. C

Lesson 18   pages 71–74
Exercise 1   Mapping
Your Guess and Definition answers will vary. Possible responses to Other Forms items follow.
1. *n.* counterfeiter; *vi.* or *vt.* counterfeits, counterfeited, counterfeiting
2. *n. pl.* galaxies; *adj.* galactic
3. *n.* investor; *n. pl.* investments; *vi.* or *vt.* invest, invests, invested, investing
4. *n. pl.* knapsacks
5. *n.* luxury, luxuriance, luxuriancy, luxuriousness, luxuriation; *vi.* luxuriate, luxuriates, luxuriated, luxuriating; *adj.* luxuriant; *adv.* luxuriantly, luxuriously
6. *n.* ornament, ornamentation, ornamenter; *vt.* ornaments, ornamented, ornamenting; *adv.* ornamentally
7. *n.* relation, relater, relationship, relative, relativeness, relativism, relativity, relator; *vt.* relates, related, relating; *adj.* relatable, related, relational, relative; *adv.* relatively
8. *n.* requestor, requester; *n. pl.* requests; *vt.* requests, requested, requesting
9. *n.* solitude, solitariness; *n. pl.* solitaries; *adv.* solitarily
10. *n.* transparence, transparency, transparentness; *adv.* transparently

Exercise 2   Context Clues

11. (I) counterfeit	16. (G) investment
12. (F) requests	17. (J) luxurious
13. (A) knapsack	18. (B) transparent
14. (E) ornamental	19. (C) relate
15. (D) solitary	20. (H) galaxy

Exercise 3   Like Meanings and Opposite Meanings
21. B   22. A   23. C   24. D   25. C   26. B   27. A
28. C   29. C   30. D

Lesson 19   pages 75–78
Exercise 1   Mapping
Your Guess and Definition answers will vary. Possible responses to Other Forms items follow.
1. *n.* appropriateness, appropriation, appropriator; *vt.* appropriates, appropriated, appropriating; *adj.* appropriative, appropriable; *adv.* appropriately
2. *n.* assumption, assumer; *vt.* assumes, assumed, assuming; *adj.* assuming, assumed, assumable, assumptive
3. *n.* contribution, contributor, contributory; *vi.* or *vt.* contributes, contributed, contributing; *adj.* contributory, contributive
4. *n.* cultivation, cultivator, cultivability; *vt.* cultivates, cultivated, cultivating; *adj.* cultivated, cultivable, cultivatable
5. *n.* gorgeousness; *adv.* gorgeously
6. *n.* heartiness; *adj.* heartier, heartiest; *adv.* heartily
7. *n.* invitation, invitee; *vt.* invite, invites, invited, inviting; *adj.* invitatory, invitational, inviting; *adv.* invitingly
8. *n.* occasionalism; *n. pl.* occasions; *adj.* occasional; *adv.* occasionally
9. *n.* ordinariness, ordinary; *adj.* ordinary
10. *n.* quantitativeness, quantitation; *n. pl.* quantities; *vt.* quantitates, quantitated, quantitating; *adj.* quantitative; *adv.* quantitatively

Exercise 2   Context Clues

11. (C) appropriate	16. (A) ordinarily
12. (H) hearty	17. (E) quantity
13. (I) occasion	18. (B) cultivated
14. (J) assumed	19. (G) inviting
15. (F) gorgeous	20. (D) contributed

Exercise 3   Like Meanings and Opposite Meanings
21. B   22. C   23. A   24. D   25. B   26. C   27. C
28. A   29. C   30. B

Lesson 20   pages 79–82
Exercise 1   Mapping
Your Guess and Definition answers will vary. Possible responses to Other Forms items follow.
1. *n.* boaster, boastfulness; *vi.* or *vt.* boasts, boasted, boasting; *adj.* boastful; *adv.* boastfully, boastingly
2. *n. pl.* contrasts; *vt.* contrasts, contrasted, contrasting; *adj.* contrastive, contrastable
3. *n. pl.* disadvantages; *vt.* disadvantaged, disadvantaging; *adj.* disadvantaged, disadvantageous; *adv.* disadvantageously
4. *n.* elimination, eliminator; *vt.* eliminates, eliminated, eliminating; *adj.* eliminatory, eliminative
5. *n.* exportation, exporter; *n. pl.* exports; *vt.* exports, exported, exporting; *adj.* exportable
6. *n. pl.* forefathers
7. *n.* importation, importer, importance; *n. pl.* imports; *vt.* imports, imported, importing; *adj.* important, importable

8. *n.* inaccuracy; *adv.* inaccurately
9. *n.* precipitateness, precipitator;
   vi. or *vt.* precipitates, precipitated, precipitating;
   adj. precipitous, precipitative; *adv.* precipitately,
   precipitously
10. *n.* traditionalism, traditionist; *n. pl.* traditions;
   adj. traditional, traditionalistic; *adv.* traditionally

Exercise 2   Context Clues

11. (H) boasts
12. (A) contrast
13. (E) import
14. (C) tradition
15. (J) disadvantage
16. (B) precipitation
17. (I) exported
18. (G) forefathers
19. (F) eliminated
20. (D) inaccurate

Exercise 3   Like Meanings and Opposite Meanings

21. C   22. B   23. B   24. B   25. A   26. C   27. B
28. A   29. D   30. A

Lesson 21   pages 83–86
Exercise 1   Mapping
*Your Guess and Definition answers will vary. Possible
responses to Other Forms items follow.*

1. *n.* appreciation, appreciator, appreciativeness;
   vi. or *vt.* appreciates, appreciated, appreciating;
   adj. appreciative, appreciable, appreciatory;
   adv. appreciatively, appreciably
2. *n.* Braille; *vt.* Brailled, Brailling
3. *n.* entertainment, entertainer;
   vi. or *vt.* entertains, entertained, entertaining;
   adj. entertaining; *adv.* entertainingly
4. *n.* genuineness; *adv.* genuinely
5. *n.* informant, information, informer;
   vi. or *vt.* informs, informed, informing;
   adj. informative, informatory; *adv.* informatively
6. *n. pl.* inspirations; *vi.* or *vt.* inspire, inspired,
   inspiring; *adj.* inspirational, inspiratory;
   adv. inspirationally
7. *n. pl.* mammoths
8. *n. pl.* texts; *adj.* textual, textuary; *adv.* textually
9. *n. pl.* themes; *vt.* themes, themed, theming;
   adj. thematic; *adv.* thematically
10. *n.* visualization; *vi.* or *vt.* visualize, visualizes,
   visualized, visualizing; *adv.* visually

Exercise 2   Context Clues

11. (J) visual
12. (G) theme
13. (D) informed
14. (F) inspiration
15. (B) mammoth
16. (A) genuine
17. (E) entertain
18. (I) text
19. (C) appreciate
20. (H) braille

Exercise 3   Like Meanings and Opposite Meanings

21. D   22. B   23. C   24. A   25. A   26. B   27. A
28. D   29. C   30. A

Lesson 22   pages 87–90
Exercise 1   Mapping
*Your Guess and Definition answers will vary. Possible
responses to Other Forms items follow.*

1. *n.* campaigner; *n. pl.* campaigns; *vi.* campaigns,
   campaigned, campaigning

2. *n.* characterization; *n. pl.* characteristics;
   vt. characterize, characterizes, characterized,
   characterizing; *adv.* characteristically
3. *n.* conscientiousness; *adj.* conscientious;
   adv. conscientiously
4. *n.* doubtlessness; *adv.* doubtlessly
5. *n.* fury, furiousness; *adv.* furiously
6. *n.* juvenility, juvenescence; *n. pl.* juveniles,
   juvenilia; *adj.* juvenescent
7. *n.* plotter; *n. pl.* plots; *vi.* or *vt.* plots, plotted,
   plotting
8. *n.* reducibility, reducer, reductionism, reduc-
   tionist; *n. pl.* reductions; *vi.* or *vt.* reduce,
   reduces, reduced, reducing; *adj.* reducible,
   reductional, reductionistic, reductive;
   adv. reducibly, reductively
9. *n.* urgency, urger; *n. pl.* urges, urgencies;
   vi. or *vt.* urges, urged, urging; *adj.* urgent;
   adv. urgently
10. *adj.* widespreading

Exercise 2   Context Clues

11. (E) juveniles
12. (C) doubtless
13. (G) reduction
14. (A) plot
15. (I) widespread
16. (H) furious
17. (B) campaign
18. (D) characteristic
19. (F) urge
20. (J) consciences

Exercise 3   Like Meanings and Opposite Meanings

21. B   22. C   23. D   24. C   25. A   26. B   27. B
28. A   29. A   30. B

Lesson 23   pages 91–94
Exercise 1   Mapping
*Your Guess and Definition answers will vary. Possible
responses to Other Forms items follow.*

1. *n.* applause, applauder; *vi.* or *vt.* applauds,
   applauded, applauding; *adv.* applaudingly
2. *n.* guide; *vt.* guide, guides, guided, guiding;
   adj. guidable
3. *n.* inexpensiveness; *adv.* inexpensively
4. *n.* issuance, issuer; *n. pl.* issues; *vi.* or *vt.* issues,
   issued, issuing
5. *n.* persuasion, persuasiveness, persuader;
   vt. persuades, persuaded, persuading;
   adj. persuasive, persuadable, persuasible;
   adv. persuasively
6. *n.* protestation, protester, protestor;
   n. pl. protests; *vt.* protests, protested, protesting
7. *n.* remediation; *n. pl.* remedies; *vt.* remedies,
   remedied, remedying; *adj.* remedial, remediable,
   remediational; *adv.* remedially
8. *n.* revolutionary, revolutionist; *n. pl.* revolutions,
   revolutionaries; *vt.* revolutionize, revolution-
   izes, revolutionized, revolutionizing; *vt.* revolve,
   revolves, revolved, revolving; *adj.* revolutionary,
   revolvable, revolving
9. *n.* temporariness; *adj.* temporal; *adv.* temporarily
10. *n.* villainy; *n. pl.* villains; *adj.* villainous;
   adv. villainously

Exercise 2   Context Clues

11. (B) inexpensive
12. (A) issue
13. (E) persuade
14. (C) protests
15. (J) applaud
16. (G) guidance
17. (I) villains
18. (F) revolution
19. (D) remedy
20. (H) temporary

Exercise 3   Like Meanings and Opposite Meanings

21. A   22. B   23. C   24. D   25. C   26. B   27. C
28. A   29. D   30. A

Lesson 24   pages 95–98
Exercise 1   Mapping

Your Guess and Definition answers will vary. Possible responses to Other Forms items follow.

1. *n.* adjustment, adjuster, adjustor; *vi.* or *vt.* adjusts, adjusted, adjusting; *adj.* adjustable, adjustive; *adv.* adjustably
2. *n.* balloter; *n. pl.* ballots; *vi.* ballots, balloted, balloting
3. *n.* candidacy, candidature; *n. pl.* candidates, candidacies
4. *n.* corporatist, corporatism, corporator; *n. pl.* corporations; *adj.* corporate; *adv.* corporately
5. *vi.* or *vt.* disgusts, disgusted, disgusting; *adj.* disgusted, disgustful, disgusting; *adv.* disgustedly, disgustingly, disgustfully
6. *n.* dissolution, dissolvent, dissolver; *vi.* or *vt.* dissolves, dissolved, dissolving; *adj.* dissoluble, dissolvable
7. *n.* employee, employment, employability; *n. pl.* employers; *vt.* employ, employs, employed, employing; *adj.* employable
8. *n.* foulness; *adv.* foully
9. *n.* hazardousness; *n. pl.* hazards; *adj.* hazardous; *adv.* hazardously
10. *n.* merchandiser, merchandising; *vi.* or *vt.* merchandises, merchandised, merchandising

Exercise 2   Context Clues

11. (F) hazard
12. (A) dissolves
13. (I) ballot
14. (G) adjust
15. (B) foul
16. (H) candidate
17. (E) merchandised
18. (D) corporations
19. (C) employers
20. (J) disgusts

Exercise 3   Like Meanings and Opposite Meanings

21. B   22. C   23. C   24. D   25. A   26. A   27. C
28. D   29. A   30. A

Lesson 25   pages 99–102
Exercise 1   Mapping

Your Guess and Definition answers will vary. Possible responses to Other Forms items follow.

1. *n.* absorbency, absorption, absorbability, absorber; *vt.* absorbs, absorbed, absorbing; *adj.* absorbent, absorbing, absorbable, absorbtive; *adv.* absorbingly
2. *n.* complainant, complainer; *n. pl.* complaints; *vi.* complains, complained, complaining
3. *n.* cooperation, cooperativeness, cooperator, cooperationist; *vi.* cooperates, cooperated, cooperating; *adj.* cooperative; *adv.* cooperatively

4. *n.* debtor; *n. pl.* debts
5. *n.* mourner, mournfulness; *vi.* or *vt.* mourn, mourns, mourned, mourning; *adj.* mournful; *adv.* mournfully, mourningly
6. *n.* offensiveness, offender; *n. pl.* offenses; *vi.* or *vt.* offend, offends, offended, offending; *adj.* offensive; *adv.* offensively
7. *n.* omission, omitter; *vt.* omits, omitted, omitting; *adj.* omissive, omissible; *adv.* omissively
8. *n.* regretter, regretfulness; *n. pl.* regrets; *vt.* regrets, regretted, regretting; *adj.* regretful, regrettable; *adv.* regretfully, regrettably
9. *n.* securance, secureness, securer; *n. pl.* securities; *vi.* or *vt.* secure, secures, secured, securing; *adj.* secure, securable; *adv.* securely
10. *n.* tenseness; *n. pl.* tensions; *vi.* or *vt.* tense, tenses, tensed, tensing; *adj.* tense, tensile, tenser, tensest; *adv.* tensely

Exercise 2   Context Clues

11. (C) complaint
12. (A) mourning
13. (J) absorbed
14. (E) tension
15. (G) regret
16. (H) debt
17. (I) omit
18. (D) security
19. (F) cooperation
20. (B) offense

Exercise 3   Like Meanings and Opposite Meanings

21. C   22. D   23. A   24. D   25. B   26. D   27. B
28. C   29. D   30. A

Lesson 26   pages 103–106
Exercise 1   Mapping

Your Guess and Definition answers will vary. Possible responses to Other Forms items follow.

1. *n.* amateurishness, amateurism; *n. pl.* amateurs; *adj.* amateurish; *adv.* amateurishly
2. *n.* duplication, duplicator; *n. pl.* duplicates; *vt.* duplicates, duplicated, duplicating; *adj.* duplicatable, duplicable, duplicative
3. *n.* intruder, intrusiveness; *vi.* or *vt.* intrude, intrudes, intruded, intruding; *adj.* intrusive; *adv.* intrusively
4. *n.* keenness; *vi.* or *vt.* keens, keened, keening; *adv.* keenly
5. *n.* privatism; *n. pl.* privacies; *adj.* private, privatist, privatistic; *adv.* privately
6. *n.* rebellion, rebeldom, rebelliousness; *n. pl.* rebels; *vi.* rebels, rebelled, rebelling; *adj.* rebellious; *adv.* rebelliously
7. *n.* residence, residency; *n. pl.* residents; *vi.* reside, resides, resided, residing; *adj.* residential, residentiary; *adv.* residentially
8. *adj.* self-respecting
9. *n.* simplification, simplifier; *vt.* simplify, simplifies, simplified, simplifying; *adj.* simplistic; *adv.* simply, simplistically
10. *n.* sympathizer; *n. pl.* sympathies; *vi.* sympathize, sympathizes, sympathized, sympathizing; *adj.* sympathetic; *adv.* sympathetically, sympathizingly

Exercise 2   Context Clues

11. (H) rebel
12. (B) duplicates
13. (I) simplify
14. (J) resident
15. (E) amateur

16. (C) intrusion
17. (F) privacy
18. (G) sympathy
19. (A) self-respect
20. (D) keen

Exercise 3   Like Meanings and Opposite Meanings

21. A   22. B   23. A   24. C   25. A   26. A   27. D
28. A   29. D   30. C

Lesson 27   pages 107–110
Exercise 1   Mapping
Your Guess and Definition answers will vary. Possible responses to Other Forms items follow.

1. *n.* captive, captor, captivation; *n. pl.* captivities; *vt.* capture, captures, captured, capturing; *adj.* captive; *adv.* captivatingly
2. *vi.* or *vt.* decreases, decreased, decreasing; *adv.* decreasingly
3. *n.* eavesdropper; *vi.* eavesdrops, eavesdropped, eavesdropping
4. *n.* massacrer; *n. pl.* massacres; *vt.* massacres, massacred, massacring
5. *n.* migration, migrant; *vi.* migrates, migrated, migrating; *adj.* migratory, migrant, migrational
6. *n.* preyer; *vi.* preys, preyed, preying
7. *n.* prohibition, prohibitionist, prohibiter, prohibitor; *vt.* prohibits, prohibited, prohibiting; *adj.* prohibitive, prohibitory; *adv.* prohibitively
8. *n.* survivor, survivorship, survivalist, survivability; *vt.* survive, survives, survived, surviving; *adj.* survivable
9. *n.* threatener; *n. pl.* threats; *vi.* or *vt.* threaten, threatens, threatened, threatening; *adv.* threateningly
10. *n.* tragedian, tragedienne, tragicalness; *n. pl.* tragedies; *adj.* tragic, tragical; *adv.* tragically

Exercise 2   Context Clues

11. (I) eavesdrop
12. (F) captivity
13. (C) survival
14. (A) prey
15. (E) decrease

16. (D) threat
17. (H) prohibit
18. (G) tragedy
19. (J) massacre
20. (B) migrate

Exercise 3   Like Meanings and Opposite Meanings

21. C   22. A   23. C   24. D   25. D   26. C   27. C
28. B   29. A   30. D

Lesson 28   pages 111–114
Exercise 1   Mapping
Your Guess and Definition answers will vary. Possible responses to Other Forms items follow.

1. *n.* benefaction, benefactor, beneficence, beneficiary; *n. pl.* benefits; *vi.* or *vt.* benefits, benefited, benefiting; *adj.* beneficent, beneficial; *adv.* beneficently
2. *n.* obviousness; *adv.* obviously
3. *n.* recklessness; *adv.* recklessly
4. *n.* resemblance; *vt.* resembles, resembled, resembling
5. *n.* responsibleness; *n. pl.* responsibilities; *adj.* responsible; *adv.* responsibly

6. *n.* severity, severeness; *n. pl.* severities; *adj.* severer, severest; *adv.* severely
7. *n.* suburbanite, suburbia, suburbanization; *n. pl.* suburbs; *vi.* or *vt.* suburbanize, suburbanizes, suburbanized, suburbanizing; *adj.* suburban, suburbicarian
8. *adv.* unfortunately
9. *n.* unity; *vi.* or *vt.* unites, united, uniting; *adj.* united, unitive; *adv.* unitedly
10. *n.* vocalist, vocalism, vocalization, vocalizer; *vi.* or *vt.* vocalize, vocalizes, vocalized, vocalizing; *adj.* vocalic; *adv.* vocally, vocalically

Exercise 2   Context Clues

11. (A) suburb
12. (I) obvious
13. (D) vocal
14. (G) unfortunate
15. (B) benefit

16. (E) reckless
17. (H) responsibility
18. (F) united
19. (J) resemble
20. (C) severe

Exercise 3   Like Meanings and Opposite Meanings

21. A   22. D   23. B   24. C   25. D   26. C   27. A
28. B   29. B   30. D

Lesson 29   pages 115–118
Exercise 1   Mapping
Your Guess and Definition answers will vary. Possible responses to Other Forms items follow.

1. *n. pl.* anthems
2. *n. pl.* compliments; *vt.* compliments, complimented, complimenting; *adj.* complimentary; *adv.* complimentarily
3. *n.* courtesy, courteousness; *adv.* courteously
4. *n.* engagement; *vi.* or *vt.* engages, engaged, engaging; *adj.* engaged, engaging; *adv.* engagingly
5. *n.* justification, justifier, justifiability; *vi.* or *vt.* justifies, justified, justifying; *adj.* justifiable, justificatory, justificative; *adv.* justifiably
6. *n.* nomination, nominee, nominator; *vt.* nominates, nominated, nominating; *adj.* nominative
7. *n.* promoter; *n. pl.* promotions; *vt.* promote, promotes, promoted, promoting; *adj.* promotable, promotional, promotive
8. *n.* qualification, qualifier; *vt.* qualifies, qualified, qualifying; *adj.* qualified, qualifiable; *adv.* qualifiedly, qualifyingly
9. *n. pl.* rehearsals; *vi.* or *vt.* rehearse, rehearsed, rehearsing
10. *n.* specification, specificity, specifier; *vt.* specifies, specified, specifying; *adj.* specific, specifiable; *adv.* specifically

Exercise 2   Context Clues

11. (B) anthem
12. (H) compliment
13. (A) rehearsal
14. (J) nominate
15. (E) engaged

16. (I) promotions
17. (F) courteous
18. (C) justifies
19. (D) specify
20. (G) qualify

Exercise 3   Like Meanings and Opposite Meanings

21. C   22. C   23. B   24. C   25. D   26. A   27. D
28. A   29. B   30. C

Lesson 30　pages 119–122
Exercise 1　Mapping
Your Guess and Definition answers will vary. Possible responses to Other Forms items follow.

1. *n.* apology, apologist, apologizer, apologia; *vi.* apologizes, apologized, apologizing; *adj.* apologetic, apologetical; *adv.* apologetically
2. *n.* applicant, applicability, applicator; *n. pl.* applications; *vi.* or *vt.* apply, applies, applied, applying; *adj.* applicable, applicative, applicatory
3. *n.* association; *n. pl.* associates; *vi.* or *vt.* associates, associated, associating; *adj.* associative, associable, associational
4. *n.* balladeer, ballade, balladmonger, balladry; *n. pl.* ballads
5. *n.* franticness; *adv.* frantically, franticly
6. *n.* gallantry; *n. pl.* gallantries; *adv.* gallantly
7. *n.* hesitation, hesitancy, hesitance, hesitator, hesitater; *vi.* hesitates, hesitated, hesitating; *adj.* hesitant, hesitative; *adv.* hesitantly, hesitatingly, hesitatively
8. *adj.* impatient; *adv.* impatiently
9. *n. pl.* reservoirs
10. *n.* superiority; *n. pl.* superiorities; *adv.* superiorly

Exercise 2　Context Clues
11. (E) associate
12. (C) gallant
13. (B) apologize
14. (H) frantic
15. (D) reservoirs
16. (J) ballad
17. (F) hesitate
18. (I) superior
19. (G) application
20. (A) impatience

Exercise 3　Like Meanings and Opposite Meanings
21. D　22. A　23. B　24. D　25. A　26. B　27. D
28. B　29. D　30. C

▣ UNDERSTANDING NEW WORDS AND THEIR USES ▣

Lesson 1　pages 125–126
Exercise 1　Multimeaning
1. C　2. B
Exercise 2　Word Analysis
3. A　4. C　5. D　6. C
7. astonish　8. deny
9. innumerable　10. twilight

Lesson 2　pages 127–128
Exercise 1　Multimeaning
1. C　2. A
Exercise 2　Word Analysis
3. C　4. A　5. B　6. C
7. nuisance　8. aviation
9. ignore　10. bombard

Lesson 3　pages 129–130
Exercise 1　Multimeaning
1. B　2. C
Exercise 2　Word Analysis
3. D　4. C　5. C　6. A
7. foe　8. paralysis
9. error　10. congratulate

> *Note:* Encourage students to use the lists of common prefixes and suffixes on page 124 when they are working on the *Prefixes* and *Suffixes* exercises in this section

Lesson 4　pages 131–132
Exercise 1　Multimeaning
1. D　2. C
Exercise 2　Word Analysis
3. C　4. A　5. A　6. A
7. impostor　8. gasp
9. portion　10. dainty

Lesson 5　pages 133–134
Exercise 1　Multimeaning
1. A　2. B
Exercise 2　Word Analysis
3. C　4. C　5. D　6. A
7. gossip　8. ransom
9. receipt　10. nephew

Lesson 6　pages 135–136
Exercise 1　Multimeaning
1. D　2. A
Exercise 2　Word Analysis
3. C　4. D　5. A　6. C
7. notion　8. publicity
9. analyze　10. offspring

Lesson 7　pages 137–138
Exercise 1　Multimeaning
1. C　2. C
Exercise 2　Word Analysis
3. D　4. C　5. B　6. C
7. architect　8. realm
9. district　10. quarantine

Lesson 8　pages 139–140
Exercise 1　Multimeaning
1. B　2. D
Exercise 2　Word Analysis
3. B　4. D　5. D　6. C
7. feat　8. barrier
9. lieutenant　10. vicinity

Lesson 9　pages 141–142
Exercise 1　Multimeaning
1. C　2. A
Exercise 2　Word Analysis
3. B　4. B　5. B　6. A
7. yacht　8. galaxy
9. oath　10. knapsack

Lesson 10　pages 143–144
Exercise 1　Multimeaning
1. C　2. D
Exercise 2　Word Analysis
3. B　4. A　5. D　6. C
7. quantity　8. import
9. gorgeous　10. occasion

Lesson 11　pages 145–146
Exercise 1　Multimeaning
1. D　2. B
Exercise 2　Word Analysis
3. A　4. C　5. A　6. A
7. juvenile　8. widespread
9. theme　10. conscience

Lesson 12   pages 147–148
Exercise 1   Multimeaning
1. A   2. C
Exercise 2   Word Analysis
3. B   4. A   5. B   6. D
7. villain   8. applaud
9. disgust   10. persuade

Lesson 13   pages 149–150
Exercise 1   Multimeaning
1. C   2. B
Exercise 2   Word Analysis
3. C   4. D   5. B   6. D
7. tension   8. privacy
9. complaint   10. keen

Lesson 14   pages 151–152
Exercise 1   Multimeaning
1. B   2. C
Exercise 2   Word Analysis
3. A   4. C   5. C   6. C
7. suburb   8. tragedy
9. massacre   10. severe

Lesson 15   pages 153–154
Exercise 1   Multimeaning
1. B   2. D
Exercise 2   Word Analysis
3. C   4. D   5. B   6. A
7. engage   8. anthem
9. qualify   10. reservoir

CONNECTING NEW WORDS AND PATTERNS

Lesson 1   page 158
1. Synonym; (B). *Conference* and *meeting* have similar meanings, as do *people* and *persons.*
   (A) PW   (C) A   (D) PO   (E) L
2. Antonym; (E). A *descendant* comes after an individual, while an *ancestor* comes before. The two words are opposite in meaning, as are *inside* and *outside.*
   (A) CQ or S   (B) D   (C) PO   (D) PW
3. Synonym; (C). *Doubtful* and *unsure* both mean uncertain. *Hurt* and *harmed* are also synonyms.
   (A) PA   (B) A   (D) CQ   (E) L
4. Antonym; (B). *Innumerable,* a vast number, means the opposite of *few. Safe,* which means free of danger, is the opposite of *dangerous.*
   (A) S   (C) D   (D) C   (E) CQ
5. Function; (A). The function of *journalism* is to *inform,* just as the function of *comedy* is to *amuse.*
   (B) S   (C) PO   (D) CE   (E) C
6. Synonym; (C). *Legend* and *myth* have similar meanings, just as the *rhythm* of a song is nearly the same thing as its *beat.*
   (A) PW   (B) CE   (D) A   (E) PA
7. Antonym; (C). *Majority* is the opposite of *minority,* just as *odd* is the opposite of *even.*
   (A) AO   (B) PW   (D) PO   (E) CQ

8. Performer and Action; (A). You expect a *navigator* to *steer* a ship, just as you expect a *chauffeur* to *drive* a car.
   (B) F   (C) PW   (D) S   (E) CQ
9. Classification; (D). A *flag* may be classified as a *symbol,* just as a *senator* may be classified as a *politician.*
   (A) PW   (B) CE   (C) PO   (E) A
10. Synonym; (B). *Vivid* and *lively* have similar meanings, as do *necessary* and *needed.*
   (A) A   (C) L   (D) F   (E) D

Lesson 2   page 159
1. Classification; (C). *Aviation* may be classified as a *science,* just as *typing* may be classified as a *skill.*
   (A) S   (B) L   (D) PW   (E) CQ
2. Synonym; (A). *Collide* and *crash* have similar meanings, as do *toss* and *throw.*
   (B) PW   (C) CE   (D) PO   (E) A
3. Antonym; (C). *Departure* is opposite in meaning to *arrival,* just as *left* is the opposite of *right.*
   (A) PO   (B) AO   (D) CE   (E) L
4. Synonym; (A). *Disturb* and *bother* have similar meanings, as do to *show* and to *display.*
   (B) A   (C) F   (D) L   (E) C
5. Degree; (C). A *fatal* accident is worse than an accident that is merely *harmful.* Similarly, a *brilliant* person is smarter than a *bright* person.
   (A) C   (B) L   (D) PO   (E) PW
6. Part and Whole; (D). A *foundation* is part of a *structure,* just as an *introduction* is part of an *essay.*
   (A) A   (B) F   (C) L   (E) CQ
7. Synonym; (C). *Ignore* and *disregard* are similar in meaning, as are *glance* and *peek.*
   (A) CQ   (B) A   (D) C   (E) CE
8. Synonym; (B). *Incident* is similar in meaning to *event,* while *car* is another word for *automobile.*
   (A) PA   (C) C   (D) PW or L   (E) PO
9. Antonym; (C). *Mischievous* means the opposite of *well-behaved,* while *messy* means the opposite of *neat.*
   (A) CE   (B) S   (D) AO   (E) C
10. Characteristic Quality; (D). A *nuisance* is characteristically *annoying,* just as a *riddle* is characteristically *puzzling.*
   (A) L   (B) PO   (C) PW   (E) C

Lesson 3   page 160
1. Part and Whole; (A). The *abdomen* is part of the *body,* just as a *trunk* is part of an *elephant.*
   (B) CQ   (C) S   (D) A   (E) PA
2. Antonym; (C). *Caution* is the opposite of *carelessness,* just as *sound* is the opposite of *silence.*
   (A) S   (B) D   (D) CQ   (E) PW
3. Synonym; (C). A *commotion* is similar to a *disturbance,* just as something's *value* is similar to its *worth.*
   (A) PW   (B) A   (D) CE   (E) F

4. Characteristic Quality; (B). *Rubber* is characteristically *flexible*, just as *ghosts* are considered characteristically *invisible*.
   (A) S   (C) A   (D) CE   (E) PO
5. Antonym; (C). A *foe*, or enemy, is the opposite of a *friend*, just as a *beginning* is the opposite of a *conclusion*.
   (A) PA   (B) PW   (D) C   (E) D
6. Cause and Effect; (C). *Gratitude* can be the result of a *favor*. *Anger* can be the result of an *insult*.
   (A) F   (B) L   (D) PW   (E) PA
7. Characteristic Quality; (E). A *rescuer* is characteristically *heroic*, just as a *prince* is characteristically *royal*.
   (A) S   (B) PO   (C) PA   (D) F
8. Function; (B). The function of a *crane* is to *hoist*, or lift, heavy objects. In the same way, the function of a *truck* is to *transport*, or carry, goods.
   (A) C   (C) CQ   (D) S   (E) A
9. Synonym; (A). *Maximum* is similar in meaning to *greatest*, just as *least* is similar in meaning to *smallest*.
   (B) D   (C) AO or F   (D) CQ   (E) A
10. Antonym; (E). *Previous* means the opposite of *next*, just as *boring* means the opposite of *entertaining*.
    (A) PO   (B) D   (C) CE   (D) S

Lesson 4   page 161
1. Cause and Effect; (B). An *assault* can cause an *injury*, just as a *repair* can result in an *improvement*.
   (A) C   (C) PA   (D) A   (E) S
2. Characteristic Quality; (E). *Lace* is characteristically *dainty*, just as *diamonds* are characteristically *sparkling*.
   (A) A   (B) S   (C) F or C   (D) L
3. Antonym; (A). To *disguise* something is roughly the opposite of to *expose* it, while to *bore* someone is the opposite of to *entertain* that person.
   (B) S   (C) PO   (D) CE   (E) PA
4. Antonym; (E). *Earnest*, which means serious, is opposite in meaning to *joking*, just as *noisy* is opposite in meaning to *quiet*.
   (A) C   (B) CE   (C) S   (D) D
5. Cause and Effect; (D). A *gasp* can result from *surprise*, just as *tears* can result from *sorrow*.
   (A) A   (B) D   (C) C   (E) S
6. Performer and Action; (E). You expect a *bear* to *hibernate*, just as you expect a *tourist* to *travel*.
   (A) F   (B) S   (C) CE   (D) A
7. Action and Object; (D). You *inhale air*, just as you *rake leaves*.
   (A) PO   (B) C   (C) D   (E) CQ
8. Synonym; (B). *Linger* and *wait* have similar meanings, as do *talk* and *chat*.
   (A) CE   (C) A   (D) PA   (E) CQ
9. Synonym; (A). *Requirement* and *necessity* have similar meanings, as do the nouns *help* and *assistance*.
   (B) L   (C) A   (D) PO   (E) CQ

10. Characteristic Quality; (C). A *vacuum* is characteristically *empty*, just as *lightning* is characteristically *bright*.
    (A) S   (B) C   (D) PW   (E) F

Lesson 5   page 162
1. Classification; (E). *Automation* may be classified as a type of *system*, just as a *democracy* may be classified as a kind of *government*.
   (A) CE   (B) A   (C) PW   (D) PO
2. Synonym; (B). *Bureau*, when it refers to a government office, means the same as *agency*. In the same way, *piece* and *section* have similar meanings.
   (A) A   (C) L   (D) PW   (E) C
3. Characteristic Quality; (E). *Gasoline* is characteristically *flammable*, just as *cotton* is characteristically *absorbent*.
   (A) A   (B) C   (C) S   (D) D
4. Synonym; (C). *Lunar* is similar in meaning to *moonlike*, just as *sunny* is similar in meaning to *bright*.
   (A) PO   (B) A   (D) D   (E) F
5. Location; (C). *Medicines* can be found in a *pharmacy*, just as *spices* can be found in the *kitchen*.
   (A) CQ   (B) PO   (D) PW   (E) A
6. Cause and Effect; (C). When you *pierce* something, you create a *hole*. In the same way, *dew* can cause *dampness*.
   (A) A   (B) AO   (D) PA   (E) F
7. Function; (A). The function of a *crowbar* is to *pry*, just as the function of a *razor* is to *shave*.
   (B) CQ   (C) S   (D) AO   (E) C
8. Antonym; (C). To *resign* from a job means the opposite of to *apply* for a job. Similarly, to *divide* a task is the opposite of *combining* several tasks.
   (A) CE   (B) D   (D) CQ   (E) L
9. Characteristic Quality; (C). A *statue* is characteristically *static*, or unmoving, just as the *ocean* is characteristically *salty*.
   (A) PW   (B) A   (D) C   (E) F
10. Antonym; (A). *Suspicion* means the opposite of *trust*, just as *boredom* means the opposite of *interest*.
    (B) PA   (C) S   (D) CQ   (E) L or PW

Lesson 6   page 163
1. Classification; (D). A *biography* may be classified as a *story*, just as *biology* may be classified as a *science*.
   (A) A   (B) D   (C) CQ   (E) S
2. Synonym; (A). *Debate* is similar in meaning to *argue*, just as *select* is similar in meaning to *choose*.
   (B) C   (C) A   (D) PW or L   (E) PO
3. Classification; (E). A *birth certificate* may be classified as a *document*, just as a *dictionary* may be classified as a *book*.
   (A) AO   (B) CQ   (C) D   (D) S

4. Antonym; (C). *Essential* and *unnecessary* have opposite meanings, as do *grinning* and *frowning*.
(A) S   (B) PW   (D) CE   (E) F

5. Antonym; (D). *Generous* and *stingy* have opposite meanings, as do *rude* and *polite*.
(A) L   (B) S   (C) C   (E) PO

6. Degree; (E). Things that are *identical* are alike to a greater degree than things that are *similar,* just as something that is *boiling* is much hotter than something that is *warm*.
(A) PO   (B) L   (C) S   (D) A

7. Classification; (E). *Teaching* may be classified as a *profession,* just as *silk* may be classified as a *fabric*.
(A) PA   (B) S   (C) D   (D) CE

8. Antonym; (C). *Routine* is the opposite of *unusual,* just as *planned* is the opposite of *unexpected*.
(A) S   (B) C   (D) CE   (E) PO

9. Performer and Action; (E). You expect a *scholar* to *read,* just as you expect a *pilot* to *fly*.
(A) PW   (B) PO   (C) L   (D) S

10. Synonym; (D). *Thorough* and *complete* have nearly the same meaning, as do *broad* and *wide*.
(A) CE   (B) CQ   (C) AO   (E) A

Lesson 7   page 164

1. Performer and Object; (C). An *architect* works with a *blueprint,* while a *composer* creates a *symphony*.
(A) A   (B) C   (D) F   (E) S

2. Synonym; (B). To *betray* and to *deceive* have nearly the same meaning, as do to *work* and to *labor*.
(A) A   (C) C   (D) L   (E) PO

3. Classification; (D). A *wedding* may be classified as a *ceremony,* just as *Utah* may be classified as a *state*.
(A) D   (B) S   (C) A   (E) CQ

4. Synonym; (A). *District* is similar in meaning to *section,* just as *boring* is similar in meaning to *dull*.
(B) C   (C) CE   (D) PO   (E) L

5. Antonym; (B). Something *eternal* is the opposite of something *temporary*. Similarly, *raw* is the opposite of *cooked*.
(A) S   (C) PW   (D) C   (E) CQ

6. Characteristic Quality; (B). *Roses* are characteristically *fragrant,* or sweet-smelling, just as *china* is characteristically *fragile*.
(A) PA   (C) L   (D) PW   (E) PO

7. Antonym; (A). To *ignite* a fire is the opposite of to *put out* a fire, just as *rest* is the opposite of *activity*.
(B) F   (C) D   (D) CE   (E) AO

8. Synonym; (C). *Quarantine* and *isolation* have similar meanings, as do *command* and *order*.
(A) AO   (B) A   (D) CQ   (E) CE

9. Synonym; (D). *Scheme* and *plot* have nearly the same meaning, as do *order* and *arrange*.
(A) F   (B) A   (C) L   (E) AO

10. Performer and Action; (D). A *victim* is someone who *suffers,* just as a *victor* is someone who *wins*.
(A) C   (B) CQ   (C) A   (E) L

Lesson 8   page 165

1. Synonym; (B). *Abundant* and *plentiful* have nearly the same meaning, as do *rich* and *wealthy*.
(A) CQ   (C) A   (D) C   (E) PO

2. Synonym; (B). *Descriptive* and *detailed* have nearly the same meaning, as do *still* and *motionless*.
(A) A   (C) CQ   (D) PW   (E) PO

3. Antonym; (A). *Desirable* means the opposite of *disgusting,* just as *bright* means the opposite of *faded*.
(B) S   (C) PW   (D) AO   (E) D

4. Antonym; (A). *Dramatic,* or showy, means the opposite of *dull. Comical* means the opposite of *gloomy*.
(B) S   (C) CQ   (D) L   (E) PW

5. Degree; (C). Something *extraordinary* is much rarer than something *unusual*. In the same way, something *awful* is much worse than something that is merely *bad*.
(A) CQ   (B) F   (D) A   (E) L

6. Classification; (A). *Geology* may be classified as a *science,* just as a *waltz* may be classified as a *dance*.
(B) PA   (C) A   (D) CE   (E) PW

7. Synonym; (A). *Possess* and *have* have nearly the same meaning, as do *lift* and *raise*.
(B) PA   (C) A   (D) AO   (E) L

8. Synonym; (E). *Prehistoric* is similar in meaning to *ancient,* just as *yell* is similar in meaning to *shout*.
(A) AO   (B) PA   (C) CE   (D) PW

9. Antonym; (D). To *satisfy* someone is the opposite of to *disappoint* someone, just as to *approve* means the opposite of to *reject*.
(A) PA   (B) PW   (C) CE   (E) S

10. Synonym; (C). *Terrain* and *ground* have nearly the same meaning, as do *ask* and *request*.
(A) PW   (B) A   (D) CQ   (E) F or AO

Lesson 9   page 166

1. Antonym; (C). *Ambitious,* or eager for advancement, means the opposite of *content,* or happy with what one already has, just as *large* means the opposite of *small*.
(A) S   (B) C   (D) F   (E) CQ

2. Synonym; (E). *Counterfeit* has a similar meaning to *fake,* just as *difficult* has a similar meaning to *hard*.
(A) A   (B) CE   (C) F   (D) CQ

3. Synonym; (C). *Envy* has nearly the same meaning as *jealousy,* just as *desire* has nearly the same meaning as *want*.
(A) L   (B) PW   (D) PO   (E) A

4. Degree; (B). To *exclaim* is to *say* something with a great degree of excitement. To *inspect* is to examine more carefully than merely to *glance*.
(A) AO   (C) CQ   (D) A   (E) CE

5. Part and Whole; (E). A *star* is part of a *galaxy,* just as *bark* is part of a *tree*.
(A) F   (B) CQ   (C) CE   (D) PA

6. Characteristic Quality; (D). A *shrub* is characteristically *ornamental,* just as a *tool* is characteristically *useful*.
(A) C   (B) F   (C) L   (E) A

7. Performer and Action; (D). You expect a *king* to *reign* over his subjects, just as you expect a *waiter* to *serve* food to customers.
(A) C   (B) PW   (C) L   (E) D

8. Characteristic Quality; (E). A *loner* is characteristically *solitary*, just as a *ballerina* is characteristically *graceful*.
(A) C   (B) A   (C) S   (D) PW

9. Characteristic Quality; (A). *Glass* is characteristically *transparent*, or see-through. A *window* is characteristically *breakable*.
(B) A   (C) AO   (D) PW   (E) CE

10. Part and Whole; (C). An *outfit* is part of your *wardrobe*, just as a *wrench* is part of a *tool set*.
(A) PO   (B) F   (D) CQ   (E) A

Lesson 10   page 167

1. Antonym; (C). *Appropriate* means the opposite of *unsuitable*, just as *fresh* means the opposite of *stale*.
(A) CE   (B) CQ   (D) S   (E) PW

2. Synonym; (A). *Boast* and *brag* have nearly the same meaning, as do *try* and *attempt*.
(B) A   (C) CE   (D) CQ   (E) AO

3. Action and Object; (D). You *cultivate* a *garden*, just as you *harvest* a *crop*.
(A) CE   (B) A   (C) L   (E) PA

4. Antonym; (A). *Eliminate*, which means to get rid of, means the opposite of *include*, just as *start* means the opposite of *finish*.
(B) C   (C) S   (D) AO   (E) L

5. Action and Object; (D). You can *export goods* just as you can *write* a *letter*.
(A) S   (B) D   (C) L   (D) PO

6. Synonym; (E). *Inviting* and *attractive* have similar meanings, as do *incorrect* and *wrong*.
(A) A   (B) CQ   (C) PO   (D) CE

7. Classification; (E). A *birthday* may be classified as an *occasion*, just as a *dictionary* may be classified as a *book*.
(A) S   (B) PO   (C) L   (D) PA

8. Synonym; (B). *Ordinarily* and *usually* have nearly the same meaning, as do *quickly* and *fast*.
(A) F   (C) PW   (D) CE   (E) L

9. Classification; (C). *Snow* may be classified as *precipitation*, just as *golf* may be classified as a *sport*.
(A) L   (B) S   (D) A   (E) AO

10. Synonym; (B). *Tradition* and *custom* have similar meanings, as do *filth* and *dirt*.
(A) PW   (C) CQ   (D) F or AO   (E) L

Lesson 11   page 168

1. Antonym; (B). To *appreciate*, or think highly of, is the opposite of *despise*, just as to *interest* is the opposite of to *bore*.
(A) PA   (C) CE or A   (D) S   (E) C

2. Action and Object; (E). A person *reads braille*, just as a person *writes* an *essay*.
(A) A   (B) S or D   (C) C   (D) PA

3. Performer and Action; (D). You expect a *politician* to *campaign*, just as you expect an *athlete* to *compete*.
(A) CQ   (B) PW   (C) A   (E) S

4. Function; (A). The function of a *conscience* is to *guide* one's actions, just as the function of a *brain* is to *think*.
(B) CE   (C) PW   (D) PO   (E) CQ

5. Performer and Action; (C). You expect a *performer* to *entertain* an audience, just as you expect an *author* to *write* books.
(A) A   (B) F   (D) PW   (E) S

6. Degree; (B). Someone who is *furious* is angrier than someone who is *annoyed*. Someone who is *delighted* is more pleased than someone who is merely *glad*.
(A) PW   (C) A   (D) AO   (E) L

7. Synonym; (D). *Genuine* and *real* have nearly the same meaning, as do *solo* and *alone*.
(A) A   (B) PA   (C) AO   (E) L

8. Antonym; (A). *Juvenile*, as an adjective meaning immature, is opposite in meaning to *mature*, just as *combined* is opposite in meaning to *separate*.
(B) D   (C) S   (D) L   (E) AO or F

9. Synonym; (C). *Theme* is similar in meaning to *subject*, just as *habit* is similar in meaning to *custom*.
(A) A   (B) PW   (D) AO   (E) C

10. Degree; (C). *Urge* suggests a stronger degree of persuasion than *suggest*. In the same way, to *crash* suggests a stronger degree of impact than to *bump*.
(A) F   (B) CE   (D) AO   (E) A

Lesson 12   page 169

1. Performer and Object; (D). A *voter* uses a *ballot* to vote, in the same way that a *customer* uses an *order form* to place an order.
(A) PW   (B) L   (C) AO   (E) S

2. Synonym; (B). *Dissolve* and *melt* are similar in meaning, as are *wash* and *cleanse*.
(A) PA   (C) C   (D) PO   (E) CQ

3. Synonym; (A). *Guidance* and *advice* are similar in meaning, as are *penalty* and *punishment*.
(B) PO   (C) A   (D) PW   (E) AO

4. Synonym; (A). *Hazard* and *danger* are similar in meaning, as are *chance* and *opportunity*.
(B) C   (C) AO   (D) CE   (E) A

5. Antonym; (C). *Inexpensive* and *costly* have opposite meanings, as do *dressy* and *casual*.
(A) C   (B) S   (D) CQ   (E) AO

6. Location; (D). *Merchandise* can be found in a *mall*, just as *groceries* can be found in a *supermarket*.
(A) PO   (B) CQ   (C) PW   (E) C

7. Antonym; (A). *Protest* roughly means the opposite of *agree*, just as *raise* means the opposite of *lower*.
(B) C   (C) AO   (D) CQ   (E) CE

8. Synonym; (B). *Remedy* and *cure* are similar in meaning, as are *memory* and *recollection*.
   (A) A   (C) CQ   (D) PW   (E) C

9. Synonym; (D). *Revolution* and *revolt* have similar meanings, as do *street* and *avenue*.
   (A) PA   (B) PO   (C) F   (E) AO

10. Antonym; (A). *Temporary,* or short-term, means the opposite of *permanent,* just as *calm* means the opposite of *upset*.
    (B) C   (C) CQ   (D) D   (E) S

Lesson 13   page 170

1. Antonym; (E). *Amateur* is the opposite of *professional,* just as *neat* is the opposite of *disorderly*.
   (A) S   (B) PO   (C) C   (D) CQ

2. Cause and Effect; (C). A *problem* can cause someone to make a *complaint,* just as *success* can cause people to give *praise*.
   (A) CQ   (B) F   (D) AO   (E) C

3. Action and Object; (E). You *pay off* a *debt,* just as you *obey* a *law*.
   (A) PO   (B) L   (C) S   (D) C

4. Synonym; (C). A *duplicate* of something is the same thing as a *copy* of it, just as someone's *position* is the same thing as his or her *location*.
   (A) F   (B) PO   (D) PW   (E) CQ

5. Cause and Effect; (A). *Death* can cause people to go into *mourning,* just as *victory* can cause people to have a *celebration*.
   (B) L   (C) AO   (D) C   (E) PA

6. Antonym; (E). To *omit* is the opposite of to *include,* just as to *pay* is the opposite of to *earn*.
   (A) PA   (B) S   (C) PW   (D) AO

7. Antonym; (B). To *rebel* is the opposite of to *obey,* just as to *bore* is roughly the opposite of to *entertain*.
   (A) S   (C) PA   (D) PW   (E) C

8. Classification; (C). *Regret* can be classified as a *feeling,* just as *pleasantness* can be classified as an *attitude*.
   (A) L   (B) AO   (D) PA   (E) CQ

9. Synonym; (B). *Self-respect* and *self-esteem* have nearly the same meaning, as do *faith* and *belief*.
   (A) C   (C) PW   (D) A   (E) AO

10. Synonym; (D). *Sympathy* is similar in meaning to *pity,* as *robbery* is similar in meaning to *theft*.
    (A) A   (B) CQ   (C) AO   (E) C or AO

Lesson 14   page 171

1. Antonym; (D). *Obvious,* which means clearly seen, is opposite in meaning to *hidden,* just as *completed* and *unfinished* have opposite meanings.
   (A) S   (B) D   (C) F or AO   (E) AO

2. Characteristic Quality; (E). *Prey,* a hunted animal, is characteristically *hunted,* just as an *artist* is characteristically *inspired,* or impelled to create.
   (A) F   (B) AO   (C) CE   (D) C

3. Antonym; (D). *Prohibit* means the opposite of *allow,* just as *defend* means roughly the opposite of *attack*.
   (A) PO   (B) CQ or C   (C) S   (E) PA

4. Antonym; (A). *Reckless* means the opposite of *careful,* just as *clumsy* means the opposite of *graceful*.
   (B) C   (C) L   (D) S   (E) D

5. Degree; (D). Things that *match* are more alike in appearance than things that *resemble* one another. In the same way, to *demand* something is to request it much more strongly than to *suggest* it.
   (A) L   (B) PW   (C) CQ   (E) AO

6. Synonym; (C). *Responsibility* is similar in meaning to *duty,* just as *job* is similar in meaning to *occupation*.
   (A) C   (B) PO   (D) A   (E) CQ

7. Synonym; (B). The *suburbs* of a city are nearly the same as its *outskirts,* just as the word *areas* can be used to refer to the *sections* of a town.
   (A) CE   (C) C   (D) L   (E) F

8. Cause and Effect; (D). A *tragedy* can cause *suffering,* just as a *delay* can cause *tardiness*.
   (A) PW   (B) D   (C) C   (E) AO

9. Antonym; (A). To *unite* is the opposite of to *divide,* just as to *work* is the opposite of to *loaf*.
   (B) C   (C) PO   (D) L   (E) AO

10. Characteristic Quality; (C). A *parrot* is characteristically *vocal,* or talkative, just as a *library* is characteristically *quiet*.
    (A) F   (B) S   (D) C   (E) L

Lesson 15   page 172

1. Classification; (E). A *ballad* may be classified as a *song,* just as a *portrait* may be classified as a *painting*.
   (A) A   (B) D   (C) PW   (D) CE

2. Antonym; (E). To *compliment* means the opposite of to *insult,* just as to *disappoint* means the opposite of to *please*.
   (A) PO   (B) PA   (C) C   (D) S

3. Antonym; (C). *Courteous* is opposite in meaning to *impolite,* just as *expensive* is nearly opposite in meaning to *cheap*.
   (A) PA   (B) CQ   (D) S   (E) C

4. Degree; (A). Someone who is *frantic* is more unsettled than someone who is *upset*. In the same way, someone who is *wild* is more active than someone who is *lively*.
   (B) L   (C) C   (D) A   (E) PA

5. Characteristic Quality; (C). A *prince* is characteristically *gallant,* just as a *ball* is characteristically *round*.
   (A) PW   (B) S   (D) A   (E) PO

6. Synonym; (A). To *hesitate* and to *pause* are similar in meaning, just as to *walk* and to *stroll* are similar in meaning.
   (B) PW   (C) L   (D) C   (E) A

7. Cause and Effect; (C). *Delays* can cause *impatience,* just as *dryness* can cause *thirst.*
   (A) D   (B) PA   (D) S   (E) PW
8. Synonym; (B). A *rehearsal,* or practice, is similar to a *drill,* just as a *tune* is similar to a *melody.*
   (A) A   (C) AO   (D) F   (E) PW
9. Function; (E). The function of a *reservoir* is to *store* water, just as the function of a *paper clip* is to *join* pieces of paper.
   (A) S   (B) A   (C) PA   (D) D
10. Degree; (E). *Superior* suggests greater quality than does *average,* just as *love* suggests stronger affection than does *like.*
    (A) AO   (B) PA   (C) CQ   (D) C

READING NEW WORDS IN CONTEXT

Lesson 1   pages 175–178
1. B   2. D   3. A   4. D   5. C   6. B   7. B   8. B
9. D   10. C   11. A   12. D   13. B   14. C   15. A
16. C   17. C   18. B   19. D   20. A

Lesson 2   pages 179–182
1. D   2. D   3. A   4. B   5. C   6. C   7. B   8. C
9. A   10. C   11. D   12. B   13. D   14. A   15. C
16. B   17. D   18. B   19. D   20. A

Lesson 3   pages 183–186
1. B   2. C   3. A   4. A   5. D   6. B   7. C   8. B
9. D   10. C   11. C   12. B   13. B   14. A   15. C
16. B   17. A   18. D   19. C   20. A

Lesson 4   pages 187–190
1. B   2. C   3. A   4. A   5. D   6. B   7. C   8. D
9. D   10. B   11. A   12. B   13. D   14. D   15. C
16. A   17. A   18. C   19. C   20. D

Lesson 5   pages 191–194
1. B   2. A   3. D   4. A   5. C   6. A   7. C   8. B
9. D   10. D   11. B   12. A   13. A   14. C   15. C
16. B   17. C   18. B   19. B   20. D

Lesson 6   pages 195–198
1. B   2. C   3. A   4. D   5. C   6. C   7. B   8. A
9. A   10. C   11. D   12. A   13. B   14. D   15. C
16. A   17. A   18. C   19. D   20. D

Lesson 7   pages 199–202
1. B   2. A   3. D   4. D   5. A   6. A   7. B   8. A
9. B   10. D   11. C   12. B   13. A   14. B   15. C
16. D   17. A   18. A   19. C   20. C

Lesson 8   pages 203–206
1. A   2. D   3. B   4. C   5. C   6. A   7. A   8. C
9. B   10. C   11. D   12. D   13. A   14. B   15. C
16. C   17. D   18. B   19. D   20. C

Lesson 9   pages 207–210
1. C   2. A   3. D   4. A   5. D   6. C   7. D   8. A
9. B   10. B   11. B   12. A   13. B   14. B   15. A
16. B   17. D   18. C   19. C   20. B

Lesson 10   pages 211–214
1. D   2. A   3. B   4. C   5. D   6. B   7. D   8. A
9. C   10. D   11. D   12. B   13. C   14. A   15. D
16. B   17. C   18. C   19. A   20. B

Lesson 11   pages 215–218
1. B   2. C   3. C   4. B   5. D   6. A   7. C   8. C
9. D   10. A   11. B   12. C   13. D   14. A   15. B
16. C   17. D   18. B   19. C   20. A

Lesson 12   pages 219–222
1. C   2. A   3. A   4. B   5. D   6. A   7. D   8. D
9. A   10. C   11. B   12. A   13. C   14. B   15. C
16. D   17. D   18. B   19. C   20. A

Lesson 13   pages 223–226
1. C   2. B   3. B   4. C   5. A   6. D   7. B   8. D
9. A   10. A   11. A   12. C   13. D   14. C   15. B
16. B   17. D   18. C   19. B   20. A

Lesson 14   pages 227–230
1. C   2. D   3. B   4. C   5. C   6. A   7. B   8. D
9. C   10. A   11. D   12. A   13. B   14. B   15. B
16. A   17. D   18. B   19. C   20. C

Lesson 15   pages 231–234
1. A   2. D   3. A   4. B   5. C   6. B   7. D   8. B
9. B   10. C   11. A   12. C   13. D   14. A   15. B
16. C   17. B   18. C   19. A   20. D

USING NEW WORDS ON TESTS

FORMATIVE ASSESSMENT
Test 1   page 3
1. D   2. A   3. C   4. A   5. D   6. B   7. A   8. B
9. D   10. C
Test 2   page 4
1. C   2. D   3. D   4. C   5. C   6. A   7. A   8. C
9. A   10. B
Test 3   page 5
1. D   2. D   3. A   4. A   5. D   6. A   7. D   8. B
9. D   10. B
Test 4   page 6
1. C   2. C   3. D   4. B   5. A   6. B   7. C   8. D
9. B   10. C
Test 5   page 7
1. D   2. A   3. B   4. A   5. A   6. B   7. C   8. D
9. A   10. B
Test 6   page 8
1. B   2. A   3. B   4. C   5. D   6. A   7. A   8. C
9. A   10. D
Test 7   page 9
1. D   2. B   3. B   4. A   5. A   6. D   7. B   8. B
9. C   10. D
Test 8   page 10
1. C   2. A   3. D   4. B   5. A   6. B   7. D   8. A
9. C   10. B
Test 9   page 11
1. D   2. A   3. D   4. C   5. C   6. D   7. B   8. D
9. C   10. A

Test 10   page 12
1. B   2. A   3. B   4. C   5. D   6. B   7. B   8. C
9. D   10. C

Test 11   page 13
1. A   2. C   3. A   4. D   5. B   6. A   7. A   8. A
9. B   10. D

Test 12   page 14
1. A   2. C   3. B   4. D   5. B   6. C   7. A   8. B
9. C   10. B

Test 13   page 15
1. C   2. B   3. B   4. A   5. B   6. B   7. B   8. C
9. D   10. B

Test 14   page 16
1. B   2. D   3. A   4. B   5. D   6. B   7. D   8. D
9. C   10. A

Test 15   page 17
1. B   2. A   3. C   4. D   5. A   6. C   7. D   8. C
9. B   10. C

Test 16   page 18
1. B   2. A   3. B   4. B   5. D   6. A   7. B   8. C
9. A   10. B

Test 17   page 19
1. B   2. A   3. D   4. C   5. D   6. A   7. A   8. C
9. A   10. D

Test 18   page 20
1. D   2. B   3. C   4. A   5. D   6. D   7. D   8. C
9. B   10. A

Test 19   page 21
1. B   2. D   3. C   4. B   5. D   6. A   7. D   8. C
9. B   10. D

Test 20   page 22
1. B   2. C   3. D   4. A   5. B   6. D   7. A   8. B
9. D   10. C

Test 21   page 23
1. A   2. C   3. B   4. A   5. B   6. D   7. C   8. B
9. A   10. B

Test 22   page 24
1. A   2. A   3. B   4. A   5. C   6. A   7. D   8. B
9. B   10. B

Test 23   page 25
1. C   2. C   3. B   4. A   5. B   6. C   7. D   8. A
9. C   10. D

Test 24   page 26
1. A   2. B   3. A   4. B   5. B   6. D   7. D   8. C
9. B   10. D

Test 25   page 27
1. B   2. B   3. A   4. A   5. C   6. D   7. C   8. C
9. A   10. B

Test 26   page 28
1. B   2. D   3. A   4. B   5. B   6. C   7. B   8. C
9. D   10. A

Test 27   page 29
1. B   2. A   3. B   4. C   5. B   6. D   7. A   8. A
9. A   10. B

Test 28   page 30
1. B   2. B   3. A   4. D   5. C   6. A   7. B   8. C
9. B   10. C

Test 29   page 31
1. D   2. A   3. A   4. B   5. B   6. A   7. C   8. C
9. A   10. C

Test 30   page 32
1. D   2. C   3. B   4. A   5. B   6. C   7. B   8. D
9. A   10. B

SUMMATIVE ASSESSMENT
Test 1 Part A   pages 35–40

1. majority
2. detect
3. collapse
4. astonish
5. session
6. disturb
7. generation
8. disastrous
9. mischievous
10. incident
11. exception
12. departure
13. symbols
14. twilight
15. unexpectedly
16. error
17. vivid
18. reliable
19. legend
20. descendants

21. B   22. A   23. C   24. B   25. C   26. B   27. D
28. C   29. A   30. C   31. C   32. D   33. D   34. B
35. A   36. B   37. C   38. C   39. C   40. D   41. B
42. A   43. C   44. D   45. C   46. B   47. B   48. C
49. B   50. C

Test 1 Part B   pages 41–46

51. reference
52. hoist
53. requirement
54. linger
55. disguise
56. imitate
57. conceal
58. paralysis
59. competition
60. assault
61. pierce
62. gasp
63. discomfort
64. pharmacy
65. pry
66. portion
67. hibernate
68. flexible
69. lunar
70. license

71. C   72. A   73. C   74. B   75. B   76. C   77. D
78. B   79. A   80. B   81. C   82. B   83. A   84. D
85. C   86. D   87. C   88. A   89. D   90. A   91. B
92. B   93. D   94. B   95. D   96. C   97. B   98. D
99. D   100. C

Test 2 Part A   pages 47–52

1. career
2. publicity
3. terrain
4. geology
5. possess
6. descriptive
7. scholar
8. establish
9. offspring
10. determination
11. quarantine
12. barrier
13. destination
14. sacrifice
15. routine
16. desperate
17. ceremony
18. realm
19. architect
20. fragrant

21. B   22. D   23. A   24. B   25. A   26. D   27. C
28. C   29. C   30. B   31. D   32. D   33. A   34. B
35. A   36. D   37. C   38. D   39. A   40. B   41. B
42. A   43. A   44. D   45. C   46. C   47. B   48. A
49. C   50. C

Test 2 Part B   pages 53–58

51. lieutenant
52. forefathers
53. ordinarily
54. heir
55. tradition
56. portraits
57. boast
58. assume
59. galaxy
60. occasion

61. precipitation
62. inviting
63. knapsack
64. disadvantage
65. feat
66. investment
67. quantity
68. import
69. cultivate
70. contribute

71. D 72. B 73. B 74. A 75. B 76. A 77. C
78. D 79. B 80. A 81. A 82. C 83. B 84. B
85. C 86. B 87. D 88. C 89. A 90. D 91. B
92. A 93. C 94. B 95. D 96. D 97. B 98. B
99. D 100. C

Test 3 Part A   pages 59–64

1. inspiration
2. doubtless
3. absorb
4. appreciate
5. villains
6. hazard
7. mammoth
8. reduction
9. juvenile
10. cooperate

11. protest
12. inform
13. inexpensive
14. candidate
15. temporary
16. persuade
17. remedy
18. merchandise
19. widespread
20. revolution

21. A 22. C 23. D 24. D 25. B 26. D 27. B
28. B 29. B 30. B 31. C 32. D 33. C 34. D
35. B 36. A 37. B 38. D 39. C 40. A 41. C
42. B 43. A 44. D 45. C 46. C 47. B 48. B
49. D 50. C

Test 3 Part B   pages 65–70

51. amateur
52. simplify
53. survival
54. duplicate
55. Reckless
56. application
57. obvious
58. resident
59. impatience
60. benefit

61. tragedy
62. responsibility
63. decrease
64. prey
65. rebel
66. severe
67. threat
68. justify
69. prohibit
70. rehearsal

71. D 72. A 73. B 74. A 75. B 76. D 77. A
78. C 79. D 80. A 81. C 82. B 83. B 84. D
85. A 86. C 87. C 88. C 89. B 90. B 91. D
92. B 93. A 94. D 95. C 96. C 97. B 98. A
99. C 100. D

First Course

Lesson 1 pages 3–6
Exercise 1 Mapping
Your Guess and Definition answers will vary. Possible responses to Other Forms items follow.
1. *n.* alienability, alienation; *vt.* alienate, alienates, alienated, alienating; *adj.* alienable
2. *n.* diplomat; *adv.* diplomatically
3. *n.* ghastliness; *adj.* ghastlier, ghastliest
4. *n.* hostility; *adv.* hostilely
5. *n.* humaneness; *adv.* humanely
6. *n.* memorability; *adv.* memorably
7. *n.* mortality; *adv.* mortally
8. *n. pl.* satellites
9. *n.* tranquilization; *vt.* tranquilize; *adj.* tranquiler, tranquilest; *adv.* tranquilly
10. *n. pl.* velocities

Exercise 2 Context Clues
11. (E) humane
12. (H) mortal
13. (D) memorable
14. (A) satellites
15. (C) hostile
16. (B) alien
17. (G) diplomatic
18. (F) tranquil
19. (I) ghastly
20. (J) velocity

Exercise 3 Like Meanings and Opposite Meanings
21. B 22. C 23. C 24. C 25. D 26. B 27. D
28. D 29. C 30. B

Lesson 2 pages 7–10
Exercise 1 Mapping
Your Guess and Definition answers will vary. Possible responses to Other Forms items follow.
1. *vt.* allies, allied, allying
2. *n.* aversion; *vt.* averts, averted, averting; *adj.* averse; *adv.* aversely
3. *n.* destination; *vt.* destine, destines, destined, destining
4. *n.* embracement, embracer; *vt.* embraces, embraced, embracing; *adj.* embraceable
5. *n.* fascination, fascinator; *vt.* fascinates, fascinated, fascinating; *adv.* fascinatingly
6. *n. pl.* fugitives; *adv.* fugitively
7. *n.* gawkiness; *adj.* gawkish, gawky, gawkier, gawkiest; *adv.* gawkily
8. *n.* gesturer; *vt.* gestures, gestured, gesturing; *adj.* gestural
9. *n.* invader; *vt.* invades, invaded, invading
10. *vt.* overtures, overtured, overturing

Exercise 2 Context Clues
11. (G) embrace
12. (D) fascinate
13. (B) ally
14. (H) fugitive
15. (F) destiny
16. (J) invade
17. (A) overture
18. (I) avert
19. (C) gesture
20. (E) gawk

Exercise 3 Like Meanings and Opposite Meanings
21. A 22. D 23. A 24. C 25. A 26. B 27. B
28. A 29. B 30. A

Lesson 3 pages 11–14
Exercise 1 Mapping
Your Guess and Definition answers will vary. Possible responses to Other Forms items follow.
1. *n.* abstracter, abstractness, abstraction, abstractionist; *adj.* abstractive; *adv.* abstractly, abstractively
2. *n.* absurdness, absurdist, absurdism, adsurdity; *adv.* absurdly
3. *n.* controversialist, controversy; *adv.* controversially
4. *n.* defiance; *adv.* defiantly
5. *n.* eventuality; *adv.* eventually
6. *n.* grotesqueness; *adv.* grotesquely
7. *n.* inferiority; *adv.* inferiorly
8. *adv.* merely
9. *n.* obsoleteness; *vt.* obsoleted, obsoleting; *adv.* obsoletely
10. *n. pl.* techniques

Exercise 2 Context Clues
11. (J) eventual
12. (D) grotesque
13. (E) inferior
14. (F) controversial
15. (I) mere
16. (H) defiant
17. (A) technique
18. (G) absurd
19. (B) obsolete
20. (C) abstract

Exercise 3 Like Meanings and Opposite Meanings
21. A 22. D 23. A 24. A 25. B 26. A 27. B
28. D 29. A 30. C

Lesson 4 pages 15–18
Exercise 1 Mapping
Your Guess and Definition answers will vary. Possible responses to Other Forms items follow.
1. *n.* conformer, conformism, conformist, conformity; *vt.* conforms, conformed, conforming
2. *n.* consequentialness; *adj.* consequent, consequential; *adv.* consequentially, consequently
3. *n.* deliberateness, deliberator, deliberation; *vi.* deliberates, deliberated, deliberating; *adv.* deliberately
4. *n.* distorter, distortion; *adj.* distortional
5. *n.* excessiveness; *adj.* excessive; *adv.* excessively
6. *n.* impaction; *adj.* impactive
7. *n.* offender, offense; *vi.* offends, offended, offending
8. *n.* origination, originator; *vi.* originate; *adj.* originative; *adv.* originally
9. *n. pl.* realities
10. *vi.* or *vt.* recoils, recoiled, recoiling; *adj.* recoilless

Exercise 2 Context Clues
11. (B) deliberate
12. (I) originality
13. (E) conform
14. (A) impact
15. (G) recoil
16. (D) consequences
17. (H) distorts
18. (J) reality
19. (C) excess
20. (F) offend

Exercise 3 Like Meanings and Opposite Meanings
21. C 22. A 23. D 24. A 25. A 26. A 27. C
28. C 29. B 30. D

Lesson 5 pages 19–22
Exercise 1 Mapping
Your Guess and Definition answers will vary. Possible responses to Other Forms items follow.
1. *n.* congregant, congregator, congregation; *vi.* or *vt.* congregates, congregated, congregating; *adj.* congregative, congregational
2. *adj.* haunted, haunting; *adv.* hauntingly
3. *n.* hoverer; *vi.* hovers, hovered, hovering
4. *n.* ignorer; *vt.* ignore; *adj.* ignorant; *adv.* ignorantly
5. *vt.* leashes, leashed, leashing
6. *vi.* or *vt.* loiters, loitered, loitering
7. *n.* maturation, matureness; *vt.* mature; *adj.* maturative, maturational; *adv.* maturely
8. *n. pl.* motives; *vt.* motivate; *adj.* motiveless
9. *n.* signification; *vt.* signifies, signified, signifying; *adj.* significant
10. *n.* supervision, supervisor; *vi.* or *vt.* supervises, supervised, supervising; *adj.* supervisory

Exercise 2 Context Clues
11. (H) haunt
12. (J) leash
13. (C) supervise
14. (A) congregated
15. (B) hovered
16. (E) signify
17. (D) motive
18. (I) maturity
19. (G) loiter
20. (F) ignorance

Exercise 3 Like Meanings and Opposite Meanings
21. B 22. A 23. C 24. D 25. B 26. A 27. B
28. B 29. B 30. A

Lesson 6 pages 23–26
Exercise 1 Mapping
Your Guess and Definition answers will vary. Possible responses to Other Forms items follow.
1. *n.* audibility; *adv.* audibly
2. *adv.* candidly
3. *n.* conspicuousness; *adv.* conspicuously
4. *n. pl.* diaphragms; *adj.* diaphragmatic; *adv.* diaphragmatically
5. *n.* idleness; *vi.* idles, idled, idling; *adj.* idler, idlest; *adv.* idly
6. *n.* lenience; *adv.* leniently
7. *adv.* modestly
8. *n.* notoriousness; *adv.* notoriously
9. *n.* subtleness; *adj.* subtler, subtlest; *adv.* subtlely
10. *n. pl.* thresholds

Exercise 2 Context Clues
11. (A) threshold
12. (D) audible
13. (H) subtle
14. (G) candid
15. (F) notorious
16. (B) conspicuous
17. (E) modest
18. (J) diaphragm
19. (I) lenient
20. (C) idle

Exercise 3 Like Meanings and Opposite Meanings
21. A 22. D 23. C 24. D 25. C 26. C 27. A
28. B 29. C 30. B

Lesson 7 pages 27–30
Exercise 1 Mapping
Your Guess and Definition answers will vary. Possible responses to Other Forms items follow.
1. *n.* aggravation; *vt.* aggravates, aggravated, aggravating

2. *n.* anticipator, anticipation; *vt.* anticipates, anticipated, anticipating; *adj.* anticipatable, anticipant, anticipative, anticipatory; *adv.* anticipatively
3. *n.* calibration, calibrator; *vt.* calibrate
4. *n.* distraction; *vt.* distract, distracts, distracting; *adj.* distractive; *adv.* distractedly, distractibly, distractingly
5. *n.* eloquence; *adv.* eloquently
6. *n.* fulfiller, fulfillment; *vt.* fulfills, fulfilled, fulfilling
7. *n.* maintainer, maintenance; *vt.* maintains, maintained, maintaining; *adj.* maintainable
8. *n. pl.* phases; *vt.* phased, phasing; *adj.* phasic
9. *n.* placidity, placidness; *adv.* placidly
10. *vt.* porcelainize, porcelainizes, porcelainized, porcelainizing; *adj.* porcelaineous

Exercise 2 Context Clues
11. (J) anticipate
12. (H) caliber
13. (G) eloquent
14. (B) maintain
15. (F) phase
16. (C) fulfill
17. (A) porcelains
18. (I) placid
19. (E) aggravated
20. (D) distracted

Exercise 3 Like Meanings and Opposite Meanings
21. A 22. D 23. C 24. B 25. B 26. B 27. B
28. A 29. D 30. C

Lesson 8 pages 31–34
Exercise 1 Mapping
Your Guess and Definition answers will vary. Possible responses to Other Forms items follow.
1. *n.* dasher; *vt.* dashes, dashed, dashing; *adv.* dashingly
2. *adv.* dismally
3. *n.* flawlessness; *vi.* or *vt.* flawed; *adj.* flawless; *adv.* flawlessly
4. *n.* frailness, frailty; *adv.* frailly
5. *vt.* obligate, obligates, obligated, obligating; *adj.* obligatory; *adv.* obligatorily
6. *n.* obstinateness, obstinacy; *adv.* obstinately
7. *n.* option; *adv.* optionally
8. *n.* principalship; *adj.* principal
9. *n.* spontaneousness, spontaneity; *adv.* spontaneously
10. *n.* tiresomeness; *adv.* tiresomely

Exercise 2 Context Clues
11. (I) dashing
12. (B) tiresome
13. (H) dismal
14. (A) spontaneous
15. (J) flaws
16. (G) principally
17. (C) frail
18. (E) optional
19. (D) obligation
20. (F) obstinate

Exercise 3 Like Meanings and Opposite Meanings
21. A 22. B 23. C 24. D 25. D 26. D 27. D
28. C 29. B 30. B

Lesson 9 pages 35–38
Exercise 1 Mapping
Your Guess and Definition answers will vary. Possible responses to Other Forms items follow.
1. *n.* authentication; *vt.* authenticate; *adv.* authentically

2. *n.* comparability, comparableness, comparative-
   ness, comparison; *vt.* compare; *adj.* comparable,
   comparative; *adv.* comparably
3. *n.* contemplator, contemplation, contemplative-
   ness; *vt.* contemplates, contemplated, contem-
   plating; *adj.* contemplative; *adv.* contemplatively
4. *n.* duality, dualism, dualist; *vt.* dualize, dualizes,
   dualized, dualizing; *adj.* dualistic; *adv.* dually,
   dualistically
5. *n.* formality, formalization; *vt.* formalize,
   formalizes, formalized, formalizing;
   adv. formally
6. *n.* immortality, immortalization, immortalizer;
   vt. immortalize, immortalizes, immortalized,
   immortalizing; *adv.* immortally
7. *n.* interpretation, interpreter; *adj.* interpretable,
   interpretational, interpretative, interpretive
8. *n.* legend, legendry
9. *n.* mythicizer; *vt.* mythicize, mythicizes, mythi-
   cized, mythicizing; *adj.* mythic, mythical;
   adv. mythically
10. *n.* profoundness; *adv.* profoundly

Exercise 2   Context Clues

11. (F) comparable	16. (H) myths
12. (D) formal	17. (A) profound
13. (E) authentic	18. (I) legendary
14. (J) immortal	19. (G) interpret
15. (C) contemplate	20. (B) dual

Exercise 3   Like Meanings and Opposite Meanings
21. C   22. C   23. A   24. A   25. D   26. D   27. C
28. A   29. A   30. D

Lesson 10   pages 39–42
Exercise 1   Mapping
*Your Guess and Definition answers will vary. Possible
responses to Other Forms items follow.*
1. *vt.* cherishes, cherished, cherishing
2. *n.* consistency, consistence; *vi.* consist;
   adv. consistently
3. *adv.* crucially
4. *n.* designator, designation; *vt.* designates,
   designated, designating; *adv.* designative
5. *n.* gratifier, gratification; *vt.* gratifies, gratified,
   gratifying
6. *n.* indispensability; *adv.* indispensably
7. *n.* mythologist; *vi.* mythologize, mythologizes,
   mythologized, mythologizing; *adj.* mythological;
   adv. mythologically
8. *n.* resolver, resolution, resolvability, resolvent;
   vt. resolves, resolving; *adj.* resolvable;
   adv. resolvedly
9. *n.* versatility; *adv.* versatilely
10. *n.* vigorousness; *adj.* vigorous; *adv.* vigorously

Exercise 2   Context Clues

11. (D) crucial	16. (G) consistent
12. (C) gratified	17. (B) resolved
13. (I) indispensable	18. (H) versatile
14. (A) cherishes	19. (E) designated
15. (F) vigor	20. (J) mythology

Exercise 3   Like Meanings and Opposite Meanings
21. B   22. B   23. B   24. C   25. D   26. A   27. D
28. B   29. D   30. B

Lesson 11   pages 43–46
Exercise 1   Mapping
*Your Guess and Definition answers will vary. Possible
responses to Other Forms items follow.*
1. *n.* guarantor; *n. pl.* guarantees; *vt.* guaranteed,
   guaranteeing, guarantied, guarantying
2. *n.* illustriousness; *adv.* illustriously
3. *n.* inadequateness, inadequacy;
   adv. inadequately
4. *vt.* initialed, initialing; *adv.* initially
5. *n.* legitimation, legitimacy, legitimist,
   legitimism, legitimization; *vt.* legitimates,
   legitimated, legitimating, legitimize, legitimizes,
   legitimized, legitimizing; *adv.* legitimately
6. *n. pl.* merits; *adj.* meritless
7. *n.* moderateness, moderation; *vt.* moderates,
   moderated, moderating; *adv.* moderately
8. *n.* moralist, morality; *adj.* moralistic;
   adv. morally; moralistically
9. *n.* partiality; *adv.* partially
10. *adj.* unisonous, unisonal, unisonant;
    adv. unisonally

Exercise 2   Context Clues

11. (C) merits	16. (E) inadequate
12. (A) illustrious	17. (D) unison
13. (G) initial	18. (B) guarantee
14. (F) legitimate	19. (I) morals
15. (J) moderate	20. (H) partial

Exercise 3   Like Meanings and Opposite Meanings
21. D   22. A   23. B   24. C   25. C   26. A   27. B
28. D   29. C   30. B

Lesson 12   pages 47–50
Exercise 1   Mapping
*Your Guess and Definition answers will vary. Possible
responses to Other Forms items follow.*
1. *n.* election; *adv.* electively
2. *n.* hypocrisy; *adj.* hypocritical;
   adv. hypocritically
3. *n.* indefiniteness; *adv.* indefinitely
4. *n.* indirectness; *adv.* indirectly
5. *n.* judicature, judiciary; *adj.* judicable, judicative,
   judicatory, judicial, judicious; *adv.* judicially,
   judiciously
6. *n.* momentariness; *adv.* momentarily
7. *n.* notableness; *adv.* notably
8. *n.* prudence; *adj.* prudential; *adv.* prudently,
   prudentially
9. *n.* segregationist; *vt.* segregates, segregated,
   segregating; *adj.* segregative
10. *n.* vetoer; *n. pl.* vetoes; *vt.* vetoed, vetoing

Exercise 2   Context Clues

11. (F) notable	16. (I) segregation
12. (G) elective	17. (J) veto
13. (D) momentary	18. (C) indefinite
14. (E) indirect	19. (B) prudent
15. (A) hypocrite	20. (H) judicial

Exercise 3 Like Meanings and Opposite Meanings
21. A 22. A 23. D 24. D 25. D 26. B 27. B
28. C 29. D 30. D

Lesson 13 pages 51–54
Exercise 1 Mapping
Your Guess and Definition answers will vary. Possible responses to Other Forms items follow.
1. *n.* credibility; *adv.* credibly
2. *n.* grammarian, grammaticality, grammaticalness
3. *n.* legibility; *adv.* legibly
4. *n. pl.* manuscripts
5. *vt.* masters, mastered, mastering
6. *n.* participation, participant, participator; *vt.* participates, participated, participating; *adj.* participatory, participative
7. *n. pl.* refrains; *vt.* refrains, refrained, refraining
8. *n.* revisal, revision, reviser; *vt.* revises, revised, revising
9. *n.* tutorage, tutorship; *n. pl.* tutors; *vt.* tutors, tutored, tutoring; *adj.* tutorial
10. *n.* usability, usableness; *vt.* use, uses, used, using; *adj.* usable

Exercise 2 Context Clues
11. (J) credible
12. (E) revise
13. (A) grammatical
14. (D) legible
15. (I) tutor
16. (F) manuscript
17. (B) mastery
18. (H) participate
19. (G) refrain
20. (C) usages

Exercise 3 Like Meanings and Opposite Meanings
21. A 22. C 23. C 24. D 25. D 26. C 27. D
28. B 29. A 30. A

Lesson 14 pages 55–58
Exercise 1 Mapping
Your Guess and Definition answers will vary. Possible responses to Other Forms items follow.
1. *n.* dialogist; *n. pl.* dialogues; *vt.* dialogued, dialoguing; *adj.* dialogistic
2. *n.* editorialist, editorialization, editorializer; *vi.* or *vt.* editorialize, editorializes, editorialized, editorializing; *adv.* editorially
3. *n. pl.* faculties
4. *n. pl.* forums
5. *n.* journalism, journalist; *n. pl.* journals; *vi.* or *vt.* journalize, journalizes, journalized, journalizing; *adj.* journalistic; *adv.* journalistically
6. *n.* literariness
7. *n.* narrator; *n. pl.* narrations; *vi.* or *vt.* narrate, narrates, narrated, narrating; *adj.* narrative; *adv.* narratively
8. *n.* persuadability, persuader, persuasiveness; *vt.* persuade, persuades, persuaded, persuading; *adj.* persuadable, persuasive; *adv.* persuasively
9. *vi.* or *vt.* prosed, prosing
10. *n.* symbol; *vt.* symbols, symboled, symboling; *adj.* symbolic, symbolical; *adv.* symbolically

Exercise 2 Context Clues
11. (A) forum
12. (B) faculty
13. (F) prose
14. (E) literary

15. (J) symbolic
16. (G) narration
17. (I) dialogue
18. (H) persuasion
19. (D) editorial
20. (C) journal

Exercise 3 Like Meanings and Opposite Meanings
21. A 22. C 23. B 24. D 25. C 26. C 27. B
28. D 29. C 30. B

Lesson 15 pages 59–62
Exercise 1 Mapping
Your Guess and Definition answers will vary. Possible responses to Other Forms items follow.
1. *n.* adherer, adherence; *vt.* adheres, adhered, adhering; *adj.* adherent
2. *n.* gouger; *vt.* gouges, gouged, gouging
3. *n.* maneuverability, maneuverer; *n. pl.* maneuvers; *adj.* maneuverable
4. *n. pl.* minorities
5. *n. pl.* opponents
6. *n.* penetrant, penetration; *vt.* penetrates, penetrated, penetrating; *adj.* penetrative; *adv.* penetratingly, penetratively
7. *n.* recommender, recommendation; *vt.* recommends, recommended, recommending; *adj.* recommendable, recommendatory
8. *n.* tactician; *adj.* tactical; *adv.* tactically
9. *n.* yard; *n. pl.* yards
10. *n.* yielder; *vt.* yields, yielded, yielding

Exercise 2 Context Clues
11. (C) adhere
12. (H) penetrate
13. (B) gouge
14. (G) recommend
15. (F) maneuvers
16. (A) tactics
17. (D) minority
18. (J) yardage
19. (E) opponents
20. (I) yield

Exercise 3 Like Meanings and Opposite Meanings
21. D 22. A 23. C 24. D 25. A 26. D 27. D
28. B 29. B 30. C

Lesson 16 pages 63–66
Exercise 1 Mapping
Your Guess and Definition answers will vary. Possible responses to Other Forms items follow.
1. *n.* expander; *vt.* expands, expanded, expanding; *adj.* expandable
2. *n.* fatigability; *vi.* or *vt.* fatigues, fatigued, fatiguing; *adj.* fatigable
3. *adj.* hardier, hardiest
4. *n.* intellection, intellectuality; *adj.* intellective
5. *n. pl.* obstacles
6. *adj.* official
7. *n.* oppositionist; *adj.* oppositional
8. *n.* pursuance, pursuer; *vt.* pursues, pursued, pursuing; *adj.* pursuant
9. *n. pl.* scholarships
10. *vt.* totaled, totaling; *adj.* total

Exercise 2 Context Clues
11. (B) officially
12. (I) opposition
13. (G) pursue
14. (E) hardy
15. (A) scholarship
16. (C) expand
17. (J) totally
18. (F) fatigues
19. (H) obstacle
20. (D) intellect

Exercise 3   Like Meanings and Opposite Meanings
21. C   22. D   23. A   24. B   25. D   26. C   27. D
28. A   29. D   30. B

Lesson 17   pages 67–70
Exercise 1   Mapping
Your Guess and Definition answers will vary. Possible responses to Other Forms items follow.
1. *n.* adoptee, adopter, adoption; *vt.* adopts, adopted, adopting; *adj.* adoptable, adoptive; *adv.* adoptively
2. *vi.* or *vt.* anguishes, anguished, anguishing
3. *vt.* blemishes, blemished, blemishing
4. *n. pl.* crises
5. *n.* immaturity, immatureness; *adv.* immaturely
6. *n.* inhabiter, inhabitability; *vt.* inhabits, inhabited, inhabiting; *adj.* inhabitable
7. *n.* intolerability, intolerableness; *adv.* intolerably
8. *adv.* maternally
9. *n.* rivalry; *vt.* rivaled, rivaling
10. *n.* self-consciousness; *adv.* self-consciously
Exercise 2   Context Clues
11. (F) intolerable   16. (I) adopt
12. (C) maternal   17. (B) blemish
13. (J) rivaled   18. (D) anguish
14. (E) crisis   19. (H) inhabit
15. (A) self–conscious   20. (G) immature
Exercise 3   Like Meanings and Opposite Meanings
21. B   22. A   23. C   24. B   25. C   26. B   27. A
28. C   29. B   30. D

Lesson 18   pages 71–74
Exercise 1   Mapping
Your Guess and Definition answers will vary. Possible responses to Other Forms items follow.
1. *n.* acuteness; *adv.* acutely
2. *n.* hesitator, hesitater, hesitation; *vi.* hesitates, hesitated, hesitating; *adj.* hesitative; *adv.* hesitatingly, hesitatively
3. *n.* hysteria; *adj.* hysteric; *adv.* hysterically
4. *n.* irritableness, irritation; *vt.* irritate, irritates, irritated, irritating; *adj.* irritant; *adv.* irritably
5. *n.* ridiculousness; *vt.* ridicules, ridiculed, ridiculing; *adj.* ridiculous; *adv.* ridiculously
6. *n. pl.* tendencies; *vi.* tend, tends, tended, tending
7. *n.* timidity, timidness; *adv.* timidly
8. *n. pl.* turmoils
9. *n.* vagueness; *adj.* vaguer, vaguest; *adv.* vaguely
10. *n.* wretch, wretchedness; *adv.* wretchedly
Exercise 2   Context Clues
11. (J) timid   16. (D) irritable
12. (E) hesitation   17. (I) ridiculed
13. (B) acute   18. (C) tendency
14. (H) hysterical   19. (G) turmoil
15. (A) wretched   20. (F) vague
Exercise 3   Like Meanings and Opposite Meanings
21. A   22. D   23. B   24. B   25. B   26. A   27. C
28. D   29. C   30. A

Lesson 19   pages 75–78
Exercise 1   Mapping
Your Guess and Definition answers will vary. Possible responses to Other Forms items follow.
1. *n.* barbarian, barbarism, barbarity; *vt.* barbarize, barbarizes, barbarized, barbarizing; *adj.* barbaric; *adv.* barbarically, barbarously
2. *n.* baronage, baroness
3. *n. pl.* canopies; *vt.* canopied, canopying
4. *n. pl.* eras
5. *n. pl.* fortresses
6. *adj.* grand
7. *n.* monarch, monarchism, monarchist; *n. pl.* monarchies; *adj.* monarchal, monarchical, monarchistic; *adv.* monarchally, monarchially
8. *n.* pageantry
9. *n.* patroness, patronage
10. *vt.* proclaim, proclaims, proclaimed, proclaiming
Exercise 2   Context Clues
11. (D) fortress   16. (A) pageant
12. (F) era   17. (H) canopy
13. (I) grandeur   18. (G) patron
14. (C) barbarous   19. (J) proclamation
15. (E) monarchy   20. (B) baron
Exercise 3   Like Meanings and Opposite Meanings
21. C   22. B   23. C   24. A   25. C   26. D   27. B
28. C   29. C   30. D

Lesson 20   pages 79–82
Exercise 1   Mapping
Your Guess and Definition answers will vary. Possible responses to Other Forms items follow.
1. *n.* absoluteness, absolutism, absolutist; *adv.* absolutely
2. *n.* banishment; *vt.* banishes, banished, banishing
3. *n. pl.* beacons
4. *n.* illusionism, illusionist; *adj.* illusional, illusionary, illusionistic, illusory; *adv.* illusorily
5. *n.* lurer; *vt.* lures, lured, luring
6. *n.* peril, perilousness; *adv.* perilously
7. *n. pl.* statuses
8. *n.* toiler; *vt.* toils, toiled, toiling
9. *n.* valiance, valiancy; *adv.* valiantly
10. *n.* vengefulness; *adj.* vengeful; *adv.* vengefully
Exercise 2   Context Clues
11. (I) absolute   16. (D) status
12. (C) perilous   17. (A) illusion
13. (B) banished   18. (J) toil
14. (E) lure   19. (F) valiant
15. (H) beacons   20. (G) vengeance
Exercise 3   Like Meanings and Opposite Meanings
21. D   22. D   23. D   24. B   25. D   26. A   27. B
28. D   29. C   30. D

Lesson 21   pages 83–86
Exercise 1   Mapping
Your Guess and Definition answers will vary. Possible responses to Other Forms items follow.
1. *n.* antisepsis; *vt.* antisepticize; *adj.* antiseptical; *adv.* antiseptically

2. *n.* edibleness; *adv.* edibly
3. *vt.* endure; *adj.* endurable; *adv.* endurably, enduringly
4. *n.* glucoside; *adj.* glucosidic
5. *n.* immunity, immunization; *vt.* immunize; *adj.* immune
6. *n.* nutritionist, nutritiousness; *adj.* nutritional; *adv.* nutritionally, nutritiously
7. *adv.* optically
8. *adj.* organismic, organismal; *adv.* organismically
9. *n.* parasitism, parasitization; *vt.* parasitize; *adj.* parasitic, parasitical; *adv.* parasitically
10. *n.* pigmentation; *vi.* or *vt.* pigmentize; *adj.* pigmentary

Exercise 2   Context Clues

11. (I) optical
12. (E) antiseptic
13. (J) organisms
14. (B) edible
15. (G) pigment
16. (F) endurance
17. (D) parasites
18. (A) nutrition
19. (C) immune
20. (H) glucose

Exercise 3   Like Meanings and Opposite Meanings

21. B   22. A   23. C   24. C   25. D   26. C   27. C
28. C   29. B   30. D

Lesson 22   pages 87–90
Exercise 1   Mapping
Your Guess and Definition answers will vary. Possible responses to Other Forms items follow.

1. *n.* camouflager; *vi.* or *vt.* camouflages, camouflaged, camouflaging
2. *n.* habitability, habitation; *adj.* habitable; *adv.* habitably
3. *n.* mammology; *adj.* mammalian
4. *n.* naturalism, naturalization; *vt.* naturalize; *adj.* natural, naturalistic; *adv.* naturally, naturalistically
5. *adv.* nocturnally
6. *n.* preservationist, preserver; *vt.* preserve; *adj.* preservative, preservable
7. *n.* season, seasonableness; *adj.* seasonable; *adv.* seasonably, seasonally
8. *n.* temperance, temperateness; *adv.* temperately
9. *adj.* undergrown
10. *n.* zoologist; *adj.* zoologic, zoological; *adv.* zoologically

Exercise 2   Context Clues

11. (A) camouflage
12. (F) seasonal
13. (G) habitat
14. (H) mammals
15. (C) temperate
16. (B) naturalist
17. (I) zoology
18. (D) nocturnal
19. (E) undergrowth
20. (J) preservation

Exercise 3   Like Meanings and Opposite Meanings

21. A   22. A   23. C   24. B   25. D   26. B   27. D
28. C   29. A   30. B

Lesson 23   pages 91–94
Exercise 1   Mapping
Your Guess and Definition answers will vary. Possible responses to Other Forms items follow.

1. *n.* competence, competency; *adv.* competently

2. *n.* computation, computability; *vt.* computes, computed, computing; *adj.* computational, computable
3. *n.* diverseness, diversification, diversion, diversionist, diversity; *vt.* diversify; *adj.* diversionary; *adv.* diversely
4. *adj.* efficient; *adv.* efficiently
5. *vt.* exceeds, exceeded, exceeding; *adv.* exceedingly
6. *n.* fundamentalism, fundamentalist; *adv.* fundamentally
7. *n.* futileness, futility; *adv.* futilely
8. *n.* percentile
9. *adj.* prestigious; *adv.* prestigiously
10. *n.* substantiality, substantialness, substantiation, substantiator; *vt.* substantiate; *adj.* substantiative; *adv.* substantially

Exercise 2   Context Clues

11. (C) compute
12. (I) exceed
13. (B) diverse
14. (E) efficiency
15. (D) fundamental
16. (H) futile
17. (J) percentage
18. (G) substantial
19. (F) prestige
20. (A) competent

Exercise 3   Like Meanings and Opposite Meanings

21. C   22. B   23. B   24. D   25. D   26. A   27. B
28. B   29. D   30. B

Lesson 24   pages 95–98
Exercise 1   Mapping
Your Guess and Definition answers will vary. Possible responses to Other Forms items follow.

1. *n.* canceler, cancellation; *vt.* cancels, canceled, canceling; *adj.* cancelable
2. *n.* compensation, compensator; *vt.* compensates, compensated, compensating; *adj.* compensable, compensative, compensatory
3. *n.* economist, economy, economizer; *vi.* or *vt.* economize; *adj.* economic; *adv.* economically
4. *n.* finance, financier; *vt.* finance; *adv.* financially
5. *n.* logic, logicality, logicalness; *adv.* logically
6. *n. pl.* memorandums or memoranda
7. *n.* metropolis, metropolitanism, metropolitization; *vt.* metropolitanize
8. *n.* recognizability; *vt.* recognize, recognizes, recognized, recognizing; *adj.* recognizable, recognitory, recognitive; *adv.* recognizably
9. *n.* stationer
10. *n.* utilization, utilizer; *n. pl.* utilities; *vt.* utilize; *adj.* utilizable

Exercise 2   Context Clues

11. (C) economical
12. (H) utility
13. (J) stationery
14. (B) recognition
15. (A) metropolitan
16. (F) cancel
17. (E) compensates
18. (I) memorandum
19. (G) logical
20. (D) financial

Exercise 3   Like Meanings and Opposite Meanings

21. A   22. D   23. D   24. B   25. C   26. B   27. B
28. B   29. C   30. C

Lesson 25 pages 99–102

Exercise 1 Mapping

Your Guess and Definition answes will vary. Possible responses to Other Forms items follow.

1. *n.* accordance; *v.* accords, accorded, according; *adj.* accordant; *adv.* accordingly
2. *n.* approximation; *vt.* approximates, approximated, approximating; *adv.* approximately
3. *n.* coincidence; *vi.* coincides, coincided, coinciding; *adj.* coincident; *adv.* coincidentally
4. *n. pl.* debris
5. *n.* elaborateness, elaboration, elaborator; *vt.* elaborates, elaborated, elaborating; *adj.* elaborative; *adv.* elaborately
6. *n.* infrequency, infrequence; *adv.* infrequently
7. *vt.* kerneled, kerneling
8. *adv.* manually
9. *n.* mechanization; *vt.* mechanize; *adj.* mechanistic; *adv.* mechanistically
10. *n.* surplusage

Exercise 2 Context Clues

11. (A) accords
12. (J) debris
13. (D) approximate
14. (C) infrequent
15. (B) elaborate
16. (G) manual
17. (E) coincides
18. (F) mechanisms
19. (H) kernels
20. (I) surplus

Exercise 3 Like Meanings and Opposite Meanings

21. A   22. B   23. C   24. D   25. A   26. B   27. D
28. A   29. C   30. B

Lesson 26 pages 103–106

Exercise 1 Mapping

Your Guess and Definition answers will vary. Possible responses to Other Forms items follow.

1. *n.* abruptness, abruption; *adv.* abruptly
2. *n.* commitment; *vt.* commits, committed, committing; *adj.* committable
3. *n.* confirmation; *vt.* confirms, confirmed, confirming; *adj.* confirmable, confirmatory, confirmative; *adv.* confirmedly
4. *n.* inertia, inertness; *adv.* inertly
5. *n.* infiniteness, infinity; *adv.* infinitely
6. *adj.* magnitudinous
7. *adj.* probabilistic; probable; *adv.* probably
8. *n.* radiance; *vi.* radiates, radiated, radiating; *adj.* radiant; *adv.* radiantly
9. *n.* randomness, randomization; *vt.* randomize, randomizes, randomized, randomizing; *adv.* randomly
10. *n.* repellence, repellency; *vt.* repels, repelled, repelling; *adj.* repellent; *adv.* repellently

Exercise 2 Context Clues

11. (J) confirms
12. (B) abrupt
13. (A) probability
14. (D) repel
15. (H) magnitude
16. (I) commit
17. (F) random
18. (E) radiate
19. (G) infinite
20. (C) inert

Exercise 3 Like Meanings and Opposite Meanings

21. A   22. A   23. D   24. D   25. C   26. B   27. A
28. D   29. D   30. A

Lesson 27 pages 107–110

Exercise 1 Mapping

Your Guess and Definition answers will vary. Possible responses to Other Forms items follow.

1. *n.* aerialist; *adv.* aerially
2. *n.* barrenness; *adv.* barrenly
3. *n.* exoticism; *adv.* exotically
4. *n.* geologist, geology; *vi.* or *vt.* geologize, geologizes, geologized, geologizing; *adv.* geologically
5. *n.* glacier, glaciation; *vt.* glaciate, glaciates, glaciated; *adj.* glacial; *adv.* glacially
6. *n.* globalization; *vt.* globalize, globalizes, globalized, globalizing; *adv.* globally
7. *n.* majesty; *adj.* majestic; *adv.* majestically
8. *n.* navigability, navigation, navigator; *vi.* navigate, navigates, navigated, navigating; *adj.* navigational; *adv.* navigably, navigationally
9. *n. pl.* tributaries; *adv.* tributarily
10. None.

Exercise 2 Context Clues

11. (C) exotic
12. (D) geological
13. (E) glacial
14. (I) global
15. (F) barren
16. (G) majestic
17. (A) navigable
18. (H) aerial
19. (J) via
20. (B) tributary

Exercise 3 Like Meanings and Opposite Meanings

21. C   22. D   23. B   24. C   25. D   26. C   27. B
28. C   29. D   30. C

Lesson 28 pages 111–114

Exercise 1 Mapping

Your Guess and Definition answers will vary. Possible responses to Other Forms items follow.

1. *n.* alternative, alternation; *vi.* or *vt.* alternates, alternated, alternating; *adj.* alternative; *adv.* alternately, alternatively
2. *n.* challenger; *n. pl.* challenges; *vt.* challenges, challenged, challenging; *adj.* challengeable
3. *n.* effecter, effectiveness; *adj.* effective; *adv.* effectively
4. *vt.* encounters, encountered, encountering
5. *n.* incredibility; *adj.* incredulous; *adv.* incredibly, incredulously
6. *n.* inquisitiveness, inquiry, inquisition, inquisitor; *vi.* inquire, inquires, inquired, inquiring; *adj.* inquisitorial; *adv.* inquisitively, inquisitorially
7. *n.* propellant, propeller; *vt.* propels, propelled, propelling; *adj.* propellent
8. *n.* universalness, universalism, universalist, universality, universalization; *vt.* universalize; *adj.* universalistic
9. *n.* unpredictability; *adj.* unpredictive; *adv.* unpredictably, unpredictively
10. *adv.* vitally

Exercise 2 Context Clues

11. (I) encounter
12. (G) challenge
13. (J) unpredictable
14. (F) incredible
15. (E) vital
16. (H) inquisitive
17. (C) universal
18. (D) propels
19. (A) alternate
20. (B) effect

Exercise 3 Like Meanings and Opposite Meanings
21. C 22. A 23. D 24. D 25. B 26. A 27. B
28. C 29. B 30. C

Lesson 29 pages 115–118
Exercise 1 Mapping
Your Guess and Definition answers will vary. Possible responses to Other Forms items follow.
1. *n. pl.* capacities
2. *n.* intermediateness, intermediacy, intermediation, intermediator; *vi.* intermediates, intermediated, intermediating; *adv.* intermediately
3. *n.* intricacy, intricateness; *adv.* intricately
4. *n.* minimization, minimizer; *n. pl.* minimums; *vt.* minimize
5. *n.* perpetuation; *vt.* perpetuate; *adv.* perpetually
6. *vi.* or *vt.* pivots, pivoted, pivoting; *adj.* pivotal; *adv.* pivotally
7. *n.* promptness; *adv.* promptly
8. *n.* receptionist, receptiveness, receptivity; *vt.* receive; *adj.* receptive
9. *n.* speculator, speculation; *vi.* speculates, speculated, speculating; *adj.* speculative; *adv.* speculatively
10. *n.* stabilization, stabilizer; *vt.* stabilize

Exercise 2 Context Clues
11. (G) capacity
12. (F) intricate
13. (D) perpetual
14. (B) prompted
15. (A) speculate
16. (J) stability
17. (C) reception
18. (I) pivot
19. (H) minimum
20. (E) intermediate

Exercise 3 Like Meanings and Opposite Meanings
21. C 22. C 23. A 24. D 25. C 26. C 27. B
28. B 29. C 30. B

Lesson 30 pages 119–122
Exercise 1 Mapping
Your Guess and Definition answers will vary. Possible responses to Other Forms items follow.
1. *n.* excluder, exclusion; *vt.* excludes, excluded, excluding; *adj.* excludable, exclusionary
2. *n.* involuntariness; *adv.* involuntarily
3. *n. pl.* precautions; *adj.* precautionary
4. *n.* preciseness, precision; *adv.* precisely
5. *n. pl.* preliminaries; *adv.* preliminarily
6. *n.* proportionment, proportionality; *n. pl.* proportions; *vt.* proportions, proportioned, proportioning; *adj.* proportionate, proportional; *adv.* proportionately, proportionally
7. *n.* proposal; *vt.* propose; *adj.* propositional
8. None.
9. *n.* submergence; *vt.* submerge; *adj.* submergible
10. *n.* termination, terminator; *vt.* terminates, terminated, terminating; *adj.* terminal, terminative, terminational

Exercise 2 Context Clues
11. (F) stationary
12. (I) exclude
13. (B) submerged
14. (J) terminate
15. (C) proposition
16. (G) involuntary
17. (H) precautions
18. (E) proportion
19. (A) precise
20. (D) preliminary

Exercise 3 Like Meanings and Opposite Meanings
21. B 22. D 23. A 24. C 25. B 26. C 27. B
28. A 29. C 30. C

Lesson 1 pages 125–126
Exercise 1 Multimeaning
1. B 2. C
Exercise 2 Word Analysis
3. C 4. D 5. C 6. A
7. ghastly 8. velocity
9. invade 10. fascinate

Note: Encourage students to use the lists of common prefixes and suffixes on page 124 when they are working on the *Prefixes* and *Suffixes* exercises in this section

Lesson 2 pages 127–128
Exercise 1 Multimeaning
1. B 2. C
Exercise 2 Word Analysis
3. D 4. A 5. B 6. A
7. eventual 8. mere
9. technique 10. obsolete

Lesson 3 pages 129–130
Exercise 1 Multimeaning
1. D 2. D
Exercise 2 Word Analysis
3. B 4. D 5. A 6. B
7. motive 8. notorious
9. haunt 10. supervise

Lesson 4 pages 131–132
Exercise 1 Multimeaning
1. A 2. C
Exercise 2 Word Analysis
3. D 4. B 5. B 6. D
7. frail 8. obligation
9. porcelain 10. flaw

Lesson 5 pages 133–134
Exercise 1 Multimeaning
1. C 2. B
Exercise 2 Word Analysis
3. A 4. C 5. C 6. B
7. cherish 8. gratify
9. resolve 10. designate

Lesson 6 pages 135–136
Exercise 1 Multimeaning
1. B 2. D
Exercise 2 Word Analysis
3. C 4. B 5. B 6. C
7. moral 8. elective
9. illustrious 10. partial

Lesson 7 pages 137–138
Exercise 1 Multimeaning
1. C 2. B
Exercise 2 Word Analysis
3. B 4. A 5. B 6. A
7. participate 8. refrain
9. journal 10. prose

Lesson 8   pages 139–140
Exercise 1   Multimeaning
1. D   2. C
Exercise 2   Word Analysis
3. D   4. B   5. C   6. B
7. yield   8. intellect
9. opposition   10. expand

Lesson 9   pages 141–142
Exercise 1   Multimeaning
1. C   2. B
Exercise 2   Word Analysis
3. B   4. D   5. A   6. C
7. inhabit   8. maternal
9. ridicule   10. adopt

Lesson 10   pages 143–144
Exercise 1   Multimeaning
1. D   2. C
Exercise 2   Word Analysis
3. B   4. C   5. B   6. B
7. vengeance   8. fortress
9. patron   10. banish

Lesson 11   pages 145–146
Exercise 1   Multimeaning
1. B   2. C
Exercise 2   Word Analysis
3. A   4. C   5. A   6. A
7. pigment   8. optical
9. nutrition   10. edible

Lesson 12   pages 147–148
Exercise 1   Multimeaning
1. B   2. C
Exercise 2   Word Analysis
3. A   4. C   5. D   6. A
7. financial   8. logical
9. substantial   10. percentage

Lesson 13   pages 149–150
Exercise 1   Multimeaning
1. C   2. D
Exercise 2   Word Analysis
3. B   4. A   5. A   6. C
7. kernel   8. debris
9. infrequent   10. probability

Lesson 14   pages 151–152
Exercise 1   Multimeaning
1. C   2. C
Exercise 2   Word Analysis
3. B   4. B   5. B   6. B
7. encounter   8. via
9. vital   10. glacial

Lesson 15   pages 153–154
Exercise 1   Multimeaning
1. C   2. C
Exercise 2   Word Analysis
3. A   4. D   5. C   6. A
7. reception   8. stationary
9. precise   10. minimum

CONNECTING NEW WORDS AND PATTERNS

Lesson 1   page 158
1. Synonym; (D). *Alien* is similar in meaning to *foreign,* just as *normal* is similar in meaning to *usual.*
   (A) F   (B) CQ   (C) C   (E) A
2. Synonym; (A). *Diplomatic* is similar in meaning to *tactful,* just as *polite* is similar in meaning to *well-mannered.*
   (B) CQ   (C) PW   (D) A   (E) PO
3. Antonym; (D). *Embrace* and *reject* are opposite in meaning, as are *accept* and *deny.*
   (A) C   (B) D or C   (C) AO   (E) S or F
4. Degree; (C). *Gawk* suggests *looking* intensely at something, as *pry* suggests *asking* too aggressively about something.
   (A) CQ   (B) CE   (D): PW   (E) F
5. Characteristic Quality; (C). A *gesture* is characteristically *expressive,* just as a *letter* is characteristically a *written* document.
   (A) C   (B) PW   (D) L   (E) D
6. Degree; (B). *Ghastly* suggests a greater degree of dreadfulness than *unpleasant* does, just as *overpowering* suggests a greater degree of strength than *strong* does.
   (A) PO   (C) AO   (D) L   (E) A
7. Characteristic Quality; (B). An *enemy* is characteristically *hostile,* just as a *friend* is characteristically *caring.*
   (A) A   (C) CE   (D) PW   (E) L
8. Synonym; (D). *Memorable* is similar in meaning to *remarkable,* just as *regular* is similar in meaning to *ordinary.*
   (A) PW or AO   (B) CQ   (C) CE   (E) A
9. Part and Whole; (E). An *overture* is the first part of an *opera,* just as an *introduction* is the first part of an *essay.*
   (A) C   (B) A   (C) L   (D) F or S
10. Classification; (E). A *moon* can be classified as a *satellite,* just as a *sun* can be classified as a *star.*
    (A) AO or F   (B) F   (C) A   (D) PO

Lesson 2   page 159
1. Synonym; (B). *Consequence* and *result* have nearly the same meaning, as do *solution* and *answer.*
   (A) A   (C) D   (D) C   (E) PO
2. Characteristic Quality; (C). *Politics* is characteristically *controversial,* just as a *maze* is characteristically *complicated.*
   (A) AO or A   (B) S or D   (D) D   (E) CE
3. Antonym; (B). A *defiant* person is the opposite of a *cooperative* person, as a *hurtful* action is the opposite of a *helpful* action.
   (A) PO   (C) S or D   (D) AO   (E) CQ
4. Synonym; (D). *Deliberate* and *purposeful* have nearly the same meaning, as do *fortunate* and *lucky.*
   (A) F   (B) C   (C) D   (E) A

5. Synonym; (D). *Distort* and *twist* have nearly the same meaning, as do *throw* and *toss*.
   (A) A   (B) C   (C) L   (E) PO
6. Degree; (E). *Grotesque* suggests a greater degree of strangeness than *odd* does, just as *deadly* suggests a greater degree of destructiveness than *harmful* does.
   (A) A or AO or CE   (B) PW   (C) AO   (D) S
7. Antonym; (A). *Inferior* and *superior* are opposite in meaning, as are *boring* and *interesting*.
   (B) S   (C) D   (D) PO   (E) C
8. Synonym; (B). *Originality* and *freshness* have nearly the same meaning, as do *enthusiasm* and *eagerness*.
   (A) AO   (C) PW   (D) A   (E) CQ
9. Antonym; (A). *Reality* is the opposite of *fantasy*, just as *fact* is the opposite of *fiction*.
   (B) PA   (C) L   (D) CE   (E) C
10. Synonym; (A). *Recoil* and *retreat* have nearly the same meaning, as do *begin* and *start*.
    (B) CQ   (C) D   (D) AO or F   (E) L

Lesson 3   page 160

1. Synonym; (E). *Candid* and *frank* have nearly the same meaning, as do *honest* and *truthful*.
   (A) CQ   (B) C   (C) PW   (D) PO
2. Classification; (D). The *diaphragm* can be classified as a *muscle*, just as a *peach* can be classified as a *fruit*.
   (A) PW   (B) F   (C) PA   (E) D
3. Performer and Action; (C). You expect a *ghost* to *haunt*, just as you expect a *leprechaun* to *trick* people.
   (A) S or D   (B) PO   (D) C   (E) PW
4. Performer and Action; (C). You expect a *hummingbird* to *hover*, just as you expect a *squirrel* to *scamper*.
   (A) D   (B) AO   (D) S or CE   (E) L
5. Antonym; (E). *Idle*, or inactive, means the opposite of *busy*, just as *serious* means the opposite of *joking*.
   (A) PO   (B) CQ   (C) F   (D) C
6. Antonym; (D). *Ignorance* and *knowledge* are opposite in meaning, as are *health* and *sickness*.
   (A) D   (B) AO   (C) PA   (E) F
7. Performer and Object; (C). A *trainer* of animals uses a *leash*, just as a *gymnast* uses a *balance beam*.
   (A) AO   (B) L   (D) CQ   (E) PA
8. Antonym; (D). A *lenient* parent is the opposite of a *strict* parent, just as a *harsh* climate is the opposite of a *mild* climate.
   (A) CQ   (B) CE   (C) C   (E) AO
9. Antonym; (B). *Modest* and *vain* are opposite in meaning, as are *fearless* and *afraid*.
   (A) S   (C) F   (D) CQ   (E) C
10. Antonym; (A). *Subtle* and *obvious* have opposite meanings, as do *clear* and *confused*.
    (B) L   (C) C   (D) CE   (E) D

Lesson 4   page 161

1. Antonym; (C). To *aggravate*, or worsen, is the opposite of to *improve*, just as to *damage* is the opposite of to *repair*.
   (A) S   (B) F   (D) PW   (E) PO

2. Synonym; (D). *Dashing* and *stylish* have nearly the same meaning, as do *lively* and *exciting*.
   (A) A   (B) PW   (C) PA   (E) F
3. Antonym; (A). *Dismal* and *cheerful* have opposite meanings, as do *disappointed* and *delighted*.
   (B) AO   (C) CE   (D) PO   (E) F
4. Synonym; (C). A *flaw* is similar to a *defect*, just as an *error* is almost the same thing as a *mistake*.
   (A) D   (B) F   (D) PW   (E) C
5. Antonym; (C). *Frail*, or weak, means the opposite of *sturdy*, just as *wet* means the opposite of *dry*.
   (A) S   (B) CE   (D) C   (E) L
6. Antonym; (B). *Maintaining* something is the opposite of *neglecting* it, just as *creating* something is the opposite of *destroying* it.
   (A) C   (C) D   (D) PW   (E) PO
7. Synonym; (B). *Obligation* and *duty* have nearly the same meaning, as do *task* and *job*.
   (A) PA   (C) PW   (D) F   (E) D
8. Synonym; (A). *Phase* is similar in meaning to *stage*, just as *zone* is similar in meaning to *area*.
   (B) F   (C) PW   (D) CQ   (E) C
9. Characteristic Quality; (D). *Laughter* is characteristically *spontaneous*, or unplanned, just as a *celebration* is characteristically *joyous*.
   (A) D   (B) A   (C) C   (E) L
10. Synonym; (E). *Tiresome* and *boring* have nearly the same meaning, as do *irritable* and *touchy*.
    (A) CE   (B) AO   (C) PW   (D) A

Lesson 5   page 162

1. Synonym; (B). *Consistent* is similar in meaning to *regular*, just as *usual* is similar in meaning to *ordinary*.
   (A) AO   (C) PW   (D) C   (E) PO
2. Synonym; (A). *Contemplate* and *consider* have nearly the same meaning, as do *admit* and *confess*.
   (B) C   (C) D   (D) CQ   (E) CE
3. Antonym; (E). *Crucial* and *unimportant* are opposite in meaning, as are *loud* and *silent*.
   (A) S   (B) L   (C) C   (D) CE
4. Characteristic Quality; (C). A *tuxedo* is characteristically *formal*, or dressy, just as *satin* is characteristically *smooth*.
   (A) PA   (B) A   (D) L   (E) PW
5. Synonym; (D). *Indispensable* and *essential* both mean necessary or required, just as *nice* and *pleasant* both mean agreeable.
   (A) AO   (B) C   (C) A   (E) PA
6. Action and Object; (D). You *interpret*, or determine the meaning of, *symbols*, just as you *deliver* a *speech*.
   (A) S   (B) L   (C) D   (E) PA
7. Degree; (A). *Legendary* suggests even greater renown than *well known* does, just as *demand* suggests greater urgency and force than *request* does.
   (B) AO   (C) A   (D) PO   (E) L

8. Characteristic Quality; (D). A *myth* is characteristically *traditional*, or passed down through generations, just as a *feather* is *light*.
   (A) PO   (B) A   (C) F   (E) D

9. Part and Whole; (B). A *legend* is part of a culture's *mythology*, just as a *tail* is part of a *cat*.
   (A) A   (C) L   (D) CQ   (E) F

10. Synonym; (A). *Vigor* and *strength* have nearly the same meaning, as do *delicateness* and *fragility*.
    (B) C   (C) F   (D) L   (E) CE

Lesson 6   page 163

1. Synonym; (A). A *guarantee* is similar to a *promise*, just as a *sign* is similar to an *indication*.
   (B) AO   (C) L   (D) D   (E) CQ

2. Characteristic Quality; (C). A *hypocrite*, one whose actions are inconsistent with his or her words, is characteristically *insincere*, just as a *thief* is characteristically *dishonest*.
   (A) D   (B) PW   (D) S   (E) PO

3. Synonym; (E). *Illustrious* and *famous* have nearly the same meaning, as do *silly* and *foolish*.
   (A) C   (B) PA   (C) D   (D) L

4. Antonym; (B). *Indefinite* and *certain* are opposite in meaning, as are *confusing* and *clear*.
   (A) PA   (C) PW   (D) F   (E) S

5. Part and Whole; (A). An *initial* is one part of a *name*, just as a *title* is one part of a *book*.
   (B) S   (C) D   (D) AO   (E) CQ

6. Synonym; (C). *Merit* is similar in meaning to *worth*, just as *ability* is similar in meaning to *skill*.
   (A) PW   (B) F or CE   (D) D   (E) PO

7. Synonym; (C). *Moderate* and *mild* have nearly the same meaning, as do *easy* and *simple*.
   (A) D   (B) PW   (D) CE   (E) C

8. Antonym; (E). *Momentary* and *permanent* are opposite in meaning, as are *brief* and *endless*.
   (A) PO   (B) CQ   (C) S   (D) L

9. Synonym; (A). When *partial* is used to describe someone who favors one person over another, *partial* and *unfair* have nearly the same meaning. *Raw* and *uncooked* are also similar in meaning.
   (B) A   (C) CQ   (D) C   (E) L

10. Action and Object; (C). You can *veto*, or refuse to approve, a *proposal*, just as you can *accept* an *invitation*.
    (A) CE   (B) C   (D) S   (E) PO

Lesson 7   page 164

1. Synonym; (D). *Credible* and *believable* have nearly the same meaning, as do *loyal* and *faithful*.
   (A) C   (B) L   (C) D   (E) F

2. Part and Whole; (E). A *teacher* is part of the *faculty*, just as a *singer* is part of the *choir*.
   (A) L   (B) C   (C) S or AO or D   (D) PA

3. Characteristic Quality; (C). A *forum*, or assembly, is characteristically *public*, just as *garbage* is characteristically *smelly*.
   (A) AO   (B) C   (D) PW   (E) A

4. Synonym; (C). A *journal* is the same as a *diary*, just as a *tale* is the same as a *story*.
   (A) C   (B) PW   (D) CQ   (E) CE

5. Synonym; (A). *Legible* and *readable* have similar meanings, as do *gentle* and *tender*.
   (B) F   (C) PW   (D) CQ   (E) CE

6. Characteristic Quality; (E). An *author* is characteristically *literary*, just as a *chemist* is characteristically *scientific*.
   (A) F or CE   (B) C   (C) L   (D) PW

7. Performer and Object; (B). A *writer* produces a *manuscript*, while a *chef* follows a *recipe*.
   (A) CE or AO   (C) PW   (D) PA   (E) A

8. Cause and Effect; (B). *Practice* can cause *mastery* of a skill, just as *repetition* can cause *memorization* of information.
   (A) C   (C) D   (D) AO   (E) A

9. Synonym; (D). A *persuasion*, or strong belief, is similar to an *opinion*, just as a *thought* is similar to an *idea*.
   (A) AO   (B) D   (C) CQ   (E) L

10. Location; (B). A *tutor* can be found in a *classroom*, just as a *chef* can be found in a *restaurant*.
    (A) A   (C) PA   (D) D   (E) PO

Lesson 8   page 165

1. Synonym; (A). To *adhere* and to *stick* have similar meanings, as do to *hint* and to *suggest*.
   (B) F   (C) CQ   (D) PO   (E) L

2. Antonym; (C). To *expand* and to *contract* are opposite in meaning, as are to *grow* and to *wither*.
   (A) S   (B) CQ   (D) D   (E) L

3. Synonym; (D). *Fatigue* means almost the same thing as *exhaustion*, just as *energy* and *power* have similar meanings.
   (A) F   (B) L   (C) PW   (E) CE

4. Degree; (C). To *gouge* is to cut more deeply than to *scratch*, just as to *pound* is to beat more forcefully than to *tap*.
   (A) F   (B) S   (D) PW   (E) C

5. Antonym; (E). *Hardy* and *weak* are opposite in meaning, as are *dry* and *moist*.
   (A) S   (B) C   (C) D   (D) PW

6. Antonym; (E). An *opponent* is the opposite of a *teammate*, just as an *enemy* is the opposite of a *friend*.
   (A) S   (B) AO   (C) CQ   (D) C

7. Synonym; (B). *Pursue* is similar in meaning to *chase*, just as *start* is similar in meaning to *begin*.
   (A) PO   (C) AO   (D) CQ   (E) C

8. Synonym; (D). *Recommend* is similar in meaning to *advise*, just as *order* is similar in meaning to *command*.
   (A) PW   (B) CQ   (C) C   (E) A

9. Performer and Object; (C). A *student* receives a *scholarship*, just as an *employee* receives a *paycheck*.
   (A) A   (B) PW   (D) F or CE   (E) L

10. Degree; (D). *Totally* and *partly* suggest two different degrees of completeness, just as *soggy* and *damp* suggest two different degrees of wetness.
   (A) PW   (B) AO or F   (C) CE   (E) A

Lesson 9   page 166

1. Synonym; (C). When *acute* and *sharp* describe hearing or pain, for example, they have nearly the same meaning, just as *plain* and *simple* have nearly the same meaning.
   (A) D   (B) L   (D) A   (E) CQ

2. Action and Object; (C). You *adopt* a *plan*, just as you *borrow* a *book*.
   (A) PA   (B) CQ   (D) PO or PA   (E) PW

3. Synonym; (D). *Anguish* has nearly the same meaning as *agony*, just as *happiness* has nearly the same meaning as *gladness*.
   (A) PA   (B) C   (C) PW   (E) CE

4. Cause and Effect; (E). *Hesitation* can be caused by *uncertainty*, just as *damage* can be caused by a *storm*.
   (A) PW   (B) C   (C) S   (D) A

5. Synonym; (B). *Hysterical* and *wild* have nearly the same meaning, as do *tame* and *gentle*.
   (A) CE   (C) A   (D) PW   (E) PO

6. Antonym; (C). *Irritable* and *calm* are opposite in meaning, as are *evil* and *good*.
   (A) CQ   (B) C   (D) L   (E) S

7. Cause and Effect; (D). *Ridicule* can cause *embarrassment*, just as *praise* can cause *confidence*.
   (A) S   (B) A   (C) PA   (E) AO

8. Antonym; (D). *Timid* means the opposite of *confident*, just as *attached* means the opposite of *separated*.
   (A) PW   (B) CQ   (C) C   (E) S

9. Antonym; (A). *Vague* means the opposite of *definite*, just as *overcast* weather is the opposite of *clear* weather.
   (B) D   (C) S   (D) CE   (E) PA

10. Degree; (D). *Wretched* suggests a greater degree of sadness than *unhappy* does, just as *excellent* suggests a greater degree of *quality* than *adequate* does.
    (A) S   (B) CE   (C) L or PW   (E) CQ

Lesson 10   page 167

1. Synonym; (A). *Barbarous* and *cruel* have similar meanings, as do *polite* and *well-mannered*.
   (B) CQ   (C) A   (D) PW   (E) C

2. Classification; (D). A *baron* may be classified as a *nobleman*, just as a *truck* may be classified as a *vehicle*.
   (A) S   (B) PA   (C) PW   (E) CQ

3. Function; (B). The function of a *beacon*, or signal, is to *warn* people of danger, just as the function of *money* is to *buy* things.
   (A) CQ   (C) A   (D) L   (E) PW

4. Function; (C). The function of a *fortress* is to *protect*, just as the function of a *weapon* is to *harm*.
   (A) L   (B) A   (D) S   (E) PW

5. Synonym; (E). *Grandeur* is similar in meaning to *magnificence*, just as *courage* is similar in meaning to *bravery*.
   (A) CQ   (B) C   (C) F   (D) CE

6. Classification; (C). A *monarchy* can be classified as a *government* ruled by a king or queen, just as *French* can be classified as a *language*.
   (A) CE or PW   (B) CQ   (D) AO   (E) PO

7. Performer and Action; (D). You expect a *patron* to *support* something or someone financially, just as you expect a *teacher* to *instruct* someone.
   (A) C   (B) CQ   (C) F   (E) L

8. Antonym; (A). *Perilous*, which means full of danger, is opposite in meaning to *safe*. *Uneasy* and *calm* also have opposite meanings.
   (B) S   (C) D   (D) PA   (E) C

9. Cause and Effect; (E). *Toil*, or work, can cause *exhaustion*, just as *success* can cause *pride*.
   (A) S   (B) A   (C) C   (D) PW

10. Antonym; (D). *Vengeance* and *forgiveness* are opposite in meaning, as are *roughness* and *smoothness*.
    (A) L   (B) PO or PA   (C) C   (E) AO

Lesson 11   page 168

1. Antonym; (C). *Edible*, which means eatable, is opposite in meaning to *poisonous*, just as *fresh* is opposite in meaning to *stale*.
   (A) D   (B) PO   (D) CQ   (E) PA

2. Synonym; (C). *Endurance* and *patience* have similar meanings, as do *truthfulness* and *honesty*.
   (A) PO   (B) PW   (D) L   (E) CQ

3. Classification; (B). *Glucose* is a type of *sugar*, just as *spaghetti* is a type of *food*.
   (A) CQ   (C) S   (D) F   (E) CE

4. Characteristic Quality; (A). A *habitat* is characteristically a *natural* environment, just as the *ocean* is characteristically *deep*.
   (B) S or D   (C) CE or D   (D) A   (E) F

5. Classification; (B). A *whale* is classified as a *mammal*, just as a *termite* is classified as an *insect*.
   (A) CE   (C) PO or L   (D) AO   (E) D

6. Performer and Object; (E). *Naturalists* study *trees*, just as *beauticians* work with *hair*.
   (A) CQ   (B) PW   (C) AO   (D) PA

7. Function; (D). The function of *nutrition* is to *nourish*, just as the function of *exercise* is to *strengthen*.
   (A) CQ   (B) PW   (C) D   (E) AO

8. Synonym; (C). *Organism* means nearly the same thing as *living thing*, just as *trousers* means nearly the same thing as *pants*.
   (A) PO   (B) CE   (D) CQ   (E) L

9. Synonym; (B). A *temperate* climate is the same as a *mild* climate. *Excited* and *thrilled* also have the same meaning.
   (A) L   (C) C   (D) PW   (E) AO

10. Classification; (B). *Zoology* is classified as a *science*, just as *German* is a *language*.
    (A) A   (C) PO   (D) S   (E) E

Lesson 12   page 169

1. Action and Object; (C). You can *cancel* an *appointment,* just as you can *plan* a *party.*
   (A) C   (B) F   (D) L   (E) PW
2. Degree; (C). *Competent* suggests a lesser level of performance than *excellent* does, just as *naughty* suggests a lesser degree of wickedness than *evil* does.
   (A) CQ   (B) AO   (D) PW   (E) C
3. Antonym; (D). *Efficiency* is the opposite of *wastefulness,* just as *tenderness* is the opposite of *roughness.*
   (A) C   (B) PO   (C) S or D   (E) CE
4. Synonym; (B). *Fundamental* and *basic* have nearly the same meaning, as do *difficult* and *hard.*
   (A) PA   (C) F   (D) A   (E) L
5. Antonym; (B). A *futile* action is the opposite of an *effective* action, just as a *valuable* thing is the opposite of a *worthless* thing.
   (A) PA   (C) C   (D) AO   (E) PW
6. Synonym; (E). *Logical* and *reasonable* have nearly the same meaning, as do *keen* and *sharp.*
   (A) CE   (B) PO   (C) PA   (D) PW
7. Function; (D). The function of a *memorandum* is to *remind,* just as the function of a *story* is to *entertain.*
   (A) PW   (B) PA   (C) CQ   (E) AO
8. Cause and Effect; (B). *Recognition,* or approval, can cause someone to feel *pride. Approval* can also cause a person to feel *pleasure.*
   (A) CQ   (C) C   (D) PO   (E) L
9. Location; (B). *Stationery* can be found in a *desk,* just as *folders* can be found in a *file cabinet.*
   (A) F   (C) D   (D) CQ   (E) S
10. Classification; (C). *Electricity* is classified as a *utility,* just as a *piano* is classified as an *instrument.*
    (A) L   (B) AO   (D) D   (E) F

Lesson 13   page 170

1. Characteristic Quality; (C). A *cliff* is characteristically *abrupt,* or steep, just as a *peak* is characteristically *high.*
   (A) PW   (B) F   (D) D   (E) PA
2. Cause and Effect; (B). *Debris* can be caused by *destruction,* just as *ashes* can be caused by *fire.*
   (A) S   (C) AO   (D) PA   (E) PW
3. Synonym; (D). *Elaborate* is similar in meaning to *complicated,* just as *ornamented* is similar in meaning to *decorated.*
   (A) C   (B) CE   (C) CQ   (E) L
4. Antonym; (D). *Infinite* and *limited* have opposite meanings, as do *lengthy* and *brief.*
   (A) PO   (B) F   (C) S   (E) D
5. Synonym; (E). An *infrequent* occurrence is the same as an *uncommon* occurrence, just as a *regular* happening is the same as an *everyday* happening.
   (A) A   (B) CQ   (C) PA   (D) AO

6. Characteristic Quality; (B). A *kernel,* the center of something, is characteristically *central,* just as a *plate* is characteristically *circular.*
   (A) AO   (C) C   (D) S   (E) A
7. Function; (C). The function of a *manual* is to *instruct,* just as the function of a *wheelchair* is to *transport.*
   (A) D   (B) C   (D) S   (E) L
8. Part and Whole; (D). A *mechanism* is part of a *clock,* just as a *skeleton* is part of a *body.*
   (A) C   (B) F   (C) CQ   (E) D
9. Antonym; (A). *Repel* and *attract* have opposite meanings, as do *push* and *pull.*
   (B) PA   (C) CQ   (D) D   (E) F
10. Synonym; (C). *Surplus* and *extra* have nearly the same meaning, as do *crooked* and *bent.*
    (A) PA   (B) C   (D) L   (E) PO

Lesson 14   page 171

1. Antonym; (D). A *barren* field is the opposite of a *fertile* field, just as being *poor* is the opposite of being *rich.*
   (A) AO   (B) F   (C) PO   (E) CQ
2. Characteristic Quality; (D). An *encounter* is characteristically *unexpected,* just as a *party* is characteristically *noisy.*
   (A) PA   (B) D   (C) C   (E) PO
3. Synonym; (C). *Exotic* and *foreign* have similar meanings, as do *regular* and *ordinary.*
   (A) PW   (B) D   (D) CQ   (E) PA
4. Degree; (C). *Incredible* suggests a greater degree of strangeness than *unusual* does, just as *gorgeous* suggests a greater degree of beauty than *attractive* does.
   (A) C   (B) S or CE   (D) PA   (E) CQ
5. Characteristic Quality; (D). A *chimpanzee* is characteristically *inquisitive,* or curious, just as an *eel* is characteristically *slippery.*
   (A) C   (B) AO or F   (C) D   (E) L
6. Characteristic Quality; (B). An *ocean* is characteristically *navigable,* allowing the passage of ships, just as a *whistle* is characteristically *shrill.*
   (A) AO   (C) D   (D) C   (E) PW
7. Function; (C). The function of a *propeller* is to *propel,* or move something forward, just as the function of a *rudder* is to *steer.*
   (A) PO   (B) PW   (D) D   (E) CQ
8. Degree; (D). A *tributary* is a smaller stream of water than a *river,* just as a *path* is a smaller and less–developed route than a *street.*
   (A) PA   (B) L   (C) AO   (E) CE
9. Characteristic Quality; (A). A *surprise* is characteristically *unpredictable,* just as a *fire* is characteristically *hot.*
   (B) C   (C) L   (D) F or PO   (E) S
10. Synonym; (C). *Vital* and *essential* have nearly the same meaning, as do *wanted* and *desired.*
    (A) CE   (B) F   (D) L   (E) PW

Lesson 15   page 172

1. Antonym; (D). *Exclude* and *include* have opposite meanings, as do *arrive* and *leave*.
   (A) AO   (B) PA   (C) F   (E) S
2. Antonym; (C). *Intricate,* or complex, means the opposite of *simple,* just as *fancy* means the opposite of *plain.*
   (A) PA   (B) L   (D) CQ   (E) PW
3. Characteristic Quality; (E). A *hiccup* is characteristically *involuntary,* just as *enlistment* in this country is characteristically *voluntary.*
   (A) L   (B) S   (C) AO   (D) PO
4. Synonym; (E). *Perpetual* is similar in meaning to *eternal,* just as *attached* is similar in meaning to *joined.*
   (A) D   (B) PW   (C) CE   (D) CQ
5. Cause and Effect; (D). *Safety* is the effect of using *precaution,* just as *tiredness* is the effect of *sleeplessness.*
   (A) C or PW   (B) PO   (C) L   (E) PW
6. Synonym; (D). *Prompt* and *quick* have nearly the same meaning, as do *safe* and *secure.*
   (A) PW   (B) D   (C) CE   (E) C
7. Synonym; (A). *Speculate* and *think* have nearly the same meaning, as do *ask* and *request.*
   (B) PW   (C) F   (D) C   (E) AO
8. Antonym; (C). *Stationary,* or still, means the opposite of *movable,* just as *broken* means the opposite of *fixed.*
   (A) AO   (B) CQ   (D) CE   (E) F
9. Characteristic Quality; (D). A *sunken ship* is characteristically *submerged,* or underwater, just as a pirate's *treasure* is characteristically *buried.*
   (A) PO   (B) CE   (C) C   (E) L
10. Antonym; (B). *Terminate* and *start* have opposite meanings, as do *finish* and *begin.*
    (A) PO   (C) CQ   (D) C   (E) CE

READING NEW WORDS IN CONTEXT

Lesson 1   pages 175–178
1. A   2. C   3. C   4. A   5. D   6. C   7. B   8. B
9. D   10. C   11. C   12. D   13. D   14. A   15. A
16. B   17. C   18. D   19. B   20. C

Lesson 2   pages 179–182
1. C   2. A   3. A   4. C   5. D   6. C   7. D   8. A
9. B   10. C   11. D   12. D   13. A   14. B   15. C
16. B   17. B   18. A   19. A   20. C

Lesson 3   pages 183–186
1. D   2. C   3. A   4. B   5. C   6. D   7. D   8. C
9. A   10. B   11. C   12. B   13. B   14. D   15. A
16. B   17. B   18. B   19. C   20. D

Lesson 4   pages 187–190
1. A   2. A   3. D   4. A   5. C   6. B   7. B   8. D
9. D   10. D   11. D   12. D   13. C   14. B   15. B
16. A   17. D   18. C   19. D   20. A

Lesson 5   pages 191–194
1. A   2. B   3. C   4. D   5. B   6. C   7. D   8. A
9. C   10. B   11. D   12. A   13. C   14. C   15. C
16. D   17. C   18. A   19. D   20. B

Lesson 6   pages 195–198
1. D   2. D   3. B   4. A   5. C   6. D   7. D   8. C
9. B   10. A   11. D   12. D   13. A   14. D   15. A
16. C   17. A   18. D   19. D   20. C

Lesson 7   pages 199–202
1. A   2. D   3. B   4. B   5. D   6. C   7. D   8. C
9. B   10. A   11. C   12. D   13. B   14. A   15. A
16. B   17. C   18. D   19. C   20. C

Lesson 8   pages 203–206
1. C   2. C   3. B   4. C   5. A   6. D   7. D   8. B
9. C   10. B   11. C   12. D   13. D   14. A   15. D
16. C   17. D   18. A   19. B   20. C

Lesson 9   pages 207–210
1. B   2. C   3. A   4. C   5. B   6. B   7. D   8. C
9. D   10. C   11. A   12. B   13. B   14. A   15. C
16. D   17. B   18. A   19. C   20. C

Lesson 10   pages 211–214
1. A   2. B   3. C   4. D   5. D   6. C   7. C   8. C
9. A   10. A   11. D   12. A   13. D   14. C   15. D
16. A   17. B   18. B   19. B   20. D

Lesson 11   pages 215–218
1. B   2. D   3. C   4. A   5. C   6. B   7. B   8. D
9. A   10. A   11. C   12. C   13. D   14. B   15. A
16. D   17. D   18. D   19. C   20. C

Lesson 12   pages 219–222
1. C   2. B   3. C   4. D   5. A   6. B   7. A   8. C
9. D   10. B   11. D   12. B   13. B   14. C   15. A
16. D   17. B   18. C   19. A   20. D

Lesson 13   pages 223–226
1. A   2. D   3. D   4. C   5. B   6. A   7. B   8. C
9. D   10. C   11. C   12. D   13. A   14. C   15. A
16. D   17. A   18. B   19. A   20. D

Lesson 14   pages 227–230
1. C   2. C   3. B   4. A   5. A   6. D   7. C   8. B
9. C   10. B   11. C   12. C   13. D   14. A   15. D
16. C   17. D   18. D   19. B   20. C

Lesson 15   pages 231–234
1. A   2. A   3. B   4. B   5. D   6. C   7. C   8. A
9. C   10. C   11. A   12. B   13. B   14. A   15. B
16. C   17. D   18. D   19. C   20. B

USING NEW WORDS ON TESTS

FORMATIVE ASSESSMENT
Test 1   page 3
1. B   2. D   3. A   4. B   5. D   6. A   7. C   8. B
9. D   10. A
Test 2   page 4
1. C   2. C   3. C   4. C   5. A   6. C   7. C   8. B
9. A   10. D

Test 3   page 5

1. D   2. D   3. C   4. D   5. C   6. B   7. B   8. C
9. A   10. D

Test 4   page 6

1. C   2. C   3. A   4. C   5. B   6. A   7. B   8. B
9. B   10. D

Test 5   page 7

1. A   2. B   3. A   4. B   5. C   6. D   7. B   8. A
9. C   10. C

Test 6   page 8

1. A   2. C   3. C   4. B   5. A   6. C   7. D   8. C
9. C   10. A

Test 7   page 9

1. D   2. B   3. C   4. B   5. B   6. A   7. D   8. B
9. B   10. D

Test 8   page 10

1. A   2. A   3. A   4. B   5. A   6. C   7. C   8. B
9. D   10. D

Test 9   page 11

1. C   2. C   3. A   4. D   5. C   6. B   7. A   8. A
9. A   10. C

Test 10   page 12

1. C   2. A   3. A   4. B   5. C   6. D   7. D   8. A
9. B   10. C

Test 11   page 13

1. B   2. A   3. A   4. C   5. A   6. B   7. D   8. B
9. D   10. C

Test 12   page 14

1. C   2. C   3. B   4. D   5. B   6. A   7. A   8. C
9. A   10. D

Test 13   page 15

1. C   2. D   3. C   4. B   5. A   6. B   7. B   8. C
9. A   10. D

Test 14   page 16

1. A   2. C   3. B   4. B   5. C   6. D   7. D   8. A
9. B   10. A

Test 15   page 17

1. A   2. C   3. A   4. B   5. C   6. D   7. B   8. B
9. C   10. D

Test 16   page 18

1. C   2. A   3. A   4. D   5. C   6. A   7. B   8. D
9. B   10. C

Test 17   page 19

1. B   2. A   3. B   4. D   5. D   6. C   7. D   8. B
9. A   10. C

Test 18   page 20

1. C   2. A   3. D   4. C   5. B   6. B   7. D   8. A
9. C   10. A

Test 19   page 21

1. C   2. A   3. B   4. C   5. D   6. B   7. D   8. A
9. C   10. C

Test 20   page 22

1. B   2. B   3. C   4. C   5. A   6. D   7. A   8. A
9. D   10. B

Test 21   page 23

1. C   2. C   3. C   4. A   5. D   6. D   7. A   8. A
9. B   10. B

Test 22   page 24

1. A   2. C   3. C   4. B   5. B   6. A   7. D   8. D
9. B   10. C

Test 23   page 25

1. B   2. B   3. D   4. B   5. A   6. C   7. D   8. A
9. C   10. D

Test 24   page 26

1. C   2. A   3. B   4. C   5. D   6. D   7. A   8. A
9. B   10. B

Test 25   page 27

1. B   2. B   3. B   4. D   5. D   6. B   7. A   8. C
9. C   10. C

Test 26   page 28

1. A   2. B   3. A   4. B   5. C   6. C   7. A   8. A
9. C   10. B

Test 27   page 29

1. C   2. D   3. B   4. B   5. C   6. D   7. B   8. C
9. C   10. A

Test 28   page 30

1. D   2. A   3. C   4. D   5. C   6. B   7. B   8. A
9. D   10. B

Test 29   page 31

1. A   2. C   3. A   4. B   5. C   6. B   7. D   8. C
9. B   10. A

Test 30   page 32

1. D   2. B   3. A   4. C   5. A   6. B   7. A   8. C
9. D   10. A

SUMMATIVE ASSESSMENT

Test 1 Part A   pages 35–40

1. consequence
2. inferior
3. caliber
4. distract
5. contemplate
6. comparable
7. defiant
8. motive
9. consistent
10. dashing
11. threshold
12. maturity
13. fulfill
14. versatile
15. fascinate
16. anticipate
17. legendary
18. resolve
19. obsolete
20. conspicuous

21. B   22. D   23. A   24. A   25. C   26. B   27. C
28. B   29. D   30. A   31. D   32. C   33. A   34. C
35. A   36. C   37. D   38. C   39. D   40. A   41. A
42. B   43. D   44. C   45. B   46. D   47. D   48. C
49. A   50. C

Test 1 Part B   pages 41–46

51. abstract
52. controversial
53. conform
54. absurd
55. designate
56. porcelain
57. deliberate
58. spontaneous
59. crucial
60. technique
61. profound
62. grotesque
63. distort
64. aggravate
65. gawk
66. offend
67. originality
68. gratify
69. vigor
70. impact

71. B   72. A   73. D   74. C   75. C   76. A   77. A
78. D   79. C   80. C   81. D   82. A   83. C   84. A
85. D   86. C   87. C   88. B   89. B   90. A   91. C
92. A   93. C   94. B   95. D   96. C   97. C   98. D
99. C   100. B

Test 2 Part A   pages 47–52

1. elective	11. minority
2. judicial	12. segregate
3. participate	13. moral
4. status	14. pursue
5. timid	15. hesitation
6. legitimate	16. tactics
7. revise	17. initial
8. adhere	18. momentary
9. intellect	19. partial
10. obstacle	20. tendency

21. A 22. B 23. D 24. D 25. B 26. B 27. A
28. D 29. A 30. B 31. A 32. C 33. B 34. A
35. C 36. C 37. B 38. A 39. C 40. D 41. B
42. A 43. B 44. C 45. A 46. D 47. B 48. C
49. D 50. C

Test 2 Part B   pages 53–58

51. era	61. opponent
52. turmoil	62. refrain
53. notable	63. persuasion
54. officially	64. illusion
55. totally	65. inadequate
56. credible	66. crisis
57. valiant	67. intolerable
58. unison	68. fatigue
59. veto	69. guarantee
60. adopt	70. recommend

71. B 72. D 73. B 74. B 75. C 76. A 77. B
78. A 79. D 80. C 81. A 82. D 83. B 84. A
85. D 86. B 87. B 88. B 89. D 90. A 91. C
92. A 93. D 94. A 95. D 96. C 97. A 98. B
99. C 100. B

Test 3 Part A   pages 59–64

1. zoology	11. tributary
2. magnitude	12. majestic
3. naturalist	13. camouflage
4. mammal	14. challenge
5. habitat	15. navigable
6. preservation	16. effect
7. barren	17. global
8. glacial	18. organism
9. seasonal	19. vital
10. undergrowth	20. precautions

21. B 22. D 23. A 24. C 25. D 26. C 27. A
28. A 29. C 30. A 31. A 32. C 33. A 34. A
35. C 36. D 37. C 38. B 39. D 40. B 41. A
42. D 43. C 44. B 45. A 46. B 47. D 48. C
49. D 50. C

Test 3 Part B   pages 65–70

51. speculate	61. logical
52. diverse	62. precise
53. accord	63. efficiency
54. futile	64. utility
55. competent	65. elaborate
56. capacity	66. minimum
57. exceed	67. proposition
58. preliminary	68. exclude
59. fundamental	69. radiate
60. manual	70. terminate

71. B 72. A 73. B 74. C 75. A 76. A 77. B
78. A 79. D 80. B 81. B 82. A 83. C 84. B
85. A 86. D 87. C 88. B 89. C 90. D 91. D
92. B 93. B 94. D 95. B 96. D 97. C 98. A
99. A 100. C

Second Course

Lesson 1 pages 3–6
Exercise 1 Mapping
Your Guess and Definition answers will vary. Possible responses to Other Forms items follow.

1. *n.* appallingness; *vt.* appall; *adv.* appallingly
2. *n.* contagion; *adv.* contagiously
3. *n.* eminence, eminency; *adv.* eminently
4. *adj.* epidemical; *adv.* epidemically
5. *n.* intention, intender; *vt.* or *vi.* intend; *adj.* intentioned; *adv.* intentionally
6. *n. pl.* myriads
7. *n.* picturesqueness; *adv.* picturesquely
8. *n.* probability; *adj.* probabilistic; *adv.* probably
9. *n.* romanticism, romanticist, romanticization; *vi.* or *vt.* romanticize; *adv.* romantically
10. *n.* ruthlessness; *adv.* ruthlessly

Exercise 2 Context Clues
11. (E) probable
12. (G) ruthless
13. (A) epidemics
14. (C) myriad
15. (B) appalling
16. (D) romantic
17. (I) eminent
18. (J) picturesque
19. (H) intentional
20. (F) contagious

Exercise 3 Like Meaning and Opposite Meanings
21. A 22. A 23. C 24. B 25. B 26. D 27. C 28. B 29. C 30. D

Lesson 2 pages 7–10
Exercise 1 Mapping
Your Guess and Definition answers will vary. Possible responses to Other Forms items follow.

1. *n.* abuser, abusiveness; *vt.* abuses, abused, abusing; *adj.* abusive, abusable; *adv.* abusively
2. *n.* bafflement, baffler; *vt.* baffles, baffled, baffling
3. *n.* barbarian, barbarity; *vt.* or *vi.* barbarize; *adj.* barbaric; *adv.* barbarically
4. *n.* bewilderment; *vt.* bewilders, bewildered, bewildering; *adv.* bewilderingly
5. *n.* calamitousness; *adv.* calamitously
6. *n.* deceiver, deceit, deceitfulness; *vt.* deceives, deceived, deceiving; *adj.* deceivable, deceitful; *adv.* deceivingly, deceitfully
7. *n.* folklorist; *adj.* folkloric, folkloristic
8. *n. pl.* knolls
9. *adj.* novel, novelistic; *adv.* novelistically
10. *n.* sincereness; *adj.* sincere, sincerer, sincerest; *adv.* sincerely

Exercise 2 Context Clues
11. (H) knoll
12. (B) calamity
13. (E) deceive
14. (I) sincerity
15. (F) baffle
16. (C) barbarism
17. (G) abuse
18. (D) novelties
19. (J) bewilder
20. (A) folklore

Exercise 3 Like Meanings and Opposite Meanings
21. D 22. B 23. C 24. A 25. B 26. C 27. A 28. C 29. C 30. A

Lesson 3 pages 11–14
Exercise 1 Mapping
Your Guess and Definition answers will vary. Possible responses to Other Forms items follow.

1. *n.* aggressiveness, aggressivity, aggression, aggressor; *vi.* aggress; *adv.* aggressively
2. *adj.* catastrophic; *adv.* catastrophically
3. *n.* ecologist; *adj.* ecological, ecologic
4. *n.* ferociousness, ferocity; *adv.* ferociously
5. *n.* inevitability, inevitableness; *adv.* inevitably
6. *n.* intelligibility; *adv.* intelligibly
7. *n. pl.* sanctuaries
8. *adj.* sinewy
9. *n.* stratagem, strategist; *vi.* strategize; *adj.* strategic, strategical; *adv.* strategically
10. *n.* validness, validity, validation; *vt.* validate; *adv.* validly

Exercise 2 Context Clues
11. (B) strategy
12. (E) inevitable
13. (H) catastrophe
14. (G) aggressive
15. (C) sinews
16. (F) ferocious
17. (J) valid
18. (A) ecology
19. (D) sanctuary
20. (I) intelligible

Exercise 3 Like Meanings and Opposite Meanings
21. C 22. A 23. D 24. C 25. A 26. A 27. C 28. C 29. B 30. A

Lesson 4 pages 15–18
Exercise 1 Mapping
Your Guess and Definition answers will vary. Possible responses to Other Forms items follow.

1. *adj.* adventitious, adventive
2. *n.* ally; *vt.* or *vi.* ally; *adj.* allied
3. *n.* defiance; *vt.* defies, defied, defying; *adj.* defiant; *adv.* defiantly
4. *n.* despicableness; *vt.* despises, despised, despising; *adj.* despicable; *adv.* despicably
5. *vt.* or *vi.* integrate
6. *vt.* or *vi.* menaces, menaced, menacing; *adv.* menacingly
7. *n. pl.* misdeeds
8. *n.* nourisher, nourishment; *vt.* nourishes, nourished, nourishing; *adv.* nourishingly
9. *n.* pacifist, pacifism, pacifier; *vt.* pacifies, pacified, pacifying; *adj.* pacifiable, pacific, pacifistic; *adv.* pacifistically
10. *n.* sustainer, sustainableness, sustainment, sustenance; *vt.* sustains, sustained, sustaining; *adj.* sustainable

Exercise 2 Context Clues
11. (I) defy
12. (D) misdeeds
13. (C) menaces
14. (A) integrity
15. (J) alliance
16. (E) despise

17. (G) pacified   19. (H) advent
18. (F) nourish   20. (B) sustains

Exercise 3   Like Meanings and Opposite Meanings
21. C   22. C   23. B   24. B   25. D   26. A   27. D
28. A   29. C   30. D

Lesson 5   pages 19–22
Exercise 1   Mapping
Your Guess and Definition answers will vary. Possible responses to Other Forms items follow.
1. *vt.* accessorize; *adj.* accessorial
2. *vt.* badgers, badgered, badgering
3. *n.* calculability, calculator; *vt.* or *vi.* calculate; *adj.* calculable, calculative; *adv.* calculably, calculatedly
4. *n.* complementarity; *vt.* complements, complemented, complementing; *adj.* complementary, complemental
5. *n.* conversion, converter, convertibility; *vt.* converts, converted, converting; *adj.* conversional, conversionary, convertible
6. *n.* customariness; *adv.* customarily
7. *n.* galleria; *vt.* galleries, galleried, gallerying
8. *n.* intervener, intervention, interventionist, interventionism; *vi.* intervenes, intervened, intervening
9. *adj.* valorous; *adv.* valorously
10. *n.* vitalization; *vt.* vitalize; *adj.* vital

Exercise 2   Context Clues
11. (C) calculation   16. (I) intervened
12. (A) gallery   17. (D) accessories
13. (G) customary   18. (J) valor
14. (F) badger   19. (H) complemented
15. (B) vitality   20. (E) converted

Exercise 3   Like Meanings and Opposite Meanings
21. A   22. A   23. C   24. A   25. C   26. C   27. A
28. D   29. C   30. A

Lesson 6   pages 23–26
Exercise 1   Mapping
Your Guess and Definition answers will vary. Possible responses to Other Forms items follow.
1. *n.* adjacency; *adv.* adjacently
2. *n.* attainability, attainment; *vt.* or *vi.* attains, attained, attaining; *adj.* attainable
3. *n.* decease; *vi.* decease, deceases, deceasing
4. *n.* fragility
5. *n.* glorification, glorifier; *vt.* glorifies, glorified, glorifying; *adj.* glorifiable
6. *n.* harmoniousness, harmonization, harmonizer, harmony; *vt.* or *vi.* harmonize; *adv.* harmoniously
7. *n.* incomparability; *adv.* incomparably
8. *n.* multicoloration, multicoloring
9. *n.* polluter, pollution, pollutant; *vt.* pollutes, polluted, polluting
10. *n.* pulverulence, pulverization, pulverizer; *vt.* pulverizes, pulverized, pulverizing; *adj.* pulverulent, pulverizable

Exercise 2   Context Clues
11. (C) fragile   16. (E) incomparable
12. (G) harmonious   17. (J) adjacent
13. (B) pulverized   18. (H) pollute
14. (I) glorify   19. (F) deceased
15. (D) attain   20. (A) multicolored

Exercise 3   Like Meanings and Opposite Meanings
21. C   22. C   23. A   24. C   25. D   26. A   27. A
28. D   29. B   30. C

Lesson 7   pages 27–30
Exercise 1   Mapping
Your Guess and Definition answers will vary. Possible responses to Other Forms items follow.
1. *n.* confederate, confederacy; *vi.* or *vt.* confederate; *adj.* confederative
2. *n.* delegation; *vt.* delegates, delegated, delegating
3. *n.* discordance, discordancy; *vi.* discords, discorded, discording; *adv.* discordantly
4. *n.* felinity; *adv.* felinely
5. *n.* foresightedness; *adj.* foresighted; *adv.* foresightedly
6. *n.* isolationist, isolationism, isolator; *vt.* isolate; *adj.* isolable, isolated, isolate
7. *n. pl.* menageries
8. *n.* phenomenalism, phenomenalist, phenom; *n. pl.* phenomena; *adj.* phenomenal; *adv.* phenomenally
9. *n. pl.* posterities
10. *n.* revelator; *vt.* reveal; *adj.* revelatory

Exercise 2   Context Clues
11. (D) menagerie   16. (H) foresight
12. (B) isolation   17. (J) phenomenon
13. (I) revelation   18. (C) delegate
14. (F) discord   19. (G) feline
15. (E) posterity   20. (A) confederation

Exercise 3   Like Meanings and Opposite Meanings
21. B   22. A   23. A   24. D   25. B   26. B   27. D
28. D   29. C   30. C

Lesson 8   pages 31–34
Exercise 1   Mapping
Your Guess and Definition answers will vary. Possible responses to Other Forms items follow.
1. *n.* adequacy, adequateness; *adv.* adequately
2. *n.* advantage; *vt.* advantage; *adv.* advantageously
3. *n.* descent, descendant, descender; *vi.* descends, descended, descending; *adj.* descendant, descendible
4. *n.* enhancement, enhancer
5. *n.* gnarl; *vt.* or *vi.* gnarl; *adj.* gnarly
6. *n.* incitation, incitement, inciter; *vt.* incites, incited, inciting
7. *n.* inflexibility, inflexibleness; *adv.* inflexibly
8. *n.* inheritance, inheritability, inheritableness, inheritor; *adj.* inheritable

9. *n.* inquisition, inquisitor, inquisitiveness; *adj.* inquisitorial; *adv.* inquisitively, inquisitorially

10. *n.* mutuality, mutualism, mutualization; *vt.* or *vi.* mutualize; *adv.* mutually

Exercise 2   Context Clues
11. (G) descend
12. (C) inquisitive
13. (H) adequate
14. (I) enhance
15. (F) inflexible
16. (J) mutual
17. (B) inherited
18. (D) gnarled
19. (A) advantageous
20. (E) incite

Exercise 3   Like Meanings and Opposite Meanings
21. C   22. B   23. D   24. C   25. A   26. B   27. B
28. D   29. B   30. C

Lesson 9   pages 35–38
Exercise 1   Mapping
Your Guess and Definition answers will vary. Possible responses to Other Forms items follow.
1. *n.* adaptability, adaptation, adapter; *adj.* adaptable, adaptational, adaptive; *adv.* adaptively
2. *n.* assumer; *vt.* assume; *adj.* assumable, assumed, assuming, assumptive
3. *n. pl.* bases; *vt.* base; *adj.* basic; *adv.* basically
4. *n.* controversialist; *vt.* controvert; *adj.* controvertible, controversial; *adv.* controversially, controvertibly
5. *n.* impeller, impulsion; *adj.* impellent
6. *n.* omitter; *vt.* omit; *adj.* omissive, omissible; *adv.* omissively
7. *n.* petitioner; *adj.* petitionary
8. *n.* potentiality; *adv.* potentially
9. *n.* primitiveness, primitivism, primitivist; *adv.* primitively
10. *n.* restoration, restorer, restorative; *vt.* restores, restored, restoring; *adj.* restorable

Exercise 2   Context Clues
11. (J) impels
12. (D) potential
13. (I) restore
14. (C) assumption
15. (B) controversy
16. (H) adapted
17. (E) basis
18. (A) petition
19. (G) omission
20. (F) primitives

Exercise 3   Like Meanings and Opposite Meanings
21. A   22. C   23. C   24. B   25. D   26. C   27. A
28. C   29. D   30. A

Lesson 10   pages 39–42
Exercise 1   Mapping
Your Guess and Definition answers will vary. Possible responses to Other Forms items follow.
1. *n.* consecutiveness, consecution; *adv.* consecutively
2. *n.* creation, creator, creativity, creativeness; *vt.* create; *adv.* creatively
3. *n.* durability; *adv.* durably
4. *n.* feasibility, feasibleness; *adv.* feasibly
5. *n.* hilariousness, hilarity; *adv.* hilariously
6. *n.* immenseness, immensity; *adv.* immensely
7. *n.* ingeniousness; *adv.* ingeniously
8. *n.* insolubility, insolubleness; *adv.* insolubly

9. *n.* punctuality, punctualness; *adv.* punctually
10. *n.* sterility, sterilization, sterilant, sterilizer; *vt.* sterilize

Exercise 2   Context Clues
11. (C) immense
12. (A) creative
13. (E) insoluble
14. (D) consecutive
15. (B) feasible
16. (H) sterile
17. (J) durable
18. (G) ingenious
19. (F) hilarious
20. (I) punctual

Exercise 3   Like Meanings and Opposite Meanings
21. A   22. D   23. B   24. A   25. C   26. B   27. D
28. A   29. B   30. C

Lesson 11   pages 43–46
Exercise 1   Mapping
Your Guess and Definition answers will vary. Possible responses to Other Forms items follow.
1. *n.* aristocracy; *adj.* aristocratic; *adv.* aristocratically
2. *n.* censor, censoriousness; *vt.* censor; *adj.* censorial; *adv.* censorially
3. *n. pl.* decades
4. *n.* emigration, emigrant, émigré
5. *n.* famishment; *vt.* or *vi.* famish; *adj.* famished
6. *adj.* or *adv.* fortnightly
7. *adj.* malnourished
8. *n.* moral, morality, moralist; *vi.* moralize; *adv.* morally, moralistically
9. *n.* optimum, optimist; *adj.* optimistic; *adv.* optimistically
10. *n.* refugee

Exercise 2   Context Clues
11. (E) emigrate
12. (J) malnutrition
13. (A) aristocrat
14. (G) refuge
15. (H) censorship
16. (F) optimism
17. (I) morale
18. (C) fortnight
19. (B) famine
20. (D) decade

Exercise 3   Like Meanings and Opposite Meanings
21. A   22. D   23. A   24. B   25. D   26. D   27. B
28. A   29. C   30. B

Lesson 12   pages 47–50
Exercise 1   Mapping
Your Guess and Definition answers will vary. Possible responses to Other Forms items follow.
1. *n.* anxiousness; *adj.* anxious; *adv.* anxiously
2. *vt.* boycotts, boycotted, boycotting
3. *n.* burliness
4. *adj.* multitudinous; *adv.* multitudinously
5. *n. pl.* nationalities
6. *n.* pamphleteer; *vi.* pamphleteers
7. *n. pl.* predicaments
8. *n.* propagandism, propagandist; *vt.* propagandize; *adj.* propagandistic; *adv.* propagandistically
9. *n.* resoluteness, resolution; *vt.* resolve; *adv.* resolutely
10. *n.* urbanization, urbanism, urbanist, urbanite, urbia, urbanology, urbanologist; *vt.* urbanize; *adj.* urbanistic

Exercise 2   Context Clues
11. (C) anxiety
12. (A) urban
13. (I) boycott
14. (F) multitude
15. (B) nationality
16. (E) pamphlets
17. (G) predicaments
18. (H) propaganda
19. (D) resolute
20. (J) burly

Exercise 3   Like Meanings and Opposite Meanings
21. A   22. B   23. A   24. C   25. D   26. C   27. D
28. B   29. A   30. C

Lesson 13   pages 51–54
Exercise 1   Mapping
Your Guess and Definition answers will vary. Possible responses to Other Forms items follow.
1. *n.* bankruptcy; *vt.* bankrupts, bankrupted, bankrupting
2. *n.* boisterousness; *adv.* boisterously
3. *n.* childlikeness
4. *n.* dilapidation; *vi.* or *vt.* dilapidate
5. *n.* fraud, fraudulence, fraudulency; *adv.* fraudulently
6. *n.* hospitality, hospice; *adv.* hospitably
7. *n.* impulsiveness, impulsion, impulse; *adv.* impulsively
8. *n.* meddlesomeness; *vi.* meddle
9. *n.* premiership
10. *n.* riot, rioter; *vt.* or *vi.* riot

Exercise 2   Context Clues
11. (E) boisterous
12. (J) hospitable
13. (C) bankrupt
14. (H) fraudulent
15. (B) impulsive
16. (G) meddlesome
17. (I) dilapidated
18. (A) premiere
19. (F) riotous
20. (D) childlike

Exercise 3   Like Meanings and Opposite Meanings
21. A   22. A   23. C   24. D   25. C   26. C   27. A
28. A   29. B   30. B

Lesson 14   pages 55–58
Exercise 1   Mapping
Your Guess and Definition answers will vary. Possible responses to Other Forms items follow.
1. *n.* acceptability; *vt.* accept; *adj.* acceptable, acceptant; *adv.* acceptably
2. *n.* circular, circulation, circulator; *vt.* or *vi.* circulates, circulated, circulating; *adj.* circulative, circulatory
3. *n.* exaggerator; *vt.* exaggerate; *adj.* exaggerative; *adv.* exaggeratedly
4. *n.* grief, grievousness; *vt.* or *vi.* grieves, grieved, grieving; *vt.* aggrieve; *adj.* grievous; *adv.* grievously
5. *n.* immigration, immigrant; *vt.* or *vi.* immigrates, immigrated, immigrating; *adj.* immigrant
6. *vt.* or *vi.* intensify; *adj.* intensive; *adv.* intensively
7. *n.* jubilee, jubilance; *vi.* jubilate; *adj.* jubilant; *adv.* jubilantly
8. *vt.* privileges, privileged, privileging
9. *vi.* thrives, thrived, thriving; *adj.* thriving
10. *vt.* upbraids, upbraided, upbraiding

Exercise 2   Context Clues
11. (H) acceptance
12. (D) grieve
13. (C) immigrate
14. (A) intensity
15. (E) exaggeration
16. (I) jubilation
17. (B) thrives
18. (J) upbraid
19. (G) privilege
20. (F) circulate

Exercise 3   Like Meanings and Opposite Meanings
21. D   22. C   23. D   24. C   25. D   26. C   27. B
28. A   29. D   30. C

Lesson 15   pages 59–62
Exercise 1   Mapping
Your Guess and Definition answers will vary. Possible responses to Other Forms items follow.
1. *n.* dedicator, dedication; *vt.* dedicates, dedicated, dedicating; *adj.* dedicatory, dedicative
2. *n.* deposal, deposition; *vt.* deposes, deposed, deposing; *adj.* deposable
3. *n.* dispensation, dispensator, dispensatory, dispenser; *vt.* dispenses, dispensed, dispensing; *adj.* dispensational
4. *n.* dissection, dissector; *vt.* dissects, dissected, dissecting; *adj.* dissectable
5. *vt.* exert; *adj.* exertive
6. *n. pl.* havens
7. *n.* humidification, humidifier; *vt.* humidify; *adj.* humid
8. *n. pl.* mementos or mementoes
9. *n.* restraint, restrainer; *vt.* restrains, restrained, restraining; *adj.* restrainable; *adv.* restrainedly
10. *n.* tumultousness; *adj.* tumultuary, tumultuous; *adv.* tumultuously

Exercise 2   Context Clues
11. (A) humidity
12. (G) dedicate
13. (D) mementos
14. (E) deposed
15. (F) restrain
16. (J) dissect
17. (B) tumult
18. (H) dispensed
19. (C) haven
20. (I) exertion

Exercise 3   Like Meanings and Opposite Meanings
21. A   22. C   23. D   24. D   25. B   26. B   27. C
28. A   29. B   30. D

Lesson 16   pages 63–66
Exercise 1   Mapping
Your Guess and Definition answers will vary. Possible responses to Other Forms items follow.
1. *n. pl.* hampers; *vt.* hampers, hampered, hampering
2. *n.* imperativeness; *adv.* imperatively
3. *n.* imposition; *vt.* imposes, imposed, imposing; *adv.* imposingly
4. *n.* inconsiderateness, inconsideration; *adv.* inconsiderately
5. *n.* interception, interceptor; *vt.* intercepts, intercepted, intercepting; *adj.* interceptive
6. *n.* liability
7. *n.* negligence, negligibility; *adv.* negligently, negligibly

8. *n.* presumer, presumption, presumptuousness; *vt.* presumes, presumed, presuming; *adj.* presumable, presumptive, presumptuous; *adv.* presumably, presumedly, presumptively, presumptuously
9. *n.* recuperation, recuperator; *vt.* recuperates, recuperated, recuperating; *adj.* recuperative, recuperatory
10. *n.* spaciousness; *adv.* spaciously

Exercise 2   Context Clues

11. (I) hamper	16. (F) recuperate
12. (B) imperative	17. (E) presume
13. (D) inconsiderate	18. (C) negligent
14. (J) intercepted	19. (H) liable
15. (A) spacious	20. (G) impose

Exercise 3   Like Meanings and Opposite Meanings

21. D   22. B   23. B   24. B   25. D   26. C   27. D
28. A   29. B   30. D

Lesson 17   pages 67–70
Exercise 1   Mapping
Your Guess and Definition answers will vary. Possible responses to Other Forms items follow.

1. *n.* aromatization; *vt.* aromatize; *adj.* aromatic; *adv.* aromatically
2. *n.* capitalism, capitalist; *vt.* capitalize; *adj.* capitalistic; *adv.* capitalistically
3. *n.* elegance; *adv.* elegantly
4. *n.* frequenter, frequentation; *vt.* frequent; *adj.* frequent, frequentative; *adv.* frequently
5. *n.* graciousness; *adv.* graciously
6. *n.* haughtiness; *adj.* haughtier, haughtiest; *adv.* haughtily
7. *n.* manageability, manageableness; *vt.* manage; *adv.* manageably
8. *n.* monopolist, monopolization, monopolizer; *vt.* monopolize; *adj.* monopolistic; *adv.* monopolistically
9. *n.* occupancy, occupation; *vt.* occupy; *adj.* occupational; *adv.* occupationally
10. *n.* probationer; *vt.* probate; *adj.* probationary, probational

Exercise 2   Context Clues

11. (A) capital	16. (B) elegant
12. (G) haughty	17. (F) occupant
13. (C) gracious	18. (J) aroma
14. (H) manageable	19. (I) probation
15. (E) monopoly	20. (D) frequency

Exercise 3   Like Meanings and Opposite Meanings

21. C   22. B   23. D   24. A   25. D   26. B   27. C
28. A   29. B   30. B

Lesson 18   pages 71–74
Exercise 1   Mapping
Your Guess and Definition answers will vary. Possible responses to Other Forms items follow.

1. *n.* baster; *vt.* bastes, basted, basting
2. *n.* diminution, diminutive; *vt.* diminishes, diminished, diminishing; *adj.* diminishable, diminutive; *adv.* diminutively

3. *n.* dismantlement, dismantler; *vt.* dismantles, dismantled, dismantling
4. *n.* embarrassment; *vt.* embarrasses, embarrassed, embarrassing; *adv.* embarrassingly
5. *n.* population; *vt.* populates, populated, populating; *adj.* populous
6. *n.* prearrangement; *vt.* prearranges, prearranged, prearranging
7. *n.* remoteness; *adj.* remoter, remotest; *adv.* remotely
8. *n.* rigidity; *vt.* or *vi.* rigidify; *adv.* rigidly
9. *n.* saturator, saturability, saturation; *vt.* saturates, saturated, saturating; *adj.* saturable, saturant
10. *n.* sedateness, sedation, sedative; *vt.* sedates, sedated, sedating; *adj.* sedative; *adv.* sedately

Exercise 2   Context Clues

11. (B) prearrange	16. (G) saturates
12. (E) dismantle	17. (I) sedate
13. (D) remote	18. (F) embarrassed
14. (J) populate	19. (C) basting
15. (H) rigid	20. (A) diminished

Exercise 3   Like Meanings and Opposite Meanings

21. A   22. C   23. C   24. C   25. D   26. A   27. B
28. C   29. D   30. B

Lesson 19   pages 75–78
Exercise 1   Mapping
Your Guess and Definition answers will vary. Possible responses to Other Forms items follow.

1. *n.* accessibility; *adj.* accessible; *adv.* accessibly
2. *n.* accommodator, accommodationist; *vt.* accommodate; *adj.* accommodative; *adv.* accommodatingly
3. *n.* circumnavigation, circumnavigator; *vt.* circumnavigates, circumnavigated, circumnavigating
4. *n.* evacuator, evacuee, evacuation; *vt.* evacuates, evacuated, evacuating; *adj.* evacuative
5. *n.* liberation, liberator; *vt.* liberates, liberated, liberating
6. *n.* notifier, notification; *vt.* notifies, notified, notifying; *adj.* notifiable
7. *n. pl.* pleasantries
8. *n.* provisioner, provisionary; *n. pl.* provisions; *vt.* provisions, provisioned, provisioning; *adj.* provisional, provisionary; *adv.* provisionally
9. *n. pl.* regimes
10. *n.* remorsefulness; *adj.* remorseful; *adv.* remorsefully

Exercise 2   Context Clues

11. (D) liberated	16. (I) circumnavigated
12. (F) notify	17. (C) regime
13. (E) access	18. (B) accommodations
14. (J) pleasantries	19. (H) remorse
15. (A) provisions	20. (G) evacuate

Exercise 3   Like Meanings and Opposite Meanings

21. C   22. B   23. D   24. A   25. B   26. B   27. A
28. C   29. D   30. B

Lesson 20 pages 79–82

Exercise 1 Mapping

Your Guess and Definition answers will vary. Possible responses to Other Forms items follow.

1. *n.* adeptness; *adv.* adeptly
2. *n.* dinginess; *adj.* dingier, dingiest; *adv.* dingily
3. *n.* disagreeableness, disagreement; *vi.* disagree; *adv.* disagreeably
4. *n.* humiliation; *vt.* humiliates, humiliated, humiliating
5. *n.* jeopardy; *vt.* jeopardizes, jeopardized, jeopardizing
6. *vt.* or *vi.* maroons, marooned, marooning
7. *n.* massager; *vt.* massages, massaged, massaging
8. *n.* persistence, persistency; *vi.* persist; *adv.* persistently
9. *n.* thrift, thriftiness; *adj.* thriftier, thriftiest; *adv.* thriftily
10. *n.* verifier, verification; *vt.* verifies, verified, verifying; *adj.* verifiable, verificational; *adv.* verifiably

Exercise 2 Context Clues

11. (C) disagreeable
12. (E) thrifty
13. (G) humiliate
14. (I) verified
15. (J) jeopardize
16. (A) adept
17. (D) dingy
18. (F) persistent
19. (B) massage
20. (H) marooned

Exercise 3 Like Meanings and Opposite Meanings

21. D 22. D 23. A 24. A 25. A 26. C 27. A
28. B 29. D 30. A

Lesson 21 pages 83–86

Exercise 1 Mapping

Your Guess and Definition answers will vary. Possible responses to Other Forms items follow.

1. *vi.* aspire; *adj.* aspiring; *adv.* aspiringly
2. *n.* diplomatist, diplomacy; *adj.* diplomatic; *adv.* diplomatically
3. *n. pl.* forewords
4. *n.* obituarist
5. *n.* premiership
6. *vi.* puns, punned, punning
7. *n. pl.* sables
8. *vt.* salute; *adj.* salutatory
9. *n.* satirist, satirizer; *vt.* satirize; *adj.* satiric, satirical; *adv.* satirically
10. *n. pl.* tariffs

Exercise 2 Context Clues

11. (H) tariff
12. (J) satire
13. (E) salutation
14. (I) sable
15. (D) pun
16. (G) premier
17. (C) obituary
18. (F) foreword
19. (A) diplomat
20. (B) aspiration

Exercise 3 Like Meanings and Opposite Meanings

21. C 22. A 23. D 24. B 25. A 26. B 27. C
28. D 29. A 30. D

Lesson 22 pages 87–90

Exercise 1 Mapping

Your Guess and Definition answers will vary. Possible responses to Other Forms items follow.

1. *n.* blockader; *vt.* blockades, blockaded, blockading
2. *n.* confiscation, confiscator; *vt.* confiscates, confiscated, confiscating; *adj.* confiscable, confiscatory
3. *n.* generation, generator; *vt.* generates, generated, generating; *adj.* generative
4. *n.* indelibility; *adv.* indelibly
5. *n.* neutralism, neutrality, neutralization, neutralizer; *vt.* neutralize; *adj.* neutralist, neutralistic; *adv.* neutrally
6. *n.* obscureness, obscurant, obscurity; *vt.* obscures, obscured, obscuring; *adv.* obscurely
7. *adj.* pewter
8. *n.* quaintness; *adv.* quaintly
9. *n.* quencher; *adj.* quenchable, quenchless
10. *n.* urgency; *vt.* urge; *adv.* urgently

Exercise 2 Context Clues

11. (E) quaint
12. (H) quenched
13. (G) urgent
14. (J) blockade
15. (C) neutral
16. (I) confiscate
17. (B) generate
18. (A) indelible
19. (D) obscure
20. (F) pewter

Exercise 3 Like Meanings and Opposite Meanings

21. D 22. B 23. A 24. C 25. C 26. A 27. B
28. C 29. A 30. D

Lesson 23 pages 91–94

Exercise 1 Mapping

Your Guess and Definition answers will vary. Possible responses to Other Forms items follow.

1. *n.* activation, activator; *vt.* activates, activated, activating
2. *n.* charitableness; *adv.* charitably
3. *n.* colossus; *adv.* colossally
4. *n.* confidant, confidence; *vt.* or *vi.* confides, confided, confiding
5. *n.* eccentricity
6. *n.* invariability; *adv.* invariably
7. *n.* latency; *adv.* latently
8. *n.* pettiness; *adv.* pettily
9. *n.* piousness; *adv.* piously
10. *vt.* or *vi.* tarnishes, tarnished, tarnishing

Exercise 2 Context Clues

11. (J) latent
12. (C) activate
13. (F) petty
14. (A) charitable
15. (E) pious
16. (D) colossal
17. (G) tarnish
18. (B) invariable
19. (I) eccentric
20. (H) confided

Exercise 3 Like Meanings and Opposite Meanings

21. B 22. C 23. A 24. A 25. C 26. B 27. C
28. C 29. D 30. A

Lesson 24   pages 95–98
Exercise 1   Mapping
Your Guess and Definition answers will vary. Possible responses to Other Forms items follow.

1. *vt.* afflict; *adj.* afflictive
2. *n.* clarification; *vt.* or *vi.* clarifies, clarified, clarifying
3. *vt.* deduce; *adj.* deductive; *adv.* deductively
4. *n.* disintegration, disintegrator; *vt.* or *vi.* disintegrates, disintegrated, disintegrating; *adj.* disintegrative
5. *n.* essayer, essayist; *vt.* essays, essayed, essaying; *adj.* essayistic
6. *n.* proposition; *vt.* propose; *adj.* propositional
7. *adj.* sarcastic; *adv.* sarcastically
8. *n.* succession; *vt.* or *vi.* succeed
9. *adj.* summital
10. *adj.* temperamental

Exercise 2   Context Clues
11. (E) clarify
12. (D) disintegrate
13. (A) essays
14. (J) proposal
15. (B) sarcasm
16. (H) successor
17. (I) affliction
18. (G) summit
19. (C) temperament
20. (F) deduction

Exercise 3   Like Meanings and Opposite Meanings
21. B   22. C   23. A   24. D   25. B   26. D   27. B
28. C   29. B   30. D

Lesson 25   pages 99–102
Exercise 1   Mapping
Your Guess and Definition answers will vary. Possible responses to Other Forms items follow.

1. *n.* anonymity, anonym; *adv.* anonymously
2. *n.* casualness; *adv.* casually
3. *vi.* climaxes, climaxed, climaxing; *adj.* climactic; *adv.* climactically
4. *vt.* or *vi.* contemporize; *adj.* contemporaneous; *adv.* contemporaneously
5. *n.* famine; *vt.* or *vi.* famish, famishes, famishing
6. *n.* fiction, fictionalization; *vt.* fictionalize; *adj.* fictional, fictive; *adv.* fictitiously, fictionally, fictively
7. *vt.* or *vi.* fragments, fragmented, fragmenting; *adj.* fragmentary, fragmental
8. *n.* literalization, literality, literalness; *vt.* literalize; *adv.* literally
9. *vi.* occur; *adj.* occurrent
10. *n.* therapist; *adj.* therapeutic; *adv.* therapeutically

Exercise 2   Context Clues
11. (A) contemporary
12. (I) climax
13. (E) casual
14. (B) anonymous
15. (G) literal
16. (J) occurrence
17. (D) therapy
18. (F) famished
19. (H) fragment
20. (C) fictitious

Exercise 3   Like Meanings and Opposite Meanings
21. B   22. A   23. C   24. D   25. C   26. C   27. B
28. D   29. B   30. B

Lesson 26   pages 103–106
Exercise 1   Mapping
Your Guess and Definition answers will vary. Possible responses to Other Forms items follow.

1. *n.* condemnation; *vt.* condemns, condemned, condemning; *adj.* condemnatory
2. *n.* dictator, dictation; *vt.* or *vi.* dictates, dictated, dictating; *adj.* dictatorial; *adv.* dictatorially
3. *n.* dilution; *vt.* dilutes, diluted, diluting
4. *n.* dispatcher; *vt.* dispatches, dispatched, dispatching
5. *n.* emphasis; *vt.* emphasizes, emphasized, emphasizing; *adj.* emphatic; *adv.* emphatically
6. *n.* endorsement, endorser; *vt.* or *vi.* endorses, endorsed, endorsing; *adj.* endorsable
7. *n.* falterer; *vi.* falters, faltered, faltering; *adv.* falteringly
8. *n.* improvisation, improviser; *vt.* or *vi.* improvises, improvised, improvising
9. *n.* intriguer; *vt.* or *vi.* intrigues, intrigued, intriguing; *adv.* intriguingly
10. *n.* modification; *vt.* or *vi.* modifies, modified, modifying

Exercise 2   Context Clues
11. (H) endorse
12. (B) condemn
13. (E) falter
14. (C) dictate
15. (J) improvise
16. (A) dispatch
17. (F) intrigues
18. (G) modify
19. (D) emphasize
20. (I) dilute

Exercise 3   Like Meanings and Opposite Meanings
21. A   22. C   23. C   24. B   25. B   26. C   27. A
28. A   29. B   30. B

Lesson 27   pages 107–110
Exercise 1   Mapping
Your Guess and Definition answers will vary. Possible responses to Other Forms items follow.

1. *n.* articulation, articulator; *vt.* or *vi.* articulates, articulated, articulating; *adj.* articulatory
2. *n.* categorization; *vt.* categorize; *adj.* categorical; *adv.* categorically
3. *n.* demolition; *vt.* demolishes, demolished, demolishing
4. *vt.* deny
5. *n.* detachment, detachability; *vt.* detaches, detached, detaching; *adj.* detachable; *adv.* detachedly
6. *vt.* distract; *adj.* distracted; *adv.* distractedly
7. *n.* illumination, illuminator; *vt.* illuminates, illuminated, illuminating; *vt.* illumine
8. *vt.* or *vi.* incline; *adj.* inclined
9. *adj.* spherical; *adv.* spherically
10. *n.* testimony, testifier; *vt.* or *vi.* testifies, testified, testifying

Exercise 2   Context Clues
11. (I) category
12. (C) illuminate
13. (F) testify
14. (J) detached
15. (D) inclination
16. (G) demolishes
17. (B) distractions
18. (H) denial
19. (A) articulate
20. (E) sphere

Exercise 3   Like Meanings and Opposite Meanings
21. D   22. A   23. D   24. C   25. C   26. B   27. D
28. A   29. B   30. C

Lesson 28   pages 111–114
Exercise 1   Mapping
Your Guess and Definition answers will vary. Possible responses to Other Forms items follow.
1. *n.* derivation; *vt.* or *vi.* derives, derived, deriving; *adj.* derivative, derivable; *adv.* derivatively
2. *n.* eligibility; *adv.* eligibly
3. *n.* extent, extensiveness, extensity; *adv.* extensively
4. *n.* implication; *vt.* implies, implied, implying; *adj.* implicit; *adv.* implicitly
5. *n.* miscellany; *adv.* miscellaneously
6. *n.* seclusion; *vt.* seclude; *adj.* seclusive
7. *n.* superficiality; *adv.* superficially
8. *n.* tangibility; *adv.* tangibly
9. *n.* transition; *vt.* or *vi.* transits, transitted, transitting; *adj.* transitory, transitional
10. *n.* uniqueness; *adv.* uniquely

Exercise 2   Context Clues
11. (I) secluded   16. (D) derive
12. (F) superficial   17. (A) eligible
13. (H) tangible   18. (C) extensive
14. (E) transit   19. (B) imply
15. (G) unique   20. (J) miscellaneous

Exercise 3   Like Meanings and Opposite Meanings
21. A   22. B   23. C   24. D   25. A   26. B   27. D
28. B   29. D   30. B

Lesson 29   pages 115–118
Exercise 1   Mapping
Your Guess and Definition answers will vary. Possible responses to Other Forms items follow.
1. *n.* commuter; *vt.* or *vi.* commutes, commuted, commuting
2. *n.* congestion; *vt.* or *vi.* congests, congested, congesting
3. *n.* consideration, considerateness; *vt.* or *vi.* consider; *adv.* considerately
4. *vt.* or *vi.* hypothesize; *adj.* hypothetical; *adv.* hypothetically
5. *vi.* malfunctions, malfunctioned, malfunctioning
6. *vt.* or *vi.* rebates, rebated, rebating
7. *n.* synthesis; *n. pl.* syntheses; *vt.* synthesize; *adv.* synthetically
8. *n.* technologist; *vt.* or *vi.* technologize
9. *n.* titan
10. *n.* warrant, warrantee, warrantor; *adj.* warrantable

Exercise 2   Context Clues
11. (G) malfunction   16. (C) synthetic
12. (E) technology   17. (F) titanic
13. (B) hypothesis   18. (J) commute
14. (H) warranty   19. (I) congested
15. (D) rebate   20. (A) considerate

Exercise 3   Like Meanings and Opposite Meanings
21. A   22. D   23. B   24. B   25. B   26. D   27. C
28. B   29. C   30. D

Lesson 30   pages 119–122
Exercise 1   Mapping
Your Guess and Definition answers will vary. Possible responses to Other Forms items follow.
1. *adj.* aeronautical
2. *adj.* antibiotic
3. *n. pl.* automatons
4. *vt.* or *vi.* erode
5. *adj.* homicidal; *adv.* homicidally
6. *n. pl.* hydraulics; *adv.* hydraulically
7. *n.* parasite, parasitism; *vt.* parasitize; *adv.* parasitically
8. *adv.* photogenically
9. *n. pl.* planetariums or planetaria
10. *n.* respirator; *vt.* or *vi.* respire; *adj.* respiratory

Exercise 2   Context Clues
11. (J) homicide   16. (G) photogenic
12. (D) parasitic   17. (C) antibiotics
13. (H) aeronautics   18. (A) erosion
14. (I) planetarium   19. (F) automaton
15. (E) hydraulic   20. (B) respiration

Exercise 3   Like Meanings and Opposite Meanings
21. A   22. D   23. B   24. C   25. B   26. D   27. B
28. B   29. B   30. B

⧩ **UNDERSTANDING NEW WORDS AND THEIR USES**

Lesson 1   pages 125–126
Exercise 1   Multimeaning
1. D   2. A
Exercise 2   Word Analysis
3. A   4. A   5. B   6. A
7. appalling   8. barbarism
9. knoll   10. novelty

Lesson 2   pages 127–128
Exercise 1   Multimeaning
1. B   2. B
Exercise 2   Word Analysis
3. C   4. A   5. C   6. C
7. advent   8. catastrophe
9. ferocious   10. intelligible

Lesson 3   pages 129–130
Exercise 1   Multimeaning
1. A   2. C
Exercise 2   Word Analysis
3. C   4. B   5. A   6. C
7. convert   8. glorify
9. fragile   10. deceased

Lesson 4   pages 131–132
Exercise 1   Multimeaning
1. D   2. D
Exercise 2   Word Analysis
3. B   4. D   5. C   6. B
7. posterity   8. gnarled
9. inflexible   10. phenomenon

Note: Encourage students to use the lists of common prefixes and suffixes on page 124 when they are working on the *Prefixes* and *Suffixes* exercises in this section.

Lesson 5   pages 133–134
Exercise 1   Multimeaning
1. B   2. C
Exercise 2   Word Analysis
3. D   4. A   5. C   6. B
7. sterile   8. adapt
9. feasible   10. omission

Lesson 6   pages 135–136
Exercise 1   Multimeaning
1. D   2. C
Exercise 2   Word Analysis
3. C   4. D   5. D   6. B
7. burly   8. urban
9. nationality   10. boycott

Lesson 7   pages 137–138
Exercise 1   Multimeaning
1. A   2. D
Exercise 2   Word Analysis
3. C   4. A   5. D   6. A
7. riotous   8. boisterous
9. jubilation   10. immigrate

Lesson 8   pages 139–140
Exercise 1   Multimeaning
1. C   2. A
Exercise 2   Word Analysis
3. A   4. A   5. C   6. C
7. haven   8. humidity
9. recuperate   10. dispense

Lesson 9   pages 141–142
Exercise 1   Multimeaning
1. B   2. D
Exercise 2   Word Analysis
3. D   4. A   5. A   6. B
7. diminish   8. saturate
9. monopoly   10. populate

Lesson 10   pages 143–144
Exercise 1   Multimeaning
1. D   2. B
Exercise 2   Word Analysis
3. B   4. C   5. A   6. C
7. liberate   8. pleasantry
9. humiliate   10. evacuate

Lesson 11   pages 145–146
Exercise 1   Multimeaning
1. A   2. D
Exercise 2   Word Analysis
3. D   4. C   5. C   6. B
7. obituary   8. pun
9. indelible   10. tariff

Lesson 12   pages 147–148
Exercise 1   Multimeaning
1. B   2. C
Exercise 2   Word Analysis
3. C   4. A   5. A   6. B
7. pious   8. petty
9. summit   10. successor

Lesson 13   pages 149–150
Exercise 1   Multimeaning
1. C   2. C
Exercise 2   Word Analysis
3. D   4. C   5. A   6. B
7. modify   8. climax
9. falter   10. dictate

Lesson 14   pages 151–152
Exercise 1   Multimeaning
1. B   2. C
Exercise 2   Word Analysis
3. A   4. C   5. B   6. D
7. sphere   8. unique
9. imply   10. secluded

Lesson 15   pages 153–154
Exercise 1   Multimeaning
1. C   2. A
Exercise 2   Word Analysis
3. D   4. B   5. A   6. A
7. hypothesis   8. erosion
9. hydraulic   10. homicide

CONNECTING NEW WORDS AND PATTERNS

Lesson 1   page 158
1. Characteristic Quality; (E). *Abuse* is characteristically *cruel*, just as a *celebration* is characteristically *joyful*.
   (A) D   (B) F   (C) AO   (D) PW
2. Degree; (B). *Appalling* means very *upsetting*, just as *fascinating* means very *interesting*.
   (A) PO   (C) C   (D) CE   (E) L
3. Synonym; (D). *Baffle* is similar in meaning to *confuse*, just as *attempt* is similar in meaning to *try*.
   (A) CE   (B) C   (C) CQ   (E) PW
4. Cause and Effect; (C). A *calamity*, or disaster, can cause *distress*, just as *winning* can cause *happiness*.
   (A) PO   (B) CQ   (D) PA   (E) AO
5. Performer and Action; (D). You expect a *liar* to *deceive* you, just as you expect a *hero* to *rescue* you.
   (A) CQ   (B) A   (C) C   (E) S or AO
6. Cause and Effect; (A). An *epidemic*, or mass illness, can cause *fear*, just as a *puzzle* can cause *confusion*.
   (B) PO   (C) D or S   (D) C   (E) S
7. Degree; (C). A *knoll* is a smaller hill than a *mountain*. A *ditch* is a shallower trough than a *canyon*.
   (A) L   (B) PW   (D) CQ   (E) AO
8. Performer and Object; (A). A *novelty* is the creation of an *inventor*, just as a *symphony* is the creation of a *composer*.
   (B) L   (C) PA   (D) PW   (E) CE

9. Antonym; (E). *Probable* and *unlikely* have opposite meanings, as do *sad* and *happy*.
   (A) L   (B) PO   (C) F   (D) C
10. Synonym; (B). *Ruthless* is similar in meaning to *merciless*, just as *famous* is similar in meaning to *well-known*.
    (A) PA   (C) CQ   (D) A   (E) CE

Lesson 2   page 159

1. Synonym; (D). *Advent* is similar in meaning to *arrival*, just as *faithfulness* is similar in meaning to *loyalty*.
   (A) D   (B) F   (C) C   (E) CQ
2. Cause and Effect; (B). *Confusion* can result from *catastrophe*, just as *sorrow* can result from *death*.
   (A) PO   (C) A   (D) PW   (E) C
3. Degree; (C). To *despise* something is to *dislike* it very strongly. In the same way, to *enrage* someone is to *annoy* that person greatly.
   (A) S   (B) CE   (D) PA   (E) PW
4. Classification; (E). *Ecology* may be classified as a *science*, just as *algebra* may be classified as a branch of *mathematics*.
   (A) L or AO   (B) F   (C) CQ   (D) PO
5. Antonym; (A). *Ferocious* and *gentle* are opposite in meaning, as are *pleased* and *dissatisfied*.
   (B) PO   (C) AO   (D) D   (E) L
6. Characteristic Quality; (B). A *menace*, or danger, is characteristically *frightening*, just as *silk* is characteristically *smooth*.
   (A) F   (C) PO   (D) S   (E) A
7. Function; (D). The function of *food* is to *nourish*, just as the function of a *raincoat* is to *protect*.
   (A) AO   (B) D   (C) C   (E) PW
8. Antonym; (E). *Pacify* and *provoke* have opposite meanings, as do *refuse* and *accept*.
   (A) C   (B) PO   (C) L   (D) D
9. Part and Whole; (C). A *sinew* is part of a *leg*, just as an *axle* is part of a *truck*.
   (A) S   (B) F or AO   (D) PO   (E) CQ
10. Synonym; (B). *Strategy* is similar in meaning to *method*, just as *intention* is similar in meaning to *purpose*.
    (A) CE   (C) PA   (D) C   (E) PW

Lesson 3   page 160

1. Classification; (D). A *belt* may be classified as an *accessory*, just as a *bracelet* may be classified as a type of *jewelry*.
   (A) AO   (B) S   (C) PA   (E) CE
2. Classification; (D). A *badger* is a type of *animal*, just as *granite* is a type of *rock*.
   (A) L   (B) CQ   (C) PA   (E) PO
3. Performer and Object; (B). A *math whiz* makes *calculations*, while a *chemist* works with *formulas*.
   (A) S   (C) PW   (D) D   (E) CE
4. Antonym; (B). *Customary* behavior is the opposite of *unusual* behavior, as a *thoughtful* action is the opposite of an *inconsiderate* action.
   (A) PW   (C) F   (D) PO   (E) C

5. Characteristic Quality; (E). An *egg* is characteristically *fragile*, or breakable, just as the *desert* is characteristically *dry*.
   (A) CE   (B) A   (C) S   (D) PO
6. Location; (D). A *painting* can be found in a *gallery*, just as an *easel* can be found in a *studio*.
   (A) PW   (B) CE   (C) D   (E) CQ
7. Antonym; (C). *Glorify* and *degrade* have opposite meanings, as do *succeed* and *fail*.
   (A) CQ   (B) L   (D) C   (E) F
8. Characteristic Quality; (D). A *rainbow* is characteristically *multicolored*, just as a *pillow* is characteristically *soft*.
   (A) A   (B) L   (C) F   (E) PA
9. Action and Object; (D). People *pollute rivers*, and a gardener *trims* a *lawn*.
   (A) C   (B) A   (C) CE   (E) PO
10. Synonym; (E). *Vitality* and *energy* have nearly the same meaning, as do *sadness* and *sorrow*.
    (A) CQ   (B) PA   (C) AO   (D) PW

Lesson 4   page 161

1. Degree; (E). *Adequate* is a lesser quality of performance than *excellent*, just as *tired* is a lesser degree of exhaustion than *frazzled*.
   (A) S   (B) PA   (C) PW   (D) C
2. Performer and Action; (C). You expect a *delegate* to *represent* others, just as you expect an *actor* to *perform*.
   (A) C   (B) CQ   (D) F   (E) S
3. Antonym; (D). *Descend* and *rise* have opposite meanings, as do *shove* and *pull*.
   (A) PO   (B) CQ   (C) D   (E) PW
4. Antonym; (C). *Discord* and *harmony* have opposite meanings, as do *war* and *peace*.
   (A) CQ   (B) F   (D) D   (E) PW
5. Function; (C). The function of a *decoration* is to *enhance*, just as the function of *fertilizer* is to *enrich*.
   (A) C   (B) AO   (D) D   (E) CE
6. Part and Whole; (C). *Whiskers* are part of a *feline*, or cat, just as a *paw* is part of a *kitten*.
   (A) PO   (B) S   (D) AO   (E) C
7. Performer and Action; (B). You expect an *heiress* to *inherit*, just as you expect a *thief* to steal.
   (A) S   (C) L   (D) PW   (E) CQ
8. Synonym; (C). *Inquisitive* is similar in meaning to *curious*, just as *eager* is similar in meaning to *anxious*.
   (A) CE   (B) S   (D) AO   (E) PA
9. Cause and Effect; (B). *Isolation* can cause *loneliness*, as *experience* can increase *confidence*.
   (A) PA   (C) PW   (D) L   (E) PO
10. Characteristic Quality; (B). A *menagerie* of animals is characteristically *caged*, just as a *crime* is characteristically *illegal*.
    (A) S   (C) PW   (D) C   (E) AO

Lesson 5   page 162

1. Synonym; (E). *Basis* is similar in meaning to *foundation*, as *sign* is similar in meaning to *indication*.
   (A) CQ   (B) F   (C) PW   (D) D

2. Characteristic Quality; (D). An *artist* is characteristically *creative*, just as a *chemist* is characteristically *scientific*.
   (A) PO   (B) CE   (C) S   (E) L

3. Synonym; (D). *Controversy* is similar in meaning to *dispute*, as *promise* is similar in meaning to *pledge*.
   (A) PA   (B) CQ   (C) AO   (E) C

4. Characteristic Quality; (E). *Leather* is characteristically *durable*, or long-lasting, just as *sand* is characteristically *gritty*.
   (A) PW   (B) F   (C) AO   (D) L

5. Degree; (D). *Hilarious* means very *funny*, just as *nasty* means very *unpleasant*.
   (A) PA   (B) A   (C) PW   (E) CE

6. Degree; (C). *Immense* means very *large*, just as *frantic* means very *nervous*.
   (A) PO   (B) L   (D) S   (E) E

7. Characteristic Quality; (D). An *inventor* is characteristically *ingenious*, or inventive, just as a *monkey* is characteristically *curious*.
   (A) PW   (B) PA   (C) F   (E) PO

8. Synonym; (D). *Primitive* and *crude* are similar in meaning, as are *complex* and *complicated*.
   (A) PW   (B) L   (C) PA   (E) C

9. Synonym; (A). *Punctual* and *prompt* have similar meanings, as do *thoughtful* and *considerate*.
   (B) CQ   (C) AO   (D) PO   (E) CE

10. Antonym; (E). *Sterile* is the opposite of *fertile*, just as *fresh* is the opposite of *stale*.
    (A) D   (B) S or CQ   (C) PW   (D) L

Lesson 6   page 163

1. Classification; (D). A *princess* is a type of *aristocrat*, just as a *sailboat* is a type of *vessel*.
   (A) AO   (B) A   (C) PA   (E) PW

2. Characteristic Quality; (A). A professional *football player* is characteristically *burly*, just as a *ballet dancer* is characteristically *graceful*.
   (B) S   (C) C   (D) PA   (E) F

3. Cause and Effect; (D). A *famine* can result from a *war*, just as *destruction* is the likely result of a *hurricane*.
   (A) A   (B) CQ   (C) L   (E) D

4. Cause and Effect; (D). *Malnutrition* can cause *death*, just as a *fever* can cause *sweating*.
   (A) AO   (B) L   (C) PA   (E) A

5. Synonym; (C). *Multitude* and *crowd* are similar in meaning, just as *ceremony* and *service* are similar in meaning.
   (A) AO   (B) PO   (D) C   (E) CQ

6. Classification; (D). A *pamphlet* may be classified as a *publication*, just as *sandals* may be classified as *footwear*.
   (A) PW   (B) A   (C) CE   (E) PA

7. Function; (E). The function of *propaganda* is to *persuade*, just as the function of a *newspaper* is to *inform*.
   (A) C   (B) CE   (C) PW   (D) L

8. Characteristic Quality; (A). A *refuge* is characteristically *safe*, just as an *anchor* is characteristically *heavy*.
   (B) S   (C) F   (D) L   (E) D

9. Synonym; (D). *Resolute* and *determined* have similar meanings, as do *steady* and *regular*.
   (A) A   (B) C   (C) PO   (E) AO

10. Antonym; (C). *Urban* and *rural* have opposite meanings, as do *firm* and *unsteady*.
    (A) L   (B) PO   (D) C   (E) F

Lesson 7   page 164

1. Antonym; (A). *Boisterous* and *calm* have opposite meanings, as do *violent* and *peaceful*.
   (B) PA   (C) AO   (D) PW   (E) PO

2. Synonym; (C). *Childlike* and *innocent* are similar in meaning, as are *ripe* and *mature*.
   (A) PA   (B) A   (D) D   (E) CQ

3. Characteristic Quality; (E). *Old ruins* are characteristically *dilapidated*, or in poor condition, just as *parachuting* is characteristically *dangerous*.
   (A) L   (B) A   (C) C   (D) F

4. Synonym; (A). *Grieve* and *mourn* have similar meanings, as do *haul* and *carry*.
   (B) CE   (C) F   (D) AO   (E) CQ

5. Degree; (A). A *hospitable* person is much friendlier than a merely *civil* person. And to *search* means to look more thoroughly than to *peek*.
   (B) CQ   (C) C   (D) CE   (E) AO

6. Cause and Effect; (D). *Victory* can cause *jubilation*, or celebration, just as *loss* can cause *sadness*.
   (A) PO   (B) S   (C) PA   (E) F

7. Characteristic Quality; (B). A *toddler* is characteristically *meddlesome*, just as a *miser* is characteristically *stingy*.
   (A) L   (C) PA   (D) A   (E) C

8. Degree; (C). *Riotous* means very *lively*, while *shudder* means to *quiver* violently.
   (A) PO   (B) CE   (D) PA   (E) A

9. Antonym; (C). *Upbraid*, or criticize, means the opposite of *praise*, just as *shout* means the opposite of *whisper*.
   (A) PA   (B) PW   (D) PO   (E) C

10. Antonym; (A). *Bankrupt* means the opposite of *rich*, just as *torn* means the opposite of *mended*.
    (B) D   (C) C   (D) L   (E) CQ

Lesson 8   page 165

1. Performer and Action; (A). You expect a *biologist* to *dissect* something, just as you expect a *professor* to *teach*.
   (B) F   (C) S   (D) AO   (E) CE

2. Characteristic Quality; (E). A *haven* is characteristically *safe*, just as *treasure* is characteristically *valuable*.
   (A) PW   (B) A   (C) D   (D) PO

3. Antonym; (D). *Hamper* and *help* have opposite meanings, as do *criticize* and *praise*.
(A) C (B) L (C) S (E) PA

4. Characteristic Quality; (C). *Humidity* is characteristically *damp,* just as *sleet* is characteristically *cold.*
(A) D (B) AO (D) L (E) PW

5. Synonym; (B). *Inconsiderate* is similar in meaning to *selfish,* just as *evil* is similar in meaning to *wicked.*
(A) CE (C) C (D) PW (E) CQ

6. Function; (D). The function of a *memento* is to *remind,* just as the function of an *exploration* is to *discover.*
(A) PO (B) PW (C) D (E) CQ

7. Performer and Action; (B). You expect a *patient* to *recuperate,* just as you expect a *physician* to *examine* someone.
(A) C (C) D (D) PW (E) CE

8. Function; (D). The function of a *seat belt* is to *restrain* someone, just as the function of a *reservoir* is to *hold* water.
(A) D (B) A (C) PW (E) CQ

9. Characteristic Quality; (B). A *mansion* is characteristically *spacious,* or roomy, just as the *sea* is characteristically *salty.*
(A) AO (C) PW (D) S (E) PA

10. Synonym; (E). *Tumult* and *uproar* have similar meanings, as do *confusion* and *disorder.*
(A) L (B) D (C) CQ (D) F or L

Lesson 9   page 166

1. Cause and Effect; (C). An *aroma,* or smell, is the effect of *baking,* just as an *accident* can be the result of *speeding.*
(A) AO (B) F (D) PO (E) C

2. Action and Object; (B). You *baste* a *turkey,* just as you *trim* a *tree.*
(A) PA (C) CE (D) L (E) CQ

3. Performer and Object; (C). An *investor* works with *capital,* just as a *realtor* works with *land.*
(A) C (B) CE (D) L (E) PW

4. Antonym; (E). *Elegant* and *crude* have opposite meanings, as do *serious* and *amusing.*
(A) S (B) C (C) L (D) PW

5. Antonym; (D). *Haughty,* or standoffish, means the opposite of *friendly,* just as *wealthy* means the opposite of *poor.*
(A) D (B) F (C) AO (E) CQ

6. Synonym; (E). *Occupant* and *resident* have the same meaning, as do *shrub* and *bush.*
(A) PW (B) F (C) C (D) D

7. Synonym; (A). *Remote* is similar in meaning to *distant,* as *hard* is similar in meaning to *difficult.*
(B) C (C) D (D) PO (E) L

8. Antonym; (B). *Rigid,* or stiff, means the opposite of *flexible,* just as *damaged* means the opposite of *repaired.*
(A) PO (C) AO (D) PA (E) PW

9. Antonym; (A). *Sedate,* or calm, and *rowdy* have opposite meanings, as do *protect* and *endanger.*
(B) PW (C) CE (D) C (E) D

10. Degree; (C). When you *moisten* something, you don't wet it as thoroughly as when you *saturate* it, just as when you *sprinkle* something you don't dispense as much water as when you *pour* water onto it.
(A) CQ (B) L (D) C (E) S

Lesson 10   page 167

1. Synonym; (D). *Dingy* and *shabby* have similar meanings, as do *private* and *personal.*
(A) C (B) A (C) F (E) PW

2. Degree; (C). Something that is *disagreeable* is not as bad as something that is *horrible,* while a *difficult* task is not as hard as an *impossible* task.
(A) PA (B) A (D) CQ (E) PW

3. Action and Object; (C). You *evacuate* a *building,* and you *entertain* a *crowd.*
(A) S (B) A (D) L (E) CQ

4. Antonym; (B). *Humiliate* and *flatter* have opposite meanings, as do *criticize* and *compliment.*
(A) L (C) PW (D) PO (E) S

5. Antonym; (A). *Liberate,* or free, and *capture* have opposite meanings, as do *feed* and *starve.*
(B) CE or D (C) S (D) AO (E) PW

6. Classification; (D). *Maroon* may be classified as a *color,* just as a *diamond* may be classified as a *gem.*
(A) AO (B) F (C) L (E) PW

7. Cause and Effect; (A). *Massage* results in *relaxation,* just as *exercise* results in improved *fitness.*
(B) CQ (C) C (D) PW (E) L

8. Synonym; (E). *Notify* and *inform* have similar meanings, as do *fasten* and *attach.*
(A) PW (B) D (C) PO (D) CE

9. Cause and Effect; (C). *Remorse* can result from *wrongdoing,* just as *forgiveness* can be gained from an *apology.*
(A) F (B) AO (D) PW (E) PA

10. Degree; (D). Someone who is *miserly* holds on to his or her money even more tightly than someone who is *thrifty.* Similarly, the acts of a *wicked* person are more harmful than the acts of a *mischievous* person.
(A) F (B) CQ (C) CE (E) C

Lesson 11   page 168

1. Synonym; (B). *Aspiration* and *ambition* have nearly the same meaning, as do *wish* and *desire.*
(A) F (C) CQ (D) AO (E) C

2. Action and Object; (A). The police *confiscate,* or take away, someone's *weapon,* as a robber *robs* a *bank.*
(B) PW (C) PA (D) CQ (E) L

3. Performer and Action; (B). You expect a *diplomat* to *represent* a nation, just as you expect a *captain* to *lead* a team.
(A) S (C) PW (D) C (E) D

4. Function; (A). The function of a *foreword* is to *introduce* something, while the function of a *conclusion* is to *summarize* something.
(B) A (C) PW (D) L (E) AO

5. Synonym; (E). *Generate* and *produce* are similar in meaning, as are *contribute* and *give*.
   (A) PW (B) PA (C) A (D) CQ
6. Antonym; (C). *Obscure,* or vague, means the opposite of *clear,* just as *private* means the opposite of *public.*
   (A) L (B) C or CE (D) S (E) PO
7. Characteristic Quality; (B). *Pewter* is a *gray* metal, and a *lemon* is a *sour* fruit.
   (A) CE (C) S (D) A (E) PO
8. Function; (A). The function of a *beverage* is to *quench* thirst, just as the function of a *sponge* is to *absorb* water.
   (B) C (C) CQ (D) PO (E) PW
9. Classification; (D). A *sable* is a type of *mammal,* just as a *maple* is a type of *tree.*
   (A) S (B) CE (C) AO (E) PA
10. Part and Whole; (A). A *salutation,* or greeting, is part of a *letter,* just as the *trunk* is part of a *tree.*
    (B) S (C) PO (D) CQ (E) D

Lesson 12   page 169
1. Cause and Effect; (E). *Affliction* can cause *suffering,* just as *treatment* for a disease can cause *healing.*
   (A) S (B) C (C) AO (D) PO
2. Antonym; (A). *Charitable,* or generous, means the opposite of *stingy,* just as *stubborn,* or unyielding, means the opposite of *flexible.*
   (B) S (C) CQ (D) F (E) D
3. Action and Object; (D). You *confide* a *secret,* just as you *tell* a *tale.*
   (A) F (B) L (C) CQ (E) PW
4. Synonym; (B). *Disintegrate* and *decay* are similar in meaning, as are *build* and *construct.*
   (A) C (C) CE (D) A (E) AO
5. Part and Whole; (C). A *conclusion* is part of an *essay,* just as a *chapter* is part of a *textbook.*
   (A) PA (B) C (D) A (E) S
6. Antonym; (D). *Petty* and *important* have opposite meanings, as do *innocent* and *guilty.*
   (A) PO (B) S (C) L (E) CQ
7. Characteristic Quality; (E). A *believer* is characteristically *pious,* just as an *artist* is characteristically *talented.*
   (A) PO (B) L (C) S (D) AO
8. Part and Whole; (C). A *summit* is part of a *mountain,* just as a *mouth* is part of a *river.*
   (A) PA (B) L (D) A (E) PO
9. Synonym; (A). *Tarnish* and *disgrace* have similar meanings, as do *need* and *require.*
   (B) CE (C) C (D) PO (E) PW
10. Synonym; (B). *Temperament* is similar in meaning to *manner,* as *region* is similar in meaning to *area.*
    (A) PA (C) CQ (D) D (E) PW

Lesson 13   page 170
1. Synonym; (C). *Casual* and *informal* have nearly the same meaning, as do *regular* and *ordinary.*
   (A) CQ (B) PO (D) F (E) D

2. Action and Object; (A). You *condemn* a *building,* and you *sign* a *contract.*
   (B) S (C) C (D) PA (E) A
3. Action and Object; (E). You *dispatch,* or send off, an *ambulance,* just as you *send* a *telegram.*
   (A) CE (B) S (C) L (D) PW
4. Synonym; (E). To *emphasize* a point means about the same thing as to *stress* a point, just as to *realize* the difficulty of a situation means the same thing as to *understand* the difficulty of a situation.
   (A) C (B) PA (C) CQ (D) L
5. Action and Object; (D). You *endorse,* or sign, the back of a *check,* just as congress *raises* *taxes.*
   (A) PW (B) PA (C) CQ (E) D
6. Degree; (A). *Famished* means very *hungry,* just as *skinny* means very *slim.*
   (B) CQ (C) L (D) C (E) A
7. Antonym; (E). *Fictitious* and *real* have opposite meanings, as do *worried* and *unconcerned.*
   (A) PW (B) PA (C) AO (D) D
8. Characteristic Quality; (D). A *fragment* is characteristically *incomplete,* just as *chrome* is characteristically *shiny.*
   (A) A (B) AO (C) PW (E) CE
9. Performer and Action; (B). You expect an *actor* to *improvise,* just as you expect a *poet* to *recite* poetry.
   (A) L (C) S (D) C (E) PW
10. Synonym; (D). *Modify* and *alter* are similar in meaning, as are *copy* and *imitate.*
    (A) PW (B) PO (C) AO (E) D

Lesson 14   page 171
1. Degree; (E). To *demolish* is to *damage* completely, just as to *recover* is to *improve* completely.
   (A) L (B) CQ (C) CE (D) PW or PA
2. Antonym; (C). *Denial* is the opposite of *acceptance,* as *encouragement* is the opposite of *disapproval.*
   (A) F (B) PA (D) PW (E) L
3. Synonym; (D). *Detach* and *disconnect* have similar meanings, as do *mend* and *repair.*
   (A) D (B) PO (C) CQ (E) C
4. Synonym; (A). *Eligible* and *qualified* have nearly the same meaning, as do *ready* and *prepared.*
   (B) A (C) L (D) D (E) C
5. Function; (B). The function of a *lantern* is to *illuminate,* or provide light, just as the function of a *refrigerator* is to *chill* food.
   (A) AO (C) A (D) PW (E) CQ
6. Antonym; (E). *Secluded* and *public,* or open, have opposite meanings, as do *deserted* and *crowded.*
   (A) PA (B) L or PW (C) F (D) PO
7. Characteristic Quality; (D). A *sphere* is characteristically *round,* just as a *rose* is characteristically *fragrant.*
   (A) C (B) PA (C) L (E) D
8. Characteristic Quality; (A). A *scrape* is characteristically *superficial,* or near the surface, while a *gash* is characteristically *deep.*
   (B) L (C) PW (D) PA (E) F

9. Synonym; (B). *Tangible* and *touchable* have similar meanings, as do *odd* and *strange*.
   (A) PO (C) CE (D) PA (E) AO
10. Performer and Action; (B). You expect a *witness* to *testify* in court, just as you expect a *shopper* to *spend* money.
   (A) CQ (C) AO (D) D (E) C

Lesson 15 page 172

1. Function; (E). The function of *antibiotics* is to help *heal* the sick, in the same way, the function of *vaccinations* is to *protect* against disease.
   (A) CE (B) PO (C) A (D) CQ
2. Synonym; (A). An *automaton* is similar to a *robot*, just as a *bureau* is similar to a *dresser*.
   (B) F (C) PO (D) C (E) PW
3. Synonym; (B). *Congest* and *clog* are similar in meaning, as are *employ* and *hire*.
   (A) A (C) D or L (D) CQ (E) PW
4. Characteristic Quality; (D). A *hypothesis*, or theory, is characteristically *unproven*, just as a *lie* is characteristically *untrue*.
   (A) PO (B) A (C) PW (E) PA
5. Antonym; (C). *Parasitic*, when used to describe someone who lives at the expense of others, means about the opposite of *independent*, just as *damaged* means about the opposite of *perfect*.
   (A) L (B) F (D) CQ (E) S
6. Characteristic Quality; (D). A *fashion model* is characteristically *photogenic*, just as *steel* is characteristically *strong*.
   (A) PO (B) PW (C) AO (E) C
7. Classification; (B). A *planetarium* may be classified as a *building*, just as an *orange* may be classified as a *fruit*.
   (A) D (C) PO (D) CQ (E) PW
8. Synonym; (E). *Respiration* and *breathing* have nearly the same meaning, as do *exchange* and *trade*.
   (A) PA (B) L (C) CQ (D) AO
9. Antonym; (B). *Synthetic* and *natural* are opposite in meaning, just as *ill* and *healthy* are.
   (A) PA (C) C (D) CE (E) PW
10. Function; (A). The function of a *warranty*, or guarantee, is to *assure* a purchaser, just as the function of an *investigation* is to *solve* a crime.
   (B) S (C) PA (D) AO (E) CQ

READING NEW WORDS IN CONTEXT

Lesson 1 pages 175–178
1. A 2. C 3. B 4. B 5. D 6. C 7. C 8. D
9. C 10. B 11. C 12. A 13. B 14. A 15. B
16. C 17. D 18. D 19. C 20. B

Lesson 2 pages 179–182
1. C 2. A 3. B 4. C 5. D 6. C 7. D 8. D
9. A 10. A 11. C 12. B 13. B 14. A 15. B
16. C 17. D 18. D 19. A 20. B

Lesson 3 pages 183–186
1. B 2. D 3. A 4. C 5. A 6. C 7. C 8. A
9. C 10. B 11. A 12. B 13. B 14. D 15. B
16. C 17. D 18. D 19. C 20. B

Lesson 4 pages 187–190
1. A 2. A 3. B 4. B 5. D 6. C 7. C 8. B
9. C 10. C 11. A 12. B 13. B 14. A 15. B
16. C 17. D 18. D 19. C 20. B

Lesson 5 pages 191–194
1. D 2. D 3. B 4. B 5. A 6. C 7. C 8. A
9. C 10. C 11. D 12. B 13. B 14. D 15. B
16. C 17. A 18. D 19. C 20. B

Lesson 6 pages 195–198
1. D 2. A 3. B 4. B 5. D 6. C 7. C 8. A
9. A 10. C 11. D 12. B 13. A 14. B 15. A
16. C 17. C 18. D 19. D 20. B

Lesson 7 pages 199–202
1. C 2. A 3. D 4. A 5. B 6. C 7. B 8. D
9. C 10. A 11. C 12. D 13. A 14. C 15. D
16. B 17. D 18. B 19. A 20. D

Lesson 8 pages 203–206
1. B 2. A 3. B 4. B 5. D 6. A 7. C 8. D
9. C 10. C 11. B 12. B 13. D 14. A 15. B
16. C 17. A 18. A 19. C 20. A

Lesson 9 pages 207–210
1. A 2. A 3. C 4. B 5. C 6. B 7. D 8. D
9. C 10. C 11. A 12. B 13. A 14. A 15. B
16. C 17. D 18. D 19. C 20. B

Lesson 10 pages 211–214
1. C 2. A 3. B 4. C 5. D 6. C 7. C 8. D
9. C 10. C 11. B 12. C 13. B 14. A 15. A
16. D 17. C 18. D 19. B 20. B

Lesson 11 pages 215–218
1. C 2. A 3. B 4. B 5. D 6. C 7. A 8. D
9. C 10. C 11. A 12. B 13. A 14. A 15. B
16. C 17. D 18. B 19. C 20. B

Lesson 12 pages 219–222
1. A 2. B 3. D 4. C 5. B 6. A 7. C 8. D
9. A 10. B 11. D 12. B 13. A 14. D 15. B
16. A 17. C 18. A 19. A 20. B

Lesson 13 pages 223–226
1. B 2. A 3. B 4. B 5. D 6. A 7. A 8. C
9. C 10. A 11. B 12. C 13. D 14. A 15. B
16. C 17. D 18. C 19. D 20. B

Lesson 14 pages 227–230
1. A 2. A 3. B 4. B 5. D 6. C 7. C 8. D
9. C 10. A 11. C 12. B 13. B 14. A 15. B
16. C 17. D 18. D 19. D 20. B

Lesson 15 pages 231–234
1. D 2. D 3. B 4. B 5. A 6. C 7. C 8. A
9. C 10. C 11. D 12. B 13. D 14. B 15. C
16. A 17. A 18. C 19. B 20. C

FORMATIVE ASSESSMENT

Test 1   page 3
1. B   2. D   3. C   4. B   5. D   6. A   7. B   8. A
9. B   10. A

Test 2   page 4
1. B   2. A   3. A   4. B   5. A   6. C   7. D   8. C
9. B   10. D

Test 3   page 5
1. A   2. B   3. D   4. D   5. C   6. A   7. A   8. C
9. A   10. B

Test 4   page 6
1. C   2. B   3. B   4. D   5. A   6. A   7. D   8. D
9. C   10. B

Test 5   page 7
1. D   2. A   3. C   4. C   5. A   6. C   7. B   8. B
9. C   10. B

Test 6   page 8
1. A   2. D   3. B   4. C   5. D   6. A   7. A   8. C
9. C   10. D

Test 7   page 9
1. B   2. D   3. C   4. C   5. A   6. A   7. A   8. B
9. D   10. D

Test 8   page 10
1. C   2. D   3. A   4. C   5. C   6. B   7. D   8. B
9. B   10. B

Test 9   page 11
1. A   2. B   3. A   4. C   5. D   6. A   7. B   8. D
9. C   10. A

Test 10   page 12
1. D   2. C   3. C   4. B   5. C   6. D   7. B   8. A
9. D   10. A

Test 11   page 13
1. D   2. C   3. B   4. C   5. A   6. B   7. B   8. D
9. D   10. C

Test 12   page 14
1. A   2. B   3. D   4. A   5. C   6. D   7. B   8. D
9. B   10. A

Test 13   page 15
1. C   2. A   3. A   4. A   5. B   6. C   7. A   8. D
9. D   10. B

Test 14   page 16
1. A   2. C   3. D   4. B   5. A   6. D   7. C   8. A
9. C   10. D

Test 15   page 17
1. B   2. A   3. B   4. C   5. D   6. C   7. B   8. B
9. A   10. C

Test 16   page 18
1. D   2. A   3. C   4. B   5. B   6. A   7. A   8. C
9. B   10. A

Test 17   page 19
1. B   2. C   3. D   4. A   5. A   6. C   7. D   8. A
9. A   10. B

Test 18   page 20
1. C   2. B   3. D   4. D   5. C   6. A   7. A   8. C
9. B   10. A

Test 19   page 21
1. C   2. C   3. D   4. A   5. D   6. A   7. D   8. D
9. B   10. B

Test 20   page 22
1. C   2. D   3. C   4. D   5. B   6. D   7. A   8. D
9. C   10. A

Test 21   page 23
1. A   2. C   3. D   4. C   5. B   6. C   7. A   8. C
9. B   10. C

Test 22   page 24
1. A   2. A   3. D   4. B   5. C   6. A   7. C   8. B
9. B   10. A

Test 23   page 25
1. B   2. D   3. C   4. D   5. C   6. B   7. A   8. A
9. A   10. A

Test 24   page 26
1. A   2. A   3. A   4. D   5. D   6. B   7. B   8. C
9. B   10. A

Test 25   page 27
1. C   2. C   3. B   4. C   5. B   6. D   7. A   8. D
9. D   10. D

Test 26   page 28
1. A   2. A   3. D   4. C   5. A   6. C   7. D   8. D
9. D   10. B

Test 27   page 29
1. C   2. D   3. B   4. B   5. B   6. C   7. A   8. C
9. C   10. B

Test 28   page 30
1. A   2. D   3. B   4. C   5. C   6. B   7. A   8. C
9. C   10. B

Test 29   page 31
1. A   2. B   3. B   4. A   5. B   6. D   7. A   8. A
9. C   10. D

Test 30   page 32
1. B   2. A   3. C   4. D   5. D   6. B   7. D   8. C
9. C   10. C

SUMMATIVE ASSESSMENT

Test 1 Part A   pages 35–40
1. enhance
2. customary
3. attain
4. confederation
5. convert
6. assumption
7. folklore
8. badger
9. calamity
10. nourish
11. ecology
12. harmonious
13. fragile
14. foresight
15. inherit
16. posterity
17. basis
18. baffle
19. deceased
20. feasible

21. B   22. D   23. A   24. A   25. C   26. B   27. C
28. B   29. D   30. A   31. D   32. A   33. A   34. C
35. A   36. C   37. D   38. C   39. A   40. A   41. B
42. B   43. D   44. C   45. B   46. C   47. B   48. D
49. D   50. C

Test 1 Part B   pages 41–46
51. potential
52. adapt
53. controversy
54. discord
55. pollute
56. appalling
57. menace
58. restore
59. immense
60. inquisitive

61. probable
62. romantic
63. strategy
64. bewilder
65. inflexible

66. pacify
67. defy
68. inevitable
69. sincerity
70. creative

71. B 72. A 73. D 74. C 75. C 76. A 77. A
78. D 79. C 80. C 81. D 82. A 83. C 84. B
85. D 86. C 87. B 88. C 89. C 90. A 91. C
92. D 93. C 94. B 95. B 96. C 97. C 98. A
99. D 100. B

Test 2 Part A   pages 47–52

1. multitude
2. nationalities
3. aristocrat
4. refuge
5. haven
6. persistent
7. immigrated
8. accommodations
9. exaggeration
10. morale

11. optimism
12. anxiety
13. urban
14. resolute
15. hospitable
16. impulsive
17. acceptance
18. fraudulent
19. thrifty
20. thrive

21. B 22. D 23. A 24. A 25. C 26. B 27. C
28. B 29. D 30. A 31. D 32. D 33. A 34. C
35. A 36. C 37. D 38. C 39. D 40. A 41. C
42. B 43. D 44. C 45. B 46. C 47. D 48. D
49. A 50. D

Test 2 Part B   pages 53–58

51. provision
52. marooned
53. burly
54. notified
55. rigid
56. gracious
57. upbraid
58. jubilation
59. grieve
60. memento

61. humidity
62. saturated
63. adept
64. predicament
65. recuperate
66. dingy
67. aroma
68. embarrassed
69. diminish
70. privilege

71. B 72. A 73. D 74. C 75. C 76. A 77. A
78. D 79. C 80. C 81. D 82. A 83. C 84. B
85. D 86. C 87. B 88. C 89. B 90. A 91. C
92. D 93. C 94. B 95. D 96. C 97. B 98. C
99. B 100. A

Test 3 Part A   pages 59–64

1. articulate
2. contemporary
3. transit
4. quaint
5. climax
6. intrigued
7. superficial
8. condemn
9. indelible
10. extensive

11. fictitious
12. unique
13. literal
14. eccentric
15. category
16. modify
17. dilute
18. distraction
19. demolished
20. emphasize

21. B 22. D 23. A 24. A 25. C 26. B 27. C
28. B 29. D 30. A 31. D 32. A 33. A 34. C
35. A 36. C 37. D 38. D 39. D 40. A 41. B
42. B 43. D 44. C 45. B 46. C 47. D 48. D
49. A 50. C

Test 3 Part B   pages 65–70

51. essay
52. generated
53. miscellaneous
54. proposal
55. falter
56. tangible
57. testify
58. inclination
59. erosion
60. imply

61. confide
62. colossal
63. pewter
64. homicide
65. pious
66. sable
67. denial
68. secluded
69. satire
70. deduction

71. B 72. A 73. D 74. C 75. C 76. A 77. A
78. D 79. C 80. D 81. D 82. A 83. C 84. B
85. D 86. C 87. B 88. C 89. B 90. A 91. C
92. D 93. C 94. B 95. D 96. C 97. D 98. D
99. C 100. C

Third Course

Lesson 1   pages 3–6
Exercise 1   Mapping
Your Guess and Definition answers will vary. Possible responses to Other Forms items follow.
1. *n.* annalist; *adj.* annalistic
2. *n.* demoralization, demoralizer; *vt.* demoralizes, demoralized, demoralizing
3. *n.* dispersal, disperser, dispersion, dispersant; *vi.* or *vt.* disperses, dispersed, dispersing; *adj.* dispersible
4. *adj.* epical; *adv.* epically
5. *n.* extreme, extremist, extremism; *n. pl.* extremities; *adj.* extreme
6. *n.* inconspicuousness; *adv.* inconspicuously
7. *n.* intactness
8. None
9. *n.* negotiation, negotiator, negotiability; *vi.* or *vt.* negotiates, negotiated, negotiating; *adj.* negotiable, negotiatory; *adv.* negotiably
10. *n.* replenishment, replenisher; *vt.* replenishes, replenished, replenishing; *adj.* replenished

Exercise 2   Context Clues
11. (H) extremity
12. (A) epic
13. (E) replenish
14. (J) negotiate
15. (C) inconspicuous
16. (I) intact
17. (F) demoralized
18. (B) dispersing
19. (D) landlocked
20. (G) annals

Exercise 3   Sentence Completion
21. D   22. A   23. D   24. B   25. E   26. B   27. A
28. C   29. D   30. A

Lesson 2   pages 7–10
Exercise 1   Mapping
Your Guess and Definition answers will vary. Possible responses to Other Forms items follow.
1. *n.* belligerence, belligerency; *adv.* belligerently
2. *n.* dexterousness; *adj.* dexterous; *adv.* dexterously
3. *n.* eradication, eradicator; *vt.* eradicates, eradicated, eradicating; *adj.* eradicable, eradicative
4. *n.* ferventness; *adv.* fervently
5. *v.* havocs, havocked, havocking
6. *n.* hideousness; *adv.* hideously
7. *n.* inflammability, inflammableness, inflamer; *vt.* inflame; *adj.* inflammatory, inflammable; *adv.* inflammably
8. *n.* manifestation, manifestant; *n. pl.* manifests; *v.* manifests, manifested, manifesting; *adj.* manifestable; *adv.* manifestly
9. *n.* meanderer; *v.* meanders, meandered, meandering; *adj.* meandrous; *adv.* meanderingly
10. *n.* recession, recessional, recess; *v.* recedes, receded, receding; *adj.* recessive

Exercise 2   Context Clues
11. (J) eradicate
12. (A) meander
13. (H) havoc
14. (G) dexterity
15. (E) manifest
16. (F) recede
17. (I) fervent
18. (D) inflammations
19. (C) belligerent
20. (B) hideous

Exercise 3   Sentence Completion
21. A   22. E   23. C   24. A   25. D   26. E   27. B
28. B   29. D   30. A

Lesson 3   pages 11–14
Exercise 1   Mapping
Your Guess and Definition answers will vary. Possible responses to Other Forms items follow.
1. *n. pl.* amities
2. *n.* chivalrousness; *adj.* chivalrous, chivalric; *adv.* chivalrously
3. *n.* devoutness; *adv.* devoutly
4. *n.* hereditariness, heredity; *adv.* hereditarily
5. *n.* medievalist, medievalism; *adv.* medievally
6. *n. pl.* potions
7. None
8. *n.* quester; *vi.* or *vt.* quests, quested, questing
9. *n.* sovereignty; *adv.* sovereignly
10. *n.* venerability, veneration, venerator, venerableness; *vt.* venerate; *adv.* venerably

Exercise 2   Context Clues
11. (D) prowess
12. (E) venerable
13. (I) medieval
14. (H) hereditary
15. (F) amity
16. (J) potions
17. (A) devout
18. (B) chivalry
19. (C) sovereign
20. (G) quest

Exercise 3   Sentence Completion
21. B   22. C   23. D   24. D   25. A   26. E   27. E
28. B   29. C   30. B

Lesson 4   pages 15–18
Exercise 1   Mapping
Your Guess and Definition answers will vary. Possible responses to Other Forms items follow.
1. *n. pl.* citadels
2. *n.* defilement, defiler; *vi.* or *vt.* defiles, defiled, defiling; *adv.* defilingly
3. *n. pl.* emissaries
4. *n.* enticement, enticer; *vt.* entices, enticed, enticing; *adv.* enticingly
5. *vt.* garbs, garbed, garbing
6. *n.* heraldry; *vt.* heralds, heralded, heralding; *adj.* heraldic
7. *n.* meditator, meditation, meditativeness; *vi.* or *vt.* meditates, meditated, meditating; *adj.* meditative; *adv.* meditatively
8. *vt.* omens, omened, omening; *adj.* ominous
9. *n.* retrievability, retriever, retrieval; *vt.* retrieves, retrieved, retrieving; *adj.* retrievable; *adv.* retrievably
10. *vt.* undergoes, underwent, undergone, undergoing

Exercise 2 Context Clues

11. (D) defile
12. (E) entice
13. (J) meditates
14. (H) undergo
15. (I) omen
16. (C) citadel
17. (G) retrieve
18. (B) emissary
19. (A) heralds
20. (F) garbs

Exercise 3 Sentence Completion

21. C   22. C   23. B   24. A   25. A   26. D   27. B
28. E   29. D   30. E

Lesson 5   pages 19–22
Exercise 1 Mapping

Your Guess and Definition answers will vary. Possible responses to Other Forms items follow.

1. *n.* agitator; *vt.* agitate, agitates, agitated, agitating; *adj.* agitative, agitational; *adv.* agitatedly
2. *n.* aloofness; *adv.* aloofly
3. *adj.* apparitional
4. *n.* benefaction
5. *vi.* copes, coped, coping
6. *n.* genealogist; *n. pl.* genealogies; *adj.* genealogical; *adv.* genealogically
7. *n.* mooring, moorage; *n. pl.* moors, moorings; *vt.* or *vi.* moors, moored, mooring
8. *n.* obsessiveness, obsessive; *vt.* obsess; *adj.* obsessional, obsessive; *adv.* obsessively
9. *n.* palatialness; *adv.* palatially
10. *n.* plaintiveness; *adv.* plaintively

Exercise 2 Context Clues

11. (A) agitation
12. (E) apparition
13. (H) cope
14. (G) moors
15. (D) palatial
16. (J) plaintive
17. (C) obsession
18. (B) genealogy
19. (F) benefactor
20. (I) aloof

Exercise 3 Sentence Completion

21. B   22. C   23. A   24. E   25. B   26. D   27. D
28. A   29. E   30. C

Lesson 6   pages 23–26
Exercise 1 Mapping

Your Guess and Definition answers will vary. Possible responses to Other Forms items follow.

1. *adj.* arrogant; *adv.* arrogantly
2. *n.* docility; *adv.* docilely
3. *n.* frivolity, frivolousness; *n. pl.* frivolities; *adv.* frivolously
4. *n.* kindler, kindling; *vi.* or *vt.* kindles, kindled, kindling
5. *vi.* seethes, seethed, seething
6. *n.* sinisterness; *adv.* sinisterly
7. *n.* smugness; *adj.* smugger, smuggest; *adv.* smugly
8. *n.* spurner; *vi.* or *vt.* spurns, spurned, spurning
9. *n.* unscrupulousness; *adv.* unscrupulously
10. *n.* yearner, yearning; *vi.* yearns, yearned, yearning

Exercise 2 Context Clues

11. (G) docile
12. (H) sinister
13. (I) unscrupulous
14. (F) seethes
15. (C) arrogance
16. (J) yearns

17. (A) kindles
18. (E) spurns
19. (D) smug
20. (B) frivolous

Exercise 3 Sentence Completion

21. D   22. A   23. D   24. E   25. C   26. A   27. B
28. B   29. D   30. C

Lesson 7   pages 27–30
Exercise 1 Mapping

Your Guess and Definition answers will vary. Possible responses to Other Forms items follow.

1. *n.* carnivore, carnivorousness; *adv.* carnivorously
2. *adv.* centrifugally
3. *n. pl.* faunas, faunae; *adj.* faunal; *adv.* faunally
4. *n. pl.* floras, florae; *adj.* floral; *adv.* florally
5. *n.* fraternizer, fraternization, fraternalism, fraternity; *vi.* fraternizes, fraternized, fraternizing; *adj.* fraternal; *adv.* fraternally
6. *n.* granulator, granulater, granularity, granulation, granule; *vi.* or *vt.* granulate; *adj.* granulative; *adv.* granularly
7. *vt.* sectors, sectored, sectoring; *adj.* sectoral, sectorial
8. *n.* stagnation, stagnancy; *vi.* stagnate; *adv.* stagnantly
9. *n.* upheaver; *n. pl.* upheavals
10. *adj.* zodiacal

Exercise 2 Context Clues

11. (E) granular
12. (D) flora
13. (H) zodiac
14. (J) sectors
15. (A) carnivorous
16. (I) centrifugal
17. (B) upheaval
18. (G) fraternize
19. (F) stagnant
20. (C) fauna

Exercise 3 Sentence Completion

21. B   22. A   23. D   24. D   25. C   26. C   27. E
28. A   29. B   30. E

Lesson 8   pages 31–34
Exercise 1 Mapping

Your Guess and Definition answers will vary. Possible responses to Other Forms items follow.

1. *n.* attributer, attributor, attribution, attributiveness, attributive; *vt.* attributes, attributed, attributing; *adj.* attributable, attributive; *adv.* attributively
2. *n.* bizarreness; *adv.* bizarrely
3. *vi.* hordes, horded, hording
4. *n.* humanitarianism
5. *n. pl.* humanoids
6. *n.* infestation, infester; *vt.* infests, infested, infesting
7. *n.* ironicalness; *adj.* ironic, ironical; *adv.* ironically
8. *n.* predator, predatoriness, predation; *adv.* predatorily
9. *n.* relevance, relevancy; *adv.* relevantly
10. *n.* toleration, tolerator, tolerability, tolerableness; *vt.* tolerates, tolerated, tolerating; *adj.* tolerant, tolerative; *adv.* tolerably, tolerantly

Exercise 2　Context Clues

11. (G) irony	16. (J) humanoid
12. (A) attribute	17. (E) tolerates
13. (B) infest	18. (F) relevant
14. (D) bizarre	19. (C) horde
15. (I) predatory	20. (H) humanitarian

Exercise 3　Sentence Completion

21. E　22. A　23. C　24. B　25. B　26. D　27. E
28. B　29. D　30. A

Lesson 9　pages 35–38
Exercise 1　Mapping

Your Guess and Definition answers will vary. Possible responses to Other Forms items follow.

1. *n.* advocator, advocacy; *vt.* advocates, advocated, advocating; *adj.* advocatory
2. *n.* alleger; *vt.* allege, alleges, alleged, alleging; *adj.* allegeable; *adv.* allegedly
3. *n.* conspirator; *vi.* conspire; *adj.* conspiratorial; *adv.* conspiratorially
4. *vi.* culminate, culminates, culminated, culminating; *adj.* culminant
5. *n.* lethality; *adv.* lethally
6. *n.* manipulation, manipulator, manipulability; *vt.* manipulates, manipulated, manipulating; *adj.* manipulative, manipulatory, manipulable, manipulatable; *adv.* manipulatory
7. *n.* misconstruction; *vt.* misconstrues, misconstrued, misconstruing
8. *n.* ominousness; *adv.* ominously
9. *n.* preposterousness; *adv.* preposterously
10. *n.* uncanniness; *adj.* uncannier, uncanniest; *adv.* uncannily

Exercise 2　Context Clues

11. (H) conspiracy	16. (G) ominous
12. (D) lethal	17. (B) misconstrue
13. (J) advocate	18. (C) culmination
14. (I) preposterous	19. (A) alleged
15. (E) manipulate	20. (F) uncanny

Exercise 3　Sentence Completion

21. A　22. C　23. E　24. D　25. B　26. E　27. C
28. A　29. B　30. D

Lesson 10　pages 39–42
Exercise 1　Mapping

Your Guess and Definition answers will vary. Possible responses to Other Forms items follow.

1. *n.* credential, credence; *vt.* credential, credentialed, credentialing
2. *n.* cumbersomeness; *vt.* cumber; *adj.* cumbrous; *adv.* cumbersomely
3. *n.* genialness, geniality; *adv.* genially
4. *n.* hoaxer; *n. pl.* hoaxes; *vt.* hoaxes, hoaxed, hoaxing
5. *n.* larcenist, larcener; *n. pl.* larcenies; *adj.* larcenous; *adv.* larcenously
6. *n.* morbidity, morbidness; *adv.* morbidly
7. *n. pl.* plaintiffs
8. *n.* prospect; *vi.* prospect; *adv.* prospectively
9. *n. pl.* quorums

10. *n.* superfluity, superfluousness; *adv.* superfluously

Exercise 2　Context Clues

11. (F) plaintiff	16. (H) prospective
12. (A) credentials	17. (C) morbid
13. (G) larceny	18. (J) superfluous
14. (I) quorum	19. (B) genial
15. (D) cumbersome	20. (E) hoax

Exercise 3　Sentence Completion

21. A　22. B　23. E　24. A　25. D　26. C　27. D
28. D　29. E　30. B

Lesson 11　pages 43–46
Exercise 1　Mapping

Your Guess and Definition answers will vary. Possible responses to Other Forms items follow.

1. *n.* blandness; *adj.* blander, blandest; *adv.* blandly
2. *n.* chronicity; *adv.* chronically
3. *n.* contempt, contemptibility, contemptibleness; *adj.* contemptuous; *adv.* contemptibly
4. *n.* diligence; *adv.* diligently
5. *n.* ideal, idealism, ideality; *adj.* ideal
6. *n.* impertinence, impertinency; *adv.* impertinently
7. *n.* incomprehension, incomprehensibility, incomprehensibleness; *adj.* incomprehensive; *adv.* incomprehensibly
8. *n.* malice, maliciousness; *adv.* maliciously
9. *n.* obtuseness, obtusity; *adv.* obtusely
10. *n.* pessimism, pessimist; *adv.* pessimistically

Exercise 2　Context Clues

11. (B) contemptible	16. (H) impertinent
12. (F) obtuse	17. (A) bland
13. (J) ideally	18. (I) pessimistic
14. (C) chronic	19. (E) malicious
15. (D) incomprehensible	20. (G) diligent

Exercise 3　Sentence Completion

21. C　22. E　23. E　24. C　25. B　26. D　27. D
28. B　29. A　30. A

Lesson 12　pages 47–50
Exercise 1　Mapping

Your Guess and Definition answers will vary. Possible responses to Other Forms items follow.

1. *n.* abhorence, abhorrer; *vt.* abhors, abhorred, abhorring; *adj.* abhorent; *adv.* abhorently
2. *n.* congenialness; *adj.* congenial; *adv.* congenially
3. *n.* cynicism, cynicalness; *n. pl.* cynics; *adj.* cynical; *adv.* cynically
4. *n.* dupability, duper, dupery; *vt.* dupes, duped, duping; *adj.* dupable
5. *n.* extroversion; *adj.* extroverted
6. *n.* gaudiness; *adj.* gaudier, gaudiest; *adv.* gaudily
7. *n.* intimacy, intimacies, intimateness; *vt.* intimate, intimates, intimated, intimating; *adv.* intimately
8. *n.* joviality; *adv.* jovially
9. *n. pl.* quotas
10. *n. pl.* tycoons

11. (F) gaudy
12. (C) jovial
13. (A) extroverts
14. (D) abhor
15. (J) quota
16. (B) congeniality
17. (I) dupe
18. (E) tycoon
19. (H) cynic
20. (G) intimate

Exercise 3   Sentence Completion
21. B   22. B   23. C   24. D   25. E   26. E   27. B
28. C   29. D   30. D

Lesson 13   pages 51–54
Exercise 1   Mapping
Your Guess and Definition answers will vary. Possible responses to Other Forms items follow.

1. *n.* acknowledgement; *vt.* acknowledges, acknowledged, acknowledging; *adj.* acknowledgeable
2. *n. pl.* adversaries; *adj.* adversarial, adversative
3. *vt.* eludes, eluded, eluding
4. *n.* exploitation, exploiter; *vt.* exploits, exploited, exploiting; *adj.* exploitable; exploitative
5. *n.* homager; *n. pl.* homages
6. *n.* implementation, implementer, implementor; *vt.* implements, implemented, implementing; *adj.* implemental
7. *n. pl.* metamorphoses; *vi.* or *vt.* metamorphose; *adj.* metamorphic
8. *n.* precedence, precedency; *vi.* or *vt.* precede; *adj.* precedential, preceding
9. *n.* surmounter; *vt.* surmounts, surmounted, surmounting; *adj.* surmountable
10. *n.* wrangler; *vi.* or *vt.* wrangles, wrangled, wrangling

Exercise 2   Context Clues
11. (B) implement
12. (J) surmount
13. (C) adversary
14. (A) wrangle
15. (I) homage
16. (H) precedent
17. (G) acknowledge
18. (D) metamorphosis
19. (F) elude
20. (E) exploits

Exercise 3   Sentence Completion
21. B   22. E   23. C   24. D   25. A   26. B   27. D
28. C   29. E   30. E

Lesson 14   pages 55–58
Exercise 1   Mapping
Your Guess and Definition answers will vary. Possible responses to Other Forms items follow.

1. *n.* addict, addiction; *vt.* addict; *adj.* addictive
2. *n.* defrauder, defraudation; *vt.* defrauds, defrauded, defrauding
3. *n.* eviction, evictor; *vt.* evicts, evicted, evicting
4. *n.* formidability, formidableness; *adv.* formidably
5. *n.* illiteracy, illiterateness; *n. pl.* illiterates; *adv.* illiterately
6. *n.* incompatibility, incompatibleness; *adv.* incompatibly
7. *n.* laxness; *adj.* laxer, laxest; *adv.* laxly
8. *n.* ostracism; *vt.* ostracizes, ostracized, ostracizing

9. *n.* solvency
10. *n.* subsequence, subsequentness; *adv.* subsequently

Exercise 2   Context Clues
11. (I) lax
12. (A) evict
13. (F) ostracize
14. (B) incompatible
15. (E) solvent
16. (C) subsequent
17. (J) formidable
18. (G) addicted
19. (D) illiterate
20. (H) defraud

Exercise 3   Sentence Completion
21. A   22. B   23. C   24. C   25. B   26. A   27. D
28. E   29. D   30. E

Lesson 15   pages 59–62
Exercise 1   Mapping
Your Guess and Definition answers will vary. Possible responses to Other Forms items follow.

1. *adj.* apathetic, apathetical; *adv.* apathetically
2. *vi.* or *vt.* cascades, cascaded, cascading
3. *n.* inductee; *vt.* induct
4. *n.* inversion; *vt.* invert; *adj.* inverted, invertible, inversive; *adv.* inversely
5. *vi.* jaunts, jaunted, jaunting
6. *n.* nausea, nauseation, nauseousness; *vi.* or *vt.* nauseates, nauseated, nauseating; *adj.* nauseated, nauseous; *adv.* nauseously, nauseatingly
7. *n.* pungency; *adv.* pungently
8. *n.* ravenousness; *adv.* ravenously
9. *n. pl.* repasts
10. *n.* tantalization, tantalizer; *vt.* tantalize; *adv.* tantalizingly

Exercise 2   Context Clues
11. (A) jaunts
12. (B) apathy
13. (I) tantalizing
14. (H) inverse
15. (E) repast
16. (G) cascade
17. (F) ravenous
18. (C) pungent
19. (D) induction
20. (J) nauseate

Exercise 3   Sentence Completion
21. A   22. C   23. E   24. B   25. A   26. D   27. A
28. B   29. B   30. E

Lesson 16   pages 63–66
Exercise 1   Mapping
Your Guess and Definition answers will vary. Possible responses to Other Forms items follow.

1. *n.* animation, animater, animator; *vt.* animate, animates, animating; *adv.* animatedly
2. *n.* benignancy; *adj.* benignant; *adv.* benignly
3. *n.* buoy, buoyancy; *vt.* buoy, buoys, buoyed, buoying; *adv.* buoyantly
4. *n.* congruence, congruency, congruousness; *n. pl.* congruences, congruencies; *adj.* congruous; *adv.* congruently, congruously
5. *n.* incandescence; *vi.* or *vt.* incandesce; *adv.* incandescently
6. *n.* incessancy, incessantness; *adv.* incessantly
7. *n.* invigoration, invigorator; *vt.* invigorate; *adj.* invigorative; *adv.* invigoratingly

8. *n.* murk, murkiness; *adj.* mirky, murkier, murkiest; *adv.* murkily
9. *n.* opaqueness, opacity; *vt.* opaqued, opaquing; *adv.* opaquely
10. *n.* oppression, oppressiveness, oppressor; *vt.* oppress; *adv.* oppressively

Exercise 2   Context Clues
11. (E) buoyant
12. (H) incandescent
13. (B) benign
14. (G) murky
15. (D) incessant
16. (I) invigorating
17. (F) opaque
18. (C) oppressive
19. (J) animated
20. (A) congruent

Exercise 3   Sentence Completion
21. B   22. A   23. E   24. D   25. A   26. C   27. C
28. A   29. D   30. B

Lesson 17   pages 67–70
Exercise 1   Mapping
Your Guess and Definition answers will vary. Possible responses to Other Forms items follow.
1. *n.* abrasion; *vt.* abrade; *adv.* abrasively
2. *n.* denotation; *vt.* denotes, denoted, denoting; *adj.* denotable, denotative; *adv.* denotatively
3. *n.* hinderer; *n. pl.* hindrances; *vt.* hinder
4. *n.* irreducibleness, irreducibility; *adv.* irreducibly
5. *n.* necessitation, necessity; *vt.* necessitates, necessitated, necessitating; *adj.* necessitative, necessitous
6. *n.* passivity, passiveness; *adv.* passively
7. *n.* reconciliation, reconciler, reconcilement, reconcilableness, reconcilability; *vt.* reconciles, reconciled, reconciling; *adj.* reconciliatory, reconcilable; *adv.* reconcilably
8. *n.* somberness; *adv.* somberly
9. *n.* turbulence, turbulency; *adv.* turbulently
10. *n.* ultimacy, ultimateness; *adv.* ultimately

Exercise 2   Context Clues
11. (F) passive
12. (I) abrasive
13. (E) reconcile
14. (H) denote
15. (C) somber
16. (A) hindrance
17. (B) turbulent
18. (J) irreducible
19. (D) ultimate
20. (G) necessitated

Exercise 3   Sentence Completion
21. C   22. D   23. A   24. A   25. A   26. D   27. B
28. C   29. A   30. E

Lesson 18   pages 71–74
Exercise 1   Mapping
Your Guess and Definition answers will vary. Possible responses to Other Forms items follow.
1. *n. pl.* adages
2. *n.* allusiveness; *vi.* allude; *adj.* allusive; *adv.* allusively
3. *n.* cadency; *n. pl.* cadences, cadencies; *adj.* cadenced, cadent, cadential
4. *n.* fallaciousness; *adj.* fallacious; *adv.* fallaciously
5. *n.* figurativeness; *adv.* figuratively
6. *n.* intensity, intensiveness; *vi.* or *vt.* intensify
7. *adj.* metaphoric, metaphorical; *adv.* metaphorically

8. *n.* potentness, potence; *adj.* potent; *adv.* potently
9. *n.* rapturousness; *vt.* raptures, raptured, rapturing; *adj.* rapturous; *adv.* rapturously
10. *n. pl.* similes

Exercise 2   Context Clues
11. (H) figurative
12. (I) intensive
13. (G) metaphors
14. (J) adage
15. (B) potency
16. (D) rapture
17. (A) simile
18. (E) cadence
19. (C) allusion
20. (F) fallacies

Exercise 3   Sentence Completion
21. A   22. D   23. E   24. B   25. B   26. C   27. A
28. A   29. C   30. E

Lesson 19   pages 75–78
Exercise 1   Mapping
Your Guess and Definition answers will vary. Possible responses to Other Forms items follow.
1. *vt.* encores, encored, encoring
2. *n.* intoner; *vi.* or *vt.* intone; *adj.* intonational
3. *vt.* inventories, inventoried, inventorying; *adj.* inventorial; *adv.* inventorially
4. *n.* orator, oration; *vi.* orate; *adj.* oratorical; *adv.* oratorically
5. *n. pl.* ovations
6. *n. pl.* patios
7. *n.* replication; *n. pl.* replicas; *vi.* or *vt.* replicate; *adj.* replicative, replicable
8. *n. pl.* rostrums, rostra; *adj.* rostral
9. *n.* soliloquizer, soliloquist; *n. pl.* soliloquies; *vi.* or *vt.* soliloquize
10. *adj.* tripodal, tripodic

Exercise 2   Context Clues
11. (C) oratory
12. (J) ovation
13. (F) replica
14. (I) encore
15. (G) intonation
16. (B) rostrum
17. (D) inventory
18. (H) soliloquies
19. (A) tripod
20. (E) patios

Exercise 3   Sentence Completion
21. B   22. A   23. E   24. B   25. C   26. D   27. A
28. B   29. E   30. B

Lesson 20   pages 79–82
Exercise 1   Mapping
Your Guess and Definition answers will vary. Possible responses to Other Forms items follow.
1. *n.* bisection; *vt.* bisects, bisected, bisecting; *adj.* bisectional; *adv.* bisectionally
2. *adj.* discreet, discretional, discretionary; *adv.* discreetly, discretionally, discretionarily
3. *adv.* hectically
4. *n.* inaudibility; *adv.* inaudibly
5. *n.* lavisher, lavishness; *vt.* lavishes, lavished, lavishing; *adv.* lavishly
6. *n.* mimicry, mimicker; *n. pl.* mimics; *vt.* mimics, mimicked, mimicking
7. *adv.* nominally
8. *n.* orthodoxy; *adv.* orthodoxly
9. *adj.* panoramic; *adv.* panoramically
10. *n.* resourcefulness; *adv.* resourcefully

Exercise 2   Context Clues
11. (C) inaudible
12. (B) bisected
13. (E) mimic
14. (F) discretion
15. (D) hectic
16. (A) panorama
17. (G) resourceful
18. (I) orthodox
19. (H) nominal
20. (J) lavish

Exercise 3   Sentence Completion
21. D   22. B   23. A   24. B   25. E   26. C   27. B
28. C   29. B   30. D

Lesson 21   pages 83–86
Exercise 1   Mapping
Your Guess and Definition answers will vary. Possible responses to Other Forms items follow.
1. *n.* assassination, assassinator; *vt.* assassinate; *adj.* assassinative
2. *n.* asterism; *n. pl.* asterisks; *vt.* asterisks, asterisked, asterisking
3. *n.* bibliographer; *adj.* bibliographical, bibliographic; *adv.* bibliographically
4. *n. pl.* brochures
5. *adj.* fatal; *adv.* fatally
6. *adj.* hygienic; *adv.* hygienically
7. *adj.* jurisdictional; *adv.* jurisdictionally
8. *n. pl.* perspectives; *adv.* perspectively
9. *adj.* recessional, recessive, recessionary; *adv.* recessively
10. *adj.* statutable, statutory

Exercise 2   Context Clues
11. (I) statutes
12. (B) asterisk
13. (C) brochures
14. (F) hygiene
15. (D) recession
16. (H) fatality
17. (E) assassin
18. (G) perspective
19. (J) jurisdiction
20. (A) bibliography

Exercise 3   Sentence Completion
21. C   22. E   23. B   24. D   25. A   26. D   27. D
28. B   29. B   30. E

Lesson 22   pages 87–90
Exercise 1   Mapping
Your Guess and Definition answers will vary. Possible responses to Other Forms items follow.
1. *n.* bilingualism; *adv.* bilingually
2. *n.* biography, biographer, biographee; *adj.* biographic; *adv.* biographically
3. *n.* chronology, chronologist; *adv.* chronologically
4. *n.* deficiency; *adv.* deficiently
5. *n.* denunciation, denouncement, denouncer; *vt.* denounces, denounced, denouncing
6. *n.* dissuasion, dissuader, dissuasiveness; *vt.* dissuades, dissuaded, dissuading; *adj.* dissuasive; *adv.* dissuasively
7. *n.* fluency; *adv.* fluently
8. *n.* galvanization, galvanizer; *vt.* galvanizes, galvanized, galvanizing
9. *n.* infamousness, infamy; *adv.* infamously
10. *n.* satire, satirist, satirizer; *vt.* satirize; *adj.* satiric; *adv.* satirically

Exercise 2   Context Clues
11. (B) denounce
12. (D) galvanized
13. (J) bilingual
14. (F) deficient
15. (E) infamous
16. (H) biographical
17. (G) satirical
18. (C) dissuade
19. (I) fluent
20. (A) chronological

Exercise 3   Sentence Completion
21. D   22. A   23. C   24. A   25. E   26. C   27. B
28. A   29. B   30. D

Lesson 23   pages 91–94
Exercise 1   Mapping
Your Guess and Definition answers will vary. Possible responses to Other Forms items follow.
1. *n.* accessibleness, access, accessibility; *vt.* access; *adv.* accessibly
2. *n.* applicability; *adv.* applicably
3. *n.* immaterialness, immaterialism, immateriality, immaterialist; *adv.* immaterially
4. *n.* inconvenience; *vt.* inconvenience; *adv.* inconveniently
5. *n.* optimism, optimist; *vi.* optimize; *adj.* optimistical; *adv.* optimistically
6. *n.* perception, perceiver, perceptivity, perceptibility; *vi.* or *vt.* perceive; *adj.* perceptive; *adv.* perceptibly, perceptively
7. *n.* ponderosity, ponderousness; *adv.* ponderously
8. *n.* prematurity, prematureness; *adv.* prematurely
9. *n.* tentativeness; *adv.* tentatively
10. *n.* trivia, triviality, trivialization, trivialism; *vt.* trivialize; *adv.* trivially

Exercise 2   Context Clues
11. (A) accessible
12. (H) ponderous
13. (B) applicable
14. (F) premature
15. (C) immaterial
16. (D) tentative
17. (J) inconvenient
18. (E) trivial
19. (I) optimistic
20. (G) perceptible

Exercise 3   Sentence Completion
21. C   22. A   23. D   24. B   25. B   26. D   27. A
28. C   29. E   30. E

Lesson 24   pages 95–98
Exercise 1   Mapping
Your Guess and Definition answers will vary. Possible responses to Other Forms items follow.
1. *n.* acclamation, acclaimer; *vt.* acclaims, acclaimed, acclaiming; *adj.* acclamatory
2. *n.* affect, affectation, affectedness, affecter; *vt.* affect; *adj.* affectable; *adv.* affectedly
3. *n.* circumscriber, circumscription; *vt.* circumscribes, circumscribed, circumscribing; *adj.* circumscriptive, circumscribable; *adv.* circumscriptively
4. *n.* clamberer; *vt.* clambers, clambered, clambering
5. *n.* incalculability, incalculableness; *adv.* incalculably
6. *n.* influence, influencer; *vt.* influence; *adv.* influentially
7. *adv.* perennially
8. *n.* poacher; *vi.* or *vt.* poaches, poached, poaching; *adj.* poachy

9. *vt.* prioritize; *adj.* prior; *adv.* priorly
10. *n.* prominency; *adj.* prominent; *adv.* prominently

Exercise 2   Context Clues

11. (G) clamber
12. (J) incalculable
13. (A) acclaim
14. (B) influential
15. (I) perennial
16. (H) poach
17. (C) affected
18. (E) priority
19. (F) prominence
20. (D) circumscribe

Exercise 3   Sentence Completion

21. A   22. B   23. A   24. D   25. E   26. C   27. D
28. D   29. B   30. C

Lesson 25   pages 99–102
Exercise 1   Mapping

Your Guess and Definition answers will vary. Possible responses to Other Forms items follow.

1. *n.* dubiousness; *adv.* dubiously
2. *vi.* or *vt.* equate; *adj.* equational; *adv.* equationally
3. *n.* essentialness, essentiality; *adj.* essential; *adv.* essentially
4. *n.* frenzy; *vt.* frenzies, frenzied, frenzying; *adv.* frenziedly
5. *adj.* gruelling; *adv.* gruelingly
6. *n.* haphazardness; *adv.* haphazardly
7. *adj.* liable
8. *n.* unkemptness
9. *adj.* vain; *adv.* vainly
10. *n.* volatileness, volatility, volatilization; *vi.* or *vt.* volatilize; *adj.* volatilizable

Exercise 2   Context Clues

11. (F) frenzied
12. (H) haphazard
13. (B) dubious
14. (A) grueling
15. (C) unkempt
16. (E) volatile
17. (D) equation
18. (I) essence
19. (G) liability
20. (J) vanity

Exercise 3   Sentence Completion

21. D   22. A   23. E   24. C   25. A   26. D   27. A
28. B   29. E   30. B

Lesson 26   pages 103–106
Exercise 1   Mapping

Your Guess and Definition answers will vary. Possible responses to Other Forms items follow.

1. *n.* autonomy, autonomist; *adv.* autonomously
2. *n.* collaboration, collaborator, collaborationist, collaborationism; *vi.* collaborates, collaborated, collaborating; *adj.* collaborative
3. *n.* depiction, depictor; *vt.* depicts, depicted, depicting
4. *n.* disruption, disruptor, disrupter; *vt.* disrupts, disrupted, disrupting; *adj.* disruptive; *adv.* disruptively
5. *n.* function; *vi.* function; *adv.* functionally
6. *n.* irksomeness; *vt.* irk; *adv.* irksomely
7. *n.* paramountcy; *adv.* paramountly
8. *n.* reluctance, reluctancy; *adv.* reluctantly
9. *n.* transcription, transcriber, transcript; *vt.* transcribes, transcribed, transcribing; *adj.* transcribable, transcriptional; *adv.* transcriptionally
10. *n.* virtuality; *adv.* virtually

Exercise 2   Context Clues

11. (D) functional
12. (F) paramount
13. (B) collaborate
14. (C) depict
15. (H) transcribe
16. (I) disrupt
17. (A) autonomous
18. (E) irksome
19. (J) virtual
20. (G) reluctant

Exercise 3   Sentence Completion

21. C   22. B   23. B   24. A   25. D   26. C   27. A
28. E   29. D   30. B

Lesson 27   pages 107–110
Exercise 1   Mapping

Your Guess and Definition answers will vary. Possible responses to Other Forms items follow.

1. *n.* conniver, connivance, connivence, connivery; *vt.* connives, connived, conniving
2. *n.* discretion, discreetness; *adv.* discreetly
3. *n.* discrimination, discriminator; *vi.* or *vt.* discriminates, discriminated, discriminating; *adj.* discriminatory, discriminative, discriminable, discriminating; *adv.* discriminatively, discriminatingly, discriminately
4. *n.* instigator, instigation; *vt.* instigates, instigated, instigating; *adj.* instigative
5. *n.* intimidation, intimidator; *vt.* intimidates, intimidated, intimidating; *adj.* intimidating
6. *n.* nimbleness; *adj.* nimbler, nimblest; *adv.* nimbly
7. *n.* raucousness; *adv.* raucously
8. *n.* skeptic, skepticism; *adj.* skeptic; *adv.* skeptically
9. *n.* transpiration; *vi.* or *vt.* transpires, transpired, transpiring
10. *n.* wryness; *vi.* or *vt.* wries, wried, wrying; *adj.* wryer, wryest; *adv.* wryly

Exercise 2   Context Clues

11. (B) nimble
12. (D) connives
13. (C) raucous
14. (G) discriminate
15. (A) skeptical
16. (J) discreet
17. (I) transpired
18. (H) instigates
19. (E) wry
20. (F) intimidate

Exercise 3   Sentence Completion

21. B   22. B   23. A   24. E   25. D   26. A   27. C
28. D   29. A   30. C

Lesson 28   pages 111–114
Exercise 1   Mapping

Your Guess and Definition answers will vary. Possible responses to Other Forms items follow.

1. *n.* alterability, alterableness; *vt.* alter; *adj.* alterable, alterative; *adv.* alterably
2. *n.* amender, amendment; *vi.* or *vt.* amend
3. *adv.* drastically
4. *n.* indivisibility, indivisibleness; *adv.* indivisibly
5. *n.* initiation, initiator; *vt.* initiate; *adj.* initiatory; *adv.* initiatively
6. *n.* interventionism, interventionist, intervener, intervenient; *vi.* intervene
7. *n.* irretrievableness, irretrievability; *adv.* irretrievably
8. *n. pl.* medleys

9. *n.* promenader; *vi.* or *vt.* promenades, promenaded, promenading
10. *n.* reprimand

Exercise 2   Context Clues
11. (F) alterations
12. (E) initiative
13. (B) irretrievable
14. (I) amends
15. (H) interventions
16. (J) medley
17. (C) reprimand
18. (G) indivisible
19. (A) promenades
20. (D) drastic

Exercise 3   Sentence Completion
21. A   22. B   23. C   24. D   25. B   26. D   27. A
28. C   29. B   30. B

Lesson 29   pages 115–118
Exercise 1   Mapping
Your Guess and Definition answers will vary. Possible responses to Other Forms items follow.

1. *n.* agileness; *adj.* agile; *adv.* agilely
2. *vi.* or *vt.* dwindles, dwindles, dwindling
3. *vi.* elapses, elapsed, elapsing
4. *n.* exasperater, exasperation; *vt.* exasperates, exasperated, exasperating; *adv.* exasperatingly
5. *n.* nonchalance; *adv.* nonchalantly
6. *n.* retraction, retractility, retractor; *vi.* or *vt.* retracts, retracted, retracting; *adj.* retractive, retractile, retractable
7. *vt.* surpasses, surpassed, surpassing; *adj.* surpassing; *adv.* surpassingly
8. *n.* susceptibility, susceptibleness, susceptiveness, susceptivity; *adj.* susceptive; *adv.* susceptibly
9. *vt.* veneers, veneered, veneering
10. *n.* wariness; *adj.* warier, wariest; *adv.* warily

Exercise 2   Context Clues
11. (E) retract
12. (D) surpass
13. (A) agility
14. (I) susceptible
15. (J) veneer
16. (H) dwindle
17. (F) wary
18. (C) exasperates
19. (B) nonchalant
20. (G) elapsed

Exercise 3   Sentence Completion
21. B   22. D   23. C   24. E   25. B   26. A   27. C
28. D   29. A   30. B

Lesson 30   pages 119–122
Exercise 1   Mapping
Your Guess and Definition answers will vary. Possible responses to Other Forms items follow.

1. *n.* assessment, assessor; *vt.* assesses, assessed, assessing; *adj.* assessable, assessorial
2. *n.* collateralization; *vt.* collateralize; *adv.* collaterally
3. *n.* compliance; *vi.* complies, complied, complying; *adj.* compliant; *adv.* compliantly
4. *n.* condolement; *vi.* condole; *adj.* condolent, condolatory
5. *n.* contamination, contaminant, contaminator; *vt.* contaminates, contaminated, contaminating; *adj.* contaminative
6. *n.* depreciation, depreciator; *vi.* or *vt.* depreciates, depreciated, depreciating; *adj.* depreciative, depreciatory

7. *n.* emergence; *vi.* emerges, emerged, emerging
8. *n.* expenditure; *vt.* expends, expended, expending; *adj.* expendable
9. *n.* immunization, immune; *vt.* immunize; *adj.* immune
10. *n.* maintainer; *vt.* maintain, maintains, maintained, maintaining; *adj.* maintainable

Exercise 2   Context Clues
11. (C) collateral
12. (H) emerges
13. (D) comply
14. (I) expend
15. (A) condolences
16. (B) assess
17. (G) contaminate
18. (F) immunity
19. (E) maintenance
20. (J) depreciate

Exercise 3   Sentence Completion
21. D   22. C   23. E   24. A   25. B   26. C   27. E
28. B   29. C   30. D

CONNECTING NEW WORDS AND PATTERNS

Lesson 1   page 126
1. (B); Antonym. *Belligerent,* which means quarrelsome, means the opposite of *peaceful. Disappointed* and *pleased* have opposite meanings.
2. (A); Synonym. *Manifest,* which means show, means the same as *reveal. Endure,* which means to hold out or last, has a meaning similar to *persist.*
3. (B); Synonym. *Meander* and *wander* have similar meanings, as do *wiggle* and *squirm.*
4. (B); Characteristic Quality. A *disciple,* or follower, is characteristically *fervent,* or devoted. An *inventor* is characteristically *creative.*
5. (E); Cause and Effect. *Practice* can result in *dexterity,* or skill. *Study* can result in *knowledge.*
6. (D); Performer and Related Action. A *diplomat* *negotiates* with other countries, just as a *lawyer* *settles* a lawsuit.
7. (C); Antonym. *Intact,* or whole, means the opposite of *damaged. Valued* means the opposite of *scorned.*
8. (D); Synonym. *Recede* and *withdraw* have similar meanings, as do *predict* and *forecast.*
9. (D); Degree. Something that is *hideous* is extremely *unattractive,* just as someone who is *overjoyed* is extremely *pleased.*
10. (E); Degree. To *replenish* something is to *provide* it again when it runs out. To *refill* something is to *fill* it again.

Lesson 2   page 127
1. (D); Synonym. An *emissary* is a *messenger,* just as a *doctor* is a *physician.*
2. (C); Characteristic Quality. A *citadel,* or hilltop fortress, is characteristically *elevated,* or high. A *courtyard,* or inner patio, is characteristically *walled.*
3. (D); Performer and Related Object. A *herald,* or messenger, delivers a *message,* just as a *mail carrier* delivers a *letter.*

4. (D); Synonym. *Medieval* and *gothic*, adjectives which refer to the period in Europe's history called the Middle Ages, have similar meanings, as do *intentional* and *purposeful*.
5. (E); Antonym. *Prowess*, which means great ability, means the opposite of *ineptitude*, or incompetence. *Pride* and *humility* are also opposite in meaning.
6. (C); Cause and Effect. Some believe a *potion* can result in *love*, just as a *sedative* can result in *calm*.
7. (C); Synonym. *Garb* and *clothing* have the same meaning, as do *makeup* and *cosmetics*.
8. (E); Synonym. *Undergo* and *endure* have similar meanings, as do *gratify* and *please*.
9. (E); Synonym. *Amity* and *friendship* have similar meanings, as do *richness* and *wealth*.
10. (B); Function. The function of an *omen* is to *foretell* the future. The function of a *crane* is to *lift* something heavy.

Lesson 3   page 128
1. (D); Performer and Related Action. A *benefactor* is someone who *helps* the needy, just as a *patron* is someone who *supports* individuals or causes.
2. (E); Synonym. *Moor*, as in to *moor* a boat, and *secure* have similar meanings, as do *speak* and *talk*.
3. (E); Antonym. *Plaintive*, which means sad, is opposite in meaning to *joyous*. *Moderate* and *excessive* are also opposite in meaning.
4. (B); Characteristic Quality. A *villain* is characteristically *sinister*, just as an *angel* is characteristically *kindly*.
5. (E); Synonym. *Cope* and *handle* possess similar meanings, as do *recall* and *remember*.
6. (A); Synonym. *Agitation* and *commotion* are similar in meaning, as are *assault* and *attack*.
7. (C); Part and Whole. A *grandparent*, like all your relatives, is a part of your *genealogy*, or family history, in the same way that an *item* is a part of a *list*.
8. (B); Antonym. *Spurn*, which means reject, is opposite in meaning to *accept*. *Forbid* and *authorize* also have opposite meanings.
9. (B); Synonym. *Kindle* and *ignite* have similar meanings, as do *conceal* and *hide*.
10. (A); Synonym. *Smug* and *self-satisfied* have similar meanings, as do *hesitant* and *unsure*.

Lesson 4   page 129
1. (B); Classification. A *rabbit* is classified as *fauna*, or animal life, just as a *tree* is classified as *vegetation*, or plant life.
2. (D); Part and Whole. *Aquarius* is one constellation within the *zodiac*, just as a *month* is one part of the *year*.
3. (E); Synonym. *Sector* and *division* have similar meanings, as do *territory* and *region*.
4. (D); Characteristic Quality. A *tiger* is characteristically *carnivorous*, or meat-eating, just as a *monkey* is characteristically *acrobatic*.

5. (D); Classification. A *daffodil* is classified as *flora*, or plant life, just as a *beaver* is classified as an *animal*.
6. (D); Performer and Related Action. One expects a *horde* of people to *wander*, just as one expects a *cast* to *perform*.
7. (D); Synonym. *Centrifugal*, which means moving out from the center, has a meaning similar to *outward*. *Heated* and *warm* also have similar meanings.
8. (B); Antonym. *Stagnant* and *moving* have opposite meanings, as do *still* and *active*.
9. (C); Part and Whole. *Contrast* is an element of *irony*, just as *conflict* is an element of *drama*.
10. (D); Degree. *Tolerate* and *endure* have similar meanings but differ in degree: *Endure* implies withstanding much greater suffering. *Torment* and *torture* are also similar, but to *torture* is more severe than to *torment*.

Lesson 5   page 130
1. (D); Synonym. *Culmination*, which means the highest point, has a meaning similar to *peak*. *Elevation* and *height* also have similar meanings.
2. (A); Synonym. *Superfluous* and *excessive* have similar meanings, as do *changeless* and *monotonous*.
3. (C); Characteristic Quality. A *host* is characteristically *genial*, or pleasant, just as a *guest* is characteristically *polite*.
4. (E); Characteristic Quality. *Credentials* are characteristically *written*, just as a *speech* is characteristically *uttered*.
5. (C); Antonym. *Preposterous*, which means senseless or ridiculous, is opposite in meaning to *sensible*. *Harmless* and *destructive* also have opposite meanings.
6. (A); Classification. *Larceny*, or theft, is classified as a *crime*. An *apple* is classified as a *fruit*.
7. (A); Performer and Related Action. An *advocate* is someone who *supports* someone else. A *winner* is someone who *triumphs*.
8. (D); Synonym. *Hoax* and *trick* have similar meanings, as do *sport* and *game*.
9. (A); Synonym. *Lethal* and *deadly* have the same meaning, as do *vital* and *essential*.
10. (E); Performer and Related Action. A *plaintiff* is someone who *sues*, or files a lawsuit. A *tailor* is someone who *sews* clothing.

Lesson 6   page 131
1. (D); Degree. *Abhor*, which means hate, is stronger in meaning than *dislike*. *Idolize*, which means worship, is stronger in meaning than *admire*.
2. (E); Synonym. All four words mean ongoing.
3. (E); Characteristic Quality. An *ant* is characteristically *diligent*, or hard-working, just as a *bee* is characteristically *busy*.

4. (B); Antonym. *Contemptible* and *admirable* have opposite meanings, as do *handsome* and *ugly*.

5. (A); Synonym. *Impertinent*, which means rude, has a meaning similar to *impolite*. *Reverent* and *respectful* also have similar meanings.

6. (A); Synonym. *Jovial* and *jolly* have similar meanings, as do *valuable* and *precious*.

7. (A); Antonym. *Malicious*, or mean, is opposite in meaning to *kind*. *Scarce* and *abundant* are also opposite in meaning.

8. (D); Synonym. *Obtuse*, or dense, has a meaning similar to *dull*. *Common* and *ordinary* also have similar meanings.

9. (E); Synonym. *Quota* and *share* have similar meanings, as do *portion* and *part*.

10. (A); Synonym. *Dupe* and *deceive* have similar meanings, as do *fool* and *trick* when they are used as verbs.

Lesson 7   page 132

1. (C); Performer and Related Action. An *adversary*, or opponent, is someone who *opposes*. A teammate is someone who *plays*.

2. (E); Antonym. *Acknowledge* and *ignore* are opposite in meaning, as are *write* and *erase*.

3. (A); Synonym. *Subsequent*, which means next, has the same meaning as *following* when *following* is used as an adjective. *Last* and *final* also have the same meaning.

4. (B); Antonym. *Ostracize*, which means to keep out, is opposite in meaning to *include*. *Enter* and *exit* also have opposite meanings.

5. (E); Antonym. *Lax* and *strict* are opposite in meaning, as are *gentle* and *harsh*.

6. (D); Degree. To *exploit* is to *use* to the degree of abusing, just as to *exaggerate* is to *describe* to the degree of distorting facts.

7. (E); Action and Related Object. One *surmounts* an *obstacle*, just as one *overcomes* a *difficulty*.

8. (A); Synonym. *Elude* and *escape* have similar meanings, as do *trap* and *catch*.

9. (D); Synonym. *Defraud*, or cheat, has a meaning similar to *swindle*. *Begin* and *start* also have similar meanings.

10. (C); Degree. To *wrangle* is to *disagree* to the extent of an argument or fistfight. To *adore* is to *like* to an extreme extent.

Lesson 8   page 133

1. (D); Synonym. *Pungent* and *sharp* have similar meanings, as do *lively* and *active*.

2. (D); Degree. *Incandescent* is similar in meaning to *bright*, but much stronger, just as *gigantic* implies greater size than *big* does.

3. (B); Classification. *Breakfast* is classified as a *repast*, or meal. *Gray* is classified as a *color*.

4. (C); Synonym. *Congruent*, which means in agreement or corresponding, has a meaning similar to *harmonious*. *Precise* and *exact* also have similar meanings.

5. (A); Antonym. *Animated*, which means lively, is opposite in meaning to *depressed*. *Curious* and *disinterested* are also opposite in meaning.

6. (A); Antonym. *Apathy*, a lack of interest or feeling, is opposite in meaning to *concern*, just as *tension* is opposite in meaning to *relaxation*.

7. (B); Synonym. *Incessant*, or never ending, has a meaning similar to *constant*. *Earnest* and *sincere* also have similar meanings.

8. (E); Antonym. *Opaque* and *transparent* have opposite meanings, as do *plentiful* and *scarce*.

9. (A); Synonym. *Inverse* and *opposite* have similar meanings, as do *difficult* and *hard*.

10. (D); Antonym. *Tantalizing* and *repulsive* are opposite in meaning, as are *calming* and *upsetting*.

Lesson 9   page 134

1. (A); Synonym. *Denote*, which means signify, has the same meaning as *mean* when *mean* is a verb. *Create* and *invent* also have the same meaning.

2. (C); Function. The function of a *simile* is to *compare* two dissimilar things. The function of an *adjective* is to *modify* a noun.

3. (E); Synonym. *Rapture*, or joy, has a meaning similar to *ecstasy*, just as *magnificence* and *splendor* have similar meanings.

4. (B); Antonym. *Ultimate*, or final, means the opposite of *initial*, or first. *Fictitious*, or imaginary, means the opposite of *actual*.

5. (A); Part and Whole. *Metaphor* is a literary device used in *poetry*, just as *shading* is a technique used in *drawing*.

6. (B); Synonym. *Cadence* and *beat* have the same meaning, as do *melody* and *tune*.

7. (A); Antonym. *Hindrance*, which means obstacle, means the opposite of *help*. *Creation* and *destruction* also have opposite meanings.

8. (A); Characteristic Quality. *Sandpaper* is characteristically *abrasive*, or gritty, just as *water* is characteristically *wet*.

9. (B); Characteristic Quality. A *waterfall* is characteristically *turbulent*, just as the *sun* is characteristically *warm*.

10. (E); Characteristic Quality. An *adage* is characteristically an *old* saying. *Rain* is characteristically *wet*.

Lesson 10   page 135

1. (E); Part and Whole. A *soliloquy*, or monologue, is part of a *drama*. A *song* is part of a *musical comedy*.

2. (B); Antonym. *Inaudible*, which means unable to be heard, is opposite in meaning to *loud*. *Vague* and *prominent* are also opposite in meaning.

3. (E); Characteristic Quality. A *panorama*, which is a broad vista or view, is characteristically *wide*, just as *lace* is characteristically *delicate*.

4. (D); Antonym. *Discretion*, which means freedom to make decisions and choices, is nearly opposite in meaning to *restriction*. *Enthusiasm*, which

means intense interest, is opposite in meaning to *disinterest*.

5. (E); Antonym. *Hectic* and *calm* have opposite meanings, as do *relaxed* and *tense*.

6. (D); Antonym. *Lavish,* or extravagant, is opposite in meaning to *meager,* which means sparse or spare. *Expensive* and *cheap* are also opposite in meaning.

7. (A); Synonym. To *inventory* items in a store is the same thing as to *list* them, just as to *remark* is to *comment*.

8. (E); Degree. *Mince,* which means finely dice, is stronger in degree than *bisect,* which means cut in half. *Scrub* is stronger in degree than *wipe*.

9. (B); Part and Whole. *Intonation* is an element of *speech,* just as *melody* is an element of *music*.

10. (D); Characteristic Quality. A *tripod* is characteristically *three-legged,* just as a *bicycle* is characteristically *two-wheeled*.

Lesson 11   page 136

1. (A); Part and Whole. *Titles* of books make up a *bibliography,* just as *definitions* of words make up a *dictionary*.

2. (D); Synonym. *Infamous* and *scandalous* have similar meanings, as do *heroic* and *brave*.

3. (C); Location. A *judge* works in a *jurisdiction,* just as a *salesperson* works in a *territory*.

4. (C); Antonym. *Dissuade,* or discourage, is opposite in meaning to *encourage*. *Occupy* and *vacate* are also opposite in meaning.

5. (E); Degree. A *fatality* is a more serious casualty than an *injury* is, just as *pneumonia* is a more serious illness than a *cold*.

6. (D); Classification. *Hygiene* is classified as a *science,* just as a *doctor* is classified as a *professional*.

7. (A); Antonym. *Chronological,* which means in time order, is opposite in meaning to *random*. *Chaotic,* which can mean unsettled and disorderly, is opposite in meaning to *peaceful*.

8. (D); Function. The function of an *asterisk* is to *mark* something. The function of a *period* is to *end* a sentence.

9. (D); Antonym. *Denounce* and *praise* are nearly opposite in meaning, as are *avoid* and *encounter*.

10. (D); Classification. A *statute* is classified as a *law,* just as a *fine* is classified as a *penalty*.

Lesson 12   page 137

1. (C); Synonym. *Applicable* and *appropriate* have similar meanings, as do *strange* and *odd*.

2. (A); Antonym. *Influential* and *powerless* are opposite in meaning, as are *eternal* and *temporary*.

3. (D); Synonym. *Trivial,* or unimportant, means nearly the same as *insignificant*. *Difficult* means nearly the same as *complex*.

4. (C); Antonym. *Optimistic* and *negative* are opposite in meaning, as are *safe* and *dangerous*.

5. (D); Synonym. *Ponderous,* which means massive, has a meaning similar to *bulky. Heavy* and *weighty* also have similar meanings.

6. (D); Synonym. *Perceptible* and *noticeable* have nearly the same meaning, as do *necessary* and *needed*.

7. (C); Classification. A *perennial* is classified as a *plant,* just as a *sofa* is classified as a *furnishing*.

8. (B); Degree. To *acclaim* is to *approve* with enthusiasm. To *treasure* something is to *like* it intensely.

9. (B); Action and Related Object. Someone might *poach deer,* just as someone might *compose* a *song*.

10. (A); Synonym. *Clamber* and *climb* have nearly the same meaning, as do *scamper* and *run*.

Lesson 13   page 138

1. (C); Antonym. *Haphazard,* or disorderly, means the opposite of *systematic,* just as *hostile* means the opposite of *friendly*.

2. (D); Synonym. *Paramount,* which means ranking higher than any other, has the same meaning as *supreme. Practiced* has the same meaning as *rehearsed*.

3. (A); Synonym. *Unkempt* and *untidy* have the same meaning, as do *unorganized* and *disorderly*.

4. (A); Antonym. *Volatile,* which means changeable or shifting, means the opposite of *stable*. *Exciting* and *dull* also have opposite meanings.

5. (B); Action and Related Object. You *transcribe notes,* just as you *translate* a *language*.

6. (A); Part and Whole. An *equation* is part of *mathematics,* just as a *statement* is part of *language*.

7. (A); Degree. *Frenzied* and *upset* are similar in meaning, but *frenzied* suggests rushed activity. In the same way, *ecstatic* suggests a stronger degree of response than *pleased*.

8. (E); Antonym. *Liability* and *advantage* have nearly opposite meanings, as do *debt* and *credit*.

9. (D); Synonym. *Dubious* and *questionable* have nearly the same meaning, as do *rough* and *uneven*.

10. (E); Synonym. *Grueling* and *exhausting* have similar meanings, as do *thrilling* and *exciting*.

Lesson 14   page 139

1. (E); Synonym. *Drastic* and *severe* have nearly the same meaning, as do *stormy* and *violent*.

2. (A); Performer and Related Action. *Thugs intimidate* their victims, just as *champs celebrate* their victories.

3. (B); Synonym. To *promenade* is to *walk,* just as to *lounge* is to *lie*.

4. (D); Antonym. *Instigate,* or start, means the opposite of *halt*. *Oppose* and *promote* are also opposite in meaning.

5. (B); Characteristic Quality. A *gymnast* is characteristically *nimble,* or agile, just as a *tiger* is characteristically *wild*.

6. (E); Synonym. Taking the *initiative* in a situation is the same as taking the *first step,* just as a *regulation* is the same thing as a *rule.*

7. (A); Synonym. *Alteration* and *change* have nearly the same meaning, as do *method* and *system.*

8. (C); Part and Whole. *Songs* are part of a *medley,* just as *vegetables* are part of a *salad.*

9. (E); Antonym. *Discreet,* or cautious, means the opposite of *careless. Proud* means the opposite of *ashamed.*

10. (A); Synonym. *Indivisible* and *united* have similar meanings, as do *unspoiled* and *fresh.*

Lesson 15   page 140

1. (A); Cause and Effect. A *vaccination* can result in *immunity* to a disease, just as *exercise* can result in *strength.*

2. (A); Antonym. *Agility* is the opposite of *sluggishness,* just as *angularity* is the opposite of *roundness.*

3. (A); Synonym. *Wary* and *cautious* have the same meaning, as do *funny* and *comic.*

4. (D); Synonym. *Surpass* means nearly the same thing as *excel,* just as *harm* means nearly the same thing as *hurt.*

5. (A); Antonym. *Dwindle,* which means to lessen, is opposite in meaning to *increase. Appear* means the opposite of *vanish.*

6. (C); Synonym. *Comply* and *obey* have the same meaning, as do *adjust* and *adapt.*

7. (A); Antonym. *Contaminate,* or pollute, means the opposite of *purify. Destroy* and *build* also have opposite meanings.

8. (D); Action and Related Object. You *expend,* or use, *resources,* just as you *spend money.*

9. (A); Antonym. *Nonchalant,* or unconcerned, means the opposite of *concerned. Sloppy* and *orderly* also have opposite meanings.

10. (B); Synonym. *Retract,* which means to pull back, means nearly the same as *withdraw. Accuse* and *blame* also have nearly the same meaning.

▮ READING NEW WORDS IN CONTEXT

Lesson 1   pages 143–148
Exercise 1   Finding Synonyms
Answers will vary. The following are possible responses.

1. disaster	11. whole
2. resupply	12. deeply felt
3. depress	13. surrounded by land
4. severe difficulties	14. aggressive
5. angered	15. work out
6. give out	16. skill
7. reveal	17. horrible
8. eliminate	18. fade away
9. records	19. not noticeable
10. a story of a hero	20. wander

Exercise 2   Reading Strategically
1. D   2. A   3. B   4. D   5. C   6. D   7. E   8. A
9. B   10. E   11. A   12. C   13. D   14. C   15. B
16. A   17. E   18. B   19. B   20. C

Lesson 2   pages 149–154
Exercise 1   Finding Synonyms
Answers will vary. The following are possible responses.

1. kings	11. think seriously
2. friendship	12. search
3. of the Middle Ages	13. bring back
4. devoted	14. fortress
5. clothing	15. tempt
6. respectable	16. damage
7. inherited	17. messenger
8. code of knighthood	18. drink
9. skill	19. warning
10. endure	20. person who makes heraldry

Exercise 2   Reading Strategically
1. A   2. C   3. B   4. C   5. E   6. C   7. A   8. E
9. A   10. B   11. B   12. B   13. A   14. C   15. A
16. B   17. E   18. A   19. B   20. E

Lesson 3   pages 155–160
Exercise 1   Finding Synonyms
Answers will vary. The following are possible responses.

1. large	11. obedient
2. silly	12. sad
3. disturbance	13. excessive pride
4. family history	14. self-righteous
5. spooky	15. distant
6. ghost	16. starts a fire
7. immoral	17. rejects
8. preoccupation	18. patron
9. marshes	19. desires
10. deals with	20. boils

Exercise 2   Reading Strategically
1. D   2. A   3. B   4. A   5. C   6. E   7. B   8. E
9. B   10. C   11. D   12. C   13. C   14. C   15. B
16. A   17. E   18. A   19. A   20. C

Lesson 4   pages 161–166
Exercise 1   Finding Synonyms
Answers will vary. The following are possible responses.

1. the path of the planets	11. plants
2. characteristic	12. animals
3. weird	13. violent change
4. related	14. meat-eating
5. concerned with human beings	15. invade
6. a humanlike being	16. the opposite of an expectation
7. preying	17. gets along with
8. moving away from a center	18. large group
9. put up with	19. section
10. grainy	20. stale

Exercise 2   Reading Strategically
1. C   2. A   3. B   4. A   5. A   6. E   7. D   8. B
9. C   10. B   11. E   12. D   13. A   14. D   15. E
16. B   17. C   18. C   19. D   20. E

Lesson 5   pages 167–172
Exercise 1   Finding Synonyms
Answers will vary. The following are possible responses.

1. gruesome
2. threatening
3. deadly
4. theft
5. the high point
6. misinterpret
7. unimportant
8. control
9. difficult to deal with
10. license; important papers
11. good-natured
12. extraordinary
13. potential
14. complainant
15. ridiculous
16. defender
17. unproven
18. plot
19. sufficient number
20. trick

Exercise 2   Reading Strategically
1. C   2. A   3. B   4. E   5. D   6. D   7. C   8. B
9. E   10. A   11. B   12. D   13. C   14. B   15. C
16. D   17. A   18. E   19. E   20. E

Lesson 6   pages 173–178
Exercise 1   Finding Synonyms
Answers will vary. The following are possible responses.

1. impossible to understand
2. a scornful, or negative, person
3. dull
4. expecting the worst
5. hate
6. evil
7. hard-working
8. hateful
9. trick
10. pleasant
11. stupid
12. showy
13. an outgoing person
14. an important business person
15. perfectly
16. agreeableness
17. continually
18. limit
19. friendly
20. disrespectful

Exercise 2   Reading Strategically
1. A   2. C   3. A   4. C   5. B   6. B   7. C   8. A
9. A   10. D   11. B   12. C   13. C   14. D   15. E
16. E   17. B   18. A   19. D   20. D

Lesson 7   pages 179–184
Exercise 1   Finding Synonyms
Answers will vary. The following are possible responses.

1. mismatched
2. admit
3. respect
4. later
5. use
6. exclude
7. escape
8. example
9. difficult
10. apply
11. overcome
12. enemy
13. throw out
14. careless
15. cheat
16. unable to read
17. dependent
18. a liquid substance
19. fights
20. change

Exercise 2   Reading Strategically
1. C   2. B   3. C   4. A   5. B   6. E   7. A   8. E
9. A   10. C   11. D   12. A   13. D   14. C   15. D
16. E   17. E   18. D   19. B   20. C

Lesson 8   pages 185–190
Exercise 1   Finding Synonyms
Answers will vary. The following are possible responses.

1. enlivening
2. in agreement
3. entry
4. distressing

5. trip
6. dark
7. glowing
8. gloomy
9. indifference
10. good
11. in the opposite way
12. waterfall
13. food
14. tempting
15. sharp
16. hungry
17. to make sick
18. lively
19. continual
20. cheerful

Exercise 2   Reading Strategically
1. C   2. C   3. A   4. B   5. A   6. D   7. D   8. C
9. D   10. E   11. E   12. E   13. A   14. B   15. A
16. B   17. C   18. E   19. D   20. C

Lesson 9   pages 191–196
Exercise 1   Finding Synonyms
Answers will vary. The following are possible responses.

1. bliss
2. most
3. old saying
4. difficulty
5. mean
6. inactive
7. bring together
8. require
9. references
10. deeply
11. mistaken idea
12. stormy
13. irritating
14. not literal
15. a direct comparison
16. a comparison using the words *like* or *as*
17. rhythm
18. power
19. can't be made simpler
20. serious

Exercise 2   Reading Strategically
1. E   2. B   3. A   4. C   5. A   6. D   7. E   8. B
9. E   10. B   11. A   12. C   13. A   14. D   15. A
16. D   17. C   18. C   19. B   20. E

Lesson 10   pages 197–202
Exercise 1   Finding Synonyms
Answers will vary. The following are possible responses.

1. clever
2. prolonged applause
3. list
4. elaborate
5. platform
6. very small
7. judgment
8. frenzied
9. not loud enough to be heard
10. public speaking
11. the rise and fall of the voice
12. a private speech revealing a character's thoughts
13. a person who imitates others
14. conventional
15. a reproduction
16. a three-legged stand
17. small porch
18. a wide, unbroken scene
19. divide in two
20. repeat performance

Exercise 2   Reading Strategically
1. C   2. A   3. D   4. B   5. E   6. A   7. E   8. D
9. C   10. A   11. D   12. B   13. C   14. C   15. B
16. B   17. E   18. D   19. E   20. D

Lesson 11   pages 203–208
Exercise 1   Finding Synonyms
Answers will vary. The following are possible responses.

1. pamphlet
2. to turn aside
3. point of view
4. notorious
5. put down
6. lacking
7. inevitability
8. sarcastic
9. a list of books
10. about a person's life

11. arouse
12. law
13. authority
14. a star-shaped symbol
15. a killer
16. in time order
17. a time of economic trouble
18. able to use a language
19. written in two languages
20. cleanliness

Exercise 2   Reading Strategically
1. B   2. A   3. B   4. C   5. D   6. D   7. A   8. A
9. E   10. C   11. D   12. E   13. A   14. B   15. C
16. B   17. D   18. E   19. C   20. D

Lesson 12   pages 209–214
Exercise 1   Finding Synonyms
Answers will vary. The following are possible responses.
1. perpetual
2. touched
3. hopeful
4. climb
5. limit
6. unimportant
7. noticeable
8. having an influence
9. most important thing
10. beyond measure
11. a state of importance
12. hesitant
13. praises
14. relevant
15. available
16. lacking significance
17. someone who trespasses
18. heavy
19. awkward
20. too early

Exercise 2   Reading Strategically
1. D   2. E   3. C   4. B   5. A   6. B   7. C   8. E
9. D   10. E   11. A   12. A   13. C   14. C   15. B
16. D   17. E   18. A   19. E   20. B

Lesson 13   pages 215–220
Exercise 1   Finding Synonyms
Answers will vary. The following are possible responses.
1. major
2. doubtful
3. show
4. a balanced group of elements
5. most essential part
6. hesitant
7. irritating
8. drawback
9. explosive
10. conceitedness
11. work together
12. independent
13. careless
14. difficult
15. wildly excited
16. write down
17. effective
18. disturb
19. almost
20. messy

Exercise 2   Reading Strategically
1. A   2. B   3. B   4. C   5. C   6. D   7. E   8. C
9. B   10. A   11. D   12. E   13. D   14. B   15. E
16. D   17. A   18. E   19. C   20. D

Lesson 14   pages 221–226
Exercise 1   Finding Synonyms
Answers will vary. The following are possible responses.
1. disbelieving
2. close
3. scold
4. plot
5. enterprise
6. changes
7. major
8. occur
9. secretive
10. make afraid
11. start
12. an action to stop something
13. cannot be recovered
14. twisted
15. have prejudice
16. rowdy
17. a dance

18. agile
19. collection
20. something given as an apology

Exercise 2   Reading Strategically
1. D   2. B   3. C   4. A   5. A   6. B   7. C   8. B
9. D   10. C   11. A   12. C   13. C   14. B   15. D
16. B   17. A   18. C   19. E   20. B

Lesson 15   pages 227–232
Exercise 1   Finding Synonyms
Answers will vary. The following are possible responses.
1. facade
2. casual
3. frustrate
4. vulnerable
5. cautious
6. evaluate
7. spend
8. security
9. exceed
10. decrease
11. protection
12. pass
13. expression of sorrow
14. pollute
15. take back
16. upkeep
17. dropped in value
18. nimbleness
19. exit
20. go along with

Exercise 2   Reading Strategically
1. E   2. E   3. A   4. B   5. C   6. C   7. A   8. C
9. D   10. B   11. A   12. A   13. B   14. C   15. E
16. B   17. C   18. C   19. C   20. A

USING NEW WORDS ON TESTS

FORMATIVE ASSESSMENT
Test 1   page 3
1. C   2. C   3. B   4. E   5. C   6. E   7. D   8. A
9. D   10. D
Test 2   page 4
1. A   2. B   3. E   4. C   5. D   6. A   7. E   8. D
9. C   10. B
Test 3   page 5
1. E   2. B   3. D   4. B   5. B   6. E   7. A   8. C
9. D   10. D
Test 4   page 6
1. D   2. A   3. B   4. D   5. B   6. E   7. C   8. C
9. C   10. B
Test 5   page 7
1. B   2. D   3. C   4. C   5. C   6. D   7. D   8. E
9. B   10. A
Test 6   page 8
1. A   2. A   3. D   4. C   5. B   6. C   7. B   8. E
9. C   10. A
Test 7   page 9
1. B   2. A   3. D   4. B   5. D   6. C   7. C   8. E
9. A   10. A
Test 8   page 10
1. E   2. B   3. D   4. B   5. C   6. A   7. D   8. C
9. C   10. A
Test 9   page 11
1. D   2. B   3. E   4. A   5. D   6. C   7. A   8. B
9. E   10. C
Test 10   page 12
1. D   2. E   3. D   4. A   5. C   6. B   7. C   8. C
9. A   10. A

Test 11   page 13
1. D   2. A   3. D   4. E   5. A   6. C   7. A   8. D
9. C   10. B
Test 12   page 14
1. D   2. B   3. D   4. E   5. C   6. E   7. B   8. B
9. D   10. A
Test 13   page 15
1. A   2. C   3. B   4. C   5. D   6. B   7. E   8. A
9. C   10. C
Test 14   page 16
1. D   2. C   3. A   4. E   5. E   6. B   7. B   8. D
9. B   10. B
Test 15   page 17
1. D   2. E   3. A   4. B   5. C   6. A   7. B   8. C
9. A   10. D
Test 16   page 18
1. C   2. E   3. B   4. C   5. B   6. B   7. C   8. E
9. D   10. A
Test 17   page 19
1. B   2. D   3. A   4. C   5. A   6. A   7. B   8. E
9. C   10. D
Test 18   page 20
1. A   2. E   3. D   4. B   5. C   6. C   7. C   8. E
9. B   10. D
Test 19   page 21
1. A   2. E   3. A   4. B   5. E   6. C   7. A   8. A
9. D   10. C
Test 20   page 22
1. E   2. D   3. C   4. A   5. D   6. C   7. A   8. C
9. B   10. D
Test 21   page 23
1. B   2. C   3. A   4. C   5. A   6. E   7. A   8. D
9. C   10. D
Test 22   page 24
1. D   2. B   3. D   4. C   5. E   6. D   7. C   8. D
9. D   10. A
Test 23   page 25
1. C   2. A   3. B   4. B   5. E   6. B   7. A   8. A
9. C   10. D
Test 24   page 26
1. B   2. A   3. A   4. D   5. C   6. C   7. C   8. C
9. B   10. E
Test 25   page 27
1. C   2. A   3. B   4. E   5. A   6. C   7. C   8. D
9. B   10. D
Test 26   page 28
1. C   2. C   3. A   4. B   5. C   6. B   7. E   8. D
9. B   10. D
Test 27   page 29
1. E   2. C   3. B   4. D   5. E   6. B   7. D   8. B
9. A   10. B
Test 28   page 30
1. C   2. B   3. C   4. C   5. B   6. E   7. A   8. A
9. A   10. D
Test 29   page 31
1. B   2. C   3. B   4. E   5. C   6. A   7. D   8. B
9. B   10. A
Test 30   page 32
1. C   2. A   3. D   4. A   5. C   6. D   7. C   8. A
9. D   10. E

SUMMATIVE ASSESSMENT

Test 1 Part A   pages 35–38
1. D   2. B   3. D   4. A   5. C   6. A   7. B   8. E
9. B   10. C   11. C   12. E   13. C   14. B   15. D
16. D   17. C   18. A   19. E   20. B
Test 1 Part B   pages 39–43
21. A   22. B   23. E   24. D   25. D   26. C   27. B
28. B   29. E   30. C   31. A   32. D   33. A   34. B
35. C   36. A   37. E   38. D   39. C   40. B   41. E
42. A   43. C   44. B   45. A   46. D   47. C   48. E
49. E   50. A   51. C   52. B   53. C   54. B   55. A
56. D   57. E   58. E   59. C   60. C   61. B   62. A
63. D   64. B   65. B   66. A   67. A   68. C   69. D
70. E
Test 1 Part C   pages 44–46
71. (E); Synonym. *Amity* and *friendship* have similar meanings, as do *richness* and *wealth*.
72. (A); Synonym. *Assault* and *attack* are similar in meaning, as are *agitation* and *commotion*.
73. (D); Characteristic Quality. A *tiger* is characteristically *carnivorous,* or meat-eating, just as a *monkey* is characteristically *acrobatic.*
74. (D); Performer and Related Action. One expects a *cast* to *perform,* just as one expects a *horde* of people to *wander.*
75. (D); Synonym. *Centrifugal,* which means moving out from the center, has a meaning similar to *outward. Heated* and *warm* also have similar meanings.
76. (A); Synonym. *Changeless* and *monotonous* have similar meanings, as do *superfluous* and *excessive.*
77. (E); Characteristic Quality. *Credentials* are characteristically *written,* just as a *speech* is characteristically *uttered.*
78. (C); Part and Whole. *Conflict* is an element of *drama,* just as *contrast* is an element of *irony.*
79. (D); Part and Whole. *France* is a country in *Europe,* just as *Aquarius* is a constellation in the *zodiac.*
80. (B); Classification. A *rabbit* is classified as *fauna,* or animal life, just as a *tree* is classified as *vegetation,* or plant life.
81. (A); Classification. A *tree* is classified as *flora,* or plant life, just as *yellow* is classified as a *color.*
82. (C); Part and Whole. A *grandparent,* like all your relatives, is a part of your *genealogy,* or family history, in the same way that an *item* is a part of a *list.*
83. (C); Characteristic Quality. *Sugar* is characteristically *granular,* just as *mayonnaise* is characteristically *smooth.*
84. (C); Cause and Effect. An *infection* can cause an *inflammation,* just as a *virus* can cause a *disease.*
85. (A); Classification. *Larceny,* or theft, is classified as a *crime.* An *apple* is classified as a *fruit.*
86. (C); Synonym. *Makeup* and *cosmetics* have the same meaning, as do *garb* and *clothing.*

87. (A); Synonym. *Manifest,* which means show, means the same thing as *reveal. Endure,* which means to hold out or last, has a meaning similar to *persist.*

88. (E); Synonym. *Meander* and *wander* have similar meanings, as do *wiggle* and *squirm.*

89. (D); Performer and Related Action. A *diplomat negotiates* with other countries, just as a *lawyer settles* a lawsuit.

90. (E); Performer and Related Action. A *plaintiff* is someone who *sues,* or files a lawsuit. A *tailor* is someone who *sews* clothing.

91. (D); Synonym. *Predict* and *forecast* have similar meanings, as do *recede* and *withdrawal.*

92. (D); Performer and Related Action. One expects a *quorum* of people to *decide,* just as one expects a *senate* to *debate.*

93. (E); Degree. To *replenish* something is to *provide* it again when it runs out. To *refill* something is to *fill* it again.

94. (E); Synonym. *Speak* and *talk* have similar meanings, as do *moor,* as in to *moor* a boat, and *secure.*

95. (B); Antonym. *Still* and *active* have opposite meanings, as do *stagnant* and *moving.*

96. (E); Synonym. *Territory* and *region* have similar meanings, as do *sector* and *division.*

97. (D); Degree. *Tolerate* and *endure* have similar meanings but differ in degree: *Endure* implies withstanding much greater suffering. *Torment* and *torture* are also similar, but to *torture* is more severe than to *torment.*

98. (C); Antonym. *Valued* means the opposite of *scorned. Intact,* or whole, means the opposite of *damaged.*

99. (B); Synonym. *Vital* and *essential* have the same meaning, as do *lethal* and *deadly.*

100. (B); Performer and Related Action. A *winner* is someone who *triumphs.* An *advocate* is someone who *supports* someone else.

Test 2 Part A   pages 47–50

1. D   2. B   3. A   4. B   5. C   6. E   7. E   8. D
9. A   10. B   11. B   12. A   13. D   14. E   15. C
16. C   17. A   18. B   19. A   20. D

Test 2 Part B   pages 51–55

21. D   22. B   23. A   24. B   25. C   26. E   27. E
28. D   29. A   30. B   31. B   32. A   33. D   34. E
35. C   36. C   37. E   38. A   39. B   40. C   41. D
42. B   43. A   44. B   45. C   46. E   47. E   48. D
49. A   50. B   51. C   52. A   53. D   54. E   55. C
56. C   57. E   58. A   59. B   60. D   61. D   62. B
63. A   64. B   65. C   66. E   67. E   68. D   69. A
70. B

Test 2 Part C   pages 56–58

71. (C); Characteristic Quality. *Sandpaper* is characteristically *abrasive,* or gritty, just as *milk* is characteristically *wet.*

72. (C); Degree. To *adore* is to *like* to an extreme extent. To *wrangle* is to *disagree* to the extent of an argument or a fistfight.

73. (D); Synonym. *Begin* and *start* have similar meanings. *Defraud,* or cheat, has a meaning similar to *disagree.*

74. (E); Characteristic Quality. A *bee* is characteristically *busy,* just as an *ant* is characteristically *diligent,* or hard-working.

75. (B); Synonym. *Cadence* and *beat* have the same meaning, as do *melody* and *tune.*

76. (D); Antonym. *Calming* and *upsetting* are opposite in meaning, as are *tantalizing* and *repulsive.*

77. (E); Synonym. All four words have the meaning of ongoing.

78. (B); Classification. *Yellow* is classified as a *color,* just as *breakfast* is classified as a *repast,* or meal.

79. (D); Synonym. *Common* and *ordinary* have similar meanings. *Obtuse,* or dense, has a meaning similar to *dull.*

80. (C); Synonym. *Congruent,* which means in agreement or corresponding, has a meaning similar to *harmonious. Precise* and *exact* also have similar meanings.

81. (A); Synonym. *Create* and *invent* have the same meaning. *Denote,* which means signify, has the same meaning as *mean* when *mean* is a verb.

82. (A); Antonym. *Curious* and *disinterested* are opposite in meaning. *Animated,* which means lively, is opposite in meaning to *depressed.*

83. (A); Synonym. *Elude* and *escape* have similar meanings, as do *trap* and *catch.*

84. (E); Synonym. *Impartial* and *fair* have the same meaning, as do *unbroken* and *whole.*

85. (D); Degree. *Incandescent* is similar in meaning to *bright,* but much stronger, just as *gigantic* implies greater size than *big* does.

86. (B); Synonym. *Incessant,* or never-ending, has a meaning similar to *constant. Earnest* and *sincere* also have similar meanings.

87. (E); Synonym. *Inverse* and *opposite* have similar meanings, as do *cautious* and *careful.*

88. (A); Synonym. *Jovial* and *jolly* have similar meanings, as do *valuable* and *precious.*

89. (E); Antonym. *Lax* and *strict* are opposite in meaning, as are *gentle* and *harsh.*

90. (E); Synonym. *Magnificence* and *splendor* have similar meanings, just as *rapture,* or joy, has a meaning similar to *ecstasy.*

91. (A); Antonym. *Malicious,* or mean, is opposite in meaning to *kind. Scarce* and *abundant* are also opposite in meaning.

92. (D); Antonym. *Opaque* and *transparent* have opposite meanings, as do *common* and *rare.*

93. (E); Characteristic Quality. A *panorama,* which is a broad vista or view, is characteristically *wide,* just as *lace* is characteristically *delicate.*

94. (D); Characteristic Quality. A *patio,* or outer courtyard, is characteristically *outside.* A *skyscraper* is characteristically *tall.*

95. (E); Synonym. *Portion* and *part* have similar meanings, as do *quota* and *share* (the noun form).

96. (A); Antonym. *Problem* means the opposite of *solution*. *Hindrance,* which means obstacle, means the opposite of *help*.

97. (D); Synonym. *Pungent* and *sharp* have similar meanings, as do *lively* and *active*.

98. (A); Synonym. *Reverent* and *respectful* have similar meanings. *Impertinent,* which means not showing proper respect, has a meaning similar to *rude*.

99. (D); Characteristic Quality. A *tripod* is characteristically *three-legged,* just as a *bicycle* is characteristically *two-wheeled*.

100. (E); Degree. *Scrub* is stronger in degree than *wipe*. *Mince,* which means finely dice, is stronger in degree than *bisect,* which means cut in half.

Test 3 Part A   pages 59–62
1. C   2. B   3. A   4. C   5. A   6. B   7. D   8. E
9. D   10. E   11. A   12. E   13. C   14. B   15. C
16. B   17. D   18. D   19. C   20. A

Test 3 Part B   pages 63–68
21. C   22. B   23. A   24. C   25. A   26. B   27. D
28. E   29. D   30. E   31. A   32. E   33. C   34. B
35. D   36. B   37. C   38. B   39. D   40. A   41. C
42. B   43. A   44. C   45. A   46. B   47. D   48. E
49. D   50. E   51. A   52. E   53. C   54. B   55. D
56. B   57. C   58. B   59. D   60. A   61. C   62. B
63. A   64. C   65. A   66. B   67. D   68. D   69. D
70. E

Test 3 Part C   pages 69–71
71. (E); Antonym. *Ashamed* means the opposite of *proud,* just as *discreet,* or careful, means the opposite of *careless*.

72. (B); Classification. An *asterisk* is classified as a *symbol,* just as a *house* is classified as a *building*.

73. (A); Synonym. *Clamber* and *climb* have nearly the same meaning, as do *scamper* and *run*.

74. (C); Synonym. *Comply* and *obey* have the same meaning, as do *adjust* and *adapt*.

75. (B); Action and Related Object. Someone might *compose* a *song,* just as someone might *poach deer*.

76. (A); Antonym. *Contaminate,* or pollute, means the opposite of *purify*. *Destroy* and *build* also have opposite meanings.

77. (E); Degree. A *fatality* is a more serious casualty than an *injury* is, just as *pneumonia* is a more serious illness than a *cold*.

78. (D); Synonym. *Feeling* and *emotion* have similar meanings, as do *hygiene* and *cleanliness*.

79. (A); Degree. *Frenzied,* or frantic, is stronger in degree than *upset*. *Ecstatic* is stronger in degree than *pleased*.

80. (D); Synonym. *Heroic* and *brave* have similar meanings, as do *infamous* and *scandalous*.

81. (C); Antonym. *Hostile* means the opposite of *friendly,* just as *haphazard,* or disorderly, means the opposite of *systematic*.

82. (A); Cause and Effect. A *vaccination* can result in *immunity* to a disease, just as *exercise* can result in *strength*.

83. (B); Synonym. *Initiative* and *enterprise* have similar meanings, as do *calm* and *tranquility*.

84. (A); Performer and Related Action. *Thugs intimidate* their victims, just as *champs celebrate* their victories.

85. (C); Location. A *judge* works in a *jurisdiction,* just as a *salesperson* works in a *territory*.

86. (C); Synonym. To *lounge* is to *lie,* just as to *promenade* is to *walk*.

87. (C); Part and Whole. *Songs* are part of a *medley,* just as *vegetables* are part of a *salad*.

88. (B); Characteristic Quality. A *gymnast* is characteristically *nimble,* just as a *tiger* is characteristically *wild*.

89. (C); Antonym. *Occupy* and *vacate* have opposite meanings. *Dissuade,* or discourage, is opposite in meaning to *encourage*.

90. (D); Antonym. *Oppose* and *promote* are opposite in meaning. *Instigate,* or start, means the opposite of *halt*.

91. (E); Synonym. *Original* and *fresh* have similar meanings. *Ponderous,* which means massive, has a meaning similar to *bulky*.

92. (D); Synonym. *Perceptible* and *noticeable* have nearly the same meaning, as do *necessary* and *needed*.

93. (D); Synonym. *Rough* and *uneven* have nearly the same meaning, as do *dubious* and *questionable*.

94. (C); Classification. A *sofa* is classified as a *furnishing,* just as a *perennial* is classified as a *plant*.

95. (A); Part and Whole. A *statement* is part of *language,* just as an *equation* is part of *mathematics*.

96. (D); Classification. A *statute* is classified as a *law,* just as a *fine* is classified as a *penalty*.

97. (E); Synonym. *Stormy* and *violent* have nearly the same meaning, as do *drastic* and *severe*.

98. (C); Synonym. *Strange* and *odd* have similar meanings, as do *applicable* and *appropriate*.

99. (B); Action and Related Object. You *transcribe notes,* just as you *translate* a *language*.

100. (A); Synonym. *Unorganized* and *disorderly* have the same meaning, as do *unkempt* and *tidy*.

Fourth Course

Lesson 1   pages 3–6
Exercise 1   Mapping
Your Guess and Definition answers will vary. Possible responses to Other Forms items follow.
1. *n.* acquitter, acquittance; *vt.* acquit
2. *n.* asserter, assertion, assertiveness; *vt.* asserts, asserting; *adj.* assertive, assertable, assertional, assertory; *adv.* assertively
3. *n.* condescendence, condescension, condescender; *vi.* condescends, condescending; *adj.* condescending; *adv.* condescendingly
4. *n.* contempt, contemptuousness; *adv.* contemptuously
5. *n.* elitism, elitist; *adj.* elitist
6. *n.* evolvement, evolution, evolutionist, evolutionism; *vi.* or *vt.* evolves, evolving; *adj.* evolvable, evolutional, evolutionistic, evolutionary; *adv.* evolutionally, evolutionistically, evolutionarily
7. *vi.* or *vt.* fortify; *adj.* fortitudinous
8. *n.* inarticulateness; *adv.* inarticulately
9. *n.* mentorship; *n. pl.* mentors
10. *n.* notoriousness; *adj.* notorious; *adv.* notoriously

Exercise 2   Context Clues
11. (E) fortitude
12. (G) condescended
13. (D) evolved
14. (I) notoriety
15. (A) asserted
16. (J) acquittal
17. (H) elite
18. (B) mentor
19. (C) inarticulate
20. (F) contemptuous

Exercise 3   Sentence Completion
21. E   22. D   23. C   24. B   25. A   26. C   27. E
28. D   29. A   30. B

Lesson 2   pages 7–10
Exercise 1   Mapping
Your Guess and Definition answers will vary. Possible responses to Other Forms items follow.
1. *n.* analogue, analogist, analogousness; *vi.* or *vt.* analogize; *adj.* analogous, analogical; *adv.* analogically, analogously
2. *n.* antiquary, antique, antiqueness, antiquarianism, antiquation, antiquatedness; *vt.* antiquate; *vi.* or *vt.* antique; *adj.* antique, antiquarian, antiquated; *adv.* antiquely
3. *n.* elector; *vi.* or *vt.* elect; *adj.* electoral
4. *n.* ethic, ethicalness, ethicality, ethicist, ethician; *n. pl.* ethics; *adv.* ethically
5. *n.* excerption; *n. pl.* excerpts; *vt.* excerpts, excerpted, excerpting
6. *n.* heretic, hereticalness; *adj.* heretical; *adv.* heretically
7. *n.* paternalism, paternalist, paternity; *adj.* paternalistic; *adv.* paternally, paternalistically
8. *n.* pauperism, pauperization; *vt.* pauperize
9. *n.* posthumousness; *adv.* posthumously
10. *n.* prophet, prophecy, prophesier, propheticalness; *vi.* or *vt.* prophesy; *adj.* prophetical; *adv.* prophetically

Exercise 2   Context Clues
11. (H) paupers
12. (C) excerpt
13. (E) analogy
14. (B) ethical
15. (D) prophetic
16. (I) heresy
17. (A) paternal
18. (F) antiquity
19. (J) posthumous
20. (G) electorate

Exercise 3   Sentence Completion
21. D   22. C   23. E   24. D   25. E   26. C   27. C
28. A   29. D   30. B

Lesson 3   pages 11–14
Exercise 1   Mapping
Your Guess and Definition answers will vary. Possible responses to Other Forms items follow.
1. *n.* amiability, amiableness; *adv.* amiably
2. *n.* anthropologist; *adj.* anthropological; *adv.* anthropologically
3. *n. pl.* bayous
4. *n.* grimacer; *n. pl.* grimaces; *vi.* grimaces, grimaced, grimacing
5. *n.* indomitableness; *adv.* indomitably
6. *n.* malleability, malleableness; *adv.* malleably
7. *n.* melodrama, melodramatist; *n. pl.* melodramatics; *adv.* melodramatically
8. *vi.* succumbs, succumbed, succumbing
9. *adj.* visaged
10. *n.* whim, whimsy, whimsicality, whimsicalness; *adv.* whimsically

Exercise 2   Context Clues
11. (C) malleable
12. (G) amiable
13. (D) anthropology
14. (J) melodramatic
15. (B) grimace
16. (F) indomitable
17. (H) succumb
18. (A) bayou
19. (I) whimsical
20. (E) visage

Exercise 3   Sentence Completion
21. C   22. E   23. B   24. D   25. A   26. D   27. B
28. C   29. B   30. E

Lesson 4   pages 15–18
Exercise 1   Mapping
Your Guess and Definition answers will vary. Possible responses to Other Forms items follow.
1. *n.* apprehensiveness, apprehension, apprehensibility; *vt.* apprehend; *adj.* apprehensible; *adv.* apprehensively, apprehensibly
2. *n.* callousness; *vi.* or *vt.* callouses, calloused, callousing; *adv.* callously
3. *n.* commendation, commendableness; *vt.* commend; *adj.* commendatory; *adv.* commendably
4. *n.* indignation, indignity; *n. pl.* indignities; *adv.* indignantly
5. *n.* ineffectuality, ineffectualness; *adv.* ineffectually
6. *n.* judiciousness; *adv.* judiciously

7. *n.* mysticalness, mysticism; *n. pl.* mystics; *adj.* mystical; *adv.* mystically
8. *n.* paraphraser; *vt.* paraphrases, paraphrasing; *adj.* paraphrastic, paraphrastical, paraphrasable; *adv.* paraphrastically
9. *n.* personifier; *vt.* personify
10. None

Exercise 2   Context Clues

11. (I) callous	16. (B) commendable
12. (J) mystic	17. (D) judicious
13. (H) indignant	18. (A) personification
14. (G) verbatim	19. (E) ineffectual
15. (F) paraphrased	20. (C) apprehensive

Exercise 3   Sentence Completion

21. C   22. B   23. D   24. A   25. E   26. C   27. E
28. D   29. B   30. A

Lesson 5   pages 19–22
Exercise 1   Mapping

Your Guess and Definition answers will vary. Possible responses to Other Forms items follow.

1. *n.* affiliation; *n. pl.* affiliates; *vi.* or *vt.* affiliates, affiliated, affiliating
2. *n.* ecstasy; *adv.* ecstatically
3. *n.* encumbrance, encumbrancer; *vt.* encumbers, encumbering
4. *n.* invariability, invariableness, invariance; *adj.* invariable, invariant
5. *n.* plausibility, plausibleness; *adv.* plausibly
6. *n.* pomposity, pompousness; *adv.* pompously
7. *n.* portliness; *adj.* portlier, portliest
8. *adj.* proximate, proximateness; *adv.* proximately
9. *n.* rejuvenation, rejuvenator, rejuvenescence; *vt.* rejuvenates, rejuvenating; *adj.* rejuvenescent
10. *adv.* unprecedentedly

Exercise 2   Context Clues

11. (A) invariably	16. (H) encumbered
12. (I) proximity	17. (D) unprecedented
13. (C) affiliates	18. (B) ecstatic
14. (J) rejuvenated	19. (F) pompous
15. (E) portly	20. (G) plausible

Exercise 3   Sentence Completion

21. A   22. E   23. B   24. E   25. D   26. C   27. D
28. B   29. A   30. C

Lesson 6   pages 23–26
Exercise 1   Mapping

Your Guess and Definition answers will vary. Possible responses to Other Forms items follow.

1. *n.* ascertainment; *vt.* ascertains, ascertained, ascertaining; *adj.* ascertainable
2. *n.* atrociousness, atrocity; *adv.* atrociously
3. *vt.* compassionate; *adj.* compassionate; *adv.* compassionately
4. *n.* composedness; *vt.* compose; *adj.* composed; *adv.* composedly
5. *n.* deterioration; *vt.* deteriorates, deteriorated, deteriorating; *adj.* deteriorative
6. *n.* insipidity; *adv.* insipidly

7. *n.* lamentation; *n. pl.* laments; *vt.* laments, lamented, lamenting; *adj.* lamentable; *adv.* lamentably, lamentedly
8. *n.* loathing, loather, loathsomeness; *vt.* loathes, loathed, loathing; *adj.* loathsome; *adv.* loathsomely
9. *adv.* painstakingly
10. *n.* repression, repressiveness, repressor, represser; *vt.* represses, repressed, repressing; *adj.* repressed, repressive, repressible; *adv.* repressively

Exercise 2   Context Clues

11. (F) insipid	16. (E) ascertain
12. (D) painstaking	17. (C) repress
13. (I) deteriorate	18. (H) loathe
14. (B) lament	19. (A) composure
15. (J) compassion	20. (G) atrocious

Exercise 3   Sentence Completion

21. B   22. D   23. C   24. E   25. A   26. D   27. C
28. B   29. A   30. E

Lesson 7   pages 27–30
Exercise 1   Mapping

Your Guess and Definition answers will vary. Possible responses to Other Forms items follow.

1. *n.* aesthete, aesthetician, aestheticism; *n. pl.* aesthetics; *adj.* aesthetical; *adv.* aesthetically
2. *n.* charism; *n. pl.* charismata; *adj.* charismatic
3. *n. pl.* clichés; *adj.* clichéd
4. *n.* conception, conceivability; *vt.* conceives, conceiving; *adj.* conceivable; *adv.* conceivably
5. *n.* emphasis; *n. pl.* emphases; *vt.* emphasize; *adj.* emphatic
6. *n.* martialism, martialist; *adv.* martially
7. *n.* paradoxicalness; *n. pl.* paradoxes; *adj.* paradoxical; *adv.* paradoxically
8. *n.* prolificacy; *vt.* proliferate; *adj.* proliferous; *adv.* prolifically
9. *n.* recipience, recipiency; *n. pl.* recipients
10. *n.* wanness; *adj.* wanner, wannest; *adv.* wanly

Exercise 2   Context Clues

11. (C) martial	16. (I) charisma
12. (D) cliché	17. (J) recipients
13. (A) prolific	18. (G) emphatically
14. (F) wan	19. (E) paradoxes
15. (H) aesthetic	20. (B) conceived

Exercise 3   Sentence Completion

21. E   22. C   23. A   24. B   25. D   26. D   27. C
28. E   29. A   30. B

Lesson 8   pages 31–34
Exercise 1   Mapping

Your Guess and Definition answers will vary. Possible responses to Other Forms items follow.

1. *n.* fabrication, fabricator; *vt.* fabricates, fabricating
2. *n.* impeder; *vt.* impede
3. *n.* mediocrity; *n. pl.* mediocrities
4. *n. pl.* miens

5. *n.* opportunity, opportuneness, opportunism; *adj.* opportunistic; *adv.* opportunely, opportunistically
6. *adj.* qualmish; *adv.* qualmishly
7. *n.* reaction; *n. pl.* reactionaries; *adj.* reactional
8. *adj.* staminal
9. *n.* zealot, zealotry, zeal, zealousness; *adv.* zealously
10. *n. pl.* zephyrs

Exercise 2   Context Clues
11. (D) mien   16. (B) mediocre
12. (E) qualms   17. (I) reactionary
13. (G) zealous   18. (F) fabricated
14. (A) impediments   19. (J) stamina
15. (H) zephyr   20. (C) opportune

Exercise 3   Sentence Completion
21. D   22. C   23. E   24. C   25. B   26. A   27. B
28. E   29. C   30. D

Lesson 9   pages 35–38
Exercise 1   Mapping
Your Guess and Definition answers will vary. Possible responses to Other Forms items follow.
1. *adj.* axiomatic; *adv.* axiomatically
2. *n.* compatibility, compatibleness; *adv.* compatibly
3. *n.* compliancy; *vt.* comply; *adj.* compliant; *adv.* compliantly
4. *n.* inanimateness, inanimation; *adv.* inanimately
5. *n.* indestructibility; *adv.* indestructibly
6. *n.* innateness; *adv.* innately
7. *n.* mutability, mutableness; *adv.* mutably
8. *n.* percept, perceptibility, perceptivity, perceptiveness; *vt.* perceive; *adj.* perceptive, perceptional, perceptual; *adv.* perceptively, perceptibly, perceptually
9. *n.* prevalence; *adv.* prevalently
10. *n. pl.* recourses

Exercise 2   Context Clues
11. (D) innate   16. (H) prevalent
12. (J) recourse   17. (I) compatible
13. (B) mutable   18. (A) perception
14. (E) compliance   19. (F) axiom
15. (C) indestructible   20. (G) inanimate

Exercise 3   Sentence Completion
21. D   22. B   23. E   24. A   25. C   26. E   27. D
28. C   29. A   30. B

Lesson 10   pages 39–42
Exercise 1   Mapping
Your Guess and Definition answers will vary. Possible responses to Other Forms items follow.
1. *n.* encompassment; *vt.* encompassed, encompassing
2. *n.* implacability; *adv.* implacably
3. *n. pl.* incentives
4. *n.* militancy; *n. pl.* militants; *adv.* militantly
5. *n.* pivot; *vt.* pivot; *adv.* pivotally
6. *n.* postulator, postulation, postulant; *n. pl.* postulates; *vt.* postulates, postulated, postulating

7. *adj.* retributive, retributory; *adv.* retributively
8. *n.* stringentness, stringency; *n. pl.* stringencies; *adv.* stringently
9. *n.* transcendence, transcendency; *vt.* transcend, transcended, transcending; *adj.* transcendent, transcendental; *adv.* transcendentally
10. *n.* transitoriness; *adv.* transitorily

Exercise 2   Context Clues
11. (H) militant   16. (J) stringent
12. (G) transitory   17. (D) implacable
13. (A) incentive   18. (I) retributions
14. (B) encompasses   19. (C) pivotal
15. (E) postulate   20. (F) transcends

Exercise 3   Sentence Completion
21. A   22. C   23. E   24. D   25. E   26. B   27. C
28. D   29. A   30. E

Lesson 11   pages 43–46
Exercise 1   Mapping
Your Guess and Definition answers will vary. Possible responses to Other Forms items follow.
1. *n.* autonomist; *adj.* autonomous; *adv.* autonomously
2. *n.* besieger; *vt.* besieges, besieging
3. *n.* devastator; *vt.* devastate; *adj.* devastating; *adv.* devastatingly
4. *n.* inclemency; *adv.* inclemently
5. *n.* latitudinarian, latitudinarianism; *adj.* latitudinal; *adv.* latitudinally
6. *n.* perseveration; *vt.* persevere; *vi.* perseverate; *adj.* perseverant, perseverative; *adv.* perseveringly
7. *n.* precariousness; *adv.* precariously
8. *n.* vulnerability; *adv.* vulnerably
9. *vi.* wanes, waned, waning; *adj.* waney, wanier, waniest
10. *n.* wreaker; *vt.* wreaks, wreaked, wreaking

Exercise 2   Context Clues
11. (E) precarious   16. (I) perseverance
12. (G) devastation   17. (D) autonomy
13. (C) vulnerable   18. (J) wane
14. (A) besieged   19. (H) inclement
15. (F) wreaking   20. (B) latitude

Exercise 3   Sentence Completion
21. B   22. D   23. A   24. E   25. D   26. C   27. C
28. E   29. B   30. A

Lesson 12   pages 47–50
Exercise 1   Mapping
Your Guess and Definition answers will vary. Possible responses to Other Forms items follow.
1. *n.* appeaser, appeasement; *vt.* appeases, appeased, appeasing; *adj.* appeasable
2. *n.* archaism, archaist; *vt.* archaize; *adj.* archaistic; *adv.* archaically, archaistically
3. *n.* balminess; *adj.* balmier, balmiest; *adv.* balmily
4. *n.* beguiler, beguilement; *vi.* or *vt.* beguiles, beguiling; *adv.* beguilingly
5. *n.* commencement, commencer; *vi.* commences, commencing
6. None

7. *vt.* facsimiles, facsimiled, facsimileing
8. *n.* invincibility, invincibleness; *adv.* invincibly
9. *n. pl.* pretexts
10. *n.* vigil, vigilance; *adv.* vigilantly

Exercise 2   Context Clues
11. (J) balmy
12. (A) facsimile
13. (D) vigilant
14. (B) commenced
15. (I) archaic
16. (H) invincible
17. (F) beguiled
18. (C) appease
19. (G) pretext
20. (E) espionage

Exercise 3   Sentence Completion
21. B   22. D   23. A   24. D   25. C   26. E   27. C
28. B   29. D   30. A

Lesson 13   pages 51–54
Exercise 1   Mapping
Your Guess and Definition answers will vary. Possible responses to Other Forms items follow.
1. *vt.* coffers, coffered, coffering
2. *adj.* edificial
3. *n.* hieroglyph; *n. pl.* hieroglyphics; *adj.* hieroglyphical; *adv.* hieroglyphically
4. *n.* inaccessibility; *adv.* inaccessibly
5. *n.* innovator; *vi.* or *vt.* innovate; *adj.* innovative, innovational; *adv.* innovatively
6. *n.* junction; *adj.* junctional
7. *n.* retainment; *vt.* retain; *adj.* retainable
8. *adj.* rivulose
9. *n.* subsidy, subsidization, subsidizer; *vt.* subsidizes, subsidizing
10. *n.* tawniness; *adj.* tawnier, tawniest

Exercise 2   Context Clues
11. (D) junctures
12. (I) tawny
13. (E) hieroglyphics
14. (A) subsidized
15. (C) inaccessible
16. (J) coffer
17. (F) rivulet
18. (H) edifices
19. (G) retainers
20. (B) innovation

Exercise 3   Sentence Completion
21. B   22. D   23. E   24. B   25. C   26. C   27. D
28. A   29. C   30. B

Lesson 14   pages 55–58
Exercise 1   Mapping
Your Guess and Definition answers will vary. Possible responses to Other Forms items follow.
1. *n. pl.* apexes, apices
2. *n.* bourgeoise, bourgeoisie, bourgeoisification; *vt.* bourgeoisify
3. *adj.* canicular
4. *n.* defunctness; *adj.* defunctive
5. None
6. *n.* meagerness; *adv.* meagerly
7. *n.* obliteration, obliterator; *vt.* obliterates, obliterating; *adj.* obliterative
8. *n.* ossification, ossicle; *vi.* or *vt.* ossifies, ossifying; *adj.* ossiferous, osseous, ossicular, ossiculate
9. *n.* perceiver; *vi.* or *vt.* perceives, perceived, perceiving; *adj.* perceivable; *adv.* perceivably
10. *n.* ravager; *vi.* or *vt.* ravages, ravaged, ravaging

Exercise 2   Context Clues
11. (B) canine
12. (C) ossified
13. (I) meager
14. (E) ravages
15. (D) apex
16. (G) defunct
17. (A) perceive
18. (H) bourgeois
19. (J) influx
20. (F) obliterated

Exercise 3   Sentence Completion
21. E   22. C   23. A   24. B   25. D   26. C   27. A
28. E   29. B   30. D

Lesson 15   pages 59–62
Exercise 1   Mapping
Your Guess and Definition answers will vary. Possible responses to Other Forms items follow.
1. *v.* buffets, buffeted, buffeting
2. *n.* delectability, delectation; *adv.* delectably
3. *vi.* ensues, ensued, ensuing
4. *n.* expedience, expediency; *adj.* expediential; *adv.* expediently
5. *n.* facilitator, facilitation; *vt.* facilitates, facilitated, facilitating; *adj.* facilitative
6. *n. pl.* hors d'oeuvres
7. *vi.* or *vt.* lapses, lapsed, lapsing; *adj.* lapsable, lapsible
8. *n.* palatability, palatableness; *adv.* palatably
9. *n. pl.* steppes
10. *n.* succulence, succulency; *adv.* succulently

Exercise 2   Context Clues
11. (B) ensue
12. (F) succulent
13. (E) facilitate
14. (G) steppes
15. (A) hors d'oeuvre
16. (J) expedient
17. (I) palatable
18. (C) buffet
19. (H) lapse
20. (D) delectable

Exercise 3   Sentence Completion
21. E   22. A   23. C   24. B   25. E   26. A   27. D
28. C   29. B   30. D

Lesson 16   pages 63–66
Exercise 1   Mapping
Your Guess and Definition answers will vary. Possible responses to Other Forms items follow.
1. *vi.* abounds, abounded, abounding
2. *adj.* aptitudinal; *adv.* aptitudinally
3. *n.* astuteness; *adv.* astutely
4. *n.* conduciveness; *vi.* conduce
5. *adv.* erratically
6. *n.* pastoralism, pastorale, pastoralist, pastorate; *adv.* pastorally
7. *n.* quantitativeness, quantitation; *vt.* quantitate; *adv.* quantitatively
8. *n.* recurrence; *vi.* recurs, recurred, recurring; *adj.* recurrent; *adv.* recurrently
9. *n.* requisition
10. *adj.* zenithal; *adv.* zenithward

Exercise 2   Context Clues
11. (D) quantitative
12. (A) zenith
13. (G) astute
14. (I) recur
15. (B) conducive
16. (E) erratic
17. (C) abound
18. (J) pastoral
19. (F) requisite
20. (H) aptitudes

Exercise 3 Sentence Completion
21. E   22. C   23. A   24. D   25. B   26. C   27. E
28. C   29. A   30. D

Lesson 17   pages 67–70
Exercise 1   Mapping
Your Guess and Definition answers will vary. Possible responses to Other Forms items follow.
1. *n.* annihilator, annihilation; *vt.* annihilates, annihilating; *adj.* annihilable, annihilative
2. *n.* concessionaire, concessioner, concessionary; *adj.* concessionary, concessive
3. *n.* decimation, decimator; *vt.* decimates, decimating
4. *n.* dispersal, disperser, dispersion; *vi.* or *vt.* disperses, dispersed, dispersing; *adj.* dispersible, dispersive; *adv.* dispersively
5. *n.* diversionist; *vt.* divert; *adj.* diversionary
6. *n.* evasion, evader; *vi.* or *vt.* evades, evaded, evading; *adj.* evadable, evasive
7. *n.* flagrance, flagrancy; *adv.* flagrantly
8. *adj.* insolent; *adv.* insolently
9. *n.* purger; *vi.* or *vt.* purges, purged, purging
10. *n.* sadist, sadism; *adv.* sadistically

Exercise 2   Context Clues
11. (E) insolence
12. (J) sadistic
13. (B) diversion
14. (F) annihilated
15. (D) purge
16. (G) dispersing
17. (C) concession
18. (H) flagrant
19. (I) decimated
20. (A) evaded

Exercise 3   Sentence Completion
21. B   22. D   23. E   24. A   25. C   26. D   27. E
28. A   29. C   30. B

Lesson 18   pages 71–74
Exercise 1   Mapping
Your Guess and Definition answers will vary. Possible responses to Other Forms items follow.
1. *adj.* clement; *adv.* clemently
2. *n.* harassment, harasser; *vt.* harasses, harassing
3. *n.* inhibitor, inhibiter; *vt.* inhibit; *adj.* inhibitive, inhibitory
4. *n.* mandator, mandate; *n. pl.* mandatories; *vt.* mandate; *adj.* mandatary; *adv.* mandatorily
5. *n.* mannerist; *adj.* mannerist, manneristic, mannered
6. *n.* meticulousness, meticulosity; *adv.* meticulously
7. *adj.* mettlesome, mettled
8. *vi.* or *vt.* protocols, protocoled, protocoling
9. *n.* submissiveness; *n. pl.* submissions; *vi.* or *vt.* submit, submits, submitted, submitting; *adj.* submissive; *adv.* submissively
10. *n. pl.* ultimatums, ultimata

Exercise 2   Context Clues
11. (J) protocol
12. (B) harassed
13. (D) mettle
14. (I) ultimatums
15. (C) clemency
16. (H) mannerism

17. (F) inhibitions
18. (E) meticulous
19. (A) submission
20. (G) mandatory

Exercise 3   Sentence Completion
21. D   22. A   23. C   24. E   25. B   26. D   27. C
28. A   29. E   30. D

Lesson 19   pages 75–78
Exercise 1   Mapping
Your Guess and Definition answers will vary. Possible responses to Other Forms items follow.
1. *n.* admirability, admiration; *vt.* admire, admires, admired, admiring; *adj.* admirable
2. *n. pl.* affidavits
3. *vt.* amnesties, amnestied, amnestying
4. *n. pl.* biases; *vt.* biases, biased, biasing
5. *n.* censurer; *vt.* censures, censured, censuring; *adj.* censurable; *adv.* censurably
6. *n.* diminutiveness; *adv.* diminutively
7. *n.* inalienability; *adv.* inalienably
8. *n. pl.* mosques
9. *vi.* or *vt.* rifts, rifted, rifting
10. *n.* timorousness; *adv.* timorously

Exercise 2   Context Clues
11. (D) censure
12. (H) mosque
13. (B) amnesty
14. (A) rift
15. (E) admirably
16. (I) inalienable
17. (G) bias
18. (C) timorous
19. (F) affidavit
20. (J) diminutive

Exercise 3   Sentence Completion
21. C   22. E   23. B   24. B   25. A   26. B   27. D
28. C   29. C   30. A

Lesson 20   pages 79–82
Exercise 1   Mapping
Your Guess and Definition answers will vary. Possible responses to Other Forms items follow.
1. *n.* bedlamite
2. *n.* colloquialism, colloquist, colloquium, colloquy; *n. pl.* colloquia, colloquiums, colloquies; *adv.* colloquially
3. *n.* consolidation, consolidator; *vi.* or *vt.* consolidates, consolidating
4. *n.* constituency; *n. pl.* constituents, constituencies; *adv.* constituently
5. *n.* curtailment; *vt.* curtails, curtailing
6. *n.* destitution
7. *n.* emancipation, emancipator; *vt.* emancipates, emancipated, emancipating; *adj.* emancipative, emancipatory
8. *vi.* exult; *adv.* exultantly, exultingly
9. *n.* ornateness; *adv.* ornately
10. *n.* prelusion; *n. pl.* preludes; *vi.* or *vt.* preludes, preluded, preluding; *adj.* preludial, prelusive, prelusory; *adv.* prelusively

Exercise 2   Context Clues
11. (I) ornate
12. (B) constituents
13. (H) destitute
14. (D) prelude
15. (F) colloquial
16. (J) exultant
17. (C) bedlam
18. (A) curtailed
19. (G) consolidated
20. (E) emancipate

Exercise 3   Sentence Completion
21. C   22. E   23. A   24. B   25. D   26. C   27. E
28. B   29. D   30. C

Lesson 21   pages 83–86
Exercise 1   Mapping
Your Guess and Definition answers will vary. Possible responses to Other Forms items follow.
1. *vt.* bestrides, bestrode, bestridden, bestriding
2. *adj.* casemented
3. *n.* debutant, debutante; *n. pl.* debuts; *vi.* or *vt.* debuts, debuting
4. *n.* documentarian, documentarist; *n. pl.* documentaries
5. *n.* fluctuation; *vi.* or *vt.* fluctuates, fluctuated, fluctuating; *adj.* fluctuant
6. *n.* melancholia, melancholiac; *n. pl.* melancholies; *adj.* melancholic, melancholiac; *adv.* melancholically
7. *vt.* reprieves, reprieved, reprieving
8. *n. pl.* requiems
9. *n.* theoretics, theoretician, theorist; *vi.* theorize; *adj.* theoretic; *adv.* theoretically
10. *n.* vehemence, vehemency; *adv.* vehemently

Exercise 2   Context Clues
11. (B) documentary
12. (E) reprieve
13. (J) fluctuate
14. (H) casement
15. (C) vehement
16. (A) debuted
17. (D) melancholy
18. (I) requiem
19. (F) theoretical
20. (G) bestriding

Exercise 3   Sentence Completion
21. A   22. D   23. C   24. B   25. E   26. C   27. D
28. E   29. A   30. C

Lesson 22   pages 87–90
Exercise 1   Mapping
Your Guess and Definition answers will vary. Possible responses to Other Forms items follow.
1. *vi.* or *vt.* clang; *adj.* clangorous; *adv.* clangorously
2. *vt.* enjoins, enjoined, enjoining
3. *vi.* gloats, gloated, gloating
4. *n.* indictment, indictee, indicter, indictor; *vt.* indicts, indicted, indicting; *adj.* indictable
5. *n. pl.* legacies
6. *n.* lividity, lividness
7. *n.* mortification, mortifier; *vt.* mortifies, mortified, mortifying
8. *n.* patency, patentee, patentor; *vt.* patents, patented, patenting; *adj.* patentable; *adv.* patently
9. *n.* patriarchy, patriarchate; *n. pl.* patriarchs, patriarchies; *adj.* patriarchal, patriarchic
10. *n.* wheedler; *vi.* or *vt.* wheedles, wheedled, wheedling; *adv.* wheedlingly

Exercise 2   Context Clues
11. (I) gloat
12. (A) legacy
13. (H) clangor
14. (G) wheedled
15. (F) patent
16. (D) indict
17. (J) patriarch
18. (C) mortified
19. (E) enjoin
20. (B) livid

Exercise 3   Sentence Completion
21. E   22. C   23. D   24. B   25. E   26. A   27. E
28. D   29. C   30. A

Lesson 23   pages 91–94
Exercise 1   Mapping
Your Guess and Definition answers will vary. Possible responses to Other Forms items follow.
1. *n.* botcher; *vt.* botches, botching; *adj.* botchy
2. *n.* client, clientage; *adj.* cliental
3. *n.* cloture; *vi.* or *vt.* closures, closured, closuring
4. *n.* condoler, condolence, condolement; *vi.* condoles, condoled, condoling; *adj.* condolatory
5. *n.* convention, convener; *vi.* or *vt.* convenes, convening
6. *n.* cronyism; *n. pl.* cronies
7. *n.* impartiality; *adv.* impartially
8. *n.* inertness; *adj.* inertial, inert; *adv.* inertly
9. *n. pl.* momentums, momenta
10. *n.* stipulation, stipulator; *vi.* or *vt.* stipulates, stipulated, stipulating; *adj.* stipulatory

Exercise 2   Context Clues
11. (J) closure
12. (D) inertia
13. (I) cronies
14. (G) convened
15. (A) botched
16. (H) impartial
17. (B) condole
18. (F) stipulate
19. (E) clientele
20. (C) momentum

Exercise 3   Sentence Completion
21. D   22. C   23. B   24. E   25. C   26. A   27. D
28. E   29. B   30. C

Lesson 24   pages 95–98
Exercise 1   Mapping
Your Guess and Definition answers will vary. Possible responses to Other Forms items follow.
1. *n.* arbitration, arbitrament, arbitrator, arbitress; *n. pl.* arbiters; *vi.* or *vt.* arbitrate; *adj.* arbitrable, arbitral, arbitrational
2. *vi.* or *vt.* breaches, breached
3. *n.* canter
4. *n.* equilibrist, equilibrant, equilibration, equilibrator; *vi.* or *vt.* equilibrate
5. *n.* imperceptibility, imperceptiveness; *adj.* imperceptive, impercipient; *adv.* imperceptibly
6. *n.* oblivion, obliviousness; *adv.* obliviously
7. *n.* rectifier, rectification; *vt.* rectifies, rectified, rectifying; *adj.* rectifiable
8. *n.* strategy, strategist; *vi.* strategize; *adj.* strategic, strategical; *adv.* strategically
9. *adv.* subsidiarily
10. *n.* substance, substantiality, substantialness, substantialism, substantiveness; *vt.* substantiate; *adj.* substantial, substantive; *adv.* substantivally, substantively

Exercise 2   Context Clues
11. (C) oblivious
12. (B) subsidiary
13. (H) cant
14. (D) equilibrium

15. (I) rectify
16. (A) substantially
17. (J) arbiter
18. (F) stratagem
19. (E) imperceptible
20. (G) breaching

Exercise 3   Sentence Completion
21. E   22. C   23. A   24. C   25. E   26. B   27. D
28. C   29. E   30. A

Lesson 25   pages 99–102
Exercise 1   Mapping
Your Guess and Definition answers will vary. Possible responses to Other Forms items follow.
1. *n.* debasement, debaser; *vt.* debases, debased, debasing
2. *n.* effervescence; *vi.* effervesce; *adv.* effervescently
3. *n.* explication, explicator; *vt.* explicates, explicated, explicating; *adj.* explicative, explicatory
4. *n.* immaculateness, immaculacy; *adv.* immaculately
5. *vt.* impose
6. *vi.* or *vt.* mulls, mulled, mulling
7. *n.* quibbler; *vi.* quibbles, quibbled, quibbling
8. *n.* resonance, resonator; *vi.* or *vt.* resonate; *adv.* resonantly
9. *adv.* sporadically
10. *n.* synthesist, synthesizer; *n. pl.* syntheses; *vt.* synthesize

Exercise 2   Context Clues
11. (C) mull
12. (H) imposition
13. (F) synthesis
14. (A) effervescent
15. (J) debase
16. (B) resonant
17. (D) explicated
18. (I) immaculate
19. (E) quibble
20. (G) sporadic

Exercise 3   Sentence Completion
21. B   22. E   23. A   24. D   25. C   26. C   27. B
28. E   29. A   30. D

Lesson 26   pages 103–106
Exercise 1   Mapping
Your Guess and Definition answers will vary. Possible responses to Other Forms items follow.
1. *n.* abdicator, abdication; *vi.* or *vt.* abdicates, abdicated, abdicating
2. *adj.* episodic, episodical; *adv.* episodically
3. *n.* inadvertence, inadvertency; *adv.* inadvertently
4. *n.* infallibility; *adv.* infallibly
5. *n.* itineration; *vi.* itinerate
6. *n.* naiveté, naiveness, naivety; *adv.* naively
7. *vi.* or *vt.* rankles, rankled, rankling
8. *adv.* sardonically
9. *n.* stimulus, stimulater, stimulator, stimulation; *n. pl.* stimuli; *vt.* stimulate; *adj.* stimulative
10. *n.* translucence, translucency; *adj.* translucid; *adv.* translucently

Exercise 2   Context Clues
11. (J) translucent
12. (B) itinerary
13. (H) stimulant
14. (D) infallible
15. (C) sardonic
16. (F) inadvertent
17. (A) naive
18. (I) abdicate
19. (E) rankle
20. (G) episodes

Exercise 3   Sentence Completion
21. A   22. D   23. B   24. C   25. E   26. C   27. D
28. B   29. A   30. C

Lesson 27   pages 107–110
Exercise 1   Mapping
Your Guess and Definition answers will vary. Possible responses to Other Forms items follow.
1. *n.* demureness; *adv.* demurely
2. *n.* edification, edifier; *vt.* edifies, edified
3. *n.* intermittence, intermitter; *vi.* or *vt.* intermit; *adv.* intermittently
4. *n.* intuitionism, intuitionist, intuitiveness; *vi.* intuit; *adj.* intuitive, intuitional, intuitionist, intuitable; *adv.* intuitively, intuitionally
5. *n.* irrelevance, irrelevancy; *adv.* irrelevantly
6. *n.* pallidness, pallor; *adv.* pallidly
7. *n.* redundance, redundancy; *n. pl.* redundancies; *adv.* redundantly
8. *n.* reminiscence; *vi.* reminisce; *adv.* reminiscently
9. *n.* sequela, sequacity; *n. pl.* sequels, sequelae; *adj.* sequacious; *adv.* sequaciously
10. *n. pl.* synopses; *vt.* synopsize

Exercise 2   Context Clues
11. (I) pallid
12. (F) intermittently
13. (A) redundant
14. (J) sequel
15. (C) demure
16. (B) irrelevant
17. (D) synopsis
18. (E) edifying
19. (G) intuition
20. (H) reminiscent

Exercise 3   Sentence Completion
21. C   22. B   23. E   24. A   25. C   26. D   27. E
28. C   29. B   30. A

Lesson 28   pages 111–114
Exercise 1   Mapping
Your Guess and Definition answers will vary. Possible responses to Other Forms items follow.
1. *n.* detonator, detonation; *vi.* or *vt.* detonates, detonated, detonating
2. *n.* ejector, ejection, ejectment; *vi.* or *vt.* ejects, ejected, ejecting; *adj.* ejectable, ejective
3. *n.* irrationality, irrationalism, irrationalist; *adv.* irrationally
4. *n.* jostler; *vi.* or *vt.* jostles, jostled, jostling
5. *n.* lexicographer, lexicography, lexicology, lexicologist; *n. pl.* lexica, lexicons; *adj.* lexical, lexicographic, lexicographical, lexicological; *adv.* lexicographically
6. *n.* merger, mergence; *vi.* or *vt.* merges, merged, merging
7. *n.* potence; *n. pl.* potencies; *adv.* potently
8. *n. pl.* rendezvous; *vi.* or *vt.* rendezvous, rendezvoused, rendezvousing
9. *vi.* or *vt.* seethes, seethed, seething
10. *n.* simulator, simulation; *vt.* simulates, simulated, simulating; *adj.* simulative

Exercise 2   Context Clues
11. (F) lexicon
12. (J) simulate
13. (D) eject
14. (I) rendezvous
15. (H) detonate
16. (G) potency

17. (E) irrational   19. (B) jostling
18. (C) seethe   20. (A) merge
Exercise 3   Sentence Completion
21. D   22. B   23. A   24. D   25. C   26. E   27. B
28. C   29. D   30. E

Lesson 29   pages 115–118
Exercise 1   Mapping
Your Guess and Definition answers will vary. Possible responses to Other Forms items follow.
1. *n.* decrepitude; *adv.* decrepitly
2. *n.* farcicality; *n. pl.* farces, farcicalities; *vt.* farces, farced, farcing; *adj.* farcical; *adv.* farcically
3. *n.* inconsistency, inconsistence; *adv.* inconsistently
4. *n.* irksomeness; *vt.* irk; *adv.* irksomely
5. *vi.* or *vt.* jargonize; *adj.* jargonistic
6. *n.* malignancy, malignance, malignity; *n. pl.* malignancies, malignities; *adv.* malignantly
7. *n.* obligation, obliger; *vt.* obligate, oblige; *adv.* obligatorily
8. *n.* parodist; *n. pl.* parodies; *vt.* parodies, parodied, parodying; *adj.* parodic, parodical, parodistic
9. *n.* pertinence, pertinency; *adv.* pertinently
10. *n.* rebuker; *n. pl.* rebukes; *vt.* rebukes, rebuked, rebuking
Exercise 2   Context Clues
11. (C) irksome   16. (F) rebuked
12. (A) malignant   17. (B) decrepit
13. (G) farce   18. (J) pertinent
14. (H) parody   19. (I) inconsistent
15. (D) jargon   20. (E) obligatory
Exercise 3   Sentence Completion
21. C   22. E   23. D   24. B   25. C   26. A   27. D
28. E   29. C   30. B

Lesson 30   pages 119–122
Exercise 1   Mapping
Your Guess and Definition answers will vary. Possible responses to Other Forms items follow.
1. *n.* carper; *vi.* carps, carping
2. *n.* causticity; *n. pl.* caustics; *adv.* caustically
3. *n.* coincidence; *vi.* coincide; *adj.* coincident; *adv.* coincidentally, coincidently
4. *n.* incendiarism; *n. pl.* incendiaries
5. *n.* negligibility; *adv.* negligibly
6. *n.* odiousness; *adv.* odiously
7. *n.* protrusion, protrusiveness, protruberance, protruberancy; *vi.* protrudes, protruded, protruding, protruberate; *adj.* protrudent, protrusile, protrusible, protruberant; *adv.* protrusively, protruberantly
8. *n.* scene, scenarist; *n. pl.* scenarios
9. *n.* sordidness, sordor; *adv.* sordidly
10. *n.* transitiveness, transitivity, transitoriness; *adj.* transitional, transitionary, transitive, transitory; *adv.* transitionally, transitively, transitorily

Exercise 2   Context Clues
11. (A) negligible   16. (I) caustic
12. (J) sordid   17. (C) scenario
13. (D) protrude   18. (G) transition
14. (E) carped   19. (B) odious
15. (F) incendiary   20. (H) coincidental
Exercise 3   Sentence Completion
21. C   22. D   23. A   24. E   25. B   26. B   27. D
28. C   29. E   30. B

CONNECTING NEW WORDS AND PATTERNS

Lesson 1   page 126
1. (D); Performer and Related Action. You expect a *snob* to *condescend,* or look down on others, just as you expect an *assistant* to *help.*
2. (A); Synonym. *Contemptuous* and *scornful* have the same meaning, as do *careful* and *cautious.*
3. (C); Characteristic Quality. The *elite,* or members of a distinguished group, are often considered to be characteristically *superior,* just as *heroes* are characteristically *brave.*
4. (B); Synonym. *Evolve* and *change* have the same meaning, as do *spin* and *twirl.* This is true when *change, spin,* and *twirl* are used as verbs.
5. (D); Characteristic Quality. An *excerpt,* or something taken out of a larger whole, is characteristically *selected,* just as a *play* is characteristically *performed.*
6. (B); Antonym. *Fortitude,* or strength, is opposite in meaning to *weakness,* just as *anxiety* is opposite in meaning to *calm.*
7. (D); Performer and Related Action. A *mentor,* or teacher, is someone who *advises* others, just as a *critic* is someone who *reviews* performances and other creative works.
8. (C); Synonym. *Notoriety* and *fame* have similar meanings, as do *merit* and *worth.*
9. (C); Performer and Related Action. A *pauper,* or very poor person, may sometimes *beg* for money, just as a *waiter serves* food to customers.
10. (C); Synonym. *Prophetic* and *predictive* have similar meanings, as do *remarkable* and *outstanding.*

Lesson 2   page 127
1. (D); Synonym. *Amiable,* which means friendly, has a meaning similar to *pleasant. Inviting* and *appealing* also have similar meanings.
2. (D); Antonym. *Apprehensive,* which means uneasy, is opposite in meaning to *calm. Tranquil* and *stormy* also have opposite meanings.
3. (B); Location. A *bayou,* or marshy inlet, can be found in *Louisiana,* just as a *glacier,* or enormous sheet of ice, can be found in *Alaska.*
4. (C); Characteristic Quality. A *dictator,* or tyrant, is characteristically *callous,* or unfeeling, just as a *glutton* is characteristically *greedy.*

5. (B); Synonym. *Commendable* and *praiseworthy* have similar meanings, as do *horrible* and *awful*.

6. (C); Cause and Effect. *Pain* can result in a *grimace*, just as a *joke* can result in *laughter*.

7. (A); Characteristic Quality. *Clay* is characteristically *malleable*, or easily formed, just as *rubber* is characteristically *flexible*.

8. (D); Characteristic Quality. A *soap opera* is characteristically *melodramatic*, just as a *comedy* is characteristically *funny*.

9. (C); Performer and Related Action. A *patient* is someone who may *succumb*, or give in, to illness, just as a *terrorist* is someone who may *threaten* people in order to achieve a political goal.

10. (E); Synonym. *Whimsical* and *fanciful* have similar meanings, as do *tired* and *weary*.

Lesson 3   page 128

1. (D); Degree. Something that is *atrocious*, or awful, is much worse than something that is *bad*, just as something that is *wonderful* is much better than something that is *good*.

2. (A); Cause and Effect. *Suffering* can result in *compassion*, just as a *crime* can result in *outrage*.

3. (B); Antonym. *Deteriorate* and *improve* have opposite meanings, as do *succeed* and *fail*.

4. (C); Degree. Someone who is *ecstatic* feels a greater degree of joy than someone who is *glad*. In the same way, someone who is *terrified* feels a greater degree of fear than someone who is *afraid*.

5. (C); Synonym. *Insipid*, which means tasteless, has a meaning similar to *flavorless*. *Amazing* and *astonishing* also have similar meanings.

6. (E); Degree. To *loathe* means to have stronger feelings of distaste than does to *dislike*. To *adore* means to have stronger positive feelings than does to *like*.

7. (C); Characteristic Quality. *Embroidering* is characteristically *painstaking*, requiring great care. *Parachuting* is characteristically *thrilling*.

8. (D); Antonym. *Pompous*, which means pretentious and self-important, is opposite in meaning to *humble*. *Knowledgeable* and *ignorant* are also opposite in meaning.

9. (D); Synonym. *Portly* and *stout* have the same meaning, as do *rigid* and *stiff*.

10. (C); Function. The function of a *face lift* is to *rejuvenate* a person, making him or her appear youthful again. The function of *armor* is to *protect* its wearer.

Lesson 4   page 129

1. (C); Synonym. *Emphatically* and *forcefully* have similar meanings, as do *severely* and *sternly*.

2. (C); Action and Related Object. You *fabricate*, or make up, an *excuse*, just as you *tell* a *story*.

3. (C); Synonym. An *impediment* is the same thing as an *obstacle*. *Device* is similar in meaning to *machine*.

4. (D); Characteristic Quality. *Weaponry* is characteristically *martial*, or military, just as *wool* is characteristically *soft*.

5. (B); Degree. Something that is *mediocre* is inferior to something that is *good*. In the same way, something that is *adequate* is inferior to something that is *superb*, or tremendous.

6. (C); Synonym. *Qualm* and *doubt* (when used as nouns) have the same meaning, as do *trembling* and *quaking*.

7. (C); Antonym. A *recipient*, or someone who receives, is opposite in meaning to a *donor*, someone who gives. *Buyer* and *seller* are also opposite in meaning.

8. (A); Cause and Effect. *Exercise* can result in *stamina*, or endurance, just as *difficulty* can result in *stress*.

9. (E); Antonym. *Zealous*, which means extremely enthusiastic, is opposite in meaning to *unenthusiastic*. *Timid* and *courageous* are also opposite in meaning.

10. (D); Characteristic Quality. A *zephyr*, or soft breeze, is characteristically *gentle*, just as a *bird* is characteristically *feathered*.

Lesson 5   page 130

1. (B); Characteristic Quality. *Friends* are characteristically *compatible*, or well-matched, just as *enemies* are characteristically *hostile*, or belligerent.

2. (C); Synonym. *Encompass*, which means to encircle and contain, has a meaning similar to *include*. *Gather* and *collect* also have similar meanings.

3. (C); Characteristic Quality. A *rock* is characteristically *inanimate*, or nonliving, just as *water* is characteristically *wet*.

4. (A); Synonym. An *incentive* is the same thing as a *motive*, just as a *fee* is the same thing as a *payment*.

5. (C); Antonym. *Indestructible* is opposite in meaning to *fragile*. *Quarrelsome* and *agreeable* are also opposite in meaning.

6. (B); Characteristic Quality. A *soldier* is characteristically *militant*, or aggressive, just as a *volunteer* is characteristically *charitable*, or generous.

7. (C); Synonym. *Prevalent* and *widespread* have similar meanings, as do *ordinary* and *usual*.

8. (B); Cause and Effect. *Retribution*, or punishment, can be a result of *wrongdoing*, just as *wages* are usually the result of *work*.

9. (C); Antonym. *Stringent*, which means strict, is opposite in meaning to *lax*. *Frequent* and *rare* are also opposite in meaning.

10. (E); Synonym. *Transcend*, which means to go beyond something, is similar in meaning to *surpass*. *Recall* means the same as *recollect*.

Lesson 6   page 131

1. (E); Action and Related Object. You *appease*, or satisfy, *hunger*, just as you *toss* a *coin* in the air.
2. (B); Characteristic Quality. *Armor* is characteristically *archaic*, or old-fashioned, just as an *artist* is characteristically *creative*.
3. (C); Characteristic Quality. A *breeze* is characteristically *balmy*, just as a *pepper* is characteristically *hot*.
4. (D); Antonym. *Commence*, which means start, is opposite in meaning to *finish*. *Waste* and *save* are also opposite in meaning.
5. (E); Degree. *Devastation* is a severe degree of *damage*. *Luxury*, a standard of living usually associated with the wealthy, includes *comfort* but to a much greater degree.
6. (C); Performer and Related Action. You expect a *spy* to practice *espionage*, just as you expect to find a *minister* engaged in *preaching*.
7. (D); Synonym. *Inclement* and *stormy* have similar meanings, as do *remarkable* and *noteworthy*.
8. (D); Characteristic Quality. A *superhero* is characteristically *invincible*, just as *exercise* is characteristically *invigorating*.
9. (E); Synonym. *Vigilant* and *watchful* have similar meanings, as do *observant* and *attentive*.
10. (C); Antonym. *Vulnerable*, which means easily hurt or attacked, is opposite in meaning to *strong*. *Rough* and *smooth* also have opposite meanings.

Lesson 7   page 132

1. (E); Classification. A *wolf* is classified as a *canine*, or member of the dog family, just as a *snake* is classified as a *reptile*.
2. (C); Synonym. *Defunct* and *extinct* have similar meanings. *Active* means the same as *lively*.
3. (B); Location. A *hieroglyphic*, or symbol from an alphabet of pictures, can be found in *Egypt*. In the same way, a *cactus* can be found in the *desert*.
4. (C); Characteristic Quality. An *innovation* is characteristically *new*, just as an *antique* is characteristically *old*.
5. (C); Antonym. *Meager*, which means inadequate or of a small amount, means the opposite of *abundant*. *Awkward* and *graceful* are also opposite in meaning.
6. (C); Antonym. *Obliterate*, which means to destroy or wipe out, is opposite in meaning to *create*. *Demolish* and *construct* are also opposite in meaning.
7. (B); Performer and Related Action. You expect *locusts* to *ravage* vegetation, just as you expect *bees* to *pollinate* flowers.
8. (C); Degree. A *rivulet*, which is a little stream or a brook, is a much smaller body of water than a *river*, just as a *footpath*, for the use of pedestrians only, is a much smaller trailway than a *road*.

9. (D); Function. The function of a *grant* is to *subsidize*, or provide financial support, just as the function of *money* is to *buy* goods and services.
10. (A); Synonym. *Tawny* and *tan* have similar meanings, as do *misty* and *hazy*.

Lesson 8   page 133

1. (A); Synonym. *Aptitude*, or skill, means the same thing as *ability*. *Talent* and *gift* also have the same meaning.
2. (B); Synonym. *Astute*, which means cunning or shrewd, is similar in meaning to *keen*, which means sharp-witted. *Persuasive* and *convincing* have the same meaning.
3. (D); Location. A *buffet*, or sideboard, can be found in a *dining room*, just as a *sink* can be found in a *kitchen*.
4. (E); Antonym. *Delectable*, which means very pleasing or delicious, is opposite in meaning to *displeasing*. *Delightful* and *disgusting* are also opposite in meaning.
5. (D); Part and whole. An *hors d'oeuvre* is a part of a *meal* that is served in the beginning as an appetizer. An *overture* is the opening segment of an *opera* that is performed before the first act.
6. (A); Characteristic Quality. *Food* is characteristically *palatable*, or tasty and edible, just as *perfume* is characteristically *fragrant*.
7. (C); Antonym. *Pastoral*, or characteristic of rural life, means the opposite of *urban*, or characteristic of city life. *Private* and *public* also have opposite meanings.
8. (E); Characteristic Quality. *Economics*, the study of wealth and labor, is characteristically *quantitative*, having to do with measurement. In the same way, a *safari* is characteristically *adventurous*.
9. (B); Classification. A *succulent* is classified as a kind of *plant life*, just as *granite* is classified as a kind of *rock*.
10. (B); Synonym. *Zenith* and *peak* have the same meaning. A *violin* is the same as a *fiddle*.

Lesson 9   page 134

1. (B); Degree. *Annihilate*, which means to demolish or destroy completely, has a much stronger meaning than *defeat* (when used as a verb). *Torment*, which means to torture or cause anguish, has a much stronger meaning than *bother*, which means to annoy or trouble.
2. (C); Classification. *Golf* can be classified as a *diversion*, or form of amusement, just as *carpentry* can be classified as an *occupation*.
3. (C); Synonym. To *harass* someone is the same as to *irritate* someone, just as to *hurt* someone is the same as to *harm* someone.
4. (C); Characteristic Quality. *Insolence*, or rude behavior, is characteristically *disrespectful*, just as a *celebration* is characteristically *joyous*.

5. (B); Antonym. *Mandatory,* or required, means the opposite of *optional. Hesitant* and *certain* have opposite meanings.
6. (C); Degree. *Meticulous* means scrupulous, or excessively *careful.* Something that is *fatal* is not only *harmful* but also deadly.
7. (D); Synonym. *Mettle* and *courage* have the same meaning, as do *curiosity* and *inquisitiveness.*
8. (E); Synonym. *Purge* (the verb form) and *rid* have similar meanings, as do *show* and *display* when they are used as verbs.
9. (C); Antonym. *Sadistic,* or cruel, is opposite in meaning to *kind. Mature* and *childish* are also opposite in meaning.
10. (C); Performer and Related Object. An *ultimatum* is a final demand stated by a *diplomat,* who represents his or her country in negotiations. A *cross-examination* of a witness is conducted by a *lawyer* to upset and discredit previous testimony.

Lesson 10   page 135
1. (D); Performer and Related Object. An *affidavit,* or sworn statement, is given by a *witness.* A *law* is passed by a *legislator* in Congress.
2. (D); Characteristic Quality. *Bedlam,* a state of noisy disorder, is characteristically *confused,* just as a *riot* is characteristically *violent.*
3. (C); Antonym. *Destitute,* or extremely poor, means the opposite of *wealthy,* or extremely rich. *Shy* and *bold* also have opposite meanings.
4. (B); Synonym. *Diminutive* and *tiny* have the same meaning, as do *ragged* and *tattered.*
5. (C); Degree. *Exultant,* which means exuberantly triumphant, is much stronger in meaning than *pleased,* which means satisfied. *Shocked* is similar in meaning to *surprised* but suggests a much more violent and troubled reaction.
6. (C); Location. *Worshipers* can be found in a *mosque,* or Muslim place of worship. *Fish* (the noun form) can be found in an *aquarium.*
7. (E); Synonym. *Ornate* and *fancy* have similar meanings, as do *organized* and *orderly.*
8. (C); Function. The function of a *prelude* is to *introduce* something, such as a piece of music. In the same way, the function of a *ruler* (in the sense of a measuring stick) is to *measure* something, such as height or width.
9. (A); Cause and Effect. A *rift,* or a break in a previously friendly relationship, can be the result of a *disagreement,* just as *suffering* can be the result of a *war.*
10. (D); Antonym. *Timorous,* or fearful, is opposite in meaning to *courageous. Elderly,* or old, is opposite in meaning to *youthful.*

Lesson 11   page 136
1. (C); Characteristic Quality. A *clangor* is a characteristically *loud* sound, just as a *rose* is a characteristically *fragrant* flower.

2. (C); Performer and Related Action. You expect an inexperienced *actress* to *debut* (the verb form), or give a first public performance, just as you expect a *comedian* to *amuse* an audience.
3. (E); Classification. A *documentary* is classified as *film,* just as a *ballet* is classified as *dance.*
4. (B); Degree. To *gloat* means to *enjoy* something but with a degree of malicious pleasure. When used as verbs, *glare* and *look* have similar meanings. However, *glare* means to *look* with a fierce, angry stare.
5. (A); Performer and Related Action. A *grand jury* acts to *indict,* or charge a defendant with a crime, just as a *monarch* acts to *rule.*
6. (B); Synonym. *Melancholy* and *gloom* have similar meanings, as do *tradition* and *custom.*
7. (D); Action and Related Object. You *patent* an *invention* by being granted an exclusive right to it, just as you *insure valuables* by paying to have them replaced should they be lost or stolen.
8. (C); Performer and Related Action. You expect a *patriarch,* the male leader of a group or family, to *lead* his people, just as you expect a *patron,* a person who benefits and protects others, to *support* his or her dependents.
9. (A); Performer and Related Object. A *requiem* is written by a *composer,* just as a *novel* is written by an *author.*
10. (C); Synonym. *Vehement,* which means impetuous or impassioned, has the same meaning as *passionate. Earnest* and *sincere* are also similar in meaning.

Lesson 12   page 137
1. (C); Performer and Related Action. You expect an *arbiter,* or judge, to *decide* a dispute, just as you expect an *architect* to *design* buildings.
2. (C); Synonym. *Botch* and *spoil* have similar meanings, as do *neglect* and *ignore.*
3. (B); Characteristic Quality. *Cant* is characteristically *insincere* talk, just as *conjunctions* are characteristically *connective,* joining different parts of a sentence.
4. (E); Synonym. One's *clientele* is the same thing as one's *customers,* just as *replacements* are *substitutes.*
5. (D); Performer and Related Action. You expect *members* of a group to *convene,* or meet, just as you expect *citizens* to *vote.*
6. (C); Synonym. A *crony* is a *buddy,* just as a *duty* is an *obligation.*
7. (D); Antonym. *Imperceptible,* which means unable to be perceived or seen, is opposite in meaning to *obvious. Vague* and *clear* are also opposite in meaning.
8. (C); Characteristic Quality. A *sleeper* is characteristically *oblivious,* or unaware, just as a *guard* is characteristically *watchful.*
9. (B); Antonym. *Rectify,* which means to correct or fix, means the opposite of *upset. Nourish* and *starve* are also opposite in meaning.

10. (B); Function. The function of a *stratagem*, or trick, is to *deceive*, just as the function of an *outline* is to *organize* information.

Lesson 13   page 138

1. (C); Action and Related Object. A ruler *abdicates*, or formally gives up, a *throne*, just as legislators *pass* a *law*.
2. (A); Antonym. *Effervescent*, as in having a bubbly personality, means the opposite of *listless*. *Brilliant* and *dull* also have opposite meanings.
3. (D); Synonym. *Immaculate* and *pure* have similar meanings, as do *convinced* and *certain*.
4. (D); Antonym. *Inadvertent*, which means unintended, is opposite in meaning to *intentional*. *Unconcerned* and *worried* are also opposite in meaning.
5. (B); Antonym. *Infallible*, which means incapable of error, is opposite in meaning to *unreliable*. *Ferocious* and *gentle* are also opposite in meaning.
6. (E); Performer and Related Object. Before traveling, a *traveler* develops an *itinerary*, or plan of travel. A *referee* uses a *whistle* during a game.
7. (C); Antonym. One meaning of *naive* is simple, which means the opposite of *sophisticated*. *Perfect* and *flawed* are also opposite in meaning.
8. (B); Characteristic Quality. A *cello* is characteristically *resonant*, or vibrating with sound, just as a *breeze* is characteristically *gentle*.
9. (D); Function. The function of a *stimulant* is to *activate*, just as the function of *meditation* is to *relax*.
10. (C); Characteristic Quality. *Frosted glass* is characteristically *translucent*, or partially clear, just as *frost* is characteristically *white*.

Lesson 14   page 139

1. (B); Antonym. One of the definitions of *demure*, reserved, is opposite in meaning to *flashy*. *Plain* and *fancy* are also opposite in meaning.
2. (D); Action and Related Object. You *detonate*, or set off, an *explosive*, just as you *strike* a *match*.
3. (C); Degree. *Jostle* is similar in meaning to *bump* but implies much rougher contact. In the same way, *beg* is similar in meaning to *ask*, but to *beg* is to *ask* in a pleading way.
4. (D); Classification. A *lexicon*, or dictionary, is classified as a *reference book*, just as *Judaism*, the Jewish way of life and form of worship, is classified as a *religion*.
5. (B); Synonym. *Pallid* and *pale* have the same meaning, as do *quiet* and *hushed*.
6. (D); Synonym. *Redundant*, which means unnecessarily repeated, has a meaning similar to *repetitive*. *Basic* and *elementary* also have similar meanings.
7. (C); Performer and Related Action. You expect *troops* to *rendezvous*, or meet at a designated time and place, just as you expect a group's *members* to *congregate*, or gather together.

8. (B); Antonym. *Seethe*, which means to boil, means the opposite of *freeze*. *Eat* and *fast* (the verb form) also have opposite meanings.
9. (C); Function. The function of a *sequel*, one phase of a literary work, is to *continue* a story, just as the function of a *foreword*, an introductory statement, is to *introduce* a story.
10. (D); Function. The function of a *synopsis*, which means a condensation or summary, is to *summarize* something, just as the function of a *videotape* is to *record* something.

Lesson 15   page 140

1. (D); Synonym. *Carp* and *nag* have the same meaning, as do *offend* and *insult*.
2. (C); Characteristic Quality. *Sarcasm*, which means making cutting remarks, is characteristically *caustic*, or corrosive. In the same way, a *cavity*, or hole, is characteristically *hollow*.
3. (E); Degree. *Decrepit* is similar in meaning to *worn* but means even more broken down or worn out. In the same way, *eager* is similar in meaning to *willing* but implies much greater enthusiasm.
4. (C); Characteristic Quality. A *farce*, an exaggerated, humorous play, is characteristically *funny*, just as a *tragedy*, a serious play with an unhappy ending, is characteristically *sad*.
5. (A); Characteristic Quality. *Jargon* is characteristically *unintelligible*, or impossible to understand, just as a *plateau* is characteristically *elevated*, or raised above sea level.
6. (C); Degree. Something that is *malignant* is much more dangerous or likely to cause death than something that is *harmful*. Similarly, someone who is *evil* has much more wicked intentions than someone who is *mischievous*.
7. (B); Synonym. *Negligible*, which means unimportant and easily disregarded, has a meaning similar to *insignificant*. *Critical* and *serious* also have similar meanings.
8. (C); Antonym. *Odious*, which means disgusting and offensive, is opposite in meaning to *appealing*. *Realistic* and *fantastic* are also opposite in meaning.
9. (C); Synonym. *Pertinent*, or relevant, is similar in meaning to *appropriate*. *Tiresome* and *annoying* also have similar meanings.
10. (B); Antonym. When used as verbs, *rebuke*, which means scold, and *praise* have opposite meanings. When used as verbs, *hamper* and *help* also have opposite meanings.

Lesson 1   pages 143–148
Exercise 1   Finding Synonyms
Answers will vary. The following are possible responses.

1. ancient times
2. from the father
3. a poor person
4. having to do with right and wrong
5. an unorthodox view
6. a teacher or advisor
7. a widespread but poor reputation
8. firmly declares
9. a selection
10. unable to speak clearly
11. scornful
12. voters
13. comparisons
14. a wealthy, powerful group
15. stooped
16. a verdict of not guilty
17. moral strength
18. predictive
19. grew from
20. after death

Exercise 2   Reading Strategically

1. C 2. B 3. D 4. A 5. E 6. C 7. E 8. A
9. B 10. E 11. B 12. D 13. C 14. D 15. A
16. B 17. E 18. B 19. C 20. D

Lesson 2   pages 149–154
Exercise 1   Finding Synonyms
Answers will vary. The following are possible responses.

1. mysterious
2. a marshy inlet
3. angry
4. made disapproving faces
5. faces
6. the study of human behavior and development
7. giving unliving objects human qualities
8. to retell in one's own words
9. word for word
10. friendly
11. easily formed
12. wise
13. fanciful
14. not producing a desired effect
15. unyielding
16. cruel, unfeeling
17. to give in to
18. exciting and sensational
19. anxious
20. deserving praise

Exercise 2   Reading Strategically

1. A 2. D 3. E 4. C 5. B 6. D 7. B 8. A
9. D 10. C 11. C 12. E 13. B 14. B 15. A
16. A 17. C 18. B 19. E 20. D

Lesson 3   pages 155–160
Exercise 1   Finding Synonyms
Answers will vary. The following are possible responses.

1. constantly
2. detests
3. determines
4. careful
5. burdened
6. original or without precedent
7. grieves
8. stout
9. sympathy
10. calmness
11. nearness
12. grows worse
13. arrogant, self-important
14. appalling
15. joyful
16. dull
17. restores youth
18. acceptable
19. associated with
20. controlled

Exercise 2   Reading Strategically

1. B 2. E 3. B 4. D 5. A 6. C 7. C 8. E
9. A 10. D 11. B 12. C 13. B 14. B 15. E
16. D 17. A 18. B 19. C 20. D

Lesson 4   pages 161–166
Exercise 1   Finding Synonyms
Answers will vary. The following are possible responses.

1. a gentle breeze
2. artistic
3. pale
4. eager
5. forcefully
6. create
7. well-timed
8. obstacle
9. productive
10. average
11. receiver
12. military
13. vigor, strength, and endurance
14. an overused expression
15. charm
16. apparent contradiction
17. formed
18. one who wants to return to earlier ways
19. appearance and bearing
20. doubts

Exercise 2   Reading Strategically

1. D 2. C 3. E 4. A 5. D 6. B 7. E 8. D
9. A 10. C 11. B 12. E 13. B 14. D 15. B
16. A 17. C 18. D 19. B 20. E

Lesson 5   pages 167–172
Exercise 1   Finding Synonyms
Answers will vary. The following are possible responses.

1. widespread
2. basic principles
3. relentlessly
4. agreeable
5. self-evident truths
6. contains, encircles
7. cannot be destroyed
8. punishment
9. pass beyond
10. unliving
11. central or crucial
12. obedience
13. aggressive or violent
14. inborn, inner
15. chance for help
16. understanding
17. temporary, ever-changing
18. encouragement
19. strict
20. changeable

Exercise 2   Reading Strategically

1. C 2. E 3. B 4. A 5. C 6. D 7. C 8. D
9. B 10. A 11. D 12. C 13. A 14. C 15. B
16. E 17. B 18. D 19. A 20. C

Lesson 6   pages 173–178
Exercise 1   Finding Synonyms
Answers will vary. The following are possible responses.

1. freedom
2. persistence
3. destruction
4. begins
5. cause or inflict
6. independent
7. spying
8. overwhelm or surround
9. tricked
10. weak
11. false story
12. unbeatable
13. uncertain and dangerous
14. reproduction
15. mild and pleasant
16. severe
17. alert
18. pacified
19. ancient
20. fade

Exercise 2   Reading Strategically

1. C 2. A 3. E 4. B 5. B 6. D 7. E 8. A
9. B 10. D 11. B 12. E 13. A 14. C 15. C
16. D 17. A 18. C 19. B 20. B

Lesson 7 pages 179–184
Exercise 1 Finding Synonyms
Answers will vary. The following are possible responses.

1. crossroads
2. see
3. financed
4. unreachable
5. a flowing in
6. buildings
7. highest point
8. streams
9. middle class
10. servants
11. invention
12. dog
13. extinct
14. picture writing
15. tan
16. changed into bone
17. destroyed
18. inadequate
19. violently destroying
20. chests

Exercise 2 Reading Strategically
1. E 2. A 3. B 4. B 5. D 6. B 7. C 8. D
9. E 10. B 11. A 12. C 13. D 14. A 15. C
16. E 17. D 18. C 19. A 20. B

Lesson 8 pages 185–190
Exercise 1 Finding Synonyms
Answers will vary. The following are possible responses.

1. supportive
2. high point
3. followed
4. passed
5. a plain
6. irregular
7. countryside, rural
8. assisted
9. shrewd
10. talent
11. a necessity
12. was plentiful
13. related to quantity, measurable
14. appetizers
15. a self-serve meal
16. efficient
17. tasty
18. moist and flavorful
19. delicious
20. happen again

Exercise 2 Reading Strategically
1. B 2. D 3. C 4. E 5. C 6. A 7. D 8. B
9. A 10. C 11. D 12. B 13. E 14. B 15. B
16. D 17. C 18. D 19. A 20. A

Lesson 9 pages 191–196
Exercise 1 Finding Synonyms
Answers will vary. The following are possible responses.

1. courage
2. required
3. total obedience
4. disrespect
5. a style or behavior
6. carefully
7. restraints
8. grants
9. enjoying cruelty
10. expel
11. a code of conduct
12. crush, destroy
13. avoid
14. destroy completely
15. spread
16. distraction
17. attack repeatedly
18. mercy or forgiveness
19. outrageous
20. a final demand

Exercise 2 Reading Strategically
1. A 2. E 3. B 4. D 5. C 6. A 7. B 8. C
9. C 10. D 11. B 12. C 13. E 14. A 15. E
16. B 17. C 18. A 19. E 20. C

Lesson 10 pages 197–202
Exercise 1 Finding Synonyms
Answers will vary. The following are possible responses.

1. jubilant
2. influenced, swayed
3. deserving of praise
4. can't be taken away
5. fearful
6. free

7. criticized
8. tiny
9. introduction
10. a loud, confusing place
11. informal
12. penniless
13. Muslim places of worship
14. elaborate
15. unified
16. voters
17. separation
18. pardon
19. a sworn statement
20. shortened

Exercise 2 Reading Strategically
1. C 2. D 3. D 4. A 5. E 6. B 7. C 8. D
9. A 10. B 11. B 12. E 13. B 14. D 15. C
16. A 17. B 18. D 19. E 20. D

Lesson 11 pages 203–208
Exercise 1 Finding Synonyms
Answers will vary. The following are possible responses.

1. first public appearance
2. inheritance
3. coaxed
4. a window frame with hinges
5. a loud, clanging sound
6. straddling
7. hypothetical
8. obvious
9. a male leader
10. prevent
11. charged with a crime
12. exult
13. shamed
14. temporary relief
15. furious
16. gloom
17. a film of or about actual events
18. a funeral hymn
19. passionately
20. vary

Exercise 2 Reading Strategically
1. D 2. B 3. C 4. C 5. A 6. E 7. A 8. B
9. E 10. C 11. B 12. A 13. D 14. E 15. C
16. B 17. D 18. A 19. C 20. B

Lesson 12 pages 209–214
Exercise 1 Finding Synonyms
Answers will vary. The following are possible responses.

1. objective
2. companies owned by larger companies
3. customers
4. friends
5. judge
6. bungle
7. closing
8. unaware
9. balance
10. force
11. significantly
12. hard to see
13. met
14. schemes
15. mourn
16. violation
17. correct
18. arrange, specify
19. insincere talk
20. lack of movement

Exercise 2 Reading Strategically
1. B 2. C 3. A 4. E 5. D 6. A 7. E 8. A
9. C 10. B 11. D 12. C 13. A 14. A 15. E
16. B 17. C 18. B 19. C 20. D

Lesson 13 pages 215–220
Exercise 1 Finding Synonyms
Answers will vary. The following are possible responses.

1. explain
2. thought about
3. combination
4. inexperienced
5. sarcastic
6. irritates
7. renounce office
8. make petty objections
9. route, travel plan
10. deep, rich in tone
11. never wrong
12. event

13. irregular
14. unintentionally
15. bubbly
16. something causing excitement
17. letting some light through
18. clean, pure
19. lowers worth
20. something forced

Exercise 2 Reading Strategically

1. E   2. B   3. C   4. A   5. D   6. D   7. E   8. C
9. A   10. B   11. B   12. E   13. A   14. A   15. C
16. B   17. A   18. D   19. C   20. A

Lesson 14   pages 221–226
Exercise 1   Finding Synonyms
Answers will vary. The following are possible responses.

1. insight
2. enlighten
3. dictionary
4. summary
5. unite
6. senseless
7. not applicable
8. suggestive
9. repetitive
10. strength
11. explode
12. reserved
13. be agitated
14. occasionally
15. throw out
16. shoving
17. imitated
18. pale
19. continuation
20. prearranged meeting

Exercise 2 Reading Strategically

1. B   2. C   3. E   4. A   5. D   6. C   7. E   8. B
9. B   10. C   11. D   12. A   13. C   14. B   15. D
16. E   17. B   18. C   19. A   20. C

Lesson 15   pages 227–232
Exercise 1   Finding Synonyms
Answers will vary. The following are possible responses.

1. annoying
2. changeable
3. outline of proposed events
4. something ridiculous
5. occurring together by accident
6. relevant
7. scold
8. disgusting
9. dirty and degrading
10. complain
11. worn-out
12. stick out
13. insignificant
14. an imitation
15. life-threatening
16. required
17. change
18. corrosive
19. flammable, causing fire
20. specialized language of a group

Exercise 2 Reading Strategically

1. D   2. A   3. C   4. E   5. B   6. C   7. C   8. D
9. E   10. A   11. D   12. C   13. B   14. B   15. A
16. D   17. B   18. B   19. A   20. B

▼ **USING NEW WORDS ON TESTS** ▼

FORMATIVE ASSESSMENT
Test 1   page 3
1. B   2. A   3. C   4. A   5. C   6. D   7. B   8. E
9. C   10. A
Test 2   page 4
1. D   2. B   3. A   4. D   5. C   6. D   7. E   8. C
9. B   10. E

Test 3   page 5
1. B   2. C   3. B   4. C   5. D   6. E   7. D   8. A
9. E   10. A
Test 4   page 6
1. B   2. D   3. C   4. A   5. E   6. A   7. C   8. A
9. D   10. B
Test 5   page 7
1. B   2. D   3. A   4. E   5. C   6. A   7. C   8. B
9. D   10. C
Test 6   page 8
1. D   2. D   3. C   4. A   5. D   6. E   7. B   8. D
9. B   10. A
Test 7   page 9
1. E   2. A   3. B   4. B   5. D   6. A   7. D   8. B
9. D   10. C
Test 8   page 10
1. A   2. D   3. A   4. B   5. C   6. B   7. B   8. E
9. C   10. D
Test 9   page 11
1. A   2. C   3. C   4. E   5. B   6. A   7. D   8. D
9. D   10. B
Test 10   page 12
1. D   2. E   3. E   4. D   5. A   6. B   7. A   8. C
9. D   10. B
Test 11   page 13
1. A   2. B   3. A   4. D   5. B   6. A   7. C   8. C
9. C   10. E
Test 12   page 14
1. C   2. D   3. D   4. A   5. A   6. E   7. B   8. C
9. E   10. B
Test 13   page 15
1. C   2. B   3. D   4. E   5. C   6. B   7. A   8. C
9. B   10. D
Test 14   page 16
1. D   2. B   3. C   4. D   5. A   6. B   7. E   8. A
9. A   10. C
Test 15   page 17
1. C   2. D   3. A   4. E   5. D   6. C   7. B   8. A
9. E   10. D
Test 16   page 18
1. E   2. C   3. B   4. D   5. D   6. B   7. A   8. C
9. C   10. A
Test 17   page 19
1. D   2. B   3. D   4. A   5. A   6. C   7. E   8. C
9. C   10. B
Test 18   page 20
1. B   2. B   3. E   4. D   5. B   6. E   7. A   8. A
9. D   10. C
Test 19   page 21
1. A   2. A   3. C   4. E   5. C   6. C   7. A   8. B
9. B   10. D
Test 20   page 22
1. B   2. D   3. E   4. B   5. B   6. D   7. A   8. A
9. C   10. E
Test 21   page 23
1. D   2. D   3. A   4. B   5. B   6. E   7. C   8. D
9. C   10. D
Test 22   page 24
1. D   2. B   3. B   4. D   5. B   6. C   7. C   8. D
9. E   10. A

Test 23   page 25
1. E   2. B   3. C   4. D   5. B   6. A   7. A   8. B
9. A   10. D
Test 24   page 26
1. D   2. E   3. D   4. B   5. E   6. B   7. A   8. A
9. D   10. C
Test 25   page 27
1. C   2. A   3. D   4. E   5. D   6. C   7. D   8. B
9. D   10. B
Test 26   page 28
1. C   2. B   3. C   4. D   5. A   6. D   7. C   8. B
9. C   10. A
Test 27   page 29
1. B   2. E   3. C   4. C   5. B   6. A   7. A   8. C
9. D   10. E
Test 28   page 30
1. C   2. A   3. B   4. D   5. E   6. A   7. D   8. B
9. C   10. B
Test 29   page 31
1. A   2. A   3. B   4. E   5. E   6. B   7. C   8. D
9. D   10. D
Test 30   page 32
1. C   2. E   3. D   4. A   5. C   6. A   7. B   8. D
9. B   10. C

SUMMATIVE ASSESSMENT
Test 1 Part A   pages 35–38
1. D   2. B   3. C   4. C   5. D   6. E   7. B   8. B
9. A   10. E   11. E   12. A   13. B   14. A   15. E
16. A   17. C   18. D   19. C   20. D
Test 1 Part B   pages 39–43
21. D   22. A   23. C   24. B   25. E   26. D   27. A
28. C   29. B   30. B   31. D   32. C   33. E   34. A
35. E   36. A   37. C   38. D   39. B   40. E   41. C
42. A   43. E   44. D   45. B   46. C   47. A   48. D
49. E   50. B   51. C   52. C   53. A   54. E   55. A
56. E   57. B   58. D   59. C   60. A   61. B   62. C
63. E   64. D   65. C   66. A   67. D   68. B   69. C
70. E
Test 1 Part C   pages 44–46
71. (E); Degree. To *adore* someone or something denotes stronger positive feelings than to *like* a person or thing. To *loathe* someone or something means to have stronger feelings of distaste than does to *dislike*.
72. (C); Synonym. *Analogy* and *comparison* have similar meanings, as do *similarity* and *sameness*.
73. (B); Performer and Related Action. You expect an *anthropologist* to *study*, just as you expect an *actor* to *perform*.
74. (D); Antonym. *Apprehensive*, which means uneasy, is opposite in meaning to *calm*. *Tranquil* and *stormy* also have opposite meanings.
75. (C); Antonym. *Buyer* and *seller* are opposite in meaning. A *recipient*, or someone who receives, is opposite in meaning to a *donor*, someone who gives.
76. (A); Synonym. *Careful* and *cautious* have the same meaning, as do *contemptuous* and *scornful*.
77. (B); Synonym. *Charisma* and *charm* have similar meanings, as do *talent* and *ability*.
78. (B); Antonym. *Deteriorate* and *improve* have opposite meanings, as do *succeed* and *fail*.
79. (D); Performer and Related Action. You expect an *electorate*, or the voting population, to *vote*, just as you expect an *audience* to *applaud*.
80. (C); Synonym. *Impediment* and *obstacle* have similar meanings, as do *device* and *machine*.
81. (E); Degree. Someone who is *inarticulate* cannot speak understandably, while someone who is *mute* cannot speak at all. Similarly, someone who is *willing* is less enthusiastic than someone who is *eager*.
82. (B); Synonym. *Insipid*, which means tasteless, has a meaning similar to *flavorless*. *Amazing* and *astonishing* also have similar meanings.
83. (E); Antonym. *Judicious*, which means wise, is opposite in meaning to *unwise*. *Trustworthy* and *unreliable* also have opposite meanings.
84. (B); Performer and Related Action. You expect a *mourner* to *lament*, or grieve, just as you expect a *sleeper* to *dream*.
85. (A); Characteristic Quality. *Clay* is characteristically *malleable*, just as *rubber* is characteristically *flexible*.
86. (D); Performer and Related Action. A *mentor*, or teacher, is someone who *advises* others, just as a *critic* is someone who *reviews* performances and other creative works.
87. (B); Synonym. *Notoriety* and *fame* have similar meanings, as do *merit* and *worth*.
88. (E); Classification. *Personification* may be classified as a *figure of speech*, just as a *sneaker* may be classified as *footwear*.
89. (D); Antonym. *Pompous*, or self-important, is opposite in meaning to *humble*. *Knowledgeable* and *ignorant* are also opposite in meaning.
90. (C); Synonym. *Prophetic* and *predictive* have nearly the same meaning, as do *remarkable* and *outstanding*.
91. (D); Performer and Related Action. You expect a *reactionary* to *react*; just as you expect a *novelist* to *write*.
92. (B); Synonym. *Repress* and *restrain* have similar meanings, as do *bicker* and *quarrel*.
93. (B); Cause and Effect. *Retribution*, or punishment, can be a result of *wrongdoing*, just as *wages* are usually the result of *work*.
94. (C); Performer and Related Action. A *terrorist* is someone who may *threaten* people in order to achieve a political goal, just as a *lawyer* is someone who *argues* a case.
95. (C); Characteristic Quality. *Parachuting* is characteristically *thrilling*, just as *embroidering*, or ornamental needlework, is characteristically *painstaking*.
96. (A); Characteristic Quality. A *moment* is characteristically *transitory*, just as *ice* is characteristically *cold*.

97. (C); Performer and Related Action. A *waiter serves* food to customers, just as a *pauper*, or penniless person, may sometimes *beg* for money.

98. (E); Synonym. *Whimsical* and *fanciful* have similar meanings, as do *tired* and *weary*.

99. (E); Antonym. *Zealous*, meaning extremely eager, is the opposite of *unenthusiastic*. *Timid* and *courageous* are also opposite in meaning.

100. (D); Characteristic Quality. A *zephyr*, or soft breeze, is characteristically *gentle*, just as a *bird* is characteristically *feathered*.

Test 2 Part A   pages 47–50
1. E   2. B   3. E   4. B   5. C   6. C   7. D   8. C
9. A   10. C   11. B   12. E   13. D   14. A   15. D
16. B   17. A   18. B   19. D   20. E

Test 2 Part B   pages 51–55
21. D   22. C   23. E   24. A   25. C   26. B   27. A
28. C   29. E   30. D   31. C   32. B   33. A   34. E
35. D   36. C   37. C   38. A   39. B   40. D   41. E
42. D   43. C   44. A   45. E   46. D   47. C   48. E
49. E   50. C   51. D   52. A   53. C   54. E   55. D
56. B   57. C   58. A   59. E   60. D   61. D   62. C
63. C   64. B   65. B   66. E   67. A   68. D   69. C
70. A

Test 2 Part C   pages 56–58
71. (D); Performer and Related Object. An *affidavit*, or sworn statement, is given by a *witness*. A *law* is passed by *legislators* in Congress.

72. (C); Location. *Fish* can be found in an *aquarium*, just as *worshipers* can be found in a *mosque*.

73. (C); Characteristic Quality. A *breeze* is characteristically *balmy*, just as *sleet* is characteristically *cold*.

74. (D); Characteristic Quality. *Bedlam*, a state of chaos, is characteristically *confused*, just as a *riot* is characteristically *violent*.

75. (B); Action and Related Object. You *besiege* a *fort*, just as you *plan* a *trip*.

76. (C); Synonym. *Bias* and *prejudice* have the same meaning, as do *violin* and *fiddle*.

77. (A); Antonym. *Bourgeois* means the opposite of *unconventional*, just as *colloquial* means the opposite of *formal*.

78. (D); Location. A *buffet*, or sideboard, can be found in a *dining room*, just as a *tub* can be found in a *bathroom*.

79. (D); Synonym. *Clemency* and *mercy* have the same meaning. *Essay* and *composition* are also similar in meaning.

80. (A); Function. The function of a *coffer*, or chest, is to *safeguard* valuables, just as one function of a *calculator* is to *multiply* numbers.

81. (E); Characteristic Quality. *Slang* is characteristically *colloquial*, just as an *artist* is characteristically *creative*.

82. (D); Classification. A *concession* is a type of *privilege*, just as a *fork* is a type of *utensil*.

83. (E); Degree. *Decimate*, which means to destroy or kill, is a greater degree of destruction than *harm*, just as *torment* is a greater degree of irritation than *bother*.

84. (C); Synonym. *Defunct* and *extinct* have similar meanings. *Active* means the same as *lively*.

85. (E); Cause and Effect. A *hurricane* can cause *devastation*, which means complete ruin or destruction, just as *medicine* can cause *healing*.

86. (C); Action and Related Object. You *build* an *edifice*, or building, just as you *direct* a *film*.

87. (B); Performer and Related Action. You expect a *liberator* to *emancipate*, or to set free, just as you expect a *watcher* to *observe*.

88. (C); Antonym. *Erratic* means the opposite of *regular*, just as *hesitant* means the opposite of *certain*.

89. (E); Performer and Related Action. A *frog* is likely to *leap*, just as a *canine* is likely to *howl*.

90. (C); Cause and Effect. *Harrassment* can cause *irritation*, just as *praise* can cause *pride*.

91. (B); Location. A *hieroglyphic*, a picture used to express language, can be found in *Egypt*. An *oasis* can be found in the *desert*.

92. (B); Antonym. *Latitude*, which means to be unrestricted, means the opposite of *restriction*, just as *introduction* means the opposite of *conclusion*.

93. (D); Performer and Related Object. You expect an *actor* to use a *mannerism*, just as you expect a *nurse* to use a *thermometer*.

94. (C); Degree. *Meticulous* means extremely *careful*. Something that is *fatal* is *harmful* to the point of being deadly.

95. (C); Antonym. *Obliterate*, which means to wipe out, is opposite in meaning to *create*. *Demolish* and *construct* are also opposite in meaning.

96. (C); Synonym. *Purge* and *rid* have the same meaning, as do *notify* and *inform*.

97. (E); Characteristic Quality. *Economics*, the science of wealth and labor, is characteristically *quantitative*, just as a *trek*, or journey, is characteristically *adventurous*.

98. (C); Degree. A *rivulet*, which is a little stream or brook, is a much smaller body of water than a *river*, just as a *path* is much smaller than a *road*.

99. (C); Location. A *steppe* can be found in *Russia*, just as a *coat* can be found in a *closet*.

100. (A); Performer and Related Object. An *ultimatum* is a final demand that might be stated by a *diplomat*, who represents his or her country in negotiations. A *game plan* is a strategy offered by a *coach*.

Test 3 Part A   pages 59–62
1. E   2. C   3. B   4. D   5. A   6. E   7. C   8. A
9. C   10. B   11. D   12. E   13. C   14. B   15. D
16. A   17. B   18. E   19. C   20. B

Test 3 Part B   pages 63–67

21. D 22. C 23. A 24. E 25. D 26. C 27. B
28. E 29. A 30. C 31. D 32. C 33. B 34. E
35. C 36. D 37. A 38. D 39. E 40. C 41. C
42. D 43. B 44. E 45. D 46. A 47. C 48. B
49. D 50. E 51. D 52. A 53. C 54. D 55. B
56. E 57. C 58. A 59. D 60. D 61. B 62. C
63. C 64. E 65. A 66. D 67. B 68. C 69. E
70. D

Test 3 Part C   pages 68–70

71. (C); Performer and Related Action. You expect an *arbiter*, or judge, to *decide* a dispute, just as you expect an *architect* to *design* a building.

72. (E); Characteristic Quality. *Sarcasm*, which means cutting remarks, is characteristically *caustic*. In the same way, a *cavity*, or hole, is characteristically *hollow*.

73. (B); Performer and Related Action. *Sympathizers condole* with others, just as *winners celebrate* with others.

74. (D); Synonym. *Convinced* and *certain* have similar meanings, as do *immaculate* and *pure*.

75. (C); Synonym. A *crony* is a *buddy*, just as a *duty* is an *obligation*.

76. (D); Antonym. To *debase*, or lower in some way, means the opposite of *elevate*, just as *criticize* means the opposite of *praise*.

77. (B); Antonym. *Demure* is opposite in meaning to *flashy*. *Plain* and *fancy* are also opposite in meaning.

78. (C); Synonym. *Earnest* and *sincere* have similar meanings. *Vehement*, which means impassioned, and *passionate* also have similar meanings.

79. (A); Antonym. *Effervescent*, or active and bubbly, means the opposite of *listless*. *Brilliant* and *dull* also have opposite meanings.

80. (B); Characteristic Quality. A *breeze* is characteristically *gentle*, just as a *cello* is characteristically *resonant*, or vibrating with sound.

81. (B); Degree. To *gloat* means to *enjoy* something with a great degree of malicious pleasure. To *glare* means to *look* with a fierce, angry stare.

82. (A); Performer and Related Action. A *grand jury* may *indict*, or charge a defendant with a crime, just as a *monarch* may *rule* a country.

83. (C); Antonym. *Inertia*, the tendency not to change, is the opposite of *change. Safety* and

danger are also opposite in meaning.

84. (B); Characteristic Quality. A *pest* is characteristically *irksome*, or annoying, just as a *clown* is characteristically *amusing*.

85. (E); Synonym. *Journalists* and *reporters* have nearly the same meaning, as do *clientele* and *customers*.

86. (D); Classification. A *lexicon*, or dictionary, is classified as a *reference book*, just as *Judaism* is classified as a *religion*.

87. (E); Synonym. *Locate* and *find* are similar in meaning, as are *carp* and *complain*.

88. (B); Synonym. *Melancholy* and *gloom* have similar meanings, as do *tradition* and *custom*.

89. (B); Synonym. *Pallid* and *pale* have the same meaning, as do *quiet* and *hushed*.

90. (A); Characteristic Quality. A *plateau* is characteristically *elevated*, just as *jargon* is characteristically *unintelligible*, or impossible for most people to understand.

91. (D); Synonym. *Protrude* and *jut out* have similar meanings, as do *remember* and *recall*.

92. (E); Antonym. *Rankle*, meaning to irritate, is the opposite of *soothe. Enjoy* and *dislike* are also opposite in meaning.

93. (C); Antonym. *Realistic* is opposite in meaning to *fantastic. Odious* and *appealing* are also opposite in meaning.

94. (A); Function. A *requiem* is written or performed to *honor* the dead, just as a *novel* is written to *entertain*.

95. (E); Synonym. *Sardonic* and *sarcastic* have similar meanings, as do *cheerful* and *glad*.

96. (D); Antonym. To *seethe*, or boil, means the opposite of to *freeze*, just as to *eat* means the opposite of to *fast*, or to go without food.

97. (B); Synonym. *Sporadic* and *occasional* have the same meaning, as do *considerate* and *thoughtful*.

98. (D); Synonym. Something *subsidiary* is *secondary* in rank or importance, just as something *strange* is *odd*.

99. (B); Performer and Related Object. A *chemist* produces *synthesis*, just as an *artist* produces a *statue*.

100. (C); Characteristic Quality. A *tragedy*, a serious play with an unhappy ending, is *sad*, just as a *farce*, an exaggerated, humorous play, is *funny*.

Fifth Course

Lesson 1   pages 3–6
Exercise 1   Mapping
Your Guess and Definition answers will vary. Possible responses to Other Forms items follow.

1. *n.* accentuation; *vt.* accentuates, accentuated, accentuating
2. *n.* ambiguity, ambiguousness; *adv.* ambiguously
3. *n.* comprehension, comprehensiveness; *adv.* comprehensively
4. *n.* felicitousness, felicity; *adv.* felicitously
5. *n.* impregnability; *adv.* impregnably
6. *adj.* inceptive; *adv.* inceptively
7. *n.* intricateness; *adj.* intricate; *adv.* intricately
8. *n.* introspection, introspectiveness; *vi.* introspect; *adj.* introspectional; *adv.* introspectively
9. *n.* provocation, provocativeness, provoker; *vt.* provoke; *adj.* provoking; *adv.* provocatively
10. *n.* vernacularism; *adv.* vernacularly

Exercise 2   Context Clues
11. (J) vernacular
12. (E) inception
13. (C) provocative
14. (B) accentuate
15. (G) intricacy
16. (D) introspective
17. (A) felicitous
18. (F) impregnable
19. (H) comprehensive
20. (I) ambiguous

Exercise 3   Sentence Completion
21. D   22. B   23. B   24. E   25. A   26. C   27. D
28. C   29. E   30. B

Lesson 2   pages 7–10
Exercise 1   Mapping
Your Guess and Definition answers will vary. Possible responses to Other Forms items follow.

1. *n.* allegorist, allegorization, allegorizer; *vi.* or *vt.* allegorize; *adj.* allegoric, allegorical, allegoristic; *adv.* allegorically
2. *n.* conjecturer; *n. pl.* conjectures; *vi.* or *vt.* conjectures, conjectured, conjecturing; *adj.* conjectural, conjecturable; *adv.* conjecturally, conjecturably
3. *n.* despicableness; *adv.* despicably
4. *n.* dissolution, dissoluteness; *adv.* dissolutely
5. *n.* ferociousness; *adj.* ferocious; *adv.* ferociously
6. *n.* incongruity, incongruousness; *adv.* incongruously
7. *n.* misanthropist, misanthropy; *adj.* misanthropic, misanthropical; *adv.* misanthropically
8. *n.* prolog; *vi.* prologuize
9. *n. pl.* protagonists
10. *n.* terseness; *adj.* terser, tersest; *adv.* tersely

Exercise 2   Context Clues
11. (J) prologue
12. (H) conjecture
13. (C) terse
14. (G) misanthrope
15. (E) allegory
16. (A) dissolute
17. (B) protagonist
18. (D) despicable
19. (F) incongruous
20. (I) ferocity

Exercise 3   Sentence Completion
21. B   22. D   23. A   24. D   25. E   26. A   27. C
28. E   29. B   30. B

Lesson 3   pages 11–14
Exercise 1   Mapping
Your Guess and Definition answers will vary. Possible responses to Other Forms items follow.

1. *adj.* epithetic, epithetical
2. *n.* evasion, evasiveness; *vi.* or *vt.* evade; *adv.* evasively
3. *n.* evocativeness, evocation, evocator; *vt.* evokes, evoked, evoking; *adj.* evocable, evocative; *adv.* evocatively
4. *n.* exactingness, exaction; *vt.* exact; *adv.* exactingly
5. *vt.* foreshadow, foreshadows, foreshadowed, foreshadowing
6. *n.* inference, inferrer; *vi.* or *vt.* infers, inferred, inferring; *adj.* inferential; *adv.* inferably, inferentially
7. *n.* lauder, laudability, laudableness; *vt.* laud; *adv.* laudably
8. *n.* lucidity, lucidness; *adv.* lucidly
9. *n.* scrutiny, scrutinizer; *vt.* scrutinizes, scrutinized, scrutinizing; *adj.* scrutable; *adv.* scrutinizingly
10. *n. pl.* symposia, symposiums; *adj.* symposiac

Exercise 2   Context Clues
11. (C) symposium
12. (E) foreshadow
13. (H) scrutinizing
14. (J) evasive
15. (B) infer
16. (D) lucid
17. (G) exacting
18. (F) evoke
19. (A) epithet
20. (I) laudable

Exercise 3   Sentence Completion
21. C   22. B   23. A   24. B   25. D   26. E   27. B
28. E   29. A   30. D

Lesson 4   pages 15–18
Exercise 1   Mapping
Your Guess and Definition answers will vary. Possible responses to Other Forms items follow.

1. *n.* affluence; *adv.* affluently
2. *adj.* brief; *adv.* briefly
3. *vt.* connote; *adj.* connotative, connotational; *adv.* connotatively
4. *n.* embellishment, embellisher; *vt.* embellishes, embellished, embellishing
5. *n.* imbiber, imbibition; *vt.* imbibe, imbibed, imbibing
6. *n.* nostalgia; *adv.* nostalgically
7. *n.* novitiate, noviciate
8. *n.* Philistine, philistinism, Philistinism
9. *n.* reiteration, reiterativeness, reiterator; *vt.* reiterate, reiterates, reiterating; *adj.* reiterative; *adv.* reiteratively
10. *adj.* stipendiary

Exercise 2   Context Clues

11. (D) novice
12. (H) philistine
13. (I) connotation
14. (A) nostalgic
15. (J) stipend

16. (E) affluent
17. (B) reiterated
18. (C) embellish
19. (F) brevity
20. (G) imbibes

Exercise 3   Sentence Completion

21. E   22. D   23. A   24. C   25. B   26. E   27. B
28. C   29. A   30. D

Lesson 5   pages 19–22
Exercise 1   Mapping

Your Guess and Definition answers will vary. Possible responses to Other Forms items follow.

1. *vt.* anagrammatize; *adj.* anagrammatic, anagrammatical; *adv.* anagrammatically
2. *n.* asserter, assertor, assertiveness; *vt.* assert; *adj.* assertive, assertable, assertible, assertional; *adv.* assertively
3. *n.* coherence, coherency; *vi.* or *vt.* cohere; *adv.* coherently
4. *n.* fulmination, fulminator; *vi.* or *vt.* fulminates, fulminated, fulminating; *adj.* fulminatory, fulminant
5. *n. pl.* goads; *vt.* goads, goaded, goading
6. *n.* inexplicableness, inexplicability; *adv.* inexplicably
7. *adv.* noncommitally
8. *n.* proboscidean; *n. pl.* proboscises, proboscides
9. *n.* quixotism, quixotry; *adj.* quixotical; *adv.* quixotically
10. *n. pl.* surmises; *vt.* surmises, surmised, surmising

Exercise 2   Context Clues

11. (J) anagram
12. (I) goad
13. (G) noncommittal
14. (A) assertion
15. (F) quixotic

16. (C) coherent
17. (E) fulminate
18. (H) proboscis
19. (B) inexplicable
20. (D) surmise

Exercise 3   Sentence Completion

21. B   22. C   23. D   24. E   25. B   26. C   27. C
28. B   29. E   30. A

Lesson 6   pages 23–26
Exercise 1   Mapping

Your Guess and Definition answers will vary. Possible responses to Other Forms items follow.

1. *n.* anecdotage, anecdotist; *adj.* anecdotal, anecdotic, anecdotical
2. *n.* climax; *adj.* climactical; *adv.* climactically
3. *n.* epilog
4. *n.* extemporaneousness, extemporization, extemporizer; *vi.* or *vt.* extemporize; *adj.* extempore, extemporary; *adv.* extemporaneously, extemporarily
5. *n. pl.* fidelities
6. *n. pl.* fortes
7. *n.* gourmand, gourmandise
8. *n.* hypochondria, hypochondriasis; *adj.* hypochondriacal; *adv.* hypochondriacally
9. *n.* prodigiousness; *adj.* prodigious; *adv.* prodigiously

10. *n.* stigmatism, stigmatization, stigmatist; *n. pl.* stigmata, stigmas; *vt.* stigmatize; *adj.* stigmal, stigmatic, stigmatical; *adv.* stigmatically.

Exercise 2   Context Clues

11. (I) climactic
12. (H) fidelity
13. (F) anecdotes
14. (E) gourmet
15. (C) prodigies

16. (D) forte
17. (G) epilogues
18. (A) stigma
19. (B) hypochondriac
20. (J) extemporaneous

Exercise 3   Sentence Completion

21. C   22. C   23. E   24. D   25. D   26. B   27. A
28. D   29. A   30. C

Lesson 7   pages 27–30
Exercise 1   Mapping

Your Guess and Definition answers will vary. Possible responses to Other Forms items follow.

1. *n.* bumptiousness; *adv.* bumptiously
2. *n.* citation, citator; *vt.* cites, cited, citing; *adj.* citatory, citable, citeable
3. *n.* consonance, consonancy; *adj.* consonantal; *adv.* consonantly
4. *n.* giber; *n. pl.* gibes; *vi.* or *vt.* gibes, gibed, gibing; *adv.* gibingly
5. *n. pl.* repartees
6. *n.* rudimentariness; *n. pl.* rudiments; *adj.* rudimentary, rudimental; *adv.* rudimentarily
7. *n. pl.* sanctions; *vt.* sanctions, sanctioned, sanctioning; *adj.* sanctionable
8. *n.* satiation, satiability, satiety; *vt.* satiates, satiated, satiating; *adj.* satiable; *adv.* satiably
9. *n.* subservience, subserviency; *vt.* subserve; *adv.* subserviently
10. *n.* vivaciousness, vivacity; *adv.* vivaciously

Exercise 2   Context Clues

11. (A) subservient
12. (G) rudiments
13. (I) gibes
14. (H) bumptious
15. (J) repartee

16. (E) consonant
17. (D) satiate
18. (B) sanction
19. (C) vivacious
20. (F) cited

Exercise 3   Sentence Completion

21. C   22. D   23. E   24. B   25. B   26. D   27. B
28. B   29. A   30. D

Lesson 8   pages 31–34
Exercise 1   Mapping

Your Guess and Definition answers will vary. Possible responses to Other Forms items follow.

1. *n.* comeliness; *adj.* comelier, comeliest
2. *n.* decadency; *adj.* decadent; *adv.* decadently
3. *n.* erroneousness; *adv.* erroneously
4. *n.* flaunter; *vt.* or *vi.* flaunts, flaunted, flaunting; *adv.* flauntingly
5. *n.* hypercritic, hypercriticism; *adv.* hypercritically
6. *n.* irascibility, irascibleness; *adv.* irascibly
7. *n.* miscreancy; *adj.* miscreant
8. *n.* ostentation, ostentatiousness; *adv.* ostentatiously

9. *n.* pretension, pretentiousness; *adv.* pretentiously
10. *n.* sterotyper, stereotypist, stereotypy;
    n. pl. stereotypes; *vt.* stereotype, stereotyped,
    stereotyping; *adj.* stereotypical, stereotyped,
    stereotypic

Exercise 2   Context Clues

11. (G) comely   16. (B) stereotypes
12. (E) miscreant   17. (J) pretentious
13. (I) flaunt   18. (F) ostentatious
14. (C) erroneous   19. (A) hypercritical
15. (H) decadence   20. (D) irascible

Exercise 3   Sentence Completion

21. C   22. E   23. B   24. E   25. A   26. B   27. C
28. D   29. E   30. C

Lesson 9   pages 35–38
Exercise 1   Mapping
Your Guess and Definition answers will vary. Possible responses to Other Forms items follow.

1. *n.* abridgment, abridgement, abridger;
   vt. abridge, abridges, abridging;
   adj. abridgeable, abridgable
2. *n.* emendator, emender; *vt.* emend;
   vt. emendate; *adj.* emendatory
3. *n.* finalization; *vt.* finalize
4. *n.* garrulousness, garrulity; *adv.* garrulously
5. *n. pl.* impromptus
6. *n.* invocation, invoker; *vt.* invokes, invoked,
   invoking; *adj.* invocational, invocatory
7. *n.* lucre, lucrativeness; *adv.* lucratively
8. *n.* shrewishness; *adj.* shrewish; *adv.* shrewishly
9. *n.* superciliousness; *adv.* superciliously
10. *n.* verbosity, verboseness; *adv.* verbosely

Exercise 2   Context Clues

11. (F) shrew   16. (E) invokes
12. (H) lucrative   17. (J) finality
13. (D) garrulous   18. (A) impromptu
14. (B) abridged   19. (G) supercilious
15. (I) verbose   20. (C) emendations

Exercise 3   Sentence Completion

21. C   22. A   23. E   24. D   25. C   26. A   27. D
28. B   29. E   30. A

Lesson 10   pages 39–42
Exercise 1   Mapping
Your Guess and Definition answers will vary. Possible responses to Other Forms items follow.

1. *n.* bolsterer; *n. pl.* bolsters; *vt.* bolsters, bolstered,
   bolstering
2. *adj.* expletory
3. None
4. *n.* idiom; *adv.* idiomatically
5. *n.* intangibility, intangibleness; *adv.* intangibly
6. *n.* laconism, laconicism; *adv.* laconically
7. *n.* reciprocator, reciprocation, reciprocality,
   reciprocalness, reciprocity; *vi.* or *vt.* reciprocate,
   reciprocated, reciprocating; *adj.* reciprocal,
   reciprocative, reciprocatory; *adv.* reciprocally
8. *n. pl.* subterfuges

9. *n.* tawdriness; *adj.* tawdrier, tawdriest;
    adv. tawdrily
10. *n.* wistfulness; *adv.* wistfully

Exercise 2   Context Clues

11. (F) intangible   16. (B) reciprocates
12. (J) idiomatic   17. (G) wistful
13. (C) expletives   18. (D) furor
14. (I) laconic   19. (H) subterfuge
15. (A) bolstered   20. (E) tawdry

Exercise 3   Sentence Completion

21. C   22. B   23. E   24. B   25. B   26. E   27. B
28. D   29. C   30. D

Lesson 11   pages 43–46
Exercise 1   Mapping
Your Guess and Definition answers will vary. Possible responses to Other Forms items follow.

1. *n.* ambivalence, ambivalency; *adv.* ambivalently
2. *n.* beneficence, benefice, beneficiary;
   adj. beneficial; *adv.* beneficently
3. *n.* betrothal; *vt.* betroth
4. *adv.* congenitally
5. *adj.* consensual; *adv.* consensually
6. *adv.* interminably
7. *n.* intrepidness, intrepidity; *adv.* intrepidly
8. *n.* repugnance, repugnancy; *adv.* repugnantly
9. *n.* sallowness; *vt.* sallows, sallowed, sallowing;
   adv. sallowly
10. *vi.* sorties, sortied, sortieing

Exercise 2   Context Clues

11. (E) congenital   16. (D) sortie
12. (A) consensus   17. (H) betrothed
13. (F) interminable   18. (C) intrepid
14. (J) sallow   19. (G) beneficent
15. (B) repugnant   20. (I) ambivalent

Exercise 3   Sentence Completion

21. D   22. E   23. B   24. E   25. D   26. A   27. B
28. C   29. B   30. D

Lesson 12   pages 47–50
Exercise 1   Mapping
Your Guess and Definition answers will vary. Possible responses to Other Forms items follow.

1. *adj.* adamantine; *adv.* adamantly
2. *n.* antagonist, antagonism; *vt.* antagonizes,
   antagonized, antagonizing; *adj.* antagonistic;
   adv. antagonistically
3. *n.* archivist; *vi.* or *vt.* archive; *adj.* archival
4. *n.* autocracy; *adj.* autocratic, autocratical;
   adv. autocratically
5. *n.* factiousness; *adv.* factiously
6. *n.* frustration, frustrater; *vt.* frustrates, frustrated, frustrating; *adv.* frustratingly
7. *n.* peremptoriness; *adv.* peremptorily
8. *n.* procrastinator, procrastination;
   vi. or *vt.* procrastinates, procrastinated,
   procrastinating
9. *n.* resiliency, resilience; *vt.* resile; *adv.* resiliently
10. *n.* supplicant, supplicator; *vi.* or *vt.* supplicate;
    adj. supplicatory

Exercise 2   Context Clues

11. (C) supplication   16. (A) frustrated
12. (J) resilient   17. (H) adamant
13. (E) factious   18. (B) procrastinated
14. (G) autocrat   19. (F) antagonized
15. (I) archives   20. (D) peremptory

Exercise 3   Sentence Completion

21. D   22. B   23. A   24. C   25. B   26. E   27. D
28. B   29. E   30. A

Lesson 13   pages 51–54
Exercise 1   Mapping

Your Guess and Definition answers will vary. Possible responses to Other Forms items follow.

1. *n.* exoneration, exonerator; *vt.* exonerates, exonerated, exonerating; *adj.* exonerative
2. *n.* expediter, expedition, expeditiousness; *vt.* expedites, expedited, expediting; *adj.* expeditious; *adv.* expeditiously
3. *n.* foregoer; *vt.* forgoes, forwent, forgone, forgoing
4. *n.* incoherence, incoherency, incoherentness; *adv.* incoherently
5. *n.* incredulity, incredulousness; *adv.* incredulously
6. *n.* pleb, plebe, plebeianism, plebiscite; *adj.* plebiscitary; *adv.* plebeianly
7. *n.* provoker, provocativeness; *vt.* provoke; *adj.* provocative, provoking; *adv.* provocatively, provokingly
8. *n.* querier, querist; *n. pl.* queries; *vt.* queries, queried, querying
9. *n.* secularism, secularist, secularity, secularization; *vt.* secularize; *adj.* secularistic; *adv.* secularly
10. *n. pl.* shibboleths

Exercise 2   Context Clues

11. (D) incoherent   16. (I) exonerated
12. (G) provocation   17. (J) secular
13. (E) plebeian   18. (C) expedite
14. (A) incredulous   19. (F) shibboleth
15. (H) queried   20. (B) forgo

Exercise 3   Sentence Completion

21. B   22. E   23. B   24. D   25. B   26. C   27. D
28. A   29. E   30. D

Lesson 14   pages 55–58
Exercise 1   Mapping

Your Guess and Definition answers will vary. Possible responses to Other Forms items follow.

1. *n.* blitheness, blithsomeness; *adj.* blither, blithest, blithesome; *adv.* blithely, blithesomely
2. *vt.* cedes, ceded, ceding
3. *vt.* chagrins, chagrined, chagrining
4. *n.* debonaireness; *adj.* debonaire; *adv.* debonairly
5. *n.* filiation; *adv.* filially
6. *n.* interposal, interposer, interposition; *vi.* or *vt.* interposes, interposed, interposing
7. *n.* intrinsicalness; *adj.* intrinsical; *adv.* intrinsically

8. *n.* precipitation, precipitateness, precipitator, precipitance, precipitancy; *vi.* or *vt.* precipitates, precipitated, precipitating; *adj.* precipitative, precipitable; *adv.* precipitately, precipitantly
9. *n.* proficiency; *adv.* proficiently
10. *vt.* remit; *adj.* remiss, remissible; *adv.* remissibly, remissly

Exercise 2   Context Clues

11. (G) filial   16. (J) remission
12. (D) chagrin   17. (B) interposed
13. (H) cede   18. (E) debonair
14. (I) proficient   19. (A) blithe
15. (C) precipitated   20. (F) intrinsic

Exercise 3   Sentence Completion

21. E   22. C   23. B   24. A   25. D   26. B   27. E
28. B   29. C   30. A

Lesson 15   pages 59–62
Exercise 1   Mapping

Your Guess and Definition answers will vary. Possible responses to Other Forms items follow.

1. *n.* acquiescence; *vi.* acquiesces, acquiesced, acquiescing; *adj.* acquiescent; *adv.* acquiescently
2. *vi.* altercate
3. *n.* assailant, assailer, assailment, assailableness; *vt.* assails, assailed, assailing; *adj.* assailable
4. *vt.* beleaguers, beleaguered, beleaguering
5. *n. pl.* brunts
6. *n.* deprecation, deprecator; *vt.* deprecates, deprecated, deprecating; *adj.* deprecatory, deprecative; *adv.* deprecatorily, deprecatingly
7. *n.* palliation, palliator; *vt.* palliates, palliated, palliating; *adj.* palliative; *adv.* palliatively
8. *n. pl.* phalanxes, phalanges; *adj.* phalangeal, phalangal, phalangean
9. *n. pl.* predecessors
10. *n.* redresser, redressor; *vt.* redresses, redressed, redressing; *adj.* redressable

Exercise 2   Context Clues

11. (E) palliate   16. (B) acquiesce
12. (G) assailed   17. (C) deprecated
13. (D) altercation   18. (A) beleaguered
14. (H) phalanx   19. (F) brunt
15. (J) predecessors   20. (I) redress

Exercise 3   Sentence Completion

21. C   22. B   23. E   24. A   25. D   26. B   27. E
28. D   29. A   30. C

Lesson 16   pages 63–66
Exercise 1   Mapping

Your Guess and Definition answers will vary. Possible responses to Other Forms items follow.

1. *vt.* bulwarks, bulwarked, bulwarking
2. *n. pl.* carnages
3. *n.* coalitionist
4. *n.* Exodus
5. *n.* heinousness; *adv.* heinously
6. *n.* Holocaust; *adj.* holocaustal, holocaustic
7. *n.* insidiousness; *adv.* insidiously
8. *n.* invidiousness; *adv.* invidiously

9. *n.* martyrdom, martyrology, martyrologist, martyrization, martyry; *vt.* martyrs, martyred, martyring; martyrize
10. *n.* waiver; *vt.* waives, waived, waiving

Exercise 2   Context Clues

11. (E) coalition
12. (I) insidious
13. (A) carnage
14. (G) holocaust
15. (H) martyrs
16. (D) bulwark
17. (B) exodus
18. (J) invidious
19. (F) waive
20. (C) heinous

Exercise 3   Sentence Completion

21. B   22. D   23. C   24. E   25. A   26. C   27. C
28. E   29. E   30. B

Lesson 17   pages 67–70

Exercise 1   Mapping

Your Guess and Definition answers will vary. Possible responses to Other Forms items follow.

1. *adj.* affinitive
2. *n.* arrayal; *vt.* arrays, arrayed, arraying
3. *n.* audacity, audaciousness; *adv.* audaciously
4. *n.* conviviality, convivialist; *adv.* convivially
5. *vi.* or *vt.* deigns, deigned, deigning
6. *n.* derogatoriness, derogation; *vi.* or *vt.* derogate; *adj.* derogative; *adv.* derogatorily
7. *n.* epicurean, Epicurean, epicurism, Epicureanism; *adj.* epicurean
8. *n.* fastidiousness; *adv.* fastidiously
9. *n.* ingratiation; *vt.* ingratiates, ingratiated, ingratiating; *adj.* ingratiating, ingratiatory; *adv.* ingratiatingly
10. *n.* oscillation, oscillator; *vi.* oscillates, oscillated, oscillating; *adj.* oscillational, oscillatory

Exercise 2   Context Clues

11. (E) derogatory
12. (B) convivial
13. (G) deigned
14. (A) affinity
15. (F) fastidious
16. (C) oscillate
17. (D) audacious
18. (I) epicure
19. (H) ingratiate
20. (J) arrayed

Exercise 3   Sentence Completion

21. C   22. A   23. D   24. B   25. D   26. A   27. E
28. B   29. C   30. D

Lesson 18   pages 71–74

Exercise 1   Mapping

Your Guess and Definition answers will vary. Possible responses to Other Forms items follow.

1. *n. pl.* bandies; *vt.* bandies, bandied, bandying
2. *n.* degeneracy, degenerateness, degeneration; *vi.* degenerates, degenerated, degenerating; *adj.* degenerative; *adv.* degenerately, degeneratively
3. *n.* efficaciousness, efficacy; *adv.* efficaciously
4. *n.* equestrienne, equestrianism
5. *n.* felon, felonry, feloniousness; *adj.* felonious
6. *n.* flayer; *vt.* flays, flayed, flaying
7. *n.* imperiousness; *adv.* imperiously
8. *n.* malevolence; *adv.* malevolently
9. *n.* rationalization, rationalizer, rationality, rationale; *vi.* or *vt.* rationalizes, rationalized, rationalizing
10. *n.* relenter; *vi.* or *vt.* relents, relented, relenting

Exercise 2   Context Clues

11. (G) flays
12. (B) felony
13. (C) efficacious
14. (D) rationalize
15. (A) degenerated
16. (F) imperious
17. (J) relent
18. (E) malevolent
19. (I) equestrian
20. (H) bandy

Exercise 3   Sentence Completion

21. C   22. D   23. A   24. E   25. D   26. B   27. A
28. D   29. E   30. C

Lesson 19   pages 75–78

Exercise 1   Mapping

Your Guess and Definition answers will vary. Possible responses to Other Forms items follow.

1. *n.* abashment; *vt.* abashes, abashed, abashing; *adv.* abashedly
2. *n.* auspice, auspiciousness; *adv.* auspiciously
3. *vi.* defer; *adj.* deferent, deferential; *adv.* deferentially
4. *n. pl.* demeanors
5. *vi.* guises, guised, guising
6. *adv.* immemorially
7. *n.* occultism, occultist, occultness; *vi.* or *vt.* occults, occulted, occulting; *adv.* occultly
8. *n.* purporter; *n. pl.* purports; *vt.* purports, purported, purporting; *adj.* purported; *adv.* purportedly
9. *n.* sartor, sartorius; *adv.* sartorially
10. *n.* syndic, syndication, syndicator; *vi.* or *vt.* syndicates, syndicated, syndicating

Exercise 2   Context Clues

11. (J) purported
12. (F) demeanor
13. (D) syndicate
14. (C) abashed
15. (G) guise
16. (B) occult
17. (E) auspicious
18. (A) immemorial
19. (H) deference
20. (I) sartorial

Exercise 3   Sentence Completion

21. B   22. D   23. B   24. A   25. D   26. B   27. C
28. C   29. A   30. C

Lesson 20   pages 79–82

Exercise 1   Mapping

Your Guess and Definition answers will vary. Possible responses to Other Forms items follow.

1. *n.* arbitrariness; *adv.* arbitrarily
2. *n.* browbeater; *vt.* browbeat, browbeaten, browbeating
3. *n.* bureau, bureaucrat, bureaucratese, bureaucratization; *vt.* bureaucratize; *adj.* bureaucratic; *adv.* bureaucratically
4. *n.* contrabandage, contrabandist
5. *n.* inanity; *adv.* inanely
6. *n.* politician, politicization, politicker, politico; *n. pl.* politics; *vt.* politick, politicize; *adj.* political; *adv.* politicly, politically
7. *n.* premeditation, premeditator; *vi.* or *vt.* premeditate, premeditates, premeditating; *adj.* premeditative; *adv.* premeditatedly
8. *n. pl.* proxies
9. *vt.* scapegoats, scapegoated, scapegoating
10. *n.* transience, transiency; *adv.* transiently

Exercise 2   Context Clues

11. (G) contraband	16. (C) arbitrary
12. (E) politic	17. (I) transient
13. (F) inane	18. (B) premeditated
14. (J) proxy	19. (D) browbeat
15. (A) bureaucracy	20. (H) scapegoats

Exercise 3   Sentence Completion

21. D   22. B   23. C   24. E   25. C   26. E   27. B
28. A   29. C   30. B

Lesson 21   pages 83–86
Exercise 1   Mapping

Your Guess and Definition answers will vary. Possible responses to Other Forms items follow.

1. *n.* assayer; *n. pl.* assays; *vt.* assays, assayed, assaying
2. *n.* augmentation, augmenter, augmentative; *vt.* augments, augmented, augmenting; *adj.* augmentable, augmentative, augmented
3. *n.* divergence, divergency; *vi.* or *vt.* diverges, diverged, diverging; *adj.* divergent; *adv.* divergently
4. *n.* factionalism, factiousness, factionalist, factionalization; *vi.* or *vt.* factionalize, factionalized, factionalizing; *adj.* factional, factious, factionalist; *adv.* factionally, factiously
5. *n. pl.* fjords
6. *n.* impotence, impotency; *adv.* impotently
7. *n.* inherence, inherency; *vi.* inhere; *adv.* inherently
8. *n.* subsidence; *vi.* subside, subsides, subsiding
9. *n.* unremittingness; *adv.* unremittingly
10. *n.* voguishness; *adj.* voguish

Exercise 2   Context Clues

11. (H) vogue	16. (D) inherent
12. (E) faction	17. (F) fiord
13. (G) assay	18. (I) unremitting
14. (C) impotent	19. (B) augment
15. (A) diverge	20. (J) subsided

Exercise 3   Sentence Completion

21. D   22. C   23. E   24. B   25. E   26. A   27. D
28. C   29. A   30. E

Lesson 22   pages 87–90
Exercise 1   Mapping

Your Guess and Definition answers will vary. Possible responses to Other Forms items follow.

1. *n.* abstention, abstainer, abstinence; *vi.* abstain, abstains, abstaining; *adj.* abstemious, abstentious
2. *n. pl.* catharses; *adj.* cathartic, cathartical
3. *n.* credentials
4. *n.* dissipation, dissipater, dissipator, dissipatedness; *vi.* or *vt.* dissipate, dissipates, dissipating; *adj.* dissipative, dissipated; *adv.* dissipatedly
5. *adj.* entatative
6. *n.* entomologist; *adj.* entomologic, entomological; *adv.* entomologically
7. *n.* idyl, idyllist; *n. pl.* idylls; *adj.* idyllic; *adv.* idyllically
8. *n.* omnivore, omnivorousness; *adv.* omnivorously

9. *n. pl.* prototypes; *adj.* prototypical, prototypic, prototypal
10. *n.* tepidity, tepidness; *adv.* tepidly

Exercise 2   Context Clues

11. (C) abstained	16. (A) omnivorous
12. (H) entomology	17. (B) idyll
13. (J) tepid	18. (D) catharsis
14. (I) prototype	19. (G) dissipated
15. (F) credence	20. (E) entity

Exercise 3   Sentence Completion

21. E   22. B   23. C   24. C   25. B   26. D   27. A
28. E   29. C   30. C

Lesson 23   pages 91–94
Exercise 1   Mapping

Your Guess and Definition answers will vary. Possible responses to Other Forms items follow.

1. *vt.* apprise, apprises, apprising
2. *n.* austerity, austereness; *adv.* austerely
3. *n.* bestowment, bestowal; *vt.* bestow, bestows, bestowing; *adj.* bestowable
4. None
5. *n.* circumspection; *adv.* circumspectly
6. *n.* correlation, correlativity; *n. pl.* correlates; *vt.* correlates, correlated, correlating; *adj.* correlative, correlational; *adv.* correlatively
7. *n.* elatedness; *vt.* elate; *adj.* elated; *adv.* elatedly
8. *n. pl.* enormities
9. *n.* exhaustiveness, exhaustivity, exhaustion, exhaustibility; *vt.* exhaust; *adj.* exhaustible, exhaustless; *adv.* exhaustively
10. *n.* recriminator; *vi.* or *vt.* recriminate; *adj.* recriminative, recriminatory

Exercise 2   Context Clues

11. (E) enormity	16. (B) circumspect
12. (C) camaraderie	17. (H) elation
13. (A) apprised	18. (D) austere
14. (I) recrimination	19. (F) correlate
15. (J) exhaustive	20. (G) bestowed

Exercise 3   Sentence Completion

21. C   22. D   23. A   24. E   25. D   26. B   27. C
28. D   29. A   30. E

Lesson 24   pages 95–98
Exercise 1   Mapping

Your Guess and Definition answers will vary. Possible responses to Other Forms items follow.

1. *vt.* accosts, accosted, accosting
2. *n.* appraisement, appraiser; *vt.* appraise; *adj.* appraisable; *adv.* appraisingly
3. *n.* furtiveness; *adv.* furtively
4. *n.* mercenariness; *adv.* mercenarily
5. *n.* permeation, permeability; *vt.* permeates, permeated, permeating; *adj.* permeative, permeable; *adv.* permeably
6. *n.* perniciousness; *adv.* perniciously
7. *n.* population, populousness; *vt.* populate; *adj.* populous, popular; *adv.* populously
8. *n.* proletariat, proletarianism, proletarianization, proletary; *vt.* proletarianize
9. *n.* rapaciousness, rapacity; *adv.* rapaciously

10. *n.* recalcitrance, recalcitrancy, recalcitration; *vt.* recalcitrate; *adv.* recalcitrantly

Exercise 2   Context Clues

11. (H) furtive   16. (D) rapacious
12. (B) mercenary   17. (E) recalcitrant
13. (F) permeate   18. (J) appraisal
14. (I) accost   19. (C) proletarians
15. (A) populace   20. (G) pernicious

Exercise 3   Sentence Completion

21. B   22. B   23. D   24. E   25. E   26. B   27. B
28. C   29. D   30. C

Lesson 25   pages 99–102

Exercise 1   Mapping

Your Guess and Definition answers will vary. Possible responses to Other Forms items follow.

1. *n.* acquisitiveness; *adj.* acquisitive; *adv.* acquisitively
2. *n.* alleviation, alleviator; *vt.* alleviates, alleviated, alleviating; *adj.* alleviative, alleviatory
3. *n.* brusqueness, brusquerie; *adj.* brusk; *adv.* brusquely
4. *n. pl.* debacles
5. *adj.* microcosmic, microcosmical; *adv.* microcosmically
6. *n.* rigor, rigorism, rigorist, rigorousness; *adj.* rigoristic; *adv.* rigorously
7. *n.* tenaciousness; *adj.* tenacious; *adv.* tenaciously
8. *n.* thwarter; *vt.* thwarted, thwarted, thwarting; *adv.* thwartly
9. *adv.* ulteriorly
10. *n.* wiliness; *adj.* wilier, wiliest; *adv.* wilily

Exercise 2   Context Clues

11. (E) brusque   16. (J) ulterior
12. (B) microcosm   17. (I) alleviate
13. (A) acquisition   18. (F) tenacity
14. (D) debacle   19. (H) thwart
15. (G) wily   20. (C) rigorous

Exercise 3   Sentence Completion

21. B   22. A   23. B   24. D   25. D   26. A   27. A
28. B   29. D   30. C

Lesson 26   pages 103–106

Exercise 1   Mapping

Your Guess and Definition answers will vary. Possible responses to Other Forms items follow.

1. *n.* arduousness; *adv.* arduously
2. *n. pl.* deluges; *vt.* deluges, deluged, deluging
3. *n.* enthrallment, enthralment; *vt.* enthrall, enthralls, enthralling
4. *n.* grandioseness, grandiosity; *adv.* grandiosely
5. *n.* impetuousness, impetuosity; *adv.* impetuously
6. *n.* insatiability, insatiableness, insatiateness; *adj.* insatiate; *adv.* insatiably, insatiately
7. *n.* oracle, oracularity; *adv.* oracularly
8. *n.* platitudinarian; *vt.* platitudinize; *adj.* platitudinal, platitudinous; *adv.* platitudinously
9. *n. pl.* sluices; *vi.* or *vt.* sluices, sluiced, sluicing
10. *n.* synchronism, synchronizer, synchronization, synchronousness, synchrony; *vi.* or *vt.* synchronize, synchronizes, synchronizing; *adj.* synchronic, synchronous, synchronistic, synchronistical; *adv.* synchronically, synchronistically

Exercise 2   Context Clues

11. (I) impetuous   16. (C) grandiose
12. (G) synchronized   17. (H) enthralled
13. (F) arduous   18. (E) sluice
14. (A) platitudes   19. (B) oracular
15. (J) insatiable   20. (D) deluge

Exercise 3   Sentence Completion

21. D   22. B   23. E   24. A   25. D   26. B   27. D
28. D   29. A   30. B

Lesson 27   pages 107–110

Exercise 1   Mapping

Your Guess and Definition answers will vary. Possible responses to Other Forms items follow.

1. *n.* abatement, abater, abator; *vi.* or *vt.* abates, abated, abating; *adj.* abatable
2. *n.* contriteness; *adj.* contrite; *adv.* contritely
3. *n.* effeteness; *adv.* effetely
4. *adj.* indolent; *adv.* indolently
5. *n.* inurement; *vi.* or *vt.* inures, inured, inuring
6. *n.* presumption, presumptuousness; *v.* presume; *adj.* presuming, presumable; *adv.* presumptuously, presumingly, presumably
7. *n.* propagation, propagator; *vt.* propagates, propagated, propagating; *adj.* propagable, propagative, propagational
8. *n.* protraction, protractedness, protractor; *vt.* protracts, protracted, protracting; *adj.* protractive, protractible, protractile; *adv.* protractedly
9. *adj.* quadrupedal
10. *n.* wrester; *n. pl.* wrests; *vt.* wrests, wrested, wresting

Exercise 2   Context Clues

11. (B) indolence   16. (J) abate
12. (H) wrest   17. (C) presumptuous
13. (F) propagate   18. (A) protract
14. (I) contrition   19. (D) effete
15. (G) quadruped   20. (E) inure

Exercise 3   Sentence Completion

21. C   22. E   23. E   24. C   25. A   26. C   27. E
28. B   29. E   30 B

Lesson 28   pages 111–114

Exercise 1   Mapping

Your Guess and Definition answers will vary. Possible responses to Other Forms items follow.

1. *n.* abomination, abominator; *vt.* abominate
2. *n.* concert; *vi.* or *vt.* concert; *adv.* concertedly
3. *n.* defilement, defiler; *vi.* or *vt.* defile, defiles, defiling; *adv.* defilingly
4. *n.* encroachment, encroacher; *vi.* encroaches, encroached, encroaching
5. *n.* fallibility, fallibleness; *adv.* fallibly
6. *n.* innocuousness; *adv.* innocuously
7. *n.* insularity, insularism, insulation; *vt.* insulate
8. *adj.* panacean
9. *n.* vegetation, vegetable, vegetativeness; *vi.* vegetates, vegetated, vegetating; *adj.* vegetal, vegetative, vegetive, vegetational; *adv.* vegetatively

10. *n.* vilification, vilifier; *vt.* vilifies, vilified, vilifying

Exercise 2 Context Clues

11. (H) panacea
12. (D) fallible
13. (B) concerted
14. (J) vilify
15. (G) encroach
16. (I) innocuous
17. (F) abominable
18. (C) insular
19. (E) vegetate
20. (A) defiled

Exercise 3 Sentence Completion

21. A 22. D 23. C 24. B 25. E 26. D 27. E
28. E 29. D 30. C

Lesson 29   pages 115–118

Exercise 1   Mapping

Your Guess and Definition answers will vary. Possible responses to Other Forms items follow.

1. *adj.* attrited
2. *n.* balefulness; *adv.* balefully
3. *n.* bilateralism, bilateralness; *adv.* bilaterally
4. None
5. *n. pl.* flails; *vi.* or *vt.* flails, flailed, flailing
6. *n.* haggardness; *adv.* haggardly
7. None
8. *n.* somnolence, somnolency; *adv.* somnolently
9. *n.* stotic, stoicism, stoicalness; *adj.* stoical; *adv.* stoically
10. *n.* vanquisher, vanquishment; *vt.* vanquishes, vanquished, vanquishing; *adj.* vanquishable

Exercise 2   Context Clues

11. (G) flail
12. (I) stoic
13. (B) haggard
14. (D) vanquish
15. (J) baleful
16. (F) somnolent
17. (A) entourage
18. (E) bilateral
19. (C) impunity
20. (H) attrition

Exercise 3   Sentence Completion

21. B 22. E 23. B 24. E 25. A 26. C 27. B
28. D 29. B 30. C

Lesson 30   pages 119–122

Exercise 1   Mapping

Your Guess and Definition answers will vary. Possible responses to Other Forms items follow.

1. *n.* abutment, abutter; *n. pl.* abuttals; *vi.* or *vt.* abuts, abutted, abutting
2. *n.* arability
3. None
4. *n.* girder, girdle, girdler; *vt.* girds, girded, girding; girdle
5. *n.* grade; *vi.* or *vt.* grade; *vt.* gradate; *adj.* gradational; *adv.* gradationally
6. *n.* incisor, incision, incisiveness; *vt.* incises, incised, incising; *adj.* incisive; *adv.* incisively
7. *n.* indigenousness, indigen, indigene; *adv.* indigenously
8. *n.* nurturer, nurturance; *vt.* nurtures, nurtured, nurturing; *adj.* nurturant, nurtural
9. *n.* orientation; *vi.* or *vt.* orients, oriented, orienting; orientate; *adj.* Oriental
10. *adj.* solstitial

Exercise 2   Context Clues

11. (H) arable
12. (G) gird
13. (E) incise
14. (A) gradations
15. (J) askew
16. (I) abut
17. (C) orient
18. (F) indigenous
19. (B) nurture
20. (D) solstice

Exercise 3   Sentence Completion

21. E 22. B 23. D 24. B 25. C 26. A 27. E
28. C 29. D 30. B

CONNECTING NEW WORDS AND PATTERNS

Lesson 1   page 126

1. (C); Classification. An *allegory* is classified as a *story*, just as a *ballad* is classified as a *song*.
2. (D); Antonym. *Comprehensive*, or complete, means the opposite of *limited*. *Narrow* and *wide* also have opposite meanings.
3. (C); Synonym. *Felicitous* and *appropriate* have similar meanings, as do *affluent* and *wealthy*.
4. (A); Characteristic Quality. A *lion* is characteristically *ferocious*, just as a *mouse* is characteristically *timid*.
5. (E); Antonym. *Incongruous*, which means lacking in harmony or agreement, means the opposite of *harmonious*, just as *reluctant*, or unwilling, means the opposite of *enthusiastic*.
6. (C); Synonym. *Intricacy* and *complexity* have nearly the same meaning, as do *commendation* and *praise*.
7. (C); Characteristic Quality. *Self-analysis* is by nature characteristically *introspective*, or inward-looking. A *mirror* is characteristically *reflective*.
8. (C); Part and Whole. A *prologue* is the first part of a *play*, as a *preamble* is the first part of a *constitution*.
9. (E); Classification. A *protagonist* is a type of *character* in a story, just as a *beagle* is a type of *dog*.
10. (C); Synonym. *Provocative* and *stimulating* have nearly the same meaning, as do *turbulent* and *stormy*.

Lesson 2   page 127

1. (D); Synonym. *Brevity* and *shortness* have nearly the same meaning, as do *length* and *extent*.
2. (A); Function. The function of a *connotation*, an idea associated with a word or phrase, is to *suggest* something. In the same way, the function of an *implication* is to *imply* something.
3. (E); Antonym. *Embellish*, which means decorate or improve by adding detail, means the opposite of *simplify*. *Agree* and *differ* are also opposite in meaning.
4. (C); Function. The function of an *epithet*, a descriptive name or title, is to *describe* someone, just as the function of a *solvent* is to *dissolve* something.
5. (A); Synonym. *Evoke*, which means call forth, has nearly the same meaning as *summon*. *Defy* and *resist* also have nearly the same meaning.

6. (B); Cause and Effect. To *foreshadow,* or hint at a story's outcome, can cause *anticipation,* just as to *exercise* can cause *health.*

7. (E); Action and Related Object. You *imbibe,* or drink, a *beverage,* just as you *devour* a *pastry.*

8. (D); Characteristic Quality. *Virtue* is *laudable,* or praiseworthy, just as *gibberish* is *unintelligible,* or impossible to understand.

9. (B); Characteristic Quality. A *has-been* is characteristically *nostalgic,* or longing for the past, just as a *hero* is characteristically *brave.*

10. (A); Synonym. *Reiterate* and *repeat* have the same meaning, as do *dispense,* which means to hand out, or *distribute.*

Lesson 3   page 128

1. (B); Characteristic Quality. An *anecdote,* or brief story, is characteristically *entertaining,* just as a *joke* is characteristically *amusing.*

2. (D); Synonym. *Assertion* and *claim* (as a noun) both have the same meaning, as do *beat* (as a noun) and *rhythm.*

3. (C); Characteristic Quality. The *finale,* or end of a show, is characteristically *climactic,* or most dramatic. In the same way, most people regard the *weekend* as characteristically *relaxing.*

4. (C); Antonym. *Coherent,* or clear, is opposite in meaning to *muddled. Fantastic* and *ordinary* also have opposite meanings.

5. (B); Antonym. A *forte,* someone's best skill or character strength, is opposite in meaning to *weakness,* just as *sturdiness* is opposite in meaning to *fragility.*

6. (A); Degree. *Fulminate,* which means denounce loudly, differs in degree but has a meaning similar to *disagree,* just as *enrage* and *annoy* have similar meanings but differ in degree.

7. (E); Antonym. *Goad,* which means urge on, is opposite in meaning to *restrain,* which means hold back. *Reward* and *punish* are also opposite in meaning.

8. (C); Characteristic Quality. A *mystery* is characteristically *inexplicable,* just as a *donor* is characteristically *generous.*

9. (B); Cause and Effect. A *stigma,* or mark of scorn, can cause *shame,* just as a *medal* can cause *pride.*

10. (A); Synonym. *Surmise* and *guess* have nearly the same meaning, as do *disregard* and *ignore.*

Lesson 4   page 129

1. (E); Part and Whole. A *consonant,* any letter that is not a vowel, is part of the *alphabet,* just as a *word* is part of a *sentence.*

2. (A); Cause and Effect. A *bad influence* can cause *decadence,* or moral decline, just as an *award* can cause a *celebration.*

3. (D); Antonym. *Erroneous,* which means wrong, is opposite in meaning to *correct.* In the same way, *beautiful* and *ugly* are also opposites.

4. (B); Performer and Related Action. A *peacock flaunts,* or displays, its feathers, just as a *squirrel hoards* nuts.

5. (E); Synonym. *Gibe* and *jeer* have nearly the same meaning, as do *braid* and *interweave.*

6. (B); Degree. *Hypercritical* is a greater degree of *critical,* just as *hyperactive* is a greater degree of *active.*

7. (A); Synonym. *Irascible* and *irritable* have nearly the same meaning, as do *peaceful* and *harmonious.*

8. (D); Synonym. A *miscreant* is a *villain,* just as a *meddler* is a *busybody.*

9. (E); Degree. *Ostentatious* indicates a greater degree of showiness than *noticeable. Wrathful* indicates a greater degree of anger than *annoyed.*

10. (C); Antonym. *Pretentious* is opposite in meaning to *humble,* just as *generous* is opposite in meaning to *miserly.*

Lesson 5   page 130

1. (B); Action and Related Object. You *abridge,* or shorten, a *text,* just as you *shrink fabric.*

2. (B); Characteristic Quality. An *expletive,* or curse, is characteristically *profane,* just as a *tribute* is characteristically *complimentary.*

3. (C); Characteristic Quality. A *language* is characteristically *idiomatic,* just as *customs* are characteristically *traditional.*

4. (C); Synonym. *Impromptu* and *spontaneous* have nearly the same meaning, as do *contaminated* and *polluted.*

5. (E); Characteristic Quality. *Emotion* is characteristically *intangible,* or untouchable, and *light* is characteristically *luminous,* or radiant.

6. (B); Antonym. *Lucrative* and *unprofitable* are opposite in meaning, as are *skillful* and *awkward.*

7. (E); Characteristic Quality. A *shrew,* or irritable woman, is characteristically *bad-tempered,* just as a *miser* is characteristically *stingy.*

8. (D); Synonym. *Supercilious* and *haughty* both mean proud and scornful. *Superfluous* and *excessive* both mean more than is needed.

9. (E); Antonym. *Tawdry* and *tasteful* have opposite meanings, as do *customary* and *unusual.*

10. (C); Synonym. *Verbose* and *wordy* have the same meaning, as do *verbal* and *spoken.*

Lesson 6   page 131

1. (D); Antonym. *Ambivalent* and *certain* are opposite in meaning, as are *absolute* and *conditional.*

2. (E); Location. *Documents* can be found in *archives,* just as *artwork* can be found in a *museum.*

3. (E); Classification. An *autocrat,* or dictator, is classified as a *ruler,* just as a *democracy* is classified as a *government.*

4. (C); Characteristic Quality. A *charity* is characteristically *beneficent*—that is, it does good. In the same way, a *sage* is a characteristically *wise* person.

5. (E); Degree. Being *betrothed* is a lesser degree of commitment than being *married.* Similarly, *groggy* is a lesser degree of relaxation than *asleep.*

6. (E); Synonym. *Congenital* and *inborn* have the same meaning, as do *temporary* and *impermanent.*

7. (C); Synonym. *Procrastinate* and *postpone* both mean to put off until another time. *Schedule* and *plan* also have the same meaning.

8. (E); Antonym. *Repugnant* and *attractive* are opposite in meaning, as are *reduced* and *enlarged*.

9. (A); Characteristic Quality. Someone who is *sick* is characteristically *sallow*, or grayish yellow, just as someone who is *healthy* is characteristically *bright-eyed*.

10. (B); Characteristic Quality. A *sortie*, or raid, is characteristically *sudden* and quick. An *attack* is characteristically *vigorous*.

Lesson 7   page 132

1. (E); Synonym. *Blithe* and *happy* have nearly the same meaning, as do *thoughtful* and *considerate*.

2. (D); Antonym. *Cede*, which means surrender, means the opposite of *claim*, (when *claim* is used as a noun) just as *agree* means the opposite of *dispute*.

3. (A); Performer and Related Action. A *jury exonerates*, or clears of blame, just as an *athlete competes*.

4. (B); Characteristic Quality. *Filial* behavior is characteristic of children, or *offspring*, just as a *father* is *paternal*, or fatherly.

5. (E); Synonym. *Interpose* and *interject* both mean to put in between. *Repose* and *recline* both mean to rest or lie back.

6. (A); Synonym. *Precipitate* (as an adjective) and *sudden* have nearly the same meaning, as do *profound* and *deep*.

7. (C); Antonym. *Proficient*, or competent, means the opposite of *unskilled*, just as *childish* means the opposite of *mature*.

8. (C); Cause and Effect. A *query*, or inquiry, can lead to a *response*, just as a *puncture* can lead to a *leak*.

9. (D); Cause and Effect. *Remission*, which can mean forgiveness of sins or lessening of pain or disease, can cause *relief*, just as a *fire* can cause *warmth*.

10. (C); Antonym. *Secular* and *religious* have opposite meanings, as do *passive* and *violent*.

Lesson 8   page 133

1. (A); Synonym. An *altercation* is the same thing as a *quarrel*, just as an *obligation* is the same thing as a *duty*.

2. (D); Degree. *Assail* suggests a greater degree of attack than *confront*, just as *demolish* suggests a greater degree of destruction than *damage*.

3. (B); Part and Whole. A *brunt*, or a heavy blow, is part of an *attack*, just as a *point* is part of an *argument*.

4. (A); Part and Whole or Location. A *bulwark*, or fortified wall, is part of a *fortress*, or can be found in one, just as a *seawall* is part of a *harbor* or can be found at one.

5. (E); Cause and Effect. *Carnage*, or bloody slaughter, can be caused by a *battle*, just as *rubble* can be caused by an *earthquake*.

6. (B); Degree. *Heinous*, which means evil or wicked, has a meaning similar to *bad* but to a greater degree. In the same way, *sweltering*, which means very hot, sultry, has a meaning similar to *warm* but to a greater degree.

7. (D); Antonym. *Insidious*, or devious, is opposite in meaning to *straightforward*. *Attractive* and *repulsive* also have opposite meanings.

8. (B); Synonym. *Invidious*, which means giving offense, means the same as *offensive*. *Haughty* and *proud* also have the same meaning.

9. (C); Performer and Related Action. A *martyr suffers*, and a *poet writes*.

10. (D); Part and Whole. A *soldier* is part of a *phalanx*, or military formation, just as a *cow* is part of a *herd*.

Lesson 9   page 134

1. (B); Antonym. *Affinity*, or attraction, is opposite in meaning to *repulsion*. *Virtue* and *vice* are also opposite in meaning.

2. (B); Synonym. *Array* (when it is used as a noun referring to clothing) and *finery* have nearly the same meaning, as do *act* and *deed*.

3. (D); Characteristic Quality. A *pirate* is characteristically *audacious*, or bold and daring. In the same way, a *rustler*, or thief of livestock, is characteristically *dishonest*.

4. (C); Action and Related Object. You *bandy*, or throw around, *words*, just as you *toss balls*.

5. (C); Performer and Related Action. A *queen deigns*, or condescends to her subjects, just as a *governor pardons* criminals.

6. (C); Characteristic Quality. An *insult* is derogatory, or belittling, just as *praise* is complimentary.

7. (A); Synonym. *Efficacious* and *effective* have the same meaning, as do *beneficial* and *good*.

8. (D); Performer and Related Object. An *epicure* is someone who appreciates fine *food*, just as a *fashion designer* appreciates fine *clothing*.

9. (A); Antonym. *Imperious*, which means overbearing and arrogant, is opposite in meaning to *meek*. *Wild* and *tame* are also opposite in meaning.

10. (E); Antonym. *Ingratiate*, which means to win approval, is opposite in meaning to *offend*. *Resist* and *submit* are also opposite in meaning.

Lesson 10   page 135

1. (E); Synonym. *Auspicious* and *favorable* have nearly the same meaning, as do *conspicuous* and *obvious*.

2. (B); Part and Whole. *Departments* are part of a *bureaucracy*, just as *stores* are part of a *mall*.

3. (D); Synonym. *Demeanor* and *behavior* have the same meaning, as do *faith* and *belief*.

4. (A); Performer and Related Object. An *impostor* uses a *guise* to disguise himself or herself, just as *troops* use *camouflage* to hide.

5. (B); Antonym. *Inane* and *meaningful* are opposite in meaning, as are *remote* (as an adjective) and *nearby*.

6. (B); Synonym. *Politic* and *shrewd* both mean crafty or clever. *Transparent* has the same meaning as *clear*.

7. (A); Antonym. *Premeditated,* which means planned in advance, is opposite in meaning to *spontaneous,* which means unplanned. *Simple* and *sophisticated* are also opposite in meaning.

8. (C); Synonym. *Purport* and *claim* (when claim is a verb) have nearly the same meaning, as do *suppose* and *assume.*

9. (E); Characteristic Quality. A *tailor,* or anything or anyone having to do with clothing, can be described as *sartorial,* just as a *newspaper* is characteristically *informative.*

10. (C); Performer and Related Action. One expects a *scapegoat* to *suffer,* just as one expects a *bodyguard* to *protect.*

Lesson 11   page 136

1. (E); Synonym. *Dissipate* and *scatter* have nearly the same meaning, as do *change* (when *change* is a verb) and *alter.*

2. (D); Antonym. *Diverge* and *merge* have opposite meanings, as do *divorce* and *marry.*

3. (E); Classification. *Entomology,* the study of insects, is classified as a *science.* In the same way, *poetry* is classified as *literature.*

4. (D); Synonym. *Faction* and *group* have nearly the same meaning, as do *gathering* and *congregation.*

5. (A); Classification. A *fiord* is classified as an *inlet,* just as an *apple* is classified as a *fruit.*

6. (A); Antonym. *Impotent,* which means lacking in strength, is opposite in meaning to *vigorous. Corrupt* is opposite in meaning to *honest.*

7. (B); Characteristic Quality. *Bears* are characteristically *omnivorous,* which means that they eat both animals and plants, just as *zebras* are characteristically *striped.*

8. (C); Antonym. *Subside* and *increase* have opposite meanings, as do *swell* and *shrink.*

9. (C); Degree. *Tepid,* or lukewarm, is less hot than *hot,* just as *cool* is less cold than *cold.*

10. (C); Synonym. *Vogue* and *fashion* have nearly the same meaning, as do *hazard* and *danger.*

Lesson 12   page 137

1. (C); Performer and Related Action. A *bully accosts,* just as a *security guard patrols.*

2. (E); Synonym. An *appraisal,* or estimate of value, is the same thing as a *valuation.* A *union* is the same thing as a *merger.*

3. (A); Antonym. *Circumspect,* or cautious, is opposite in meaning to *foolhardy. Astute,* or clever, is opposite in meaning to *gullible.*

4. (B); Synonym. *Correlate* and *relate* have similar meanings, as do *correct* and *rectify.*

5. (D); Antonym. *Exhaustive,* which means thorough, is opposite in meaning to *superficial. Full* and *partial* also have opposite meanings.

6. (B); Characteristic Quality. A *thief* is characteristically *furtive,* or secretive, just as a *clown* is characteristically *funny.*

7. (B); Synonym. *Permeate* and *penetrate* have similar meanings, as do *ooze* and *seep.*

8. (B); Degree. *Rapacious* is more extreme in degree than *selfish,* just as *violent* is more extreme in degree than *aggressive.*

9. (D); Degree. *Recalcitrant,* or uncooperative, suggests a greater degree of unwillingness than *reluctant,* just as *delighted* suggests a greater degree of pleasure than *satisfied.*

10. (A); Cause and Effect. *Recrimination,* or counter-accusation, can be the effect of an *accusation,* just as an *injury* can be the effect of an *accident.*

Lesson 13   page 138

1. (E); Part and Whole. An *acquisition*—something that is acquired—is part of a *collection,* just as a *member* is part of a *sorority.*

2. (E); Antonym. A *debacle,* or failure, is the opposite of a *success,* just as *contraction* is the opposite of *expansion.*

3. (C); Synonym. *Enthrall* and *spellbind* have the same meaning, as do *sway* and *influence.*

4. (E); Characteristic Quality. A *microcosm* is a small part that is characteristically *representative* of the whole. A *flag* is characteristically *symbolic.*

5. (E); Characteristic Quality. A *platitude* is a commonplace, or *trite,* remark, just as a *pet name* is an *affectionate* name.

6. (C); Synonym. *Rigorous* and *strict* have similar meanings, as do *crucial* and *important.*

7. (D); Synonym. *Synchronize* and *coordinate* have nearly the same meaning, as do *match* and *correspond.*

8. (B); Antonym. *Thwart,* which means prevent, is opposite in meaning to *assist,* just as *clasp* is opposite in meaning to *release.*

9. (A); Synonym. *Ulterior,* or hidden, means the same as *undisclosed,* just as *interior* means the same as *internal.*

10. (D); Characteristic Quality. A *trickster* is characteristically *wily,* or crafty, just as a *thinker* is characteristically *wise.*

Lesson 14   page 139

1. (A); Synonym. *Abate* and *lessen* have nearly the same meaning, as do *swell* and *increase.*

2. (B); Synonym. *Contrition* and *remorse* both mean sorrow for doing wrong. *Sensation* and *feeling* (as a noun) also have the same meaning.

3. (D); Antonym. *Defile* and *purify* have opposite meanings, as do *pollute* and *cleanse.*

4. (A); Performer and Related Action. An *intruder* is someone who *encroaches,* or intrudes, just as a *thief* is someone who *steals.*

5. (A); Antonym. *Fallible* and *perfect* are opposite in meaning, as are *famous* and *unknown.*

6. (D); Antonym. *Innocuous,* or harmless, means the opposite of *lethal,* just as *tardy,* or late, means the opposite of *early.*

7. (D); Synonym. A *panacea* is a *cure-all,* just as an *antidote* is a *remedy.*

8. (B); Synonym. *Protract* and *lengthen* have the same meaning, as do *shorten* and *abbreviate.*

9. (A); Performer and Related Action. A *slanderer vilifies*, or uses defaming language, just as a *criminal victimizes*.
10. (D); Performer and Related Action. A *purse snatcher wrests* purses from their owners, just as a *dog sniffs*.

Lesson 15   page 140
1. (E); Synonym. *Abut* and *adjoin* both have the same meaning, as do *liberate* and *release*.
2. (A); Characteristic Quality. A *garden* is characteristically *arable*, or able to support plants, just as a *cliff* is characteristically *treacherous*.
3. (A); Characteristic Quality. A *gradation*, or gentle increase or incline, is *gradual*, just as an *aggravation* is *annoying*.
4. (C); Synonym. *Incise* and *carve* have nearly the same meaning, as do *snare* and *catch*.
5. (D); Antonym. *Indigenous*, or native, means the opposite of *exotic*. *Foreign* and *familiar* are also opposite in meaning.
6. (E); Performer and Related Action. One expects a *parent* to *nurture*, or care for children, just as one expects a *general* to command an *army*.
7. (E); Function. The function of a *map* is to *orient*, or guide a traveler, just as the function of an *oven* is to *bake*.
8. (D); Part and Whole. The *solstice* is a part of *summer*, just as *Tuesday* is part of the *week*.
9. (E); Characteristic Quality. A *stoic* is characteristically *unexcitable*, just as an *eccentric* is characteristically *strange*.
10. (B); Performer and Related Action. *Conquerors vanquish*, or defeat their foes, just as *instigators initiate*, or begin, something.

READING NEW WORDS IN CONTEXT

Lesson 1   pages 143–148
Exercise 1   Finding Synonyms
Answers will vary. The following are possible responses.
1. inconsistency
2. main character
3. emphasize
4. a story that has symbolic meaning
5. inclusive
6. vague
7. complex
8. beginning
9. appropriate
10. degenerate; depraved
11. concise
12. preliminary act
13. contemplative
14. fierceness
15. contemptible
16. a person who hates all people
17. impenetrable
18. dialect; spoken language
19. guesswork; inference
20. stimulating

Exercise 2   Reading Strategically
1. A   2. C   3. B   4. E   5. B   6. D   7. A   8. B
9. C   10. E   11. B   12. C   13. D   14. D   15. A
16. B   17. B   18. E   19. D   20. E

Lesson 2   pages 149–154
Exercise 1   Finding Synonyms
Answers will vary. The following are possible responses.
1. conference or collection of essays
2. closely examine
3. elusive; slippery
4. clear
5. demanding
6. amateur; inexperienced
7. draw as a conclusion
8. salary
9. wealthy
10. briefness
11. a descriptive name
12. a person who lacks culture
13. praiseworthy
14. adorn; decorate
15. suggest something beforehand
16. longing for something past or far away
17. drink; take in
18. a suggested meaning
19. call forth
20. restate

Exercise 2   Reading Strategically
1. C   2. A   3. B   4. E   5. D   6. A   7. D   8. B
9. E   10. B   11. C   12. D   13. A   14. C   15. B
16. A   17. D   18. C   19. C   20. A

Lesson 3   pages 155–160
Exercise 1   Finding Synonyms
Answers will vary. The following are possible responses.
1. brief story
2. claim
3. strong point
4. of one who enjoys fine food
5. prod
6. unexplainable
7. someone who complains about imaginary ills
8. neutral
9. nose
10. culminating; most important
11. mark of shame
12. denounce; explode violently
13. in a logically connected way
14. conclusion; afterword
15. guess
16. improvised
17. rearrangement of letters in a word to make another word
18. faithfulness
19. highly gifted person
20. idealistic

Exercise 2   Reading Strategically
1. D   2. B   3. A   4. C   5. E   6. A   7. D   8. C
9. B   10. E   11. A   12. D   13. B   14. C   15. E
16. C   17. A   18. C   19. C   20. B

Lesson 4   pages 161–166
Exercise 1   Finding Synonyms
Answers will vary. The following are possible responses.
1. incorrect
2. overly showy
3. overly generalized view
4. affected
5. show off
6. principle
7. moral decay
8. criminal
9. support
10. harmonious
11. irritable
12. inferior
13. attractive
14. pushy
15. lively
16. comebacks
17. satisfy
18. overly severe in judgment
19. quote
20. taunt

Exercise 2   Reading Strategically
1. C   2. B   3. E   4. C   5. A   6. D   7. B   8. E
9. A   10. C   11. B   12. D   13. B   14. E   15. A
16. C   17. D   18. C   19. D   20. B

Lesson 5   pages 167–172
Exercise 1   Finding Synonyms
Answers will vary. The following are possible responses.

1. deception
2. uproar
3. profitable
4. haughty
5. reinforce
6. bad-tempered woman
7. condense
8. correction
9. gaudy; cheaply showy
10. abstract
11. return
12. yearning
13. spontaneous
14. call upon
15. curse
16. decisiveness
17. characteristic of a time or group
18. wordy
19. terse; brief
20. talkative

Exercise 2   Reading Strategically
1. E 2. C 3. A 4. B 5. D 6. B 7. A 8. B
9. E 10. A 11. C 12. B 13. D 14. D 15. A
16. C 17. B 18. E 19. A 20. C

Lesson 6   pages 173–178
Exercise 1   Finding Synonyms
Answers will vary. The following are possible responses.

1. discourage
2. generosity
3. humble request
4. inborn
5. arrogant; dictatorial
6. general agreement
7. dictatorial
8. unyielding
9. delay
10. courageous
11. mixed; conflicting
12. dissenting; quarrelsome
13. unending
14. sickly pale; grayish yellow
15. disgusting
16. buoyant
17. anger
18. place where historical records are kept
19. a raid on attackers
20. engaged

Exercise 2   Reading Strategically
1. C 2. C 3. B 4. C 5. A 6. D 7. E 8. A
9. A 10. C 11. D 12. B 13. A 14. B 15. B
16. A 17. C 18. D 19. D 20. C

Lesson 7   pages 179–184
Exercise 1   Finding Synonyms
Answers will vary. The following are possible responses.

1. essential
2. skeptical; unbelieving
3. incitement
4. hasten
5. ask
6. do without
7. skillful
8. embarassment
9. charming
10. intervene
11. password
12. common; vulgar; crude
13. lessening
14. cheerful
15. worldly
16. expected of a child
17. absolve
18. yield
19. hasten
20. unintelligible

Exercise 2   Reading Strategically
1. B 2. B 3. A 4. E 5. B 6. D 7. C 8. A
9. E 10. B 11. A 12. D 13. B 14. C 15. A
16. B 17. C 18. E 19. A 20. B

Lesson 8   pages 185–190
Exercise 1   Finding Synonyms
Answers will vary. The following are possible responses.

1. mass departure
2. attack
3. vile; wicked
4. largest part
5. relinquish
6. wily; sly
7. offensive; hateful
8. disapprove of
9. person who precedes
10. surrounded
11. destruction
12. orderly mass
13. give in
14. remedy; rectify
15. protector; supporter
16. fight
17. one who dies for a cause
18. relieve; ease
19. slaughter
20. alliance

Exercise 2   Reading Strategically
1. C 2. B 3. E 4. E 5. A 6. C 7. D 8. A
9. C 10. B 11. E 12. B 13. D 14. A 15. C
16. D 17. C 18. C 19. B 20. A

Lesson 9   pages 191–196
Exercise 1   Finding Synonyms
Answers will vary. The following are possible responses.

1. bold; insolent
2. natural attraction
3. effective
4. explain away
5. dress
6. joke
7. bring into favor
8. overbearing
9. serious crime
10. criticize severely
11. belittling
12. give in
13. pertaining to horses
14. condescend
15. a lover of fine food and drink
16. malicious
17. depraved; corrupt
18. jovial
19. particular; finicky
20. waver

Exercise 2   Reading Strategically
1. A 2. C 3. D 4. D 5. E 6. B 7. A 8. B
9. C 10. E 11. C 12. A 13. D 14. B 15. C
16. A 17. B 18. D 19. E 20. C

Lesson 10   pages 197–202
Exercise 1   Finding Synonyms
Answers will vary. The following are possible responses.

1. bearing
2. someone who is blamed for another's crimes
3. smuggled goods
4. senseless; stupid
5. intimidate
6. false appearance
7. a group that bands together to carry on business
8. claim
9. of tailors or their work
10. beyond human understanding
11. embarrass
12. planned
13. a person who stands in for another
14. temporary
15. whimsical
16. shrewd
17. respect
18. promising
19. the administration of government through departments
20. before memory

Exercise 2   Reading Strategically
1. D 2. B 3. C 4. A 5. B 6. D 7. C 8. E
9. A 10. B 11. D 12. C 13. B 14. A 15. E
16. B 17. D 18. D 19. C 20. A

Lesson 11   pages 203–208
Exercise 1   Finding Synonyms
Answers will vary. The following are possible responses.

1. fashion
2. model
3. a subgroup
4. a being
5. move away from
6. a person who studies insects
7. a narrow, steep-sided inlet
8. emotional purification

9. increase
10. believability
11. refrain
12. eating both plants and animals
13. abate
14. powerless
15. test
16. innate
17. a work about a pastoral scene
18. incessant
19. scattering
20. lukewarm

Exercise 2   Reading Strategically
1. B   2. C   3. E   4. B   5. B   6. D   7. C   8. A
9. D   10. C   11. A   12. E   13. C   14. A   15. B
16. C   17. E   18. D   19. A   20. D

Lesson 12   pages 209–214
Exercise 1   Finding Synonyms
Answers will vary. The following are possible responses.
1. thorough
2. the masses
3. spread throughout
4. notify; inform
5. to show the relationship between
6. deadly
7. great wickedness
8. countercharge
9. to approach aggressively
10. careful; prudent
11. defiant
12. motivated by a desire for money
13. assessment
14. greedy
15. joy
16. plain; ascetic
17. working class
18. friendship
19. secretive
20. to present

Exercise 2   Reading Strategically
1. D   2. A   3. E   4. C   5. B   6. A   7. C   8. C
9. E   10. B   11. B   12. A   13. C   14. E   15. D
16. A   17. B   18. E   19. D   20. C

Lesson 13   pages 215–220
Exercise 1   Finding Synonyms
Answers will vary. The following are possible responses.
1. sly; crafty
2. undisclosed
3. overused saying
4. minature world
5. difficult; demanding
6. coordinate
7. total collapse
8. captivated
9. persistence
10. unquenchable
11. act of obtaining
12. hard
13. prophet
14. relieve
15. overly grand
16. furiously moving
17. flood
18. channel
19. defeat
20. abrupt; blunt

Exercise 2   Reading Strategically
1. D   2. C   3. B   4. C   5. A   6. D   7. C   8. C
9. E   10. B   11. B   12. A   13. E   14. B   15. C
16. D   17. A   18. C   19. D   20. D

Lesson 14   pages 221–226
Exercise 1   Finding Synonyms
Answers will vary. The following are possible responses.
1. intrude
2. remorse; regret
3. capable of mistakes
4. arrogant
5. without impact
6. pull; twist
7. combined
8. reproduce
9. island; isolated
10. lessen
11. lead an inactive life
12. four-legged animals
13. horrid
14. long-term

15. lazy
16. sterile
17. cure-all
18. spoiled; fouled
19. to habituate
20. condemn

Exercise 2   Reading Strategically
1. C   2. A   3. D   4. E   5. B   6. E   7. C   8. A
9. C   10. C   11. D   12. E   13. B   14. A   15. B
16. D   17. C   18. A   19. B   20. E

Lesson 15   pages 227–232
Exercise 1   Finding Synonyms
Answers will vary. The following are possible responses.
1. to adjust; to position
2. crooked
3. gaunt
4. sleepy
5. first day of summer
6. impassive
7. defeated
8. native to the region
9. border
10. cultivable
11. surrounding
12. care for
13. attendants
14. gradual reduction
15. beating
16. freedom from punishment
17. cut
18. threatening
19. gradual change
20. mutually binding

Exercise 2   Reading Strategically
1. B   2. D   3. E   4. B   5. C   6. D   7. D   8. C
9. A   10. E   11. B   12. C   13. E   14. A   15. D
16. B   17. C   18. A   19. D   20. D

USING NEW WORDS ON TESTS

FORMATIVE ASSESSMENT
Test 1   page 3
1. A   2. A   3. D   4. C   5. C   6. E   7. D   8. E
9. A   10. D

Test 2   page 4
1. A   2. D   3. C   4. B   5. A   6. A   7. B   8. B
9. B   10. E

Test 3   page 5
1. A   2. A   3. B   4. E   5. B   6. C   7. B   8. D
9. C   10. D

Test 4   page 6
1. E   2. B   3. B   4. E   5. A   6. B   7. C   8. A
9. C   10. D

Test 5   page 7
1. B   2. A   3. D   4. B   5. E   6. B   7. B   8. D
9. C   10. C

Test 6   page 8
1. D   2. D   3. D   4. C   5. B   6. C   7. E   8. A
9. A   10. B

Test 7   page 9
1. C   2. A   3. B   4. B   5. C   6. C   7. A   8. E
9. D   10. B

Test 8   page 10
1. A   2. C   3. D   4. C   5. B   6. E   7. E   8. D
9. A   10. B

Test 9   page 11
1. C   2. D   3. D   4. C   5. D   6. C   7. A   8. B
9. E   10. B

Test 10   page 12
1. B   2. A   3. A   4. A   5. D   6. E   7. C   8. E
9. C   10. A

Test 11   page 13
1. A   2. C   3. C   4. A   5. D   6. B   7. A   8. A
9. D   10. E

Test 12   page 14
1. E   2. C   3. B   4. B   5. D   6. A   7. C   8. B
9. E   10. C

Test 13   page 15
1. D   2. B   3. B   4. E   5. D   6. B   7. C   8. E
9. A   10. D

Test 14   page 16
1. C   2. D   3. B   4. D   5. D   6. A   7. D   8. C
9. E   10. D

Test 15   page 17
1. A   2. B   3. D   4. E   5. D   6. A   7. E   8. C
9. A   10. A

Test 16   page 18
1. E   2. A   3. C   4. B   5. C   6. D   7. C   8. E
9. B   10. A

Test 17   page 19
1. B   2. B   3. D   4. A   5. C   6. E   7. C   8. B
9. A   10. D

Test 18   page 20
1. A   2. D   3. E   4. B   5. B   6. A   7. D   8. D
9. D   10. A

Test 19   page 21
1. C   2. B   3. E   4. C   5. B   6. C   7. D   8. A
9. A   10. A

Test 20   page 22
1. A   2. E   3. D   4. A   5. B   6. D   7. C   8. D
9. C   10. D

Test 21   page 23
1. D   2. C   3. C   4. C   5. B   6. A   7. B   8. C
9. D   10. B

Test 22   page 24
1. B   2. D   3. E   4. B   5. C   6. B   7. C   8. C
9. D   10. A

Test 23   page 25
1. A   2. C   3. B   4. C   5. A   6. B   7. B   8. E
9. B   10. A

Test 24   page 26
1. A   2. B   3. C   4. E   5. E   6. B   7. B   8. C
9. C   10. C

Test 25   page 27
1. B   2. D   3. A   4. B   5. C   6. B   7. A   8. D
9. C   10. E

Test 26   page 28
1. D   2. D   3. A   4. C   5. A   6. E   7. D   8. C
9. A   10. B

Test 27   page 29
1. A   2. C   3. D   4. E   5. C   6. C   7. E   8. B
9. B   10. A

Test 28   page 30
1. B   2. B   3. C   4. D   5. B   6. A   7. E   8. A
9. D   10. C

Test 29   page 31
1. C   2. E   3. C   4. E   5. D   6. A   7. B   8. A
9. B   10. B

Test 30   page 32
1. D   2. B   3. C   4. C   5. B   6. D   7. A   8. E
9. C   10. B

SUMMATIVE ASSESSMENT
Test 1 Part A   pages 35–38
1. C   2. A   3. D   4. E   5. B   6. D   7. A   8. C
9. C   10. A   11. D   12. E   13. D   14. C   15. A
16. B   17. D   18. C   19. E   20. D   21. A   22. C
23. B   24. B   25. E

Test 1 Part B   pages 39–43
26. C   27. E   28. C   29. E   30. E   31. B   32. D
33. A   34. E   35. C   36. A   37. C   38. C   39. A
40. B   41. D   42. C   43. B   44. E   45. C   46. E
47. A   48. E   49. B   50. E   51. A   52. C   53. E
54. A   55. B   56. A   57. B   58. C   59. B   60. D
61. D   62. C   63. E   64. B   65. D   66. C   67. C
68. D   69. A   70. B

Test 1 Part C   pages 44–46
71. (C); Synonym. *Agree* and *consent* have similar meanings, as do *fulminate*, which means denounce loudly, and *scold*.

72. (C); Classification. An *allegory* is classified as a *story*, just as a *ballad* is classified as a *song*.

73. (B); Characteristic Quality. An *anecdote*, or brief story, is characteristically *entertaining*, just as a *joke* is characteristically *amusing*.

74. (E); Characteristic Quality. *Assurance* is characteristically *comforting*, just as a *shrew*, or irritable woman, is characteristically *bad-tempered*.

75. (B); Antonym. *Bolster*, or strengthen, means the opposite of *undermine*, or weaken. *Open* and *close* are also opposite in meaning.

76. (E); Synonym. *Braid* and *interweave* have nearly the same meaning, as do *gibe* and *jeer*.

77. (C); Cause and Effect. *Joy* can cause *celebration*, just as *corruption* can cause *decadence*.

78. (C); Characteristic Quality. A *peak* is characteristically *climactic*, just as a *conclusion* is charactistically *final*.

79. (C); Antonym. *Consonant* and *vowel* have opposite meanings, as do *capital* and *lowercase*.

80. (D); Antonym. *Correct* and *improper* have opposite meanings, as do *lucrative* and *unprofitable*.

81. (A); Synonym. *Defy* and *resist* have nearly the same meaning. *Evoke*, which means call forth, has nearly the same meaning as *summon*.

82. (D); Characteristic Quality. A *villain* is characteristically *despicable*, just as a *murder* is characteristically *gruesome*.

83. (A); Synonym. *Disregard* and *ignore* have nearly the same meaning, as do *surmise* and *guess*.

84. (C); Function. The function of an *epithet*, a descriptive name or title, is to *describe* someone, just as the function of a *solvent* is *dissolve* something.

85. (B); Characteristic Quality. An *expletive*, or curse, is characteristically *profane*, just as a *tribute* is characteristically *complimentary*.

86. (A); Characteristic Quality. A *lion* is characteristically *ferocious*, just as a *mouse* is characteristically *timid*.

87. (C); Action and Object. You can *goad,* or urge, *oxen,* just as you can *poke cattle.*

88. (E); Antonym. *Incongruous,* which means lacking in harmony or agreement, means the opposite of *harmonious,* just as *reluctant,* or unwilling, means the opposite of *enthusiastic.*

89. (D); Degree. *Jealous* means *envious* to a greater degree. *Ostentatious* suggests a greater degree of showiness than does *conspicuous.*

90. (D); Synonym. A *meddler* is the same as a *busybody,* just as a *miscreant* is the same as a *villain.*

91. (A); Synonym. *Peaceful* and *harmonious* have nearly the same meaning, as do *irascible* and *irritable.*

92. (C); Part and Whole. A *preamble* is the first part of a *constitution,* as a *prologue* is the first part of a *play.*

93. (C); Antonym. *Pretentious* is opposite in meaning to *humble,* just as *generous* is opposite in meaning to *miserly.*

94. (E); Synonym. *Prodigy* and *genius* have similar meanings, as do *disaster* and *devastation.*

95. (A); Part and Whole. A *protagonist* is part of a *novel,* just as a *dancer* is part of a *ballet.*

96. (C); Action and Object. You can *satiate,* or satisfy, an *appetite,* just as you can *quench* a *thirst.*

97. (D); Antonym. *Stereotypical* means the opposite of *original,* just as *despondent,* or hopeless, means the opposite of *joyful.*

98. (B): Cause and Effect. A *stigma,* or mark of scorn, can cause *shame,* just as a *medal* can cause *pride.*

99. (D); Synonym. *Superfluous* and *excessive* both mean more than is needed. *Supercilious* and *haughty* both mean proud and scornful.

100. (E); Antonym. *Tawdry* and *tasteful* have opposite meanings, as do *customary* and *unusual.*

Test 2 Part A   pages 47–50
1. D   2. B   3. C   4. A   5. B   6. D   7. A   8. E
9. C   10. E   11. C   12. B   13. B   14. D   15. A
16. C   17. E   18. B   19. D   20. B   21. A   22. D
23. B   24. C   25. C

Test 2 Part B   pages 51–55
26. D   27. E   28. A   29. B   30. A   31. C   32. E
33. D   34. B   35. D   36. E   37. D   38. C   39. A
40. C   41. E   42. E   43. A   44. B   45. D   46. C
47. B   48. B   49. A   50. C   51. C   52. B   53. A
54. E   55. E   56. A   57. A   58. B   59. D   60. B
61. D   62. B   63. C   64. E   65. B   66. A   67. D
68. B   69. C   70. A

Test 2 Part C   pages 56–58
71. (D); Degree. *Assail* suggests a greater degree of attack than *confront,* just as *demolish* suggests a greater degree of destruction than *damage.*

72. (E); Classification. An *autocrat,* or dictator, is classified as a *ruler,* just as *democracy* is classified as a *government.*

73. (A); Synonym. *Betrothed* and *engaged* have the same meaning, as do *finished* and *completed.*

74. (A); Part and Whole or Location. A *breakwater* is part of a *harbor* or can be found in one, just as a *bulwark,* or fortified wall, is part of a fortress or can be found in one.

75. (B); Part and Whole. A *brunt* is part of a *blow,* just as a *thrust,* in the sense of a main point, is part of an *argument.*

76. (B); Part and Whole. *Departments* are part of a *bureaucracy,* just as *stores* are part of a *mall.*

77. (D); Antonym. *Cede,* which means surrender, means the opposite of *claim* (when *claim* is used as a verb), just as *agree* means the opposite of *dispute.*

78. (C); Characteristic Quality. *Praise* is *complimentary,* just as *insult* is *derogatory,* or belittling.

79. (E); Synonym. *Congenital* and *inherited* have the same meaning, as do *persuasive* and *convincing.*

80. (C); Synonym. *Deign* and *stoop* have the same meaning, as do *adore* and *love.*

81. (D); Synonym. *Demeanor* and *behavior* have the same meaning, as do *faith* and *belief.*

82. (D); Characteristic Quality. A *rustler,* or thief of livestock, is characteristically *dishonest.* In the same way, a *pirate* is characteristically *audacious,* or bold and daring.

83. (D); Performer and Related Action. A *jury exonerates,* or clears someone of blame, just as an *athlete competes.*

84. (D); Performer and Related Action. A *burglar* commits a *felony,* just as a *sculptor* creates *art.*

85. (D); Characteristic Quality. A *guise* is characteristically *superficial,* just as a *crime* is characteristically *offensive.*

86. (D); Antonym. *Insidious,* or devious, is opposite in meaning to *straightforward. Attractive* and *repulsive* also have opposite meanings.

87. (E); Performer and Related Action. One who was *sacrificed* may be a *martyr,* just as one who was *punished* may be a *convict.*

88. (A); Synonym. An *obligation* is the same thing as a *duty,* just as an *altercation* is the same thing as a *quarrel.*

89. (D); Part and Whole. A *soldier* is part of a *phalanx,* or military formation, just as a *cow* is part of a *herd.*

90. (A); Synonym. *Profound* and *deep* have nearly the same meaning, as do *precipitate* (as an adjective) and *sudden.*

91. (C); Synonym. *Purport* and *claim* (when claim is a verb) have nearly the same meaning, as do *suppose* and *assume.*

92. (E); Antonym. *Reduced* and *enlarged* are opposite in meaning, as are *repugnant* and *attractive.*

93. (E); Cause and Effect. *Rubble* can be caused by an *earthquake,* just as *carnage,* or bloody slaughter, can be caused by a *battle.*

94. (D); Characteristic Quality. Someone who is *sick* is characteristically *sallow,* or grayish yellow, just as someone who is *healthy* is characteristically *ruddy.*

95. (C); Synonym. *Schedule* and *plan* have the same meaning. *Procrastinate* and *postpone* both mean to put off until another time.

96. (B); Characteristic Quality. A *sortie*, or raid, is characteristically *sudden* and quick. An *attack* is characteristically *aggressive*.

97. (B); Degree. *Sweltering*, which means very hot, sultry, has a meaning similar to *warm* but to a greater degree. In the same way, *heinous*, which means evil or wicked, has a meaning similar to *bad* but to a greater degree.

98. (E); Synonym. *Thoughtful* and *considerate* have nearly the same meaning, as do *blithe* and *happy*.

99. (E); Performer and Related Action. You *hurt* a *victim*, just as you *blame* a *scapegoat*.

100. (C); Characteristic Quality. A *sage* is a characteristically *wise* person. In the same way, a *charity* is characteristically *beneficent*—that is, it does good.

Test 3 Part A   pages 59–62

1. E 2. B 3. D 4. B 5. C 6. A 7. D 8. C
9. C 10. D 11. E 12. A 13. C 14. B 15. D
16. C 17. A 18. C 19. C 20. B 21. D 22. E
23. A 24. D 25. C

Test 3 Part B   pages 63–67

26. C 27. A 28. E 29. B 30. D 31. A 32. C
33. B 34. D 35. C 36. E 37. E 38. B 39. D
40. A 41. C 42. B 43. C 44. E 45. A 46. D
47. D 48. B 49. C 50. D 51. E 52. C 53. A
54. B 55. D 56. C 57. C 58. E 59. A 60. C
61. B 62. D 63. D 64. B 65. C 66. B 67. C
68. A 69. B 70. C

Test 3 Part C   pages 68–70

71. (A); Synonym. *Appraisal, value, estimation,* and *worth* all have similar meanings.

72. (A); Antonym. *Circumspect*, or cautious, is opposite in meaning to *foolhardy*. *Astute*, or clever, is opposite in meaning to *gullible*.

73. (A); Synonym. *Correlate* and *relate* have similar meanings, as do *organize* and *order*.

74. (E); Antonym. A *debacle*, or failure, is the opposite of a *success*, just as *contraction* is the opposite of *expansion*.

75. (A); Performer and Related Object. An *intruder encroaches*, or trespasses, just as a *thief steals*.

76. (E); Classification. *Entomology*, the study of insects, is classified as a *science*. In the same way, *poetry* is classified as *literature*.

77. (A); Antonym. *Fallible* and *perfect* are opposite in meaning, as are *famous* and *unknown*.

78. (D); Characteristic Quality. A *clown* is characteristically *funny*, just as a *thief* is characteristically *furtive*, or secretive.

79. (C); Synonym. *Hazard* and *danger* have nearly the same meaning, as do *vogue* and *fashion*.

80. (E); Antonym. *Impotent*, which means ineffective, is opposite in meaning to *effective*. *Stern* is opposite in meaning to *tender*.

81. (E); Synonym. *Inherent* and *basic* have nearly the same meaning, as do *broad* and *wide*.

82. (A); Synonym. *Interior* means the same as *inside*, just as *ulterior*, or hidden, means the same as *undisclosed*.

83. (E); Synonym. *Liberate* and *release* have the same meaning, as do *abut* and *adjoin*.

84. (E); Characteristic Quality. A *microcosm* is a small part that is characteristically *representative* of the whole. A *flag* is characteristically *symbolic*.

85. (E); Performer and Related Action. One expects a *parent* to *nurture*, or care for children, just as one expects a *general* to *command* an army.

86. (E); Synonym. *Obstinate* and *stubborn* have the same meaning, as do *recalcitrant* and *uncooperative*.

87. (B); Characteristic Quality. *Humans* are characteristically *omnivorous*, which means that they eat both animals and plants, just as *zebras* are characteristically *striped*.

88. (B); Synonym. *Ooze* and *seep* have similar meanings, as do *permeate* and *penetrate*.

89. (B); Synonym. *Sensation* and *feeling* (as a noun) have the same meaning. In the same way, *contrition* and *remorse* both mean sorrow for doing wrong.

90. (B); Classification. *Softball* may be classified as a *sport*, just as a *recrimination* may be classified as a *response*.

91. (E); Degree. *Stare* is stronger in degree than *glance*, just as *wrest* is stronger in degree than *tug*.

92. (E); Characteristic Quality. Someone who is *stoic* is characteristically *unexcitable*, just as someone who is *eccentric* is characteristically *strange*.

93. (C); Synonym. *Sway* and *influence* have the same meaning, as do *enthrall* and *spellbind*.

94. (C); Antonym. *Swell* and *shrink* have opposite meanings, as do *subside* and *increase*.

95. (B); Synonym. *Tenacity*, or holding firmly, has a meaning similar to *grip*, as do *firmness* and *hold*.

96. (C); Degree. *Tepid*, or lukewarm, is less hot than *hot*, just as *cool* is less cold than *cold*.

97. (B); Performer and Related Action. *Conquerors vanquish*, or defeat their foes, just as *instigators initiate*, or begin, something.

98. (D); Antonym. *Vilify* means the opposite of *rejoice*, just as *criticize* means the opposite of *praise*.

99. (B); Degree. *Violent* is more extreme in degree than *rough*, just as *rapacious* is stronger in degree than *greedy*.

100. (D); Characteristic Quality. A *fox* is characteristically *wily*, or crafty, just as an *owl* is characteristically *wise*.

Complete Course

Lesson 1   pages 3–6
Exercise 1   Mapping
Your Guess and Definition answers will vary. Possible responses to Other Forms items follow.
1. *n.* banality; *adv.* banally
2. *n.* bellicosity; *adv.* bellicosely
3. *vt.* or *vi.* finesses, finessed, finessing
4. *n.* glibness; *adv.* glibly
5. *n.* lampoonery, lampooner, lampoonist; *vt.* lampoons, lampooned, lampooning
6. *n.* lugubriousness; *adv.* lugubriously
7. *n.* nefariousness; *adv.* nefariously
8. None
9. *n.* pseudonymity; *adj.* pseudonymous; *adv.* pseudonymously
10. *vt.* or *vi.* purloins, purloined, purloining

Exercise 2   Context Clues
11. (J) glibly
12. (E) lugubrious
13. (A) finesse
14. (H) nemesis
15. (C) purloins
16. (D) banal
17. (I) pseudonym
18. (B) lampoon
19. (G) nefarious
20. (F) bellicose

Exercise 3   Sentence Completion
21. B   22. A   23. A   24. E   25. B   26. C   27. A
28. E   29. A   30. A

Lesson 2   pages 7–10
Exercise 1   Mapping
Your Guess and Definition answers will vary. Possible responses to Other Forms items follow.
1. *n.* abjection, abjectness; *adv.* abjectly
2. *n.* admonition, admonishment; *vt.* admonishes, admonished, admonishing; *adv.* admonishingly
3. *n.* commensuration, commensurability; *adj.* commensurable; *adv.* commensurately, commensurably
4. None
5. *n.* euphemist; *vt.* or *vi.* euphemize; *adj.* euphemistic, euphemistical; *adv.* euphemistically
6. *n.* nebulosity, nebulousness; *adv.* nebulously
7. *n.* phlegm; *adj.* phlegmatical; *adv.* phlegmatically
8. *n. pl.* proprieties
9. *n.* prosaicness; *adv.* prosaically
10. *n.* revilement, reviler; *vt.* or *vi.* reviles, reviled, reviling

Exercise 2   Context Clues
11. (D) euphemism
12. (J) nebulous
13. (F) abject
14. (A) propriety
15. (C) reviled
16. (B) distraught
17. (G) admonish
18. (I) prosaic
19. (E) phlegmatic
20. (H) commensurate

Exercise 3   Sentence Completion
21. A   22. D   23. C   24. E   25. B   26. C   27. E
28. D   29. A   30. C

Lesson 3   pages 11–14
Exercise 1   Mapping
Your Guess and Definition answers will vary. Possible responses to Other Forms items follow.
1. *n.* assimilation, assimilationism, assimilationist; *vt.* or *vi.* assimilates, assimilated, assimilating; *adj.* asssimilable, assimilative, assimilatory
2. *n.* cognition, cognizance; *vt.* cognize; *adj.* cognizable
3. *n.* discursiveness; *adv.* discursively
4. None
5. *n.* farce, farcicality; *adv.* farcically
6. *n.* fortuity, fortuitousness; *adv.* fortuitously
7. *n.* hyperbolism; *vt.* or *vi.* hyperbolize; *adj.* hyperbolic, hyperbolical; *adv.* hyperbolically
8. *n. pl.* incognitos
9. *n.* mesmerist, mesmerizer, mesmerization; *vt.* mesmerize; *adj.* mesmeric; *adv.* mesmerically
10. *n.* omniscience; *adv.* omnisciently

Exercise 2   Context Clues
11. (C) incognito
12. (E) cognizant
13. (D) farcical
14. (F) discursive
15. (A) hyperbole
16. (G) omniscient
17. (H) fortuitous
18. (J) assimilate
19. (I) ennui
20. (B) mesmerism

Exercise 3   Sentence Completion
21. C   22. B   23. E   24. D   25. A   26. C   27. B
28. D   29. E   30. A

Lesson 4   pages 15–18
Exercise 1   Mapping
Your Guess and Definition answers will vary. Possible responses to Other Forms items follow.
1. *n.* adroitness; *adv.* adroitly
2. *n.* allayer; *vt.* allays, allayed, allaying
3. *n.* blazoner, blazonment, blazonry; *vt.* blazons, blazoned, blazoning
4. None
5. *n.* choler
6. *n.* colloquium, colloquist; *n. pl.* colloquies
7. *n.* conferment, conference, conferrer, conferee; *vt.* or *vi.* confers, conferred, conferring; *adj.* conferrable
8. *n. pl.* dirges
9. *n.* expatriation; *vt.* or *vi.* expatriates, expatriated, expatriating
10. *n.* feigner; *vt.* or *vi.* feigns, feigned, feigning

Exercise 2   Context Clues
11. (J) dirges
12. (B) confers
13. (F) expatriating
14. (E) colloquy
15. (I) allay
16. (C) feigned
17. (A) blazon
18. (H) choleric
19. (G) adroit
20. (D) bravado

Exercise 3   Sentence Completion
21. A   22. C   23. C   24. D   25. E   26. B   27. C
28. E   29. D   30. B

Lesson 5 pages 19–22
Exercise 1 Mapping
Your Guess and Definition answers will vary. Possible responses to Other Forms items follow.
1. *n.* amorphism, amorphousness; *adv.* amorphously
2. *n.* asceticism; *adj.* ascetical; *adv.* ascetically
3. *n.* decorousness; *adj.* decorous; *adv.* decorously
4. *n. pl.* doggerels
5. *n.* facileness; *vt.* facilitate; *adv.* facilely
6. *adj.* guileful, guileless
7. *vt.* proffers, proffered, proffering
8. None
9. *n.* sanguineness; *adj.* sanguineous; *adv.* sanguinely
10. *n.* seraph; *adv.* seraphically

Exercise 2 Context Clues
11. (A) guile
12. (I) proffered
13. (E) seraphic
14. (F) amorphous
15. (D) decorum
16. (B) protégés
17. (G) sanguine
18. (H) doggerel
19. (C) ascetics
20. (J) facile

Exercise 3 Sentence Completion
21. C 22. D 23. E 24. B 25. B 26. A 27. D
28. B 29. C 30. C

Lesson 6 pages 23–26
Exercise 1 Mapping
Your Guess and Definition answers will vary. Possible responses to Other Forms items follow.
1. *n.* dogmatism, dogmatist; *vt.* or *vi.* dogmatize; *adj.* dogmatic, dogmatical; *adv.* dogmatically
2. *n.* exhortation; *vt.* or *vi.* exhorts, exhorted, exhorting; *adj.* exhortatory, exhortative
3. *n.* inveiglement, inveigler; *vt.* inveigles, inveigled, inveigling
4. *n. pl.* nondescripts
5. *n. pl.* nonentities
6. *n.* parsimony, parsimoniousness; *adv.* parsimoniously
7. *n.* scurrility, scurrilousness; *adv.* scurrilously
8. *n. pl.* sundries
9. *n.* tacitness; *adv.* tacitly
10. *n.* vociferousness, vociferation, vociferator; *vt.* or *vi.* vociferate; *adj.* vociferant; *adv.* vociferously

Exercise 2 Context Clues
11. (G) tacit
12. (D) nondescript
13. (F) sundry
14. (A) inveigle
15. (J) dogma
16. (E) scurrilous
17. (I) parsimonious
18. (B) exhort
19. (H) nonentities
20. (C) vociferous

Exercise 3 Sentence Completion
21. E 22. C 23. B 24. D 25. C 26. A 27. E
28. D 29. B 30. C

Lesson 7 pages 27–30
Exercise 1 Mapping
Your Guess and Definition answers will vary. Possible responses to Other Forms items follow.
1. *n.* broacher; *vt.* broaches, broached, broaching
2. *n.* charlatanism, charlatanry
3. *n.* erudition; *adv.* eruditely
4. *n.* extoller, extollment; *vt.* extolls, extolled, extolling
5. *adv.* gratuitously
6. *n.* immutability, immutableness; *adv.* immutably
7. *n.* predisposition; *vt.* presdisposes, predisposed, predisposing
8. *n. pl.* prerogatives
9. *adj.* truistic
10. *n.* veneration, venerator; *vt.* venerates, venerated, venerating; *adj.* venerable

Exercise 2 Context Clues
11. (E) gratuitous
12. (A) prerogative
13. (D) venerate
14. (B) truism
15. (H) erudite
16. (J) charlatan
17. (I) extol
18. (F) broached
19. (C) predisposed
20. (G) immutable

Exercise 3 Sentence Completion
21. C 22. B 23. D 24. A 25. E 26. B 27. C
28. D 29. C 30. B

Lesson 8 pages 31–34
Exercise 1 Mapping
Your Guess and Definition answers will vary. Possible responses to Other Forms items follow.
1. *n.* absolution, absolver; *vt.* absolves, absolved, absolving; *adj.* absolvent
2. *adj.* antipathetic, antipathetical; *adv.* antipathetically
3. *n.* antipode; *adj.* antipodal, antipodean
4. *n.* indigence, indigency; *adv.* indigently
5. *n.* infringement; *vt.* infringes, infringed, infringing
6. *n.* nettler; *vt.* nettles, nettled, nettling; *adj.* nettlesome
7. *adj.* ostensive; *adv.* ostensibly
8. *n.* retroaction, retroactivity; *vi.* retroact; *adv.* retroactively
9. *n.* speciosity, speciousness; *adv.* speciously
10. *n.* subjugation, subjugator; *vt.* subjugates, subjugated, subjugating

Exercise 2 Context Clues
11. (G) infringe
12. (B) specious
13. (E) ostensibly
14. (I) absolve
15. (F) subjugate
16. (A) antipodes
17. (C) retroactive
18. (H) antipathy
19. (D) nettle
20. (J) indigent

Exercise 3 Sentence Completion
21. E 22. C 23. B 24. D 25. A 26. C 27. B
28. E 29. C 30. C

Lesson 9 pages 35–38
Exercise 1 Mapping
Your Guess and Definition answers will vary. Possible responses to Other Forms items follow.
1. *n.* abnegator; *vt.* abnegate
2. *n.* copiousness; *adv.* copiously
3. *n.* eulogium, eulogist, eulogizer; *vt.* eulogize; *adj.* eulogistic
4. *adj.* euphonic, euphonious, euphonical; *adv.* euphonically

5. *n.* extraneousness; *adv.* extraneously
6. *adv.* mundanely
7. *n.* poignancy; *adv.* poignantly
8. *n. pl.* progenies
9. *n.* sonorousness; *adv.* sonorously
10. *adj.* tenured, tenurial

Exercise 2   Context Clues
11. (C) mundane
12. (J) eulogy
13. (B) progeny
14. (D) copious
15. (H) tenure
16. (I) euphony
17. (E) sonorous
18. (F) abnegation
19. (A) poignant
20. (G) extraneous

Exercise 3   Sentence Completion
21. D   22. B   23. C   24. E   25. A   26. D   27. C
28. E   29. B   30. D

Lesson 10   pages 39–42
Exercise 1   Mapping
Your Guess and Definition answers will vary. Possible responses to Other Forms items follow.

1. *n.* ascription; *vt.* ascribes, ascribed, ascribing; *adj.* ascribable
2. *n.* elegist; *vi.* elegize; *adj.* elegiac
3. *vt.* or *vi.* engenders, engendered, engendering
4. *n.* hackney
5. *n.* homilist; *adj.* homiletic, homiletical; *adv.* homiletically
6. None
7. *adj.* idiosyncratic; *adv.* idiosyncratically
8. *n.* inconsequentiality; *adj.* inconsequent; *adv.* inconsequentially
9. *n.* introversion; *vt.* or *vi.* introverts, introverted, introverting
10. *n. pl.* paragons

Exercise 2   Context Clues
11. (I) hackneyed
12. (G) paragon
13. (D) ascribe
14. (E) inconsequential
15. (C) humdrum
16. (A) engendered
17. (H) idiosyncrasy
18. (J) elegy
19. (B) introvert
20. (F) homilies

Exercise 3   Sentence Completion
21. A   22. D   23. B   24. C   25. E   26. D   27. A
28. C   29. E   30. D

Lesson 11   pages 43–46
Exercise 1   Mapping
Your Guess and Definition answers will vary. Possible responses to Other Forms items follow.

1. *n.* aberrance, aberrancy; *adj.* aberrational, aberrant
2. *vt.* adjudges, adjudged, adjudging
3. *adj.* candid; *adv.* candidly
4. *n.* corroboration, corroborator; *vt.* corroborates, corroborated, corroborating; *adj.* corroborant
5. None
6. *adv.* diurnally
7. *n.* hercules
8. *n.* ludicrousness; *adv.* ludicrously
9. *n.* retrospection; *adj.* retrospective; *adv.* retrospectively
10. *n.* salience, saliency; *adv.* saliently

Exercise 2   Context Clues
11. (E) corroborate
12. (C) aberration
13. (D) herculean
14. (B) retrospect
15. (G) dearth
16. (H) salient
17. (A) adjudged
18. (F) diurnal
19. (J) candor
20. (I) ludicrous

Exercise 3   Sentence Completion
21. D   22. C   23. E   24. B   25. E   26. D   27. C
28. E   29. A   30. B

Lesson 12   pages 47–50
Exercise 1   Mapping
Your Guess and Definition answers will vary. Possible responses to Other Forms items follow.

1. *n.* artificer, artificiality, artifact; *adj.* artificial; *adv.* artificially
2. *n.* augur; *vt.* or *vi.* augurs, augured, auguring
3. *n.* captivation, captivator; *vt.* captivates, captivated, captivating; *adv.* captivatingly
4. *vt.* or *vi.* chicane
5. *vt.* configure; *adj.* configurational, configurative
6. *n.* deduction; *vt.* deduces, deduced, deducing; *adj.* deducible, deductive; *adv.* deductively
7. *vi.* exist
8. *vt.* or *vi.* propone
9. *n.* refutation, refutal, refuter; *vt.* refutes, refuted, refuting; *adj.* refutable; *adv.* refutably
10. *n.* scrupulosity, scrupulousness; *n. pl.* scruples; *vt.* or *vi.* scruple; *adv.* scrupulously

Exercise 2   Context Clues
11. (A) artifices
12. (G) configuration
13. (B) scrupulous
14. (D) deduce
15. (E) refute
16. (F) captivates
17. (I) proponent
18. (H) extant
19. (C) chicanery
20. (J) augury

Exercise 3   Sentence Completion
21. E   22. C   23. D   24. B   25. A   26. D   27. C
28. E   29. B   30. D

Lesson 13   pages 51–54
Exercise 1   Mapping
Your Guess and Definition answers will vary. Possible responses to Other Forms items follow.

1. *n. pl.* civilities
2. *n.* connoisseurship
3. *vt.* exhilarate; *adj.* exhilarant, exhilarative
4. *n. pl.* foibles
5. None
6. *n.* gregariousness; *adv.* gregariously
7. *n.* obsequiousness; *adv.* obsequiously
8. *adj.* patrimonial
9. *n.* precociousness, precocity; *adv.* precociously
10. *n.* punctiliousness; *adv.* punctiliously

Exercise 2   Context Clues
11. (F) gregarious
12. (G) exhilaration
13. (A) patrimony
14. (J) obsequious
15. (I) civility
16. (D) germane
17. (H) punctilious
18. (E) foible
19. (B) connoisseur
20. (C) precocious

Exercise 3   Sentence Completion
21. E   22. C   23. B   24. D   25. A   26. C   27. E
28. B   29. D   30. A

Lesson 14   pages 55–58
Exercise 1   Mapping
Your Guess and Definition answers will vary. Possible responses to Other Forms items follow.
1. *vt.* affronts, affronted, affronting
2. *n.* buffoonery; *adj.* buffoonish
3. *n.* capitulation; *vi.* capitulates, capitulated, capitulating
4. *vt.* or *vi.* effuse; *adj.* effusive
5. *vi.* guffaws, guffawed, guffawing
6. *n.* indulger, indulgence; *vt.* or *vi.* indulge; *adv.* indulgently
7. *n.* magnanimity; *adv.* magnanimously
8. *n.* munificence; *adv.* munificently
9. *n.* propitiousness; *vt.* propitiate; *adv.* propitiously
10. *n.* querulousness; *adv.* querulously

Exercise 2   Context Clues
11. (A) effusion
12. (G) querulous
13. (C) indulgent
14. (D) affront
15. (B) propitious
16. (J) munificent
17. (F) guffaw
18. (I) capitulated
19. (H) buffoon
20. (E) magnanimous

Exercise 3   Sentence Completion
21. B   22. D   23. C   24. E   25. C   26. A   27. D
28. C   29. A   30. E

Lesson 15   pages 59–62
Exercise 1   Mapping
Your Guess and Definition answers will vary. Possible responses to Other Forms items follow.
1. *n. pl.* abeyances
2. *adj.* discrepant; *adv.* discrepantly
3. *n.* homogeneity, homogeneousness; *vt.* homogenize; *adv.* homogeneously
4. *n.* illicitness; *adv.* illicitly
5. *n.* inscrutability; *adv.* inscrutably
6. *n.* inundation, inundator; *vt.* inundates, inundated, inundating; *adj.* inundatory, inundant
7. *n.* perfidy; *adv.* perfidiously
8. *n.* pervasion, pervasiveness; *vt.* pervades, pervaded, pervading; *adj.* pervasive; *adv.* pervasively
9. *adv.* primordially
10. *n.* sumptuousness; *adv.* sumptuously

Exercise 2   Context Clues
11. (I) perfidious
12. (F) illicit
13. (H) discrepancies
14. (C) inundated
15. (E) sumptuous
16. (A) inscrutable
17. (G) abeyance
18. (B) primordial
19. (D) homogeneous
20. (J) pervaded

Exercise 3   Sentence Completion
21. C   22. E   23. B   24. D   25. A   26. C   27. C
28. E   29. B   30. D

Lesson 16   pages 63–66
Exercise 1   Mapping
Your Guess and Definition answers will vary. Possible responses to Other Forms items follow.
1. *n.* chastisement, chastiser; *vt.* chastises, chastised, chastising
2. *n.* demagogy; *vi.* demagogues, demagogued, demagoguing; *adj.* demagogic; *adv.* demagogically
3. *n.* deplorer; *vt.* deplores, deplored, deploring; *adj.* deplorable; *adv.* deplorably
4. *adj.* detrimental; *adv.* detrimentally
5. *n.* emanation; *vi.* emanates, emanated, emanating; *adj.* emanative
6. *vt.* harbingers, harbingered, harbingering
7. *n.* intercession, intercessor; *vi.* intercedes, interceded, interceding; *adj.* intercessional
8. *n.* irrevocability; *adv.* irrevocably
9. *n.* obnoxiousness; *adv.* obnoxiously
10. *n.* prevarication, prevaricator; *vi.* prevaricates, prevaricated, prevaricating

Exercise 2   Context Clues
11. (B) harbinger
12. (C) emanating
13. (A) demagogue
14. (I) prevaricated
15. (F) detriment
16. (E) obnoxious
17. (G) chastised
18. (J) irrevocable
19. (D) deplore
20. (H) intercede

Exercise 3   Sentence Completion
21. C   22. A   23. B   24. D   25. C   26. E   27. E
28. D   29. C   30. B

Lesson 17   pages 67–70
Exercise 1   Mapping
Your Guess and Definition answers will vary. Possible responses to Other Forms items follow.
1. *n.* anarchist, anarchism; *adj.* anarchic; *adv.* anarchically
2. *n.* cajolery, cajoler; *vt.* or *vi.* cajoles, cajoled, cajoling; *adv.* cajolingly
3. *n.* commodiousness; *adv.* commodiously
4. *n.* ethnologist; *adj.* ethnological; *adv.* ethnologically
5. *n.* extricability, extrication; *vt.* extricates, extricated, extricating; *adj.* extricable
6. *n.* impairment; *vt.* or *vi.* impairs, impaired, impairing
7. *adv.* menially
8. None
9. *adj.* pestilent, pestilential; *adv.* pestilently, pestilentially
10. *n.* rampancy; *adv.* rampantly

Exercise 2   Context Clues
11. (H) extricated
12. (E) menial
13. (B) rampant
14. (C) cajoled
15. (F) pestilence
16. (D) anarchy
17. (J) nadir
18. (I) ethnology
19. (G) impaired
20. (A) commodious

Exercise 3   Sentence Completion
21. C   22. A   23. B   24. E   25. C   26. D   27. B
28. A   29. E   30. D

Lesson 18   pages 71–74
Exercise 1   Mapping
Your Guess and Definition answers will vary. Possible responses to Other Forms items follow.

1. *n.* cadaver, cadaverousness; *adj.* cadaveric; *adv.* cadaverously
2. *n.* consignment, consignation, consignor, consignee; *vt.* consigns, consigned, consigning; *adj.* consignable
3. *n.* elocutionist; *adj.* elocutionary
4. *n.* incorrigibleness, incorrigibility; *adv.* incorrigibly
5. *n.* maimer; *vt.* or *vi.* maims, maimed, maiming
6. *n.* residue, residuum; *adj.* residuary; *adv.* residually
7. *adj.* restitutive
8. *n.* stridence, stridency; *adv.* stridently
9. *n.* subversiveness, subverter; *vt.* subvert; *adv.* subversively
10. *n.* virus, virulence; *adv.* virulently

Exercise 2   Context Clues
11. (C) residual
12. (E) virulent
13. (I) strident
14. (F) consigning
15. (D) elocution
16. (G) subversion
17. (A) cadaverous
18. (H) incorrigible
19. (J) restitution
20. (B) maimed

Exercise 3   Sentence Completion
21. C   22. D   23. D   24. B   25. E   26. A   27. C
28. D   29. B   30. A

Lesson 19   pages 75–78
Exercise 1   Mapping
Your Guess and Definition answers will vary. Possible responses to Other Forms items follow.

1. *n.* calumniator; *vt.* or *vi.* calumniate; *adj.* calumnious; *adv.* calumniously
2. *n.* contingence; *adj.* contingent; *adv.* contingently
3. *n.* dissension, dissenter, dissentient; *vi.* dissents, dissented, dissenting; *adv.* dissentingly
4. *n.* impassivity, impassiveness; *adv.* impassively
5. *n.* litigant; *vt.* or *vi.* litigate; *adj.* litigable, litigious
6. *n.* mollifier, mollification; *vt.* mollifies, mollified, mollifying
7. *n.* recanter, recantation; *vt.* or *vi.* recants, recanted, recanting
8. *n.* retaliation; *vt.* or *vi.* retaliates, retaliated, retaliating; *adj.* retaliative, retaliatory
9. *n.* salinity; *vt.* salinize
10. *n.* sedentariness; *adv.* sedentarily

Exercise 2   Context Clues
11. (J) saline
12. (C) recant
13. (I) contingency
14. (A) litigation
15. (D) retaliate
16. (B) calumny
17. (H) sedentary
18. (G) impassively
19. (E) dissents
20. (F) mollified

Exercise 3   Sentence Completion
21. C   22. E   23. B   24. A   25. D   26. E   27. C
28. B   29. C   30. A

Lesson 20   pages 79–82
Exercise 1   Mapping
Your Guess and Definition answers will vary. Possible responses to Other Forms items follow.

1. *n.* auspiciousness; *adj.* auspicious; *adv.* auspiciously
2. *adj.* austere; *adv.* austerely
3. *n.* clandestineness; *adv.* clandestinely
4. *n.* fomentation; *vt.* foments, fomented, fomenting
5. *adj.* hiatal
6. *n.* obesity
7. *n.* solicitude, solicitousness; *adv.* solicitously
8. *n.* temerariousness; *adv.* temerariously
9. *adj.* vestigial; *adv.* vestigially
10. *n.* vindication, vindicator; *vt.* vindicates, vindicated, vindicating; *adj.* vindicatory

Exercise 2   Context Clues
11. (E) vindicate
12. (B) obese
13. (I) temerity
14. (G) austerity
15. (D) fomenting
16. (J) solicitous
17. (F) auspices
18. (A) hiatus
19. (C) clandestine
20. (H) vestige

Exercise 3   Sentence Completion
21. A   22. B   23. E   24. D   25. C   26. C   27. E
28. B   29. A   30. C

Lesson 21   pages 83–86
Exercise 1   Mapping
Your Guess and Definition answers will vary. Possible responses to Other Forms items follow.

1. *n.* differentiation; *vt.* or *vi.* differentiates, differentiated, differentiating
2. *adj.* disparate; *adv.* disparately
3. *n.* empiricism, empiricist, empiric; *adv.* empirically
4. *n.* facetiousness; *adv.* facetiously
5. *n.* officiousness; *adv.* officiously
6. *n.* quiescence; *adv.* quiescently
7. *n.* renouncement, renouncer; *vt.* or *vi.* renounces, renounced, renouncing
8. *vi.* scathe; *adv.* scathingly
9. *n. pl.* testimonials
10. *n. pl.* treatises

Exercise 2   Context Clues
11. (F) disparity
12. (C) renounced
13. (I) officious
14. (H) scathing
15. (J) facetious
16. (D) empirical
17. (B) differentiate
18. (A) treatise
19. (E) quiescence
20. (G) testimonial

Exercise 3   Sentence Completion
21. B   22. B   23. A   24. D   25. B   26. A   27. C
28. A   29. C   30. D

Lesson 22   pages 87–90
Exercise 1   Mapping
Your Guess and Definition answers will vary. Possible responses to Other Forms items follow.

1. *n.* chauvinist; *adj.* chauvinistic; *adv.* chauvinistically

2. *n.* cosmopolis, cosmopolite, cosmopolitanism
3. None
4. *n.* epitomizer; *vt.* epitomize
5. *n.* inexorability; *adv.* inexorably
6. *vt.* moots, mooted, mooting
7. *n.* regime
8. *vt.* reposit
9. *n.* sagaciousness; *adj.* sagacious; *adv.* sagaciously
10. *n.* tenuousness, tenuity; *adv.* tenuously

Exercise 2   Context Clues
11. (E) chauvinism   16. (F) repository
12. (C) epitome   17. (B) regimen
13. (A) inexorable   18. (H) sagacity
14. (D) cosmopolitan   19. (J) tenuous
15. (G) devoid   20. (I) moot

Exercise 3   Sentence Completion
21. D   22. A   23. C   24. E   25. D   26. C   27. E
28. B   29. A   30. D

Lesson 23   pages 91–94
Exercise 1   Mapping
Your Guess and Definition answers will vary. Possible responses to Other Forms items follow.
1. *vt.* bodes, boded, boding
2. *n.* burnisher; *vt.* or *vi.* burnishes, burnished, burnishing
3. *n.* coercion, coerciveness; *vt.* coerces, coerced, coercing; *adj.* coercible, coercive; *adv.* coercibly, coercively
4. *n. pl.* esoterica; *adv.* esoterically
5. *adj.* firmamental
6. *adj.* gauntleted
7. *vt.* metes, meted, meting
8. *n. pl.* misnomers
9. *vt.* mottle
10. None

Exercise 2   Context Clues
11. (D) firmament   16. (G) terra firma
12. (E) bode   17. (B) burnished
13. (A) gauntlet   18. (H) esoteric
14. (F) mottled   19. (I) mete
15. (C) misnomer   20. (J) coerce

Exercise 3   Sentence Completion
21. C   22. E   23. D   24. A   25. B   26. C   27. D
28. E   29. D   30. A

Lesson 24   pages 95–98
Exercise 1   Mapping
Your Guess and Definition answers will vary. Possible responses to Other Forms items follow.
1. *n.* acrimony, acrimoniousness; *adv.* acrimoniously
2. *vt.* or *vi.* atrophies, atrophied, atrophying; *adj.* atrophic
3. *adj.* benevolent; *adv.* benevolently
4. *vt.* consternate
5. *n.* desistance; *vi.* desists, desisted, desisting
6. *adj.* enigmatic, enigmatical; *adv.* enigmatically
7. *n.* expounder; *vt.* expounds, expounded, expounding
8. *n.* loquacity, loquaciousness; *adv.* loquaciously

9. *adj.* precursory
10. *n.* voluminosity; *adv.* voluminously

Exercise 2   Context Clues
11. (C) enigma   16. (I) atrophy
12. (D) voluminous   17. (A) expound
13. (E) consternation   18. (J) benevolence
14. (B) acrimonious   19. (F) desist
15. (H) precursor   20. (G) loquacious

Exercise 3   Sentence Completion
21. D   22. B   23. E   24. C   25. A   26. C   27. D
28. E   29. B   30. C

Lesson 25   pages 99–102
Exercise 1   Mapping
Your Guess and Definition answers will vary. Possible responses to Other Forms items follow.
1. *n.* assiduity, assiduousness; *adv.* assiduously
2. *n.* averrment; *v.* avers, averred, averring
3. *vt.* or *vi.* cease
4. *n. pl.* denizens
5. None
6. *n.* iniquitousness; *adj.* iniquitous; *adv.* iniquitously
7. *n.* inordinateness; *adv.* inordinately
8. *n.* mercurialness; *adv.* mercurially
9. *adv.* pecuniarily
10. *n.* tenability, tenableness; *adv.* tenably

Exercise 2   Context Clues
11. (I) equanimity   16. (A) denizens
12. (E) tenable   17. (G) mercurial
13. (C) inordinate   18. (B) assiduous
14. (D) aver   19. (J) iniquities
15. (H) pecuniary   20. (F) cessation

Exercise 3   Sentence Completion
21. D   22. C   23. B   24. E   25. C   26. D   27. B
28. A   29. E   30. C

Lesson 26   pages 103–106
Exercise 1   Mapping
Your Guess and Definition answers will vary. Possible responses to Other Forms items follow.
1. *n.* avariciousness; *adj.* avaricious; *adv.* avariciously
2. *n.* conciliation, conciliator; *vt.* conciliates, conciliated, conciliating; *adj.* conciliable, conciliatory, conciliative
3. *n. pl.* corollaries
4. None
5. *n.* espousal, espouser; *vt.* espouses, espoused, espousing
6. *n.* extenuation; *vt.* extenuates, extenuating
7. *vt.* or *vi.* fissures, fissured, fissuring
8. *n.* impeccability; *adj.* impeccant; *adv.* impeccably
9. *n.* incarceration, incarcerator; *vt.* incarcerates, incarcerated, incarcerating
10. *n.* queller; *vt.* quells, quelled, quelling

Exercise 2   Context Clues
11. (I) extenuated   16. (A) impeccable
12. (C) duress   17. (H) corollary
13. (B) quelled   18. (D) avarice
14. (J) incarcerated   19. (F) fissure
15. (E) conciliate   20. (G) espoused

Exercise 3   Sentence Completion
21. B   22. D   23. C   24. E   25. A   26. C   27. B
28. E   29. B   30. D

Lesson 27   pages 107–110
Exercise 1   Mapping
Your Guess and Definition answers will vary. Possible responses to Other Forms items follow.
1. *n.* caricaturist; *vt.* caricatures, caricatured, caricaturing
2. *n.* commiseration; *vt.* commiserates, commiserated, commiserating; *adj.* commiserative; *adv.* commiseratively
3. *n.* evanescence; *vi.* evanesce; *adv.* evanescently
4. *n.* festoonery; *vt.* festoons, festooned, festooning
5. *vi.* gambols, gamboled, gamboling
6. *n.* ingénue, ingenuousness; *adv.* ingenuously
7. None
8. *n.* pallidness; *adj.* pallid; *adv.* pallidly
9. *n.* remunerator; *vt.* remunerate; *adj.* remunerable, remunerative; *adv.* remuneratively
10. *n.* venality; *adv.* venally

Exercise 2   Context Clues
11. (B) gamboling   16. (F) maudlin
12. (I) renumeration   17. (A) caricatures
13. (H) pallor   18. (D) festooned
14. (E) ingenuous   19. (G) commiserate
15. (J) venal   20. (C) evanescent

Exercise 3   Sentence Completion
21. D   22. A   23. B   24. D   25. C   26. C   27. E
28. B   29. E   30. C

Lesson 28   pages 111–114
Exercise 1   Mapping
Your Guess and Definition answers will vary. Possible responses to Other Forms items follow.
1. *n.* abstrusity, abstruseness; *adv.* abstrusely
2. *n.* apostate; *vt.* apostatize
3. *n. pl.* baubles
4. None
5. *n. pl.* frescoes; *vt.* fresco
6. *n.* frugality; *adv.* frugally
7. *n.* iridescence; *adv.* iridescently
8. *n.* opulency; *adj.* opulent; *adv.* opulently
9. *n. pl.* promontories
10. *n.* usurer, usuriousness; *adj.* usurious; *adv.* usuriously

Exercise 2   Context Clues
11. (D) promontory   16. (B) apostasy
12. (J) opulence   17. (E) fresco
13. (F) abstruse   18. (C) baubles
14. (I) frugal   19. (G) iridescent
15. (A) usury   20. (H) bullion

Exercise 3   Sentence Completion
21. B   22. D   23. C   24. E   25. D   26. A   27. C
28. E   29. D   30. B

Lesson 29   pages 115–118
Exercise 1   Mapping
Your Guess and Definition answers will vary. Possible responses to Other Forms items follow.
1. *n.* absconder; *vi.* absconds, absconded, absconding
2. *n.* adjurer, adjuration; *vt.* adjures, adjured, adjuring; *adj.* adjuratory
3. *vt.* asperse
4. *n.* circumvention; *vt.* circumvents, circumvented, circumventing; *adj.* circumventive
5. *n.* ethereality, etherealness; *adv.* ethereally
6. *n.* ignominiousness; *adj.* ignominious; *adv.* ignominiously
7. *n.* maligner; *vt.* maligns, maligned, maligning
8. *n.* malingerer; *vi.* malingers, malingered, malingering
9. *adj.* prognostic
10. *n.* remonstration, remonstrator, remonstrant; *vt.* or *vi.* remonstrates, remonstrated, remonstrating; *adj.* remonstrative; *adv.* remonstratively

Exercise 2   Context Clues
11. (E) ignominy   16. (H) prognosis
12. (D) circumvent   17. (A) adjured
13. (J) malingering   18. (I) abscond
14. (F) aspersions   19. (G) maligned
15. (B) remonstrate   20. (C) ethereal

Exercise 3   Sentence Completion
21. B   22. C   23. D   24. A   25. B   26. D   27. E
28. C   29. B   30. A

Lesson 30   pages 119–122
Exercise 1   Mapping
Your Guess and Definition answers will vary. Possible responses to Other Forms items follow.
1. *n.* biennale, biennium; *adv.* biennially
2. *n.* caprice, capriciousness; *adv.* capriciously
3. *n.* elicitor, elicitation; *vt.* elicits, elicited, eliciting; *adj.* elicitable
4. *n.* emaciation; *vt.* emaciates, emaciated, emaciating
5. *n.* equivocation, equivocator, equivocality; *vi.* equivocate; *adv.* equivocally
6. *n.* extortion, extorter, extortioner, extortionist; *vt.* extorts, extorted, extorting; *adj.* extortive, extortionate, extortionary
7. *n. pl.* fiascoes
8. None
9. *n. pl.* reprisals
10. *n.* taciturnity; *adj.* tacit; *adv.* taciturnly

Exercise 2   Context Clues
11. (J) extort   16. (E) biennial
12. (I) reprisals   17. (D) emaciate
13. (H) elicit   18. (B) longevity
14. (G) taciturn   19. (C) capricious
15. (A) fiascoes   20. (F) equivocal

Exercise 3   Sentence Completion
21. D   22. C   23. B   24. E   25. A   26. C   27. D
28. E   29. C   30. B

Lesson 1   page 126

1. (C); Degree. To *admonish* suggests a lesser degree of punishment than to *condemn*. When used as verbs, *glance* means to look briefly, while *stare* means to look for a long time.
2. (E); Synonym. *Banal,* which means ordinary or insipid, has a meaning similar to *commonplace. Strange* and *unusual* have the same meaning.
3. (E); Degree. *Lugubrious* has a meaning similar to *sad,* but it also means mournful to an exaggerated or ridiculous degree. *Jubilant* has a meaning similar to *pleased* but also implies greater joy.
4. (C); Characteristic Quality. *Fog* is characteristically *nebulous,* or indefinite and vague, just as a *blanket* is characteristically *soft.*
5. (D); Characteristic Quality. A *villain* is characteristically *nefarious,* or wicked, just as a *clown* is characteristically *amusing.*
6. (A); Performer and Related Action. You expect a *nemesis,* someone who imposes retribution or punishment, to *punish* others, just as you expect a *savior* to *save* others.
7. (B); Characteristic Quality. A *loafer* is characteristically *phlegmatic,* sluggish and hard to get moving, just as an *artist* is characteristically *creative.*
8. (E); Antonym. *Prosaic,* which means ordinary, is opposite in meaning to *exceptional,* which means special and distinctive. *Fancy* and *plain* also have opposite meanings.
9. (A); Classification. A *pseudonym,* a fictitious alias assumed by an author, is classified as a *name,* just as an *actor* is classified as a *performer.*
10. (E); Performer and Related Action. You expect a *thief* to *purloin,* or steal, money, just as you expect a *surveyor* to *measure* land.

Lesson 2   page 127

1. (D); Action and Related Object. You *assimilate,* or absorb, *food,* just as you *join* an *organization.*
2. (B); Performer and Related Object. A *knight* carries a *blazon,* which can be a coat of arms, a heraldic shield, or a banner, just as a *police officer* carries a *badge.*
3. (A); Characteristic Quality. A *hothead* is characteristically *choleric,* or bad-tempered, just as a *genius* is characteristically *brilliant.*
4. (E); Degree. A *colloquy,* a formal discussion or conference, is distinguished from a *chat,* which is an informal conversation, often on light topics. A *festival* is an organized celebration, usually involving a large number of people, while a *gathering* is an informal meeting or assemblage of people.

5. (B); Synonym. *Confer* and *give* have the same meaning, as do *discover* and *find.* An alternative meaning of *confer,* to discuss, is not applicable here.
6. (D); Part and Whole. A *dirge* is a mournful song that is often part of a *funeral,* just as an *intermission,* a break between acts, is often a part of a *play.*
7. (E); Cause and Effect. *Inactivity* can result in *ennui,* or boredom, just as *labor* can result in *fatigue,* or tiredness.
8. (C); Degree. Something that is *farcical* is amusing, while something that is *hilarious* is extremely funny. In the same way, *good* implies a lesser degree of quality than *excellent.*
9. (A); Performer and Related Action. You expect a *pretender* to *feign,* or make a false show of something, just as you expect a *surgeon* to *operate* on a patient.
10. (E); Antonym. *Fortuitous,* which means accidental, is opposite in meaning to *planned. Unfortunate* and *lucky* are also opposite in meaning.

Lesson 3   page 128

1. (E); Characteristic Quality. An *ascetic* is characteristically *self-denying,* just as an *athlete* is characteristically *active.*
2. (A); Classification. *Doggerel,* or bad poetry, can be classified as a kind of *verse,* just as a *sonnet* can be classified as a kind of *poem.*
3. (B); Action and Related Object. You *preach dogma,* or a set of beliefs, just as you *teach* a *lesson.*
4. (E); Performer and Related Action. You expect an *advisor* to *exhort,* or urge, someone to do something, just as you expect a *witness* to *testify* in court.
5. (B); Antonym. *Facile,* which can mean insincere or superficial, is opposite in meaning to *sincere. Guilty* and *innocent* also have opposite meanings.
6. (B); Performer and Related Action. You expect a *deceiver* to *inveigle* others by tricking them or leading them on with deception, just as you expect a *detective* to *investigate* a case.
7. (D); Synonym. *Proffer* and *offer* have the same meaning, as do *trade* and *exchange.*
8. (C); Characteristic Quality. An *optimist* is characteristically *sanguine,* or relaxed and hopeful, just as a *mourner* is characteristically *sorrowful.*
9. (D); Antonym. *Scurrilous* language, which is coarse, indecent, and vulgar, is the opposite of *refined* language. *Flexible* and *rigid* also have opposite meanings.
10. (E); Synonym. *Seraphic* and *angelic* have the same meaning, as do *anxious* and *worried. Seraphic* specifically refers to the highest order of angels.

Lesson 4 page 129

1. (D); Performer and Related Action. You expect a *jury* to *absolve,* or forgive and release a defendant, when it renders a verdict of not guilty. In the same way, you expect a *choir* to *harmonize* when singing together.
2. (A); Cause and Effect. *Antipathy,* which means strong dislike or aversion, can result in *avoidance* of that which causes the negative feeling, just as *success* can result in *confidence.*
3. (C); Synonym. *Antipodes* and *opposites* have similar meanings, as do *friends* and *comrades.*
4. (E); Performer and Related Action. You expect a *charlatan,* one who makes false claims, to *deceive* others, just as you expect an *impostor* to *trick* others.
5. (B); Characteristic Quality. A *scholar* is characteristically *erudite,* or learned, just as a *wrestler* is characteristically *strong.*
6. (D); Antonym. *Immutable,* which means never changing, is opposite in meaning to *changeable.* *Steadfast,* which means reliable and dependable, is opposite in meaning to *fickle.*
7. (E); Antonym. *Indigent,* which means poor, means the opposite of *wealthy. Solemn* and *silly* also have opposite meanings.
8. (B); Performer and Related Action. You expect a *violator* to be someone who *infringes,* or trespasses on, the rights of others, just as you expect the members of a *team* to *cooperate* with each other.
9. (C); Classification. A *nettle* can be classified as a stinging or spiny *plant.* In the same way, a *quarter* can be classified as a *coin.*
10. (A); Synonym. *Ostensible* and *apparent* have similar meanings, as do *fragile* and *delicate.*

Lesson 5 page 130

1. (D); Classification. An *elegy,* or verse written to lament the dead, can be classified as a *poem.* A *jet* can be classified as an *airplane.*
2. (B); Function. The function of a *eulogy,* a formal speech written about a person who has died, is to *praise* its subject. In the same way, the function of a *cartoon* is to *amuse.*
3. (A); Characteristic Quality. A *euphony,* or combination of agreeable sounds, is characteristically *pleasant,* just as *lightning* is characteristically *bright.*
4. (E); Antonym. *Extraneous,* which means irrelevant or inessential, is opposite in meaning to *essential. Cautious* and *careless* also have opposite meanings.
5. (D); Performer and Related Object. You expect a *minister* to deliver a *homily,* or moralizing sermon, to a congregation, just as you expect a *doctor* to perform an *examination* of a patient.
6. (C); Performer and Related Action. You expect an *introvert,* or shy person, to *withdraw* from others, just as you expect an *entertainer* to *perform* before an audience.

7. (B); Antonym. *Mundane,* which means ordinary or commonplace, means the opposite of *exceptional. Simple* and *complex* also have opposite meanings.
8. (D); Synonym. *Paragon* and *model* have similar meanings, as do *narrative* and *story.*
9. (E); Synonym. *Progeny* and *descendants* have the same meaning, as do *kin* and *relatives.*
10. (A); Characteristic Quality. A *cello* is characteristically *sonorous,* with a deep and rich sound, just as a *bomb* is characteristically *destructive.*

Lesson 6 page 131

1. (B); Antonym. *Candor,* which means openness and honesty, means the opposite of *deceitfulness. Growth* and *decline* also have opposite meanings.
2. (B); Synonym. *Configuration* and *shape* have similar meanings. *Alteration* and *change* also have similar meanings.
3. (A); Action and Related Object. You *corroborate,* or confirm, *evidence,* just as you *confirm* a *fact.*
4. (D); Synonym. *Dearth* and *scarcity* have the same meaning, as do *exaggeration* and *overstatement.*
5. (B); Performer and Related Action. You expect a *thinker* to *deduce,* or reason things out, just as you expect a *contributor* to *give.*
6. (A); Antonym. *Diurnal,* which means occurring during the daytime, and *nocturnal,* which means occurring at night, have opposite meanings. *Urban* and *rural* also have opposite meanings.
7. (B); Antonym. *Extant,* which means still existing, is opposite in meaning to *extinct. Sheltered* and *exposed* are also opposite in meaning.
8. (E); Degree. A *herculean* task is extraordinarily *difficult,* just as something that is *fascinating* is extraordinarily *interesting.*
9. (D); Characteristic Quality. A *fool* is characteristically *ludicrous,* or absurd, just as a *comedian* is characteristically *funny.*
10. (E); Performer and Related Action. You expect a *proponent* to *support* something, just as you expect a *forerunner* to *precede* something else.

Lesson 7 page 132

1. (A); Performer and Related Action. You expect a *buffoon,* or clown, to *amuse* others, just as you expect a *proofreader* to *check* type.
2. (C); Performer and Related Action. You expect a *loser* to *capitulate,* or give up, just as you expect a *chef* to *cook.*
3. (E); Antonym. *Civility,* which means politeness, is opposite in meaning to *rudeness. Acceptance* and *rejection* are also opposite in meaning.
4. (B); Performer and Related Action. You expect a *connoisseur,* someone with fine taste and expert knowledge, to *appreciate* fine things, just as you expect a *scholar* to *study.*
5. (E); Synonym. *Foible* and *weakness* have similar meanings, as do *division* and *separation.*
6. (D); Cause and Effect. A *joke* can result in a *guffaw,* or loud laugh, just as *carelessness* can result in an *error.*

7. (C); Synonym. *Indulgent*, which means kind to excess, and *lenient* have similar meanings, as do *fortified* and *strengthened*.

8. (A); Antonym. *Magnanimous*, which means generous, is opposite in meaning to *selfish*. *Divided* and *united* also have opposite meanings.

9. (B); Degree. Someone who is *obsequious* shows an exaggerated desire to please and obey, whereas someone who is *obedient* is merely willing to follow instructions. Similarly, something that is *gigantic* is bigger than something that is *large*.

10. (B); Degree. *Punctilious* means *careful* but to a much greater degree, implying scrupulousness and precise attention to detail. In the same way, *hostile* means *unfriendly* but to a much greater degree.

Lesson 8   page 133

1. (B); Performer and Related Action. You expect a *disciplinarian* to *chastise*, or scold, someone, just as you expect a *student* to *study*.

2. (D); Classification. A *demagogue*, someone who gains power by stirring up emotions, can be classified as a *leader*, just as a *banana* can be classified as a *fruit*.

3. (B); Synonym. When used as nouns, *detriment* and *harm* have similar meanings, as do *scheme* and *plot*.

4. (E); Synonym. *Discrepancy* and *inconsistency* have the same meaning, as do *resolution* and *determination*.

5. (D); Characteristic Quality. *Bribery* is characteristically *illicit*, or illegal, just as a *skyscraper* is characteristically *tall*.

6. (A); Synonym. *Inscrutable,* or obscure and difficult to understand, is similar in meaning to *mysterious*. *Scholarly* and *learned* also have similar meanings.

7. (E); Performer and Related Action. A *peacemaker* is someone who *intercedes,* or steps between two parties that disagree. An *antagonist* is someone who *opposes* something.

8. (D); Antonym. *Obnoxious,* which means rude, is opposite in meaning to *pleasant. Ornery* and *agreeable* are also opposite in meaning.

9. (A); Antonym. *Perfidious,* which means disloyal, means the opposite of *faithful. Cordial* and *unfriendly* also have opposite meanings.

10. (E); Characteristic Quality. A *palace* is characteristically *sumptuous,* or lavish, just as a *doubter* is characteristically *skeptical*.

Lesson 9   page 134

1. (E); Cause and Effect. *Chaos* can result from *anarchy,* which is a lack of law and order, just as an *illness* can result from a *virus*.

2. (D); Synonym. To *cajole* and to *coax* have the same meaning, as do to *start* and to *begin*.

3. (E); Antonym. *Commodious,* which means roomy and spacious, is opposite in meaning to *cramped. Boundless* and *limited* also have opposite meanings.

4. (B); Classification. *Ethnology,* the study of human behavior and development, is classified as a kind of *anthropology. Pediatrics,* the medical care of infants and children, is classified as a kind of *medicine*.

5. (D); Degree. To *impair* something means to break it or make it unusable, while to *destroy* something means to obliterate or ruin it completely. In the same way, to *nibble* means to take small bites, while to *devour* means to eat voraciously.

6. (C); Antonym. *Nadir,* which means lowest point, means the opposite of *high point. Failure* and *success* also have opposite meanings.

7. (B); Characteristic Quality. A *pestilence,* or widespread, contagious, and often fatal disease, is characteristically *destructive. A benefactor* is characteristically *charitable*.

8. (D); Synonym. *Restitution,* which means giving back something that has been lost or taken away, is similar in meaning to *compensation. Consideration* and *thoughtfulness* have the same meaning.

9. (C); Antonym. *Subversion,* which means overthrow or ruin, is opposite in meaning to *establishment. Reduction* and *increase* also have opposite meanings.

10. (A); Synonym. *Virulent* and *deadly* have similar meanings. *Courageous* and *brave* have the same meaning.

Lesson 10   page 135

1. (D); Degree. One meaning of *austerity* is extreme *simplicity,* without ornamentation or luxury. *Starvation* suggests *hunger* but to a much stronger degree.

2. (B); Synonym. *Calumny* and *slander* (used as a noun) both mean a false statement that hurts someone's reputation. *Thrill* (used as a noun) and *excitement* have similar meanings.

3. (C); Performer and Related Action. You expect an *instigator* to *foment,* or stir up, trouble, just as you expect a *teacher* to *instruct* students.

4. (D); Antonym. *Impassive* and *emotional* have opposite meanings, as do *maintained* and *neglected*.

5. (A); Performer and Related Object. You expect a *lawyer* to be involved in *litigation,* or lawsuits, just as you expect a *diplomat* to be involved in *negotiation*.

6. (E); Synonym. *Mollify,* which means to appease or make less severe, has a meaning similar to *soothe. Scramble* and *mix* have the same meaning.

7. (C); Antonym. *Obese,* which means extremely overweight, has a meaning opposite to *skinny. Agitated* and *calm* also have opposite meanings.

8. (E); Synonym. *Saline* and *salty* have the same meaning, as do *coarse* and *rough*.

9. (D); Characteristic Quality. A *typist*, who stays seated much of the time, is characteristically *sedentary*, just as a *snob* is characteristically *conceited*.

10. (A); Degree. *Temerity* means rash or foolish boldness, while *nerve* means boldness without the added degree of recklessness. *Absurdity* is an extreme degree of *silliness*.

Lesson 11   page 136

1. (D); Degree. *Chauvinism* is an extreme degree of *devotion* to one's group, implying militancy and boastfulness. *Reverence* implies an extreme degree of *respect*.

2. (E); Antonym. *Facetious*, which means witty and joking, means the opposite of *serious*. *Caring* and *indifferent* also have opposite meanings.

3. (B); Synonym. *Inexorable*, which means unable to be moved or influenced by persuasion, has a meaning similar to *unrelenting*. *Intricate* and *complex* also have similar meanings.

4. (E); Characteristic Quality. A *controversy* is characteristically *moot*, or debatable, just as a *crime* is characteristically *illegal*.

5. (E); Characteristic Quality. A *meddler* is characteristically *officious*, or interfering, just as a *model* is characteristically *photogenic*.

6. (B); Synonym. *Quiescent* and *inactive* have the same meaning, as do *skeptical* and *doubting*.

7. (E); Performer and Related Object. A *soldier* follows a *regimen*, or a strict routine of diet and exercise, just as a *student* follows a *curriculum*, or prescribed course of study.

8. (B); Antonym. To *renounce*, or give up something, means the opposite of to *adopt*. *Withhold* and *give* also have opposite meanings.

9. (A); Function. The function of a *repository*, or container where things are kept, is to *contain*, just as the function of a *sieve* is to *strain*.

10. (E); Performer and Related Object. A *treatise* is a formal, systematic book or article composed by a *scholar*, just as a *memorandum* is an informative document composed by an *administrator*.

Lesson 12   page 137

1. (E); Synonym. *Acrimonious* and *bitter* have similar meanings, as do *perpetual* and *continual*.

2. (B); Cause and Effect. *Gratitude* can be a result of *benevolence*, or kindness and charity, just as *learning* can be the result of *study*.

3. (C); Performer and Related Action. You expect a *tyrant* to *coerce*, or threaten or use force against his or her subjects, just as you expect a *mourner* to *grieve* a loss.

4. (A); Cause and Effect. A *tragedy* can cause *consternation*, a bewildering fear or shock, just as a *victory* can cause *celebration*.

5. (C); Antonym. *Desist* and *persist* have opposite meanings, as do *occupy* and *vacate*.

6. (D); Characteristic Quality. An *enigma*, or riddle, is characteristically *mysterious*, just as *honey* is characteristically *sweet*.

7. (B); Location. *Stars* can be found in the *firmament*, or sky, just as *whales* can be found in the *ocean*.

8. (D); Part and Whole. A *gauntlet*, which is a metal-plated glove, is part of a suit of *armor*, just as a *bristle* is part of a *brush*.

9. (B); Synonym. *Loquacious* and *talkative* have the same meaning, as do *venomous* and *poisonous*.

10. (E); Classification. A *misnomer*, that is, a misleading or inappropriate name, can be classified as an *error*, just as a *nickel* can be classified as a *coin*.

Lesson 13   page 138

1. (B); Antonym. *Assiduous*, which means careful and diligent, is opposite in meaning to *careless*. *Prompt* and *tardy* are also opposite in meaning.

2. (D); Synonym. *Avarice* and *greed* have similar meanings, as do *vice* and *fault*.

3. (E); Performer and Related Action. You expect a *negotiator* to *conciliate*, or smooth over conflicts between opposing parties, just as you expect an *heir* to *inherit* an estate.

4. (B); Performer and Related Action. You expect a *denizen* to *inhabit* a place, just as you expect an *occupant* to *dwell* in a place.

5. (A); Synonym. *Duress*, which means the use of force or threats, is similar in meaning to *force*. *Perfection* and *flawlessness* have the same meaning.

6. (D); Antonym. *Equanimity*, which means calm and composure, is opposite in meaning to *excitability*. *Order* and *chaos* are also opposite in meaning.

7. (D); Performer and Related Action. You expect a *jailer* to *incarcerate*, or imprison, a prisoner, just as you expect a *pilot* to *fly*.

8. (C); Cause and Effect. *Iniquity*, which means wickedness, can result in *punishment*, just as *experimentation* can result in *discovery*.

9. (B); Synonym. *Inordinate* and *excessive* have similar meanings, as do *foolhardy* and *reckless*.

10. (B); Antonym. *Mercurial*, which means volatile and changeable, is opposite in meaning to *constant*. *Virtuous* and *evil* also have opposite meanings.

Lesson 14   page 139

1. (E); Characteristic Quality. A *bauble*, or trinket, is characteristically *showy*, just as *lace* is characteristically *delicate*.

2. (D); Performer and Related Action. You expect a *sympathizer* to *commiserate*, or express sympathy, just as you expect a *debater* to *argue*.

3. (B); Characteristic Quality. A *festoon*, a wreath or garland made of flowers or other materials, is characteristically *decorative*, just as a *ring* is characteristically *round*.

4. (A); Performer and Related Object. A *fresco*, a painting made on wet plaster, is created by a *painter*, just as a *blueprint*, or a design for a building, is created by an *architect*.

5. (E); Synonym. *Frugal* and *thrifty* have the same meaning, as do *evident* and *obvious*.

6. (B); Degree. *Maudlin* means excessively, often foolishly or tearfully, *sentimental*. In the same way, something that is *priceless* is *valuable* but to such a degree that a price cannot be put on it.

7. (C); Antonym. *Opulence*, or wealth, is opposite in meaning to *poverty*. *Simplicity* and *complexity* also have opposite meanings.

8. (C); Cause and Effect. An *illness* can result in *pallor*, or paleness, just as *insomnia*, or a lack of sleep, can result in *tiredness*.

9. (B); Location. A *promontory*, which is a peak of land that extends into a body of water, can be found along the *seacoast*. An *alligator* can be found in a *swamp*.

10. (D); Synonym. *Remuneration* and *compensation* have the same meaning, that of reward or pay. *Comprehension* and *understanding* have the same meaning.

Lesson 15 page 140

1. (B); Performer and Related Action. You expect a *criminal* to *abscond*, or run away to escape the law, just as you expect a *miser* to *hoard* money.

2. (D); Synonym. *Adjure* and *command* have the same meaning, as do *plead* and *beg*.

3. (C); Synonym. *Capricious*, which means erratic and inconstant, is similar in meaning to *fickle*, which means unstable and changeable. *Nonsensical* and *silly* also have similar meanings.

4. (B); Action and Related Object. A *body* can become *emaciated*, or abnormally lean, just as a *blade* can become *sharpened*.

5. (A); Antonym. One of the definitions of *ethereal* is heavenly, which is opposite in meaning to *worldly*. *Required* and *optional* also have opposite meanings.

6. (E); Characteristic Quality. A *fiasco*, which is a project that fails, is characteristically *unsuccessful*, just as a *disagreement* is characteristically *unpleasant*.

7. (E); Cause and Effect. *Wrongdoing* can result in *ignominy*, or shame and dishonor, just as *training* can result in *skill*.

8. (D); Cause and Effect. *Healthfulness* can result in *longevity*, or a long life, just as *exercise* can result in *fitness*.

9. (B); Performer and Related Action. You expect a *slanderer* to *malign*, or make damaging, false statements about another person, just as you expect a *mayor* to *govern* a city.

10. (B); Performer and Related Object. A *physician* makes a *prognosis*, or a prediction about the course of a disease, about a patient, just as a *judge* makes a *sentencing* about a defendant.

Lesson 1   pages 143–148
Exercise 1   Finding Synonyms
Answers will vary. The following are possible responses.
1. stale from overuse
2. satirize
3. pen name
4. vague
5. acceptable behavior
6. commonplace
7. stole
8. a polite term for something unpleasant
9. wicked
10. warlike
11. avenger
12. deeply sad
13. agitated
14. warn
15. delicate skill
16. miserable
17. attacks with cruel language
18. indifferent
19. insincerely
20. equal

Exercise 2   Reading Strategically
1. D   2. C   3. B   4. D   5. A   6. A   7. A   8. E
9. D   10. C   11. C   12. E   13. D   14. B   15. A
16. E   17. C   18. B   19. B   20. C

Lesson 2   pages 149–154
Exercise 1   Finding Synonyms
Answers will vary. The following are possible responses.
1. aware
2. absorbed
3. conference
4. discuss
5. obvious exaggeration
6. lessen
7. accidental
8. skillfully
9. hypnotism
10. comical
11. bad-tempered
12. all-knowing
13. rambling
14. coats of arms
15. boredom
16. funeral hymns
17. people exiled from their native lands
18. in disguise
19. pretends
20. show of false bravery

Exercise 2   Reading Strategically
1. B   2. B   3. E   4. B   5. D   6. C   7. C   8. A
9. B   10. C   11. C   12. D   13. E   14. A   15. B
16. D   17. A   18. C   19. E   20. D

Lesson 3   pages 155–160
Exercise 1   Finding Synonyms
Answers will vary. The following are possible responses.
1. implied
2. varied
3. craftiness
4. urge
5. loud and demanding
6. foulmouthed
7. coax
8. stingy
9. offers
10. hopeful
11. without recognizable qualities
12. angelic
13. unreal beings
14. badly written verse
15. smooth
16. disorganized; shapeless
17. teachings
18. one who practices disciplined self-denial
19. polite behavior
20. someone helped by an influential person

Exercise 2   Reading Strategically
1. C   2. E   3. B   4. D   5. A   6. D   7. E   8. C
9. B   10. B   11. D   12. C   13. A   14. A   15. C
16. B   17. C   18. A   19. E   20. C

Lesson 4   pages 161–166
Exercise 1   Finding Synonyms
Answers will vary. The following are possible responses.

1. revered
2. aversion
3. opposites
4. exclusive privilege
5. statement of obvious truth
6. free from blame
7. irritated
8. unchangeable
9. poor
10. conquer
11. trespassing
12. apparent
13. made susceptible to
14. praise highly
15. without justification
16. introduced
17. scholarly
18. impostor
19. seemingly true but actually false
20. applying to a date in the past

Exercise 2   Reading Strategically
1. E   2. B   3. A   4. C   5. D   6. B   7. E   8. A
9. D   10. C   11. D   12. B   13. C   14. E   15. C
16. A   17. B   18. C   19. D   20. B

Lesson 5   pages 167–172
Exercise 1   Finding Synonyms
Answers will vary. The following are possible responses.

1. produce
2. a shy, quiet person
3. self-denial
4. full of information
5. commonplace
6. having a deep, rich tone
7. offspring
8. dull
9. trite
10. unimportant
11. a long, moralizing sermon
12. tribute
13. emotionally touching
14. peculiarities
15. attributed
16. agreeableness of sound
17. irrelevant; unnecessary
18. perfect example
19. mournful poems
20. length of time in a position

Exercise 2   Reading Strategically
1. C   2. D   3. E   4. C   5. E   6. D   7. B   8. A
9. D   10. B   11. E   12. D   13. D   14. D   15. B
16. C   17. A   18. D   19. B   20. B

Lesson 6   pages 173–178
Exercise 1   Finding Synonyms
Answers will vary. The following are possible responses.

1. outline; arrangement
2. noticeable
3. still existing
4. requiring great strength
5. ridiculous
6. concluded
7. confirmed
8. lack
9. exacting; precise
10. daily
11. frankness
12. fascinated
13. deviations
14. advocates
15. omens
16. an artful trick
17. disprove
18. trickery
19. decided
20. examination of the past

Exercise 2   Reading Strategically
1. D   2. A   3. C   4. E   5. A   6. B   7. D   8. C
9. C   10. D   11. E   12. B   13. B   14. A   15. C
16. D   17. E   18. B   19. A   20. C

Lesson 7   pages 179–184
Exercise 1   Finding Synonyms
Answers will vary. The following are possible responses.

1. an expert in art or taste
2. pouring forth
3. excitement
4. sociable
5. a clown
6. laughed loudly
7. shortcomings
8. fawning
9. exact and careful
10. mature for one's age
11. pertinent
12. politeness
13. noble in spirit
14. inheritance
15. complaining
16. favorable
17. extremely generous
18. lenient
19. intentional insults
20. yielded

Exercise 2   Reading Strategically
1. B   2. C   3. A   4. D   5. A   6. A   7. E   8. C
9. D   10. B   11. A   12. E   13. E   14. C   15. A
16. C   17. B   18. A   19. C   20. E

Lesson 8   pages 185–190
Exercise 1   Finding Synonyms
Answers will vary. The following are possible responses.

1. primitive
2. mysterious
3. highly offensive
4. luxurious
5. disapproved strongly
6. damage
7. overwhelmed
8. composed of similar parts; uniform
9. a leader who stirs up people's emotions
10. forerunner
11. illegal
12. spread throughout
13. originated from
14. treacherous
15. contradiction
16. lie
17. criticized severely
18. temporary suspension
19. irreversible
20. pleaded on another's behalf

Exercise 2   Reading Strategically
1. D   2. C   3. B   4. B   5. E   6. B   7. D   8. A
9. C   10. D   11. A   12. B   13. E   14. C   15. D
16. A   17. E   18. B   19. C   20. C

Lesson 9   pages 191–196
Exercise 1   Finding Synonyms
Answers will vary. The following are possible responses.

1. release
2. lowest possible point
3. art of public speaking
4. harsh
5. spacious
6. crippled
7. corpselike
8. very contagious, often fatal diseases
9. widespread
10. deadly
11. weakened
12. state of disorder
13. overthrow of something or someone
14. of or suited to a servant
15. assigned
16. coaxed
17. remaining
18. incapable of being reformed
19. compensation
20. branch of anthropology that compares the cultures of recent societies

Exercise 2   Reading Strategically
1. C   2. D   3. B   4. C   5. E   6. D   7. A   8. E
9. B   10. A   11. D   12. C   13. C   14. E   15. A
16. D   17. B   18. B   19. C   20. E

Lesson 10 pages 197–202
Exercise 1 Finding Synonyms
Answers will vary. The following are possible responses.

1. avoid
2. rashness
3. lawsuits
4. an interruption
5. justified
6. incited
7. retracted
8. approval and support
9. salty
10. get even with
11. possible occurrence
12. not showing emotion
13. extremely overweight
14. unmoving
15. extreme simplicity
16. concerned with others
17. disagreed
18. secret
19. soothe
20. trace

Exercise 2 Reading Strategically
1. E 2. B 3. C 4. B 5. D 6. E 7. A 8. C
9. D 10. B 11. B 12. B 13. C 14. D 15. A
16. B 17. C 18. B 19. D 20. A

Lesson 11 pages 203–208
Exercise 1 Finding Synonyms
Answers will vary. The following are possible responses.

1. overbearing
2. difference
3. harsh
4. essence
5. simplistic and inspiring debate
6. quiet
7. based on direct experience
8. routine
9. distinguish
10. international
11. a place of safekeeping
12. disagree with
13. unalterable
14. a supporting statement
15. devotion to one thing and contempt for its opposite
16. flimsy
17. book
18. insightfulness
19. poking fun at
20. lacking

Exercise 2 Reading Strategically
1. A 2. C 3. D 4. C 5. A 6. D 7. D 8. D
9. C 10. B 11. C 12. A 13. A 14. B 15. A
16. D 17. A 18. C 19. E 20. A

Lesson 12 pages 209–214
Exercise 1 Finding Synonyms
Answers will vary. The following are possible responses.

1. forced
2. solid earth
3. talkative
4. give out
5. metal-plated glove
6. bitter
7. shock and resulting confusion
8. stop
9. kindness or charity
10. sky
11. spotted with different colors
12. polish
13. riddle
14. understood by few
15. foretell
16. waste away
17. extensive, filling many volumes
18. forerunner
19. explains
20. wrong name

Exercise 2 Reading Strategically
1. B 2. D 3. A 4. B 5. E 6. C 7. D 8. C
9. B 10. E 11. C 12. A 13. D 14. E 15. A
16. C 17. D 18. B 19. B 20. D

Lesson 13 pages 215–220
Exercise 1 Finding Synonyms
Answers will vary. The following are possible responses.

1. unpredictably changeable
2. inhabitants
3. diligently
4. declare
5. reasonable
6. deep cracks
7. composure
8. ending
9. faultless
10. serving as an excuse
11. greed
12. financial
13. supported
14. result
15. excessive
16. evils
17. imprisoned
18. suppressed
19. use of threats or force
20. appease

Exercise 2 Reading Strategically
1. E 2. C 3. A 4. D 5. B 6. E 7. B 8. B
9. C 10. B 11. A 12. C 13. E 14. D 15. C
16. B 17. C 18. A 19. E 20. B

Lesson 14 pages 221–226
Exercise 1 Finding Synonyms
Answers will vary. The following are possible responses.

1. paintings made on wet plaster
2. fleeting
3. high point of land extending into water
4. swirling rainbow colors
5. paleness
6. simple or innocent
7. forsaking of beliefs
8. luxury
9. trinkets
10. decorated
11. complex
12. gold or silver bars, ingots
13. pay
14. an exaggerated portrait
15. economy or thrift
16. excessively sentimental
17. sympathy
18. charging high interest on loans
19. dishonest
20. frolicking

Exercise 2 Reading Strategically
1. C 2. D 3. A 4. E 5. A 6. B 7. C 8. C
9. B 10. E 11. B 12. D 13. B 14. C 15. E
16. B 17. D 18. B 19. C 20. A

Lesson 15 pages 227–232
Exercise 1 Finding Synonyms
Answers will vary. The following are possible responses.

1. threaten
2. length of life
3. wasted away
4. pretending to be sick
5. bring forth
6. ran away
7. forecast
8. uncommunicative
9. avoid
10. unearthly
11. living or lasting for two years
12. protested
13. undecided
14. erratic
15. command
16. slander
17. injury done for injury received
18. complete failure
19. public disgrace
20. defamed

Exercise 2 Reading Strategically
1. A 2. E 3. D 4. C 5. A 6. B 7. B 8. E
9. A 10. C 11. C 12. E 13. D 14. B 15. C
16. A 17. C 18. D 19. B 20. E

FORMATIVE ASSESSMENT

Test 1   page 3
1. C   2. B   3. D   4. E   5. C   6. C   7. A   8. E
9. B   10. B

Test 2   page 4
1. C   2. D   3. D   4. C   5. B   6. A   7. A   8. D
9. C   10. E

Test 3   page 5
1. A   2. C   3. D   4. D   5. D   6. C   7. B   8. B
9. E   10. E

Test 4   page 6
1. B   2. E   3. D   4. B   5. D   6. B   7. C   8. D
9. C   10. A

Test 5   page 7
1. C   2. A   3. B   4. A   5. C   6. B   7. E   8. E
9. D   10. C

Test 6   page 8
1. D   2. C   3. A   4. E   5. B   6. B   7. B   8. A
9. A   10. C

Test 7   page 9
1. D   2. C   3. A   4. A   5. C   6. E   7. B   8. C
9. D   10. A

Test 8   page 10
1. B   2. B   3. A   4. E   5. C   6. C   7. B   8. C
9. E   10. D

Test 9   page 11
1. B   2. A   3. A   4. B   5. A   6. E   7. D   8. D
9. D   10. B

Test 10   page 12
1. D   2. B   3. E   4. E   5. C   6. E   7. D   8. A
9. C   10. D

Test 11   page 13
1. B   2. A   3. C   4. C   5. A   6. B   7. B   8. D
9. B   10. E

Test 12   page 14
1. B   2. B   3. D   4. C   5. D   6. A   7. A   8. E
9. C   10. D

Test 13   page 15
1. A   2. E   3. D   4. C   5. C   6. A   7. D   8. D
9. B   10. E

Test 14   page 16
1. C   2. B   3. B   4. C   5. A   6. A   7. E   8. D
9. A   10. B

Test 15   page 17
1. A   2. B   3. A   4. A   5. B   6. D   7. C   8. D
9. E   10. B

Test 16   page 18
1. D   2. B   3. D   4. C   5. C   6. E   7. E   8. B
9. A   10. A

Test 17   page 19
1. C   2. A   3. A   4. E   5. D   6. C   7. B   8. D
9. D   10. A

Test 18   page 20
1. B   2. E   3. D   4. C   5. B   6. D   7. A   8. B
9. C   10. A

Test 19   page 21
1. E   2. E   3. B   4. D   5. D   6. A   7. C   8. C
9. C   10. D

Test 20   page 22
1. B   2. C   3. A   4. A   5. D   6. C   7. B   8. D
9. C   10. E

Test 21   page 23
1. A   2. A   3. D   4. E   5. A   6. C   7. E   8. A
9. B   10. C

Test 22   page 24
1. A   2. E   3. D   4. B   5. C   6. E   7. B   8. C
9. B   10. C

Test 23   page 25
1. E   2. D   3. C   4. B   5. A   6. C   7. A   8. B
9. C   10. D

Test 24   page 26
1. D   2. D   3. C   4. C   5. A   6. C   7. E   8. E
9. B   10. D

Test 25   page 27
1. C   2. B   3. C   4. D   5. E   6. D   7. E   8. B
9. B   10. A

Test 26   page 28
1. B   2. C   3. D   4. B   5. E   6. D   7. A   8. C
9. C   10. C

Test 27   page 29
1. B   2. C   3. D   4. E   5. D   6. B   7. E   8. B
9. A   10. A

Test 28   page 30
1. B   2. C   3. D   4. A   5. C   6. B   7. D   8. E
9. A   10. C

Test 29   page 31
1. E   2. D   3. A   4. B   5. C   6. E   7. C   8. B
9. D   10. A

Test 30   page 32
1. D   2. A   3. A   4. D   5. C   6. B   7. A   8. B
9. D   10. E

SUMMATIVE ASSESSMENT

Test 1 Part A   pages 35–38
1. E   2. B   3. C   4. D   5. B   6. B   7. A   8. D
9. E   10. B   11. A   12. C   13. B   14. A   15. D
16. C   17. D   18. E   19. D   20. C   21. C   22. D
23. E   24. B   25. C

Test 1 Part B   pages 39–43
26. E   27. B   28. C   29. A   30. D   31. C   32. E
33. D   34. C   35. B   36. D   37. A   38. C   39. E
40. D   41. D   42. B   43. C   44. A   45. C   46. D
47. E   48. B   49. C   50. A   51. D   52. E   53. C
54. C   55. E   56. B   57. D   58. A   59. D   60. C
61. C   62. B   63. E   64. A   65. D   66. B   67. C
68. E   69. C   70. D

Test 1 Part C   pages 44–46
71. (A); Synonym. *Abject* and *miserable* have similar meanings, as do *tired* and *weary*.
72. (C); Degree. To *admonish* suggests a lesser degree of punishment than to *condemn*. *Look* suggests a lesser degree of severity than *glare*, which means to stare angrily.

73. (D); Characteristic Quality. *Mist* is characteristically *amorphous,* or shapeless, just as a *jackhammer* is characteristically *loud.*

74. (B); Performer and Related Object. A *police officer* carries a *badge,* just as a *knight* carries a *blazon,* which can be a coat of arms, a heraldic shield, or a banner.

75. (D); Antonym. *Bravado,* which means excessive confidence, is opposite in meaning to *humility,* which means humbleness. *Bravery* and *cowardice* also have opposite meanings.

76. (A); Characteristic Quality. A *genius* is characteristically *brilliant,* just as a *hothead* is characteristically *choleric,* or bad-tempered and apt to explode in anger.

77. (E); Performer and Related Action. You expect a *charlatan,* one who makes false claims, to *deceive* others, just as you expect an *impostor* to *trick* others.

78. (B); Synonym. *Distraught* and *agitated* have similar meanings, as do *fashionable* and *stylish.*

79. (C); Characteristic Quality. A *euphemism* is characteristically *inoffensive,* just as a *diamond* is characteristically *hard.*

80. (E); Degree. A *friendship* is stronger and deeper than an *acquaintance,* just as a *colloquy* is more formal than a *chat.*

81. (C); Synonym. *Glib* is similar in meaning to *insincere,* just as *evasive* is similar in meaning to *dishonest.*

82. (D); Synonym. *Guile* and *slyness* have the same meaning, as do *clamor* and *uproar.*

83. (B); Classification. A *hyperbole* can be classified as a *figure of speech,* just as a *novel* can be classified as a type of *literature.*

84. (D); Classification. A *jet* can be classified as a type of *airplane.* An *elegy,* or verse written to lament the dead, can be classified as a type of *poem.*

85. (E); Synonym. *Kin* and *relatives* have the same meaning, as do *progeny* and *descendants.*

86. (D); Antonym. *Nondescript* is opposite in meaning to *colorful. Stubborn* means the opposite of *yielding.*

87. (C); Degree. *Omniscient,* which means all-knowing, is greater in degree than *knowledgeable. Infinite,* which means endless, is greater in degree than *large.*

88. (A); Performer and Related Action. You expect a *surgeon* to *operate* on a patient, just as you expect a *trickster* to *feign,* or make a false showing of something.

89. (A); Synonym. *Ostensible* and *apparent* have the same meaning, as do *fragile* and *delicate.*

90. (D); Antonym. *Poignant,* which means pointed, is opposite in meaning to *dull,* just as *exciting* means the opposite of *boring.*

91. (B); Synonym. *Prerogative* and *privilege* have similar meanings, as do *error* and *mistake.*

92. (C); Performer and Related Action. You expect a *thief* to *purloin,* or steal, things, just as you expect a *surveyor* to *measure* land.

93. (D); Antonym. *Retroactive* and *anticipatory* are opposite in meaning, as are *hospitable* and *unfriendly.*

94. (C); Performer and Related Action. You expect a *slanderer* to *revile,* or scold, someone, just as you expect an *admirer* to *praise* someone.

95. (B); Performer and Related Action. You expect a *savior* to attempt to *save* someone, just as you expect a *nemesis,* someone who imposes retribution or punishment, to *punish* others.

96. (E); Antonym. *Solemn* means the opposite of *silly,* just as *indigent,* or poor, means the opposite of *wealthy.*

97. (E); Characteristic Quality. *Propaganda* is characteristically *specious,* or misleading, just as a *busybody* is characteristically *meddlesome.*

98. (B); Synonym. *Subjugate* and *conquer* have the same meaning. *Lose* and *misplace* have similar meanings.

99. (D); Antonym. *Tacit,* which means silent, means the opposite of *expressed,* just as *tidy* means the opposite of *messy.*

100. (A); Characteristic Quality. *Cheering* is characteristically *vociferous,* just as a *winner* is characteristically *ecstatic.*

Test 2 Part A   pages 47–50
1. D   2. B   3. A   4. C   5. E   6. C   7. B   8. E
9. A   10. B   11. D   12. C   13. C   14. E   15. A
16. B   17. D   18. B   19. A   20. D   21. C   22. A
23. C   24. D   25. C

Test 2 Part B   pages 51–55
26. D   27. C   28. A   29. B   30. E   31. D   32. C
33. E   34. A   35. B   36. D   37. C   38. C   39. E
40. A   41. D   42. B   43. D   44. C   45. E   46. A
47. D   48. C   49. B   50. E   51. C   52. A   53. D
54. D   55. E   56. B   57. C   58. C   59. A   60. D
61. E   62. C   63. B   64. D   65. C   66. A   67. B
68. D   69. C   70. E

Test 2 Part C   pages 56–58
71. (C); Synonym. *Aberration* and *abnormality* have the same meaning. *Evolution* and *development* have similar meanings.

72. (C); Antonym. *Agitated* means the opposite of *calm. Obese,* which means extremely overweight, means the opposite of *skinny.*

73. (B); Synonym. *Alteration* and *change* have the same meaning. *Configuration* and *shape* have similar meanings.

74. (E); Performer and Related Object. You expect a *prophet* to interpret an *augury,* just as you expect a *mathematician* to solve an *equation.*

75. (D); Classification. A *banana* can be classified as a *fruit,* just as a *demagogue,* or someone who gains power by stirring up people's emotions, can be classified as a *leader.*

76. (D); Synonym. *Consideration* and *thoughtfulness* have the same meaning. *Restitution*, which means giving back something that has been lost or taken away, is similar in meaning to *compensation*.

77. (C); Synonym. *Contingency* and *possibility* have similar meanings, as do *opportunity* and *chance*.

78. (A); Antonym. *Cordial* and *unfriendly* have opposite meanings. *Perfidious*, which means disloyal, means the opposite of *faithful*.

79. (E); Synonym. *Elocution* and *public speaking* have similar meanings, as do *quarrel* and *dispute*.

80. (B); Degree. Something that is *gigantic* is considered to be bigger than something that is *large*. Someone who is *obsequious* shows an excessive desire to please and obey, whereas someone who is *obedient* is merely willing to follow instructions.

81. (E); Antonym. *Gregarious*, which means friendly, is opposite in meaning to *unfriendly*. *Comical* and *tragic* also have opposite meanings.

82. (B); Antonym. *Growth* and *decline* have opposite meanings. *Candor*, which means openness and honesty, means the opposite of *deceitfulness*.

83. (A); Characteristic Quality. A *harbinger* is characteristically *informative*, just as a *vacation* is characteristically *refreshing*.

84. (B); Synonym. *Hiatus*, which means gap, and *interruption* have similar meanings, as do *silliness* and *foolishness*.

85. (D); Characteristic Quality. *Twins* are characteristically *homogeneous*, or similar, just as *ice* is characteristically *slippery*.

86. (B); Synonym. *Inundate* and *overwhelm* have similar meanings, as do *complete* and *finish*.

87. (D); Characteristic Quality. A *fool* is characteristically *ludicrous*, or absurd, just as a *comedian* is characteristically *funny*.

88. (A); Antonym. *Magnanimous*, which means generous, is opposite in meaning to *selfish*. *Divided* and *united* also have opposite meanings.

89. (D); Degree. *Munificent* is more extreme in degree than *generous*, just as *infuriating* is more extreme in degree than *annoying*.

90. (E); Performer and Related Object. An *heir* receives a *patrimony*, just as an *employee* receives a *salary*.

91. (B); Classification. A *pediatrician*, a doctor for infants and children, is classified as a kind of *physician*. *Ethnology*, the study of human behavior and development, is classified as a kind of *anthropology*.

92. (E); Degree. *Primordial*, which means primitive, suggests a greater degree of antiquity than does *early*, just as *ancient*, suggests a greater degree of age than does *old*.

93. (A); Synonym. *Procedure* and *method* have similar meanings, as do *foible* and *weakness*.

94. (A); Performer and Related Action. You expect a *proofreader* to *read* text, just as you expect a *buffoon*, or clown, to *amuse* others.

95. (B); Characteristic Quality. A *complainer* is characteristically *querulous*, just as a *trickster* is characteristically *mischievous*.

96. (B); Synonym. *Salient* and *prominent* have similar meanings, as do *alone* and *solitary*.

97. (D); Characteristic Quality. A *typist*, who stays seated much of the time, is characteristically *sedentary*, just as a *snob* is characteristically *conceited*.

98. (E); Characteristic Quality. A *doubter* is characteristically *skeptical*, just as a *palace* is characteristically *sumptuous*.

99. (D); Synonym. *Start* and *begin* have the same meaning, as do *cajole* and *coax*.

100. (B); Performer and Related Action. A *jury* may *vindicate* someone, just as the *police* may *protect* someone.

Test 3 Part A   pages 59–62

1. B 2. C 3. D 4. C 5. E 6. A 7. D 8. B
9. C 10. B 11. A 12. E 13. C 14. D 15. E
16. B 17. C 18. A 19. A 20. C 21. B 22. C
23. D 24. B 25. E

Test 3 Part B   pages 63–67

26. C 27. C 28. E 29. D 30. C 31. D 32. B
33. D 34. A 35. C 36. A 37. E 38. D 39. D
40. C 41. B 42. B 43. C 44. D 45. A 46. E
47. E 48. D 49. C 50. B 51. A 52. B 53. A
54. C 55. A 56. E 57. D 58. E 59. E 60. A
61. B 62. A 63. E 64. A 65. C 66. C 67. D
68. C 69. C 70. D

Test 3 Part C   pages 68–70

71. (D); Antonym. *Apostasy* is the opposite of *allegiance*, just as *freedom* is the opposite of *captivity*.

72. (C); Cause and Effect. an *aspersion* can cause a *bad reputation*, just as *practice* can cause *mastery*.

73. (B); Antonym. *Aver*, which means affirm, means the opposite of *deny*. *Allow* and *forbid* are also opposite in meaning.

74. (D); Part and Whole. A *bristle* is part of a *brush*, just as a *gauntlet*, a metal-plated glove, is part of a suit of *armor*.

75. (D); Action and Related Object. You *burnish*, or polish, *silverware*, just as you *baste* a *turkey*.

76. (B); Synonym. *Corollary* and *deduction* have similar meanings, as do *verification* and *proof*.

77. (C); Synonym. *Differentiate* and *distinguish* have similar meanings, as do *practice* and *rehearse*.

78. (A); Antonym. *Disparity*, which means difference, means the opposite of *similarity*, just as *reunion* means the opposite of *separation*.

79. (D); Synonym. *Espouse* and *support* have similar meanings, as do *inspect* and *examine*.

80. (C); Performer and Related Action. You expect a *commentator* to *expound*, or explain, just as you could expect a *gymnast* to *somersault*.

81. (B); Performer and Related Action. You expect a *blackmailer* to *extort*, just as you expect a *deer* to *run*.

82. (D); Performer and Related Action. You expect a *pilot* to *fly*, just as you expect a *jailer* to *incarcerate*, or imprison, a prisoner.

83. (C); Performer and Related Action. You expect a *mourner* to *grieve*, just as you expect a *tyrant* to *coerce*.

84. (B); Performer and Related Action. You expect a *miser* to *hoard* money, just as you expect a *criminal* to *abscond*, or run away.

85. (B); Synonym. *Inexorable*, which means unable to be moved or influenced by persuasion, has a meaning similar to *unrelenting*. *Intricate* and *complex* also have similar meanings.

86. (E); Performer and Related Action. You expect an *heir* to *inherit* an estate, just as you expect a *negotiator* to *conciliate*, or smooth over conflicts between opposing parties.

87. (C); Characteristic Quality. A *rainbow* is characteristically *iridescent*, which means having rainbowlike colors, just as a *mountain* is characteristically *high*.

88. (E); Characteristic Quality. *Lace* is characteristically *delicate*, just as a *bauble* is characteristically *showy*.

89. (E); Performer and Related Object. A *memorandum* is an informative document composed by an *administrator*, just as a *treatise* is a formal, systematic book or article composed by a *scholar*.

90. (A); Synonym. *Mete* and *distribute* have the same meaning, as do *surround* and *enclose*.

91. (D); Synonym. *Mottled* and *splotchy* have the same meaning as do *slim* and *slender*.

92. (C); Characteristic Quality. A *model* is characteristically *photogenic*, just as a *meddler* is characteristically *officious*, or interfering.

93. (B); Location. A *promontory*, which is a peak of land that extends into a body of water, can be found along the *seacoast*. An *alligator* can be found in a *swamp*.

94. (D); Antonym. *Remonstrate*, which means to object or protest, is opposite in meaning to *accept*. *Organize* and *confuse* are also opposite in meaning.

95. (D); Synonym. *Reprisal* and *revenge* can both mean retaliation. *Satisfaction* and *contentment* also have the same meaning.

96. (B); Cause and Effect. *Learning* can be the result of *study*, just as *gratitude* can be a result of *benevolence*, or kindness and charity.

97. (A); Antonym. *Taciturn*, or habitually silent, is opposite in meaning to *talkative*, just as *courteous* is opposite in meaning to *impolite*.

98. (C); Cause and Effect. *Insomnia*, the inability to sleep, can cause *tiredness*, just as *illness* can cause *pallor*, or paleness associated with poor health.

99. (C); Characteristic Quality. *Usury*, or lending money at an excessive rate of interest, is characteristically *unfair*. In the same way, *smuggling* is characteristically *illegal*.

100. (B); Synonym. *Venal* and *corrupt* have similar meanings, as do *temporary* and *short-lived*.

HOLT, RINEHART AND WINSTON

ISBN 0-03-043024-0

90000>

EAN

9 780030 430244